MANAGING SEX IN TH

Studies in War, Society, and the Military

Managing Sex in the
U.S. Military

Gender, Identity, and Behavior

Edited by BETH BAILEY, ALESHA E. DOAN,
SHANNON PORTILLO, *and* KARA DIXON VUIC

University of Nebraska Press
Lincoln

The University of Nebraska Press is part of a land-grant institution with campuses and programs on the past, present, and future homelands of the Pawnee, Ponca, Otoe-Missouria, Omaha, Dakota, Lakota, Kaw, Cheyenne, and Arapaho Peoples, as well as those of the relocated Ho-Chunk, Sac and Fox, and Iowa Peoples.

Library of Congress Cataloging-in-Publication Data
Names: Bailey, Beth L., 1957– editor. | Doan, Alesha E., 1972– editor. | Portillo, Shannon, editor. | Vuic, Kara Dixon, 1977– editor.
Title: Managing sex in the U.S. military: gender, identity, and behavior / edited by Beth Bailey, Alesha E. Doan, Shannon Portillo, and Kara Dixon Vuic.
Other titles: Managing sex in the United States military
Description: Lincoln: University of Nebraska Press, [2022] | Series: Studies in war, society, and the military | Includes bibliographical references and index.
Identifiers: LCCN 2021031553
ISBN 9781496219022 (hardback)
ISBN 9781496229885 (paperback)
ISBN 9781496230850 (epub)
ISBN 9781496230867 (pdf)
Subjects: LCSH: Soldiers—Sexual behavior—United States. | Soldiers—Family relationships—United States. | Sexual harassment in the military—United States. | Gay military personnel—United States. | Sexual minority military personnel—United States. | Transgender military personnel—United States. | United States—Armed Forces—Women. |
BISAC: HISTORY / Military / United States | SOCIAL SCIENCE / Women's Studies
Classification: LCC UH630 .M36 2022 | DDC 813/.54—dc25
LC record available at https://lccn.loc.gov/2021031553

Set in Minion Pro by Mikala R. Kolander.

CONTENTS

ACKNOWLEDGMENTS

This collection grew from a symposium that brought fourteen scholars and two representatives from the U.S. Army's Sexual Harassment/Assault and Prevention Office to the University of Kansas (KU) in February 2018. The purpose of that symposium was to create an opportunity for historians, policy scholars, and practitioners to discuss the U.S. military's efforts to "manage sex" from the early twentieth century to the present day. Many of the participants in that meeting wrote chapters in this book, and all helped to shape its final outline.

The editors are grateful to KU's Center for Military, War, and Society Studies and to Texas Christian University's history department and its LCpl. Benjamin W. Schmidt Professorship of War, Conflict, and Society in Twentieth-Century America for major sponsorship of the initial symposium; to Jena Gunter and the staff of KU's Institute for Policy and Social Research for their logistical support; to KU's Hall Center for the Humanities for physically hosting the meeting; and to KU PhD student Marjorie Galelli, who made both conceptual and practical contributions to this volume.

ABBREVIATIONS

ACLU — American Civil Liberties Union
AEF — American Expeditionary Forces
ANC — Army Nurse Corps
AVF — all-volunteer force
AWOL — absent without leave
CA — Civilian Affairs
CAAF — Court of Appeals for the Armed Forces
CHAMPUS — Civilian Health and Medical Program of the Uniformed Services
CMA — Court of Military Appeals
CST — Cultural Support Teams
DACOWITS — Defense Advisory Committee on Women in the Services
DADT — Don't Ask, Don't Tell
DCPC — Direct Combat Probability Coding
DOD — Department of Defense
DODI — Department of Defense Instruction
DGCAR — Direct Ground Combat and Assignment Rule
FETS — Female Engagement Teams
FRGS — Family Readiness Groups
GAO — Government Accountability Office
HQMC — Headquarters Marine Corps
LBG — Lesbian, Gay, and Bisexual
LGBTQ — Lesbian, Gay, Bisexual, Transgender, Queer
MACV — Military Assistance Command, Vietnam
MAGTF — Marine Air Ground Task Force
MISO — Military Information Support Operations

MLDC	Military Leadership Diversity Commission
MOS	Military Occupational Specialties
NCO	noncommissioned officer
NCTE	National Center for Transgender Equality
NOW	National Organization for Women
ODA	Operational Detachment Alpha
OTH	Other Than Honorable
PX	Post Exchange
RAA	Recreation and Amusement Association
R&R	Rest and Recuperation
SAPR	Sexual Assault Prevention and Response
SASC	Senate Armed Services Committee
SF	Special Forces
SFC	Sergeant First Class
SO	Special Operations
SOF	Special Operations Forces
SHAEF	Supreme Headquarters Allied Expeditionary Force
SHARP	Sexual Harassment/Assault Response and Prevention
SOGIE	Sexual Orientation, Gender Identity, and Gender Expression
SWAN	Service Women's Action Network
UCMJ	Uniform Code of Military Justice
USAREC	Army Recruiting Command
VA	Veterans Affairs
WAAC	Women's Army Auxiliary Corps
WAC	Women's Army Corps
WAF	Women in the Air Force
WASPS	Women Airforce Service Pilots
WEAL	Women's Equity Action League

MANAGING SEX IN THE U.S. MILITARY

Introduction

BETH BAILEY, ALESHA E. DOAN, SHANNON PORTILLO,
AND KARA DIXON VUIC

As the American military geared up for war in the late spring of 1917, commanders and medical officers debated how to handle an age-old problem: venereal disease. They wanted to keep the dough-boys healthy and "fit to fight," they wanted to avoid troublesome problems with French authorities, and they wanted to appease an American public worried about how war might change their sons. They decided on a multifaceted approach. General John J. Pershing forbid servicemen from visiting brothels. Chaplains and physicians lectured and distributed pamphlets on abstinence. Civilian organizations provided recreation and sports as diversion. Officers issued punishments, revoked leave privileges, withheld pay, and sent infected soldiers to segregated labor camps where they worked while being treated. Neither the carrots nor the sticks worked to the degree that they hoped. The U.S. Army boasted that it had the lowest venereal disease rates among combatants, but it still lost seven million days of active duty during the war to sexually transmitted infections.[1]

Decades later, during World War II, medical treatments mitigated the dangers of venereal disease to a degree, but commanders still confronted issues and problems of sex and sexuality. Most of them thought their men were entitled to sex, so, in some theaters, commanders provided prostitutes; in others they encouraged relationships with "respectable" local women. But at an isolated post in Greenland, commanders faced another kind of problem. Daily routines were monotonous. There were no nearby towns for the men to visit, and a year at the isolated post, one medical officer warned, was a long time for men to go without sex. He did not fear the consequences of abstinence, necessarily, but worried that the men might be tempted to have sex with each other.[2]

A captain stationed in a village in South Vietnam in 1967 did not worry as much that his men would have sex with each other. He feared that they would rape the women with whom they lived. He commanded a company of men who lived and worked among a small hamlet of South Vietnamese, and he knew he had a problem when the men started making "advances" to the women. He decided that the best solution was to find a few women to work as prostitutes. They received weekly medical exams and charged a set fee that was not too expensive for the GIs. Other commanders adopted similar systems, even as official U.S. policy deemed prostitution off-limits.[3]

About that same time, an army nurse back in the United States found out that she was pregnant. She had served in the reserves for ten years and hoped to continue her career, but the Army Nurse Corps moved to discharge her. She insisted that her responsibilities as a mother would not interfere with her work, and she explained that if she were activated, her husband and mother would care for her son. None of these plans or promises made a difference. Frustrated with a policy that seemed discriminatory toward women, the nurse sued and won an injunction in U.S district court. Army leaders were not pleased that external forces were mandating internal policies, but soon other courts and, ultimately, the Supreme Court guaranteed women equal protection in the military.[4]

Sex, in its many manifestations, has obviously demanded the attention of the U.S. military, both now and throughout that institution's history. And for the military (if not for individual service members), sex—both the act and the physiological differences between women and men—appears most frequently as a problem to be managed.

The sexual behavior of troops has presented a consistent challenge throughout U.S. history, though what worried military leaders during World War II would pass unnoticed a half-century later. In the 1940s and 1950s, for example, having sex outside marriage could destroy the reputation of "respectable" young women; female military leaders believed that such behavior by women in uniform could undermine the very existence of the women's military corps and crafted policies to keep such behavior under control. But such actions created new problems to resolve: Could female and male service members be governed by different regulations?

Military law addressed sexual behavior, and in ways that likewise changed over time. In 1917 the military defined "sodomy," when committed as part of an assault, as a criminal offense. In 1920 that definition was revised to include consensual sodomy and applied to both same-sex and non-same-sex couplings. Going further, in 1951 the Uniform Code of Military Justice (UCMJ) prohibited "unnatural carnal copulation."

Rape was also defined as a crime in the UCMJ, but military leaders worried about sexual assault in ways that went beyond the criminal behavior of an individual. The rape of a civilian by a member of the U.S. armed forces outside the United States might affect international relations. The sexual assault of fellow service members appeared endemic once the institution began paying attention; it also proved an intractable problem.

The consequences of sexual behavior posed problems for the military, or at the very least required it to create policy. High rates of venereal disease were definitely undesirable, a problem to be solved. But pregnancy also had implications. What regulations would govern pregnancy, or those who were pregnant? What about children—after all, they were the product of sexual congress—or the families of service members? What policies governed military dependents? Was it the Army Family, with "Family" capitalized to indicate its value to the institution? Was it "if the Army wanted you to have a wife it would have issued you one"? The answers depended heavily on the composition of the military, which in turn depended on a series of other decisions made about who served and on what terms. And while military regulations were intended to be universal, implementation often was not. When it came to sex, as when it came to much else, African American service members were often treated differently from their white peers.

The category of "sex" also encompasses gender, the socially constructed understandings of femininity and masculinity ascribed to women and men. While sex-as-gender posed different sorts of problems than did the sexual behavior of millions of people in uniform, managing gender was a persistent concern. In the first half of the twentieth century, Americans debated whether or not women could serve in the nation's military. In subsequent decades, the question was over the terms of service: What were the conditions of women's service? What were they allowed to do? Forbidden from doing? Would the military embrace or challenge the conventional American understandings of appropriate "sex roles"? And with the new millennium, questions arose over the definition of gender. Was the biological definition of sex sufficient? What determines gender identity? How should that issue be addressed in policy? And what about sexual identity or orientation?

In fact the military had complete control over very little when it came to sex. Decisions about who could serve and under what conditions were made by Congress, in its role of civilian oversight. They were adjudicated by the courts. They were subject to executive order. But in all cases, the military had to develop policy, to create regulations and training, and to implement the decisions on sex. Whether those decisions came from within or without, whether they reflected the preferences and assumptions of military leadership or pushed them in uncomfortable directions, they became military policy. In the end the military had to manage sex.

Why does it matter what the military did when confronted with the issue of sex? In large part it matters because the U.S. military is a massive institution, and its policies on sexual behavior, gender, and sexuality have shaped the experiences of tens of millions of Americans, sometimes in life-altering fashion. Sixteen million Americans were in uniform during World War II. Almost seven million were on active duty during the Korean War, with more than nine million serving during the Vietnam War era. And while the post–World War II military hit its highest numbers in 1968, tens of millions of people have served in the years that followed. All were subject to military regulations and policies, exposed both to military training and military culture. For better and worse, they carried their military experiences and the individual understandings born of them back to all corners of the nation.

It also matters because military service has symbolic weight in American society. The connections between the rights and (military) obligations of citizenship persist even as the nation moves into its fifth consecutive decade with an all-volunteer force. As various groups have pursued the right to serve on equal terms in the military, they have emphasized that tie: by fulfilling the obligations of citizenship, some have argued, we have earned an equal place in the nation. Thus, the military's management of sex, as applied to women, to gays and lesbians, and to trans individuals, is part of the nation's history of civil rights—as is the way that assumptions about race shaped military actions.

Finally, the discussions over how to govern sex in the military are frequently public in nature. Congressional hearings and debates—whether over regulations barring women from combat, over the future of Don't Ask, Don't Tell and "gays in the military," over family policy or sexual assault prevention—present arguments that both reflect and shape contemporary opinion.

When it comes to sex, the armed forces have different tools for managing problems—or possibilities—than do institutions in civilian society. The military is frequently given exceptional status before the law, exempted from some of the civil rights protections otherwise guaranteed. And the military's control is more absolute, conveyed through orders, enforced through regulations. But while military practices and policies are not truly comparable to civilian ones, they matter, both in and of themselves and because their influence reaches well beyond the boundaries of military service and the military as an institution.

As an institution that exerts significant influence on American society and culture, the military is an important source for historians and policy scholars interested in sex, gender, and sexuality. Historians, who study change over time, look to the military as a way to understand changing sexual behaviors, as well as how institutions sought to manage those behaviors. They seek to understand the forces and influences that have directed changes in gender norms and identities, and the military—as an institution that holds enormous power in framing popular understandings of masculinity and femininity—offers important clues for historians to pursue. Historians also seek to understand changes in the policing of sexual behaviors and identities, and here again the military's record of regulating, forbidding, or even encouraging certain practices and people is instructive.

Public policy scholars approach the military as one of the largest public institutions and public employers in the United States. They seek to understand how elected officials and leaders in each administration convey social values, priorities, and expectations via military policy and leadership. Employment protections and expectations in this massive public institution often shape and foreshadow broader social expectations. Public policy scholars focus on how policy priorities are shaped and implemented in the military, and how this might inform other aspects of public life. As the military is a public organization, designed to serve and protect citizens and overseen by elected officials, policy scholars are also concerned with questions about representation. The military does not mirror the demographics of the nation's citizenry, nor does its leadership mirror its members. These representational disparities are of great concern to policy scholars who seek to understand the implications of this disjuncture with the everyday policies and practices designed to govern the military. The absence of gender, racial, and sexual orientation representation has been consequential to the development of the military as a male-dominated organization that tightly reinforces a hypermasculine culture, which has historically manifested in disparate treatment of its members. As such the military continues to grapple with establishing and implementing successful policies that deal with deep-seated systemic issues fundamentally related to gender inequity.

Historians and policy scholars seek to understand how gender norms have changed and how they have been enforced in American society. Many have found that the military has played an important role in defining and enforcing gender norms, both within the services and outside them. For example, military officials have expressed wildly different beliefs about the relationship between sex and soldiering. For most of military history, commanders considered sex to be a matter of morale for male soldiers: they either needed sex or they deserved it as reward. That belief rationalized the regulation of prostitution, the distribution of condoms, and leave policies designed to allow men to meet local women. Yet the military has never granted women the same allowances. Guided by prevailing ideas about womanhood and sexual respectability, military officials have instituted different practices and policies regarding sex, sexual education, and prophylaxis for women and men. As increasing numbers of women integrated into the military in the wake of World War II, and especially after the beginning of the all-volunteer force in 1973, the military faced new questions about reproduction and parenthood, sexual double standards, and women's expectations of sex and family.

Scholars also attribute gender change to a range of influences, and the military offers a focused look at how grassroots activism converges with legal and policy changes to shape the lives of service members and their families. Military officials have managed their concerns about sex while considering the desires of the people it hoped to recruit and retain, along with their parents, spouses, and family members. Service members have advocated for many policy changes regarding sex and sexuality, pressuring the forces to better meet their needs and wishes. And at times they have utilized the power of the courts and Congress in their struggle. Servicewomen used the courts to force policy changes about pregnancy and parenthood. Gay men and lesbians utilized the courts and Congress to overturn Don't Ask, Don't Tell. And service members who have been victims of sexual abuse and harassment have turned to Congress to mandate policy changes. The military's policies at times led, and at times lagged behind, civilian policies on sex, but scholars have demonstrated that the two are interconnected.

Scholars also seek to understand the ways that other developments, such as science and medicine, shape the history of sexuality. In looking to the military, these scholars find that military leaders' understandings of sex, sexuality, and gender are all framed by continually changing medical, psychological, and sociological discourses. When physicians and preventive medicine officials have attempted to manage the consequences of sex, for example, their understandings of venereal disease and pregnancy reflected the state of medical science at the time. The introduction of more effective medicines, prophylaxis measures, and birth control options altered the military's responses. The introduction of penicillin, for example, freed commanders from the knowledge that a soldier who contracted gonorrhea would not be able to fight. The introduction of the birth control pill allowed many servicewomen to regulate menstruation and minimize the chance of pregnancy, thus affording them greater sexual control and freedom than their forebears enjoyed. Medical advances greatly mitigated the consequences of sex, even as new issues and concerns arose.

Relatedly, scholars have also shown that the military's understandings of sexual behavior and identity have been shaped by contemporaneous understandings of psychology. Before World War II, military officials thought of sex as a behavior, something that could be regulated, controlled, even forbidden. But as the field of psychology evolved, psychiatrists began to understand sexuality as an identity, something innate to an individual. These understandings dramatically changed the ways the military policed sex, especially sex between same-sex partners. Whereas the military's practice had been to punish sodomy as an act, for example, during World War II, military psychiatrists began to strategize ways of identifying and discharging individuals based on their *identity* as homosexual. The subsequent exclusion of gay men and lesbians from serving in the military at all, then from openly serving, had significant ramifications not only for the men and women whose lives were disrupted but also for broader notions of American citizenship and pluralism.

Scholars interested in diplomacy and foreign relations have also turned to the military as an important actor, and they have highlighted the ways that matters of sexuality have operated as points of contention or negotiation with foreign governments and domestic populations. Sexual crimes against civilians have undermined and destabilized diplomatic relationships. While cases of rape or assault have presented—and continue to present—the most difficult challenges, military officials have also had to broker negotiations and agreements about all matters of sex, including prostitution, marriage, and courtship. Even the presence of a military installation in an area raises questions and introduces potential problems when service members visit local establishments and seek out companionship. Far from a matter of private concern or of internal debate, the military's management of sex—and perhaps more important its failure to manage sexual crimes—has proved to be a matter of national concern.

As historians and policy scholars have demonstrated, the military's policies and practices have never existed in a vacuum, nor have they reflected only the desires of the military's leadership. The military has managed sex in the context of a host of social, cultural, legal, and personal factors. Military actions have both reflected and determined social, cultural, and legal trends. The essays included here deepen our understanding not only of the American military but also of the history of sex, gender, and sexuality in U.S. history.

This collection consists of five parts: (1) Behavior; (2) Family and Reproduction; (3) Orientation and Identity; (4) Sexual Assault and Prevention; and (5) Gender, Sexuality, and Combat. While this volume as a whole considers the U.S. military as an institution, some chapters focus on specific branches or organizations within the military. In the first part scholars explore how the military managed, and shaped, sexual behavior at home and abroad. While the first part considers sexual behavior broadly, the second part focuses on reproduction. The salience and official approach to reproduction and family planning issues have shifted over time for the military as an organization, particularly in the post-1973 all-volunteer force. Reproductive decision-making is also an individual-level consideration, especially for female service members; thus, this part considers these issues at both the organizational and individual level. The third part considers sexual orientation and gender identity or expression by exploring the various policies the military has put in place, comparing bans around sexual orientations and gender identities. In this part the authors contextualize these bans and policy changes, discussing how the broader push for LGBTQ rights in the United States has influenced the military's management of sexual orientation, gender identity, and expression. The fourth part, which explores the military's response to sexual assault and sexual violence, begins by historicizing the military's managing of sexual assault and considerations of sexual violence before the shift to an all-volunteer force; it then concludes with a focus on the military's contemporary response to sexual assault and sexual violence. The final part explores gender, sexuality, and combat. In it the authors examine how combat policies and societal expectations and understandings of gender and sexuality have shaped gender integration, and they discuss the ways that historical ideals of combat and masculinity have defined military culture and continue to limit gender integration in contemporary times. Collectively, the five parts of this book provide a rich consideration of how the military as an institution is positioned within the broader American political context, and how this institution has shaped historic and contemporary understanding of sex, sexuality, and gender.

Andrew Byers's chapter anchors part 1, "Behavior," and centers on the disparate policy responses the military has employed when managing soldiers' sexual behavior domestically (as compared to their behavior abroad). Byers argues that sexually "problematic" behavior came to be increasingly linked to visible evidence of sexual encounters—namely, venereal infections, marriage, or pregnancy, which military leaders believed undercut effectiveness, morale, and readiness. In seeking to curb these activities through official policy, the military opted to implement a fundamentally different strategy for managing sexual behavior during soldiers' deployment overseas built on "othering" foreign women of color. The military institutionalized regulated prostitution regimes. As Byers concludes, while the military tried to tighten its grip on soldiers' sexual behavior, it also sought to redefine same-sex relationships through a lens of pathology and criminality.

Tracking similar topics in a later period, Susan Carruthers explores the intractable problems faced by those who sought to manage sexual behavior, contending that attempts to do so have led to confusion, hypocrisy, and irresolvable challenges that persist today. Carruthers begins by arguing that the military has historically subscribed to the idea that men in uniform deserve heterosexual intercourse as a compensation for martial service. During and after World War II, the military sometimes treated prostitution as commerce, justifying it as spoils for military victories. Regardless of the attempts to regulate sexual behavior, Carruthers claims, the military's plans have always been problematic due to the often inseparable nature of emotion and sexual activity. Returning to a common theme, Carruthers suggests that the military has inserted itself into service people's sexual behavior due to its assumption that sex has purportedly dangerous consequences for unit cohesion and combat effectiveness.

Beth Bailey's chapter, which concludes part 1, examines the military's struggles over policies governing women's sexual behavior, from the creation of the Women's Army Auxiliary Corps during World War II through the army's abolishment of the Women's Army Corps (WAC) in 1978. Due in part to their experience with the sexualized accusations opponents of the WAC made during World War II—that the ranks of the WAC were filled with prostitutes and "Amazons"—the officers who led the corps through the transformations of the 1960s and 1970s continued to emphasize the importance of respectability and femininity, even as the legal standing for different regulations by gender had disappeared. Bailey's analysis traces the interaction between law, regulation, and logic in the struggles to define the acceptable parameters for WAC behavior.

Part 2, "Family and Reproduction," begins with John Worsencroft's exploration of the military's transition to an all-volunteer force in the 1970s. He highlights the history of military family policy to illustrate the significant overlap between military institutions, civilian and military lobbying organizations, and civil rights groups. Worsencroft's chapter illuminates the many ways that domestic politics and changing national values shaped the military's management of sexuality and gender. These overlapping interests created significant disagreement among constituencies and often led to unintended consequences, both inside and outside the military. Women's rights groups and their members disagreed over the proper role of women in society, particularly women's roles in the military. Worsencroft shows that each military branch saw the problem of families differently, and that their leaders pursued solutions according to the unique institutional needs and cultures of their organizations.

Focusing more specifically on women, Kara Dixon Vuic examines the military's policies about reproduction, including birth control and abortion, throughout the twentieth century. Most of these policies focused on servicewomen, whose reproductive lives were of great concern, especially during wars. Until late in the twentieth century, women in uniform were forbidden from having children. However, social changes during the Vietnam War era, including the women's movement and sexual revolution, led the military to alter reproductive policies. Vuic demonstrates that reproductive policies not only reveal the importance of pragmatic personnel considerations, but they also highlight the way the military has harnessed changing historical notions of appropriate gender roles to create the kind of force that would meet with public approval. At the same time, Vuic shows that service members and their families pressed for change and, thus, influenced military policies.

Part 3, "Orientation and Identity," tackles a range of issues related to sexual orientation and gender identity. Turning specifically to the bans on gays and lesbians and on transgender personnel in the military, Agnes Schaefer examines the historical and political context of these policies, treating them as key examples of the military's evolving understanding and management of sexual orientation and gender identity. In both cases sexual orientation and gender identity have been considered disqualifying psychological conditions and grounds for administrative discharge. Echoing a theme found in earlier chapters, Schaefer demonstrates that the concerns initially voiced about the consequences of allowing gays, lesbians, and transgender personnel to serve openly have been sidestepped by arguing that prohibiting gay service members would have negative impacts on military readiness and unit cohesion.

Taking a slightly broader view, Jacqueline Whitt examines the history-policy-advocacy nexus of LGBTQ-related policies in the U.S. military, placing them within a broader global and chronological context to emphasize the ways in which sexuality and gender have been managed within militaries. She argues that sexual orientation and gender identity or expression within the U.S. military context is inseparable from the gay rights movement and from the political history of Don't Ask, Don't Tell and its subsequent repeal. Moreover, Whitt explores how other categories of identity, such as socioeconomic class, race, and religion, intersect with sexual orientation and gender identity. Whitt suggests that this broader context is particularly important as the history of the U.S. military's management of sexual orientation and gender identity remains in flux.

Part 4, "Sexual Assault and Prevention," begins with Kellie Wilson-Buford's analysis of military officials' struggles to define "sexual assault." She maps the military's historic policies and practices to contextualize current debates and efforts at prevention. She argues that leaders have historically failed to view sexual assault as an institutional problem and instead have assumed that sexual violence was a natural consequence of military service, especially in remote locations and war zones. Wilson-Buford examines how gendered and racialized assumptions about victims' and suspected perpetrators' moral credibility minimized the scope of the problem and silenced victims. Heteronormative assumptions that men could not be victims of sexual assault simultaneously propagated institutional silence about male-on-male sexual assault. Wilson-Buford concludes that official policies implemented before the turn of the twenty-first century were often reactive and situational, rather than preventative and systematically implemented.

Amanda Boczar's chapter focuses on contemporary struggles over harassment and assault in the military. She documents how the permanent integration of women into the services after World War II, combined with changing policies toward the service of openly gay men and lesbians, negative public relations stemming from high profile events, and increased reporting by servicewomen, necessitated changes in training and punishment. Despite efforts to increase transparency and reporting, Boczar argues, the military continues to struggle to effectively manage its intractable problem of sexual assault and harassment.

Rounding out this collection, part 5, "Gender, Sexuality, and Combat," examines the history, policies, and contemporary military culture that have prevented servicewomen from fulfilling combat positions in the military. Elizabeth Mesok's chapter examines the evolution of the military's combat exclusion policies between 1948 and 2013, cautioning against an easy narrative of progress in which the 2013 repeal can be seen as the inevitable next step in women's equality. Rather, Mesok argues that the military's approach to women in combat has been shaped by its evolving understanding of gender as well as by changes in the United States' security objectives and strategies. As Mesok documents in detail, the combat exclusion policy was repealed after the military recognized the value of gender for nontraditional warfare and began to view servicewomen as a potential "combat multiplier"—a way to develop combat strength and power without increasing the actual number of troops.

Turning the analytical lens to combat and masculinity, Christopher Hamner unpacks the unexamined historical assumptions about gender that shape perceptions of combat in the military. The belief that battle is a space and activity that remains the exclusive province of men goes back centuries. Hamner contends that there is no other profession in America so thoroughly identified with maleness as soldiering, where men are expected to make war, and war is expected to make them men. An equally pervasive, and similarly unexamined, assumption about soldiers' ability to fight and to withstand the rigors and trauma of combat runs throughout much of American military history. Hamner explores the ways that different groups—military brass, civilian leaders and pundits, active-duty soldiers and officers, and combat veterans—have responded to, challenged, and shaped the debates about masculinity and masculine identity on the battlefield, as old assumptions about combat have come under increased scrutiny.

In the book's final chapter, Alesha Doan and Shannon Portillo examine service members' contemporary resistance to gender integration in Special Forces (SF) and Special Operations. Based on their empirical data, Doan and Portillo argue that most SF soldiers draw on traditional gender stereotypes and tropes to resist integration. Men, along with a surprisingly significant percentage of women, founded their opinions about integration on gender stereotypes and anecdotal experiences rather than on empirical facts. Participants largely defined gender along binary lines that were heavily steeped in patriarchal and heteronormative assumptions; these assumptions structured their behavior toward female colleagues and shaped the day-to-day cultural norms of SF. Doan and Portillo conclude that couching disapproval of gender integration in terms of "combat effectiveness" masks the systemic impact of the ways in which gender tropes reinforce military norms and behavior.

Taken as a whole, these essays provide insight into how the military has managed sex during the twentieth and twenty-first centuries. Employing historical and policy lenses, the collection demonstrates how the military as an institution has impacted social understandings of sex, sexuality, and gender equity in the United States. Each author provides a robust discussion of the policies and practices designed to regulate and shape sexual behavior, reproduction and family planning, sexual orientation and identity, sexual violence, and gender integration. Across time and issues, the authors illuminate how the successes and failures of these policy pursuits have had a lasting legacy, the contours of which continue to shape the modern military.

Notes

1. Allan M. Brandt, *No Magic Bullet: A Social History of Venereal Disease in the United States since 1880* (New York: Oxford University Press, 1985), 115.

2. "Annex #1 to Sanitary Report, April 1943, 190th Station Hospital," May 5, 1943, 5, HD 730 Neuropsychiatry 1943 Morale and Psychiatry ASF Reports, World War II Administrative Records, Z1, Record Group 112, Records of the Office of the Surgeon General (Army), National Archives and Records Administration, College Park MD.

3. Lieutenant Colonel Jesse H. Denton, interview by Lieutenant Colonel Allan R. Wetzel, Senior Officer Oral History Program, 1983, Military History Institute, Army Heritage and Education Center, Carlisle Barracks PA.

4. "Army Discriminates, Says Nurse-Mother," *American Journal of Nursing* (*AJN*) 70, no. 11 (November 1970): 2283–84; "If You're Pregnant (a Predicament in Army-ese) You May Not Have to Leave the Corps," *AJN* 71, no. 1 (July 1971): 1311.

PART 1

Behavior

ONE

The U.S. Army's Management of Sexuality at Home and Abroad, 1898–1940

ANDREW BYERS

The U.S. Army of the late nineteenth and early twentieth centuries intervened in a host of issues related to sexuality—prostitution and venereal disease, marriage and family life, sexual propriety and violence, and same-sex sexuality, among others—in ways and to a degree that twenty-first-century readers might find surprising.[1] These interventions came at a time when the army was asked to take on new missions abroad in the Caribbean, Asia, and Europe beginning in 1898. This timing was not coincidental, since military and civilian leaders came to believe that interventions in the sexual lives of American soldiers and those they came into contact with around the world were both necessary and possible in these new environments. The U.S. Army attempted to control sexual behaviors that it found particularly problematic for the institution and military effectiveness via official policy, legal enforcement, indoctrination, and military culture. Allowing soldiers the opportunity to indulge some sexual desires but not others, while guarding against the problems that sex could cause for unit readiness and morale, became one of the key balancing acts for U.S. Army planners throughout the early decades of the twentieth century.

As with many other militaries, the U.S. Army believed that soldiers' sexual activities had the potential to cause a variety of problems. The behaviors the army found troublesome included sexual encounters that resulted in venereal infections, marriage, or pregnancy, as well as those that created public embarrassment for the entire army or difficulties in relations between the army and local civilians. From the army's perspective, the biggest problem that could emerge from soldiers' sexual activities was that soldiers might contract a venereal disease, rendering them unable to perform their military duties. Infected soldiers consumed medical resources during treatment, which might take days or weeks before the diseases' symptoms abated or—after the introduction of penicillin during World War II—the diseases were cured. In an attempt to mitigate the potential damage from venereal disease, the army regulated prostitution, believing that female prostitutes were the primary vector for venereal disease, even mandating medical inspections of prostitutes by army doctors, both on the U.S.-Mexican border (1916–17) and in the Philippines (1898–1918). These inspection regimes had the secondary effect of creating a ready pool of officially sanctioned sexual partners for soldiers.

Soldiers' sexual activities could also cause problems and generate considerable ill will and even active resistance in communities surrounding military bases.[2] Rapes by servicemen of local women in friendly or occupied areas could cause significant resentment by local civilian populations, as could unacknowledged or unwanted pregnancies, making placid civil-military relations extremely difficult. Vulgar displays by soldiers, especially when such behaviors were publicly exhibited by officers, also proved embarrassing to militaries.

We can trace the army's attempts to manage sexuality over time via changes in the army's legal system, through the Articles of War (predecessor to the Uniform Code of Military Justice), which governed the regulation of sexuality in military courts. One of the most important legal changes during this period was the explicit introduction of sodomy as a criminal offense in 1917; the army used this prohibition to manage same-sex sexual contacts, which it increasingly viewed as problematic. Prior to this point, the military justice system was mostly silent, at least explicitly, on sexual matters, with very few prosecutions of cases related to the sexual behavior of soldiers. The army's policies and regulations were not created in an intellectual, legal, or medical vacuum, but rather were products of broader debates and changes in civilian society. Over time the army came to view sexual relationships between soldiers—almost all of whom were male at this time—as undesirable largely because American attitudes toward such same-sex relationships, influenced by medical and psychoanalytic experts, had changed. The army thus implicitly endorsed the perceived linkage, especially from the early 1920s onward, between same-sex sexual activities and pathologized homosexuality, which came to be equated with both effeminacy and psychological degeneracy.

The army of this period is worth studying, rather than the navy or the Marine Corps, not only because of the army's significant new overseas deployments but also because of the considerable internal change that the army underwent in the first half of the twentieth century. It increased dramatically in size and transformed demographically, incorporating many new immigrant communities. That transformation, in turn, triggered attempts to "Americanize" the army. The institution also went through serious attempts to professionalize and reform almost all aspects of its internal processes and performance. World War I likewise brought many new men, and broader socioeconomic classes of men, into the service, thus bringing more external scrutiny and calls for reform. Each of these changes played significant roles in how the army perceived and regulated sexuality over time.

In this chapter we will first work through how the army thought about and attempted to regulate prostitution, primarily as a means of mitigating the damage caused by venereal diseases because of the perceived causal relationship between prostitution and disease. Then we will explore marriage and family life in the army, the experiences of which differed significantly based on one's professional position in the army. We will also examine the army's expectations for sexual propriety and the violence that could sometimes emerge in sexual relationships. Lastly we will analyze the army's increasing interest (and interventions) in same-sex relationships because of growing fears about homosexuality. All told the army's attempts to regulate sexuality represent considerable interventions in personal and public health; the creation of normative standards of sexual behavior, including how and in what ways soldiers might engage in sexual activities and relationships; and official endorsement of particular views of sexual morality and sexual identities among soldiers.

Venereal Disease and Prostitution

The U.S. Army remained profoundly concerned about venereal disease outbreaks among soldiers throughout the early twentieth century because of the burden of treating venereal infections and the impact of these diseases on individual and unit readiness. It routinely rejected recruits who were found to be venereally infected—the most common reason for rejection of applicants in nine of the first twenty years of the twentieth century.[3] The army also sought to treat soldiers who contracted venereal diseases during their military service, mandating treatment after sexual exposure. Despite these measures venereal disease was rampant among U.S. soldiers. From 1873 through 1898, roughly 8.5 percent of Regular Army soldiers were treated for venereal disease annually.[4] In 1899 the incidence of venereal disease within the U.S. Army increased to 13.8 percent. The overall venereal disease rate continued to climb, with an average venereal disease rate from 1899 through 1910 of 14.9 percent of all soldiers infected. The primary change in the army in this period was the large-scale deployments to the Philippines.

The venereal admission rates for army units in the Philippines were significantly higher than in all other locales. In some years the annual venereal disease admission rate for the Philippine Department was more than 23 percent, with some units reaching nearly 36 percent.[5] Clearly, soldiers contracted venereal diseases in the Philippines at an alarming rate, far more than at any other station, foreign or domestic, during the first four decades of the twentieth century. The army sought to mitigate the effects of venereal disease on soldiers by, when necessary, medically inspecting and forcibly treating prostitutes and eventually American soldiers in the Philippines. The army's regulated-prostitution program had limited effects on the rate of venereal disease transmission to soldiers because there were no fully effective means available to treat venereal infections prior to the advent of antibiotics, which began to be mass produced in 1944.

In acknowledging the venereal threat, Brigadier General George H. Torney, the surgeon general of the army, stated in 1910 that "the venereal peril has come to outweigh in importance any other sanitary question which now confronts the Army, and neither our national optimism nor the Anglo-Saxon disposition to ignore a subject which is offensive to public prudery can no longer excuse a frank and honest confrontation of the problem."[6] Torney recommended a series of countermeasures for decreasing the venereal infection rate. The War Department endorsed his plan in 1912, along with a new policy of stopping pay for soldiers during their venereal treatments. The surgeon general's recommendations included the introduction of new, wholesome recreation facilities to lure soldiers away from illicit sex; the creation of temperance societies within the army, since sex and alcohol were so frequently linked in the minds of reformers; lectures on sexual health that focused on the dangers of sex; and, perhaps most important, periodic venereal inspections of soldiers and increased availability of prophylactic packages.[7] These prophylactic packages, often described as a "K-Packet," consisted of a glass syringe of chemicals packaged in wax paper that soldiers were to inject into the urethra after sex to prevent infection by syphilis.[8] Notably, they did not include condoms, which many American moralists believed would have only encouraged immoral sexual behavior.

The medical inspection program in the Philippines eventually came under tremendous criticism by domestic moral reform organizations, many of which were sharply anti-imperialist and used the issue of sexual immorality to criticize the American occupation. Nevertheless, the army continued its program in the Philippines until World War I. During the war, because the army feared that venereal disease rates would once again climb due to new overseas deployments, it embraced similar regimes of mandated medical inspections of prostitutes in France and Germany with the cooperation of the local governments. American reformers were never entirely comfortable with such regimes but were forced to acquiesce to these policies, as they were legally required under French and German law and widely accepted in both countries. Such medical inspections regimes were not tried in the continental United States because of domestic political resistance, though the army established similar programs on the U.S.-Mexican border during the Pancho Villa Expedition (1916–17) and in Honolulu (from the late nineteenth century) with the approval of territorial officials. It seems clear that the implementation of regulated prostitution regimes was only possible outside the continental United States, in places where local women were perceived as posing grave medical dangers to the soldiers they were expected to have sex with because of prevailing American beliefs about the sexual and medical impurities of non-American women.

U.S. deployments to Europe during World War I only heightened concerns about venereal disease. Four medical officers, led by Major (later Colonel) Hugh H. Young, who would head the army's newly formed urological department, accompanied General Pershing and his headquarters staff on Pershing's ship to France in May 1917.[9] These medical officers immediately began a study of "the prevention and treatment of venereal disease in the English and French armies," with a goal of designing an anti-venereal regime for the American army. The American Expeditionary Force's (AEF) sixth General Order, issued in July 1917, exclusively addressed policies for mitigating the effects of venereal disease within the U.S. Army.[10] It established prophylactic stations throughout France and mandated that all members of the AEF report to these stations for treatment within three hours of sexual exposure. It also dictated that men who contracted venereal diseases "through neglect" be court-martialed. Elaborate, detailed instructions were provided for the mandated prophylactic treatments, though army surgeons frequently complained about the inadequacy of the prophylactic stations under field conditions.[11]

Almost immediately upon the arrival of the first American soldiers in France, U.S. Army physicians detected a significant outbreak of syphilis. Army leaders and medical experts quickly investigated and blamed French prostitutes for the outbreak.[12] While some of these women were undoubtedly the source of some American soldiers' infections, the number of women found to be infected was not high enough to account for the outbreak. On October 21, 1917, the army began to venereally inspect American troops prior to embarkation in the United States. Medical authorities were surprised at the number of cases of syphilis infections discovered before the troops left the United States. The army found that the rates of venereal infections among newly arriving members of the AEF varied tremendously. In October and November

1917, the average rate for all soldiers of the A E F was approximately 1.2 percent, though some units' rates were as high as 25 to 33 percent. Rates for Black units were roughly four or five times as high as those of white units.[13] Contrary to the prejudices of some doctors and army leaders, this evidence suggests that the main vector of infection may have been from American soldiers to French prostitutes, rather than the other way around, but army leaders resisted that conclusion.

Overall, venereal infection rates differed sharply between white and Black soldiers in the A E F. While approximately 10 percent of all white soldiers contracted a venereal disease during the war, 58 percent of Blacks did.[14] Several theories have been advanced to explain this sharp disparity: white physicians may have been prone to diagnosing a variety of ailments in Blacks as sexual in origin because of racialized ideas about Black male hypersexuality, for example. Also, while many whites who were venereally infected at induction were rejected for military service, most infected Blacks were not, reflecting the prevailing idea among whites that almost all Blacks were venereally infected, and so they could not be disqualified solely for this reason. High venereal infection rates among Blacks also reflected the poor quality (or nonexistence, in some cases) of medical care available to them prior to their military service in the United States.

The U.S. Army's early twentieth-century interventions in the sexual lives of soldiers and their partners most prominently involved efforts to mitigate the effects of venereal diseases on army manpower. Because of the prevailing—and often incorrect—notion (in the army and within American society) that prostitutes were the primary source of venereal disease, the army frequently sought to attack venereal disease by medically regulating the prostitutes with whom soldiers came into contact. This created an inextricable linkage between prostitution and venereal disease and meant that civilians outside the United States were forced to accede to regular medical inspections by army doctors, facing imprisonment until their symptoms went into remission. Despite these efforts and intrusions, the army was not able to eradicate venereal diseases among soldiers.

The U.S. Army also intervened in another important way in the personal lives of its members: it forbade most enlisted men—sergeants excepted, because of their age and seniority—and some junior officers from marrying.[15] As an old saying about life in the U.S. Army went, "If the army had wanted you to have a wife, it would have issued you one." Though some enlisted soldiers did marry while in military service, with or without their commanding officer's permission, they were forbidden from reenlisting once married and were court-martialed if they attempted to conceal the fact that they were married at enlistment or reenlistment. The army ostensibly created this policy because large numbers of civilian dependents would have created a burden on the army to provide housing and support for the wives and children of soldiers. Moreover, maintaining large numbers of army families would have been especially difficult in the army's austere basing conditions abroad. Most middle-class Americans perceived enlisted military service as socially undesirable, and enlisted soldiers were also generally paid less than civilian blue-collar workers. These factors would have made supporting a wife and family financially and socially challenging, even had the army permitted marriage. The army's anti-marriage policy thus created a military culture in which most soldiers who desired romantic or sexual partnerships were forced to choose between consorting with prostitutes and risking venereal infection; violating army regulations by having illicit sexual relationships or marrying in secret, with the risk of being court-martialed when the marriage or relationship came to the official attention of the army; or marrying and then being forced to leave military service when the current term of service had ended. This dilemma was further complicated by the expectation that "respectable" women would not have sex outside marriage.

"Married men in the Army are unquestionably a burden . . . so also are married officers," wrote George Shelton, an army official, in the secretary of war's 1907 annual report.[16] In 1903 Major General Henry C. Corbin, adjutant general of the army, worked to establish policies preventing junior officers from marrying and married junior officer candidates from being commissioned. Other proponents of this view alleged that married lieutenants were not as attentive to their duties as single men, as they were distracted by their wives and domestic concerns. Some single officers charged that policies governing marriage were unfair, as married lieutenants were given special privileges in housing and other matters.[17] Ultimately, Corbin was unsuccessful in pushing through this change in army policy, though the issue arose again in 1915 when the General Staff briefly considered barring second lieutenants from marriage. Once again it was asserted that marriage was too distracting and, perhaps more important from the army's perspective, "too expensive a luxury" because of the additional costs incurred by the army in housing and transporting the families of junior officers.[18] This effort was likewise unsuccessful, and while junior officers were unofficially strongly discouraged from marrying, they were never legally prohibited from doing so. The army had to accept at least some marriages and families if it expected to retain experienced soldiers and therefore had to provide adequate pay, housing, and other benefits to support these families.

Some privates did marry, clandestinely and without the approval of their commanding officers, though they likely lived in common-law relationships more frequently than in formalized, legal marriages, especially in places like the Philippines and Hawaii, where such common-law relationships were more socially acceptable. The wives and children of noncommissioned officers generally lived on army posts. While these spouses often lacked formal education, they were integrated into base social and professional life, though the careers of noncommissioned officers could sometimes be made more difficult or even derailed by their wives and children's social missteps in interactions with officers and their families.

Sexual Propriety and Violence

The U.S. Army has created and maintained sharp, class-based, hierarchical divides between commissioned officers and enlisted men throughout its history, and the early decades of the twentieth century were no exception.[19] U.S. Army officers and enlisted men of the early twentieth century maintained separate cultures within the army, a fact that had profound implications for all aspects of these men's lives, including those that were the most intimate.

Commissioned officers, for example, were only very rarely forced to submit to intrusive and demeaning venereal inspections of their bodies, unlike enlisted men, who were court-martialed for refusing to submit to medical inspections and treatments. Officers and enlisted men received very different treatment under the military justice system and were subject to divergent expectations, surveillance, and discipline of sexual propriety and behaviors. The varying experiences of officers and enlisted men and the different ways in which the army regulated their sexual lives help shed additional light on the army's separate cultures because the army's regulation of sexuality reinforced and helped maintain its social and professional hierarchy.

The army's class structures included not just soldiers, but also their wives, families, and sex partners. The army treated these civilians very differently depending on the ranks of the men with which they were associated. Officers' wives were nearly always considered respectable women. Neither officers nor their families welcomed intrusion by enlisted men into their private spaces. Many older noncommissioned officers were also married, and their wives often accompanied them on deployments, though they formed their own family communities separate from those of officers. The army tended to consider unmarried women who interacted sexually with enlisted soldiers to be prostitutes and sources of venereal contagion, though the army often deemed them necessary for servicing soldiers' assumed sexual needs. Thus, the sex lives of these different groups of men and their civilian sex partners were regarded and regulated very differently by the army. These sharply divergent expectations and practices likewise led to different conceptions of masculinity for commissioned officers and enlisted men. Officers, for example, were deemed capable of violating the 95th Article of War, which made criminal any "conduct unbecoming an officer and a gentleman."[20] In practice this meant that officers were required to act according to fairly rigid, traditional standards of middle-class morality and social behavior at all times. However, no matter how "well-behaved" they might be, enlisted men were never held to this standard because they were never considered "gentlemen"—and thus could never violate the 95th Article of War—because of their social status and military rank. This illustrates two starkly different social constructions of masculinity embodied in two groups of men: enlisted soldiers, who were mostly from working-class backgrounds and perceived as having rough-and-tumble lifestyles that also included frequent sexual encounters with working-class women; and commissioned officers, mostly from middle- and upper-class backgrounds, who were expected to behave, at least publicly, as the American public believed men of those classes were supposed to behave toward women and in matters related to sexuality. The class structures embedded in the army's hierarchy reinforced and reified these social constructions of masculinity.

Despite these different expectations, there was a great deal of contact between officers' wives and enlisted men when no officers were present. Much of this contact stemmed from the fact that officers frequently hired enlisted soldiers to perform chores in and around the home; while officers were away, their wives supervised the soldiers' work. These interactions sometimes crossed a line, with officers' wives sometimes becoming scandalized at the remarks or insinuations made by soldiers. Soldiers found to have sexually harassed women, either the wives of officers or civilians, were usually punished severely and rarely allowed to remain in the army. Enlisted soldiers convicted of invading the intimate or domestic spaces of noncommissioned or commissioned officers and their families, usually as "peeping toms," were also treated harshly. The army made it clear that it did not tolerate sexual improprieties committed against respectable, middle-class women by their enlisted social inferiors. In some cases Black soldiers interacted with officers' white wives in ways army officials deemed inappropriate, seemingly eliciting racial anxieties in addition to social and gender concerns, which brought about severe punishments for the soldiers involved.

Army officers were bound by a set of expectations regarding matters of social (and sexual) propriety to which enlisted men were generally not held accountable. Officers faced legal reprisals for some kinds of sexual behaviors for which enlisted men were seldom prosecuted. For example, officers were court-martialed for their interactions with prostitutes because they either offended the sensibilities of their fellow officers, or because they engaged publicly in activities the army deemed immoral. The army also acted to maintain the boundaries of social propriety between officers and enlisted men. When officers publicly violated these social norms—by drinking, gambling, or discussing sex with enlisted men, for example—the army could act rapidly and decisively to convict and dismiss the offending officers.

The army was also concerned with issues of sexual violence. There are some reported instances of domestic violence at army bases in this period. When the incidents occurred in private residences and did not create public disturbances, the army did not involve itself. However, the army did initiate formal legal proceedings against soldiers who committed acts of violence against their wives or girlfriends in public. There were a relatively small number of cases involving allegations of rape by soldiers against civilian women (commissioned officers were almost never charged with such offenses, perhaps suggesting that army culture and class structures protected such men). In almost all of these cases, the character and morality of the woman who was alleged to have been raped was called into question by the defense and often led to acquittals for the accused. In several cases multiple witnesses testified—in line with the perceptions of many in that era—that the women were immoral, promiscuous, or had been romantically involved with the accused and thus successfully cast doubt on the women's claims that they had been raped.

Rape, like murder, was one of the very few capital crimes under the Articles of War, with the two crimes grouped together under the 92nd Article of War. Because federal law at the time did not define rape, the army adopted the common-law (civilian) understanding of the crime: "The having of unlawful carnal knowledge of a woman by force and without her consent." The sex act did not have to be completed to be considered rape, but rather "any penetration, however slight, of a woman's genitals is sufficient carnal knowledge, whether emission occurs or not." Husbands could not commit rape against their wives, even if the wife did not grant her consent—a man's marital privileges allowed him to legally have sex with his wife whenever he wished. All other women could be victims of rape: "The offense may be committed on a female of any age, on a man's mistress, or on a common harlot." Additionally, women who were mentally handicapped ("idiotic"), unconscious, asleep, or coerced to grant consent through violence or the threat of violence were all deemed unable to legally grant consent, and men who had sex with the women under these circumstances were guilty of committing rape. The 92nd Article of War made clear that "mere verbal protestations and a pretense of resistance do not of course show a want of consent, but the contrary, and where a woman fails to take such measures to frustrate the execution of the man's design as she is able to, and are called for by the circumstances, the same conclusion may be drawn." Women were thus required not simply to put up a token or verbal resistance to the sex act, but to resist actively. The threshold was lower for younger women, in which case "the court will demand less clear opposition than in the case of an older and intelligent female."[21] In practice, though it was technically a capital crime, soldiers who were convicted of committing rape were almost never sentenced to death during peacetime. During wartime a number of American soldiers were tried and convicted of raping French women; most were executed immediately. It seems clear that the army took seriously charges of sexual violence and harassment when they became public, but it is impossible to know how many such cases were overlooked or ignored because they did not take place in circumstances that brought them to the army's official attention. As imperfect as it was during this period, the army's understanding and treatment of rape—based as it was on civilian laws and assumptions—probably did not differ markedly from that of the civilian legal system used at the time.

Homosexuality and Same-Sex Relationships

Prior to the U.S. involvement in World War I, the U.S. Army focused narrowly on the physical act of sodomy in its legal practices, rather than on homosexuality as an identity of some soldiers.[22] While some army physicians—and occasionally other officers—who offered testimony in courts-martial suggested that certain individuals were congenitally predisposed toward moral weakness and this may have led accused soldiers to commit homosexual acts, more often the prevailing notion within the army seemed to be that same-sex sexual activity was situational, often brought about by overindulgence in alcohol. This implicit belief in "situational homosexuality" as the primary cause of such acts did not prevent relatively harsh sentences of dishonorable discharges and up to several years of hard labor in federal penitentiaries.

The 1917 revision to the army's *Manual for Courts-Martial*—which first introduced sodomy as an explicit offense—ushered in a series of new sodomy-related charges. Because there was no Federal Penal Code definition of sodomy, army courts-martial used the common-law definition of sodomy: "Sodomy at common law consists in sexual connection with any brute animal, or in sexual connection, per anum, by a man with any man or woman." The army went on to enlarge its definition of sodomy beyond that found in civil courts by noting explicitly that "penetration of the mouth of the person also constitutes this offense." Sodomy was thus an extremely broad category of offense: it could consist of bestiality, anal sex, and oral sex. There was no requirement that both parties involved in the offense be male; soldiers who had oral or anal sex with women were also guilty of sodomy. In its description of sodomy, the army made no attempt to distinguish between the active or passive participants in the act. "Both parties are liable as principals if each is adult and consents; but if either be a boy of tender age the adult alone is liable, and although the boy consent the act is still by force." (No language about female minors was included.) In one important clarification—because it often could not be proved if ejaculation had occurred—the army noted that "penetration alone is sufficient." Army regulation No. 40-105, which went into effect in 1921, created psychiatric screening standards for homosexuality that remained in effect until they were revised in 1941.[23] This regulation drew explicitly on then-prevailing psychiatric theories that considered same-sex sexual activity, often described as a form of "sexual psychopathy," to be symptomatic of grave physical, mental, and moral degeneracy, as well as effeminacy, which made such men unfit for military service.

In the United States, the 1920s also witnessed the rise of psychoanalysis and the influence of Sigmund Freud's work, which ushered in new perspectives on human sexuality, including homosexuality.[24] As the American medical and psychoanalytical communities became professionalized in the early twentieth century, their monopoly over expertise in matters psychological and sexual grew. World War I only served to give them a new sense of mission in treating an increasingly pathologized populace and expand their role in society. By war's end psychological and medical professionals, many of whom deemed themselves "sexologists"—experts in diagnosing and treating sexual dysfunctions—were regularly consulted in matters of public health and sexuality.

By the 1920s there was growing awareness of same-sex sexual attraction, which elicited considerable interest among psychoanalysts and sexologists, who increasingly viewed such behavior as pathological. Homosexuality was no longer seen as a set of behaviors, gestures, or demeanors but as a central feature of the identity of those who engaged in same-sex sexual activity. As Michel Foucault later noted, "Homosexuality appeared as one of the forms of sexuality when it was transposed from the practice of sodomy onto a kind of interior androgyny, a hermaphroditism of the soul. The sodomite had been a temporary aberration; the homosexual was now a species."[25] Freud questioned the idea that homosexuality was inborn and inherited, as previous sexologists like Magnus Hirschfeld and Richard von Krafft-Ebing, among many others, had believed. Freud instead asserted that it was the result of early childhood experiences and ultimately concluded that homosexuality, like other sexual conditions he regarded as perverse, was generally the result of interrupted sexual development.[26] To Freud heterosexuality was the normal state of mature, adult psychosexual development: "One of the tasks implicit in object choice is that it should find its way to the opposite sex."[27] Later psychoanalytic clinicians in the United States and elsewhere—including many employed by the U.S. Army—perceived homosexuality as a profound, psychopathic disturbance.

After World War I the U.S. Army prioritized eliminating homosexuality within the service. American society, the medical and psychoanalytic communities, and the army increasingly took notice of homosexual practices and began to pathologize such activities.[28] In this new, postwar environment, same-sex sexual practices came to be seen as signifying an identifiable homosexual identity for those men who engaged in these practices. Homosexuality became increasingly linked with psychiatric defects and effeminacy, neither of which was deemed acceptable for soldiers. While these fears about the dangers of homosexuality produced only sporadic investigations, they suggested considerable underlying anxieties, as well as a significant expenditure of resources to periodically root out offenders. These efforts produced a number of courts-martial for men charged with various offenses related to sexual contact with other men. Despite the growing belief that men who were sexually attracted to other men were mentally deficient or effeminate—and therefore poor soldiers—without some evidence of physical sexual acts, soldiers suspected of being homosexuals were not charged. The army seems to have developed new anxieties about homosexuality in this period, which it then projected onto soldiers accused of some behaviors that were previously treated less seriously, but it mostly focused on specific behaviors rather than wholesale sexual identities in regulating same-sex attraction.

Outcomes and Effects of Army Management of Sexuality

The U.S. Army exhibited concerns about soldiers' sexual behavior everywhere it went, though it sought to deal with the host of issues surrounding sex very differently in each setting. Expansionist U.S. foreign policy, the growth in both the size of the army and the scope of its operations across the globe, and the nation's renewed investment and interest in the U.S. Army as a result of the national mobilization of World War I all resulted in increased public scrutiny of and interest in life inside the army. The effects and outcomes of these interventions are myriad, though at least four significant effects should be highlighted here.

First, these interventions demonstrate how an institutional concern by the military—in this case the desire to mitigate the effects of venereal infections on soldiers and thereby unit readiness—can lead to large-scale interventions into civilian life. This can be seen in the public health programs intended to regulate prostitution, which had profound legal and medical implications everywhere it was tried. The U.S. Army instituted medical inspection and segregation regimes of prostitutes first in the Philippines and then later along the U.S.-Mexican border, and the army cooperated with civilian officials who maintained similar policies in Hawaii, France, and Germany. In contrast with more permissive regimes abroad, at least until negative publicity forced changes, in the continental United States the army cooperated with domestic moral reformers who sought to eliminate all traces of prostitution and other "vices" surrounding military bases within the continental United States.

Second, the interventions discussed in this chapter illustrate how reform-minded civilian constituencies could employ the military as an institution to advance a particular set of (highly ideological) behavioral norms. This played out directly during World War I, when moral and social reformers sought to use the military to create a utopian American society after the war by promoting a particular brand of traditional, white, middle-class sexual norms via the encouragement of sexual abstinence among soldiers, due to the massive influx of new, middle-class "respectable" young men who entered military service. These men, unlike professional soldiers who chose to serve in the army during peacetime, were perceived as being morally and sexually vulnerable, in need of protection from the temptations of the flesh. Many domestic reformers considered these draftees to be a source of moral renewal of the nation after the war—if they could be protected from sexual dangers and trained to reject sexual immorality. This policy failed to produce the sexual abstinence these reformers sought, just as it failed to transform broader American sexual norms after the war.

Third, these interventions demonstrate how military institutions are buffeted by a variety of forces, ideas, and debates external to the military, and how prevailing views in the larger domestic civilian context can come to impact the military's actions. The military truly is a product of its civilian environment—pathologizing homosexuality is a key example here. The army required increasingly heteronormative sexual expression of soldiers, as the institution and American society became more aware of same-sex attraction. Soldiers were expected to conform to these specific gender and sexual norms and public performances, while also being forbidden from engaging in sexual practices and behaviors deemed effeminate. The resulting set of acceptable hypermasculinized sexual behaviors constituted part of a new sexual identity for soldiers, one that army leaders believed was the most effective for promoting aggressive, militant, and therefore martial set of behaviors in the new century.

Lastly, these interventions highlight how different conceptions of masculinity can operate simultaneously within a group of men, and how these conceptions can be embraced and promoted by institutions for their own purposes. The U.S. Army seems to have embraced what scholars of masculinity have described as a changing conception of American manhood that emerged in the late nineteenth century as a result of larger cultural responses by white men to the oft-heralded disappearance of the American "frontier" defined by the increasing urbanization, bureaucratization, and industrialization of American society. The slow but steady rise in the social and political rights of women, minorities, and other groups most white American men had previously dominated also played a major role in the construction of masculinity during this period.[29] With these changes came increasing interest in martial virtues, physicality, strength, a robust male body, athleticism, competition, respect for "primitive" warriors, and virility to create what might be called "militant masculinity." American soldiers, who routinely engaged in intense physical labor and held a virtual monopoly on the legal use of violence, were able to embrace this new conception of masculinity to a greater degree than most civilian men. These constructed images of gender became central to soldiers' identities and highly charged with meaning, shaping the way that soldiers conceived of themselves as men and as soldiers. The army adopted and enlarged the concept of militant masculinity, using it to shape soldiers' sexual identities. Enlisted soldiers, some of whom were considered sexually problematic by army officials, were socialized to generate that specific kind of masculinity in their public and private lives and to behave in particular kinds of "masculine" ways. Army officers, considered "gentlemen" in military culture and law, were required to exhibit different traits of masculinity and different standards of sexual behavior from the enlisted soldiers who served under them.

In the first four decades of the twentieth century, the U.S. Army regulated practically all forms of sexual behavior and expressions by soldiers to a greater degree than ever before. While the U.S. Army in other times may have encouraged a robust, virile, and even promiscuous heterosexuality in its soldiers (or at least looked the other way in a spirit of "boys will be boys"), it tried rather assiduously between 1898 and 1940 to regulate and at times prohibit almost all forms of sexual expression, ranging from the reprehensible (rape) to the harmless (masturbation). The U.S. Army attempted to control—via official policy, legal enforcement, indoctrination, and military culture—sexual behaviors that it found problematic for the institution as a whole and its overall military effectiveness. Allowing soldiers the opportunity to indulge in some sexual desires but not others, while guarding against the problems that sex could cause for unit readiness and morale, became one of the key balancing acts that U.S. Army planners had to perform throughout the early decades of the twentieth century. The sexual behaviors the army found particularly troublesome included sexual encounters that resulted in venereal infections, marriage, or pregnancy, and those that created public embarrassment for the army or problems with civil-military relations. Over time the army increasingly viewed sexual relationships between soldiers as undesirable because of changes in the way that most Americans, led by medical and psychoanalytic experts, viewed such same-sex relationships. In regulating these sexual behaviors, the army also indirectly (and in some cases unintentionally) influenced views of sexual morality and sexual identities among soldiers. For example, in emphasizing sexual abstinence as a policy during World War I, the army publicly helped promote a brand of traditional, middle-class sexual morality favored by many influential moral reformers. It also implicitly endorsed the perceived linkage between same-sex sexual activities and pathologized homosexuality. The U.S. Army thus acted as a powerful force in the early twentieth century to manage the sexuality of soldiers and civilians alike throughout the world, wherever the army deployed, having long-term consequences on public health as well as normative sexual identities and behaviors.

Notes

1. For a more detailed exploration of the issues discussed in this chapter, see Byers, *Sexual Economy of War*.

2. Lutz, *Bases of Empire*; Höhn and Moon, *Over There*; Enloe, *Maneuvers*.

3. Coffman, *Regulars*, 97.

4. "Venereal Diseases and Alcoholism in the Regular Army in the United States," undated chart, AGO Docfile #1915426, filed with AGO Docfile #1045985, NARA. Note that this does not necessarily mean that 8.5 percent of all soldiers in the U.S. Army were admitted for newly contracting venereal diseases each year. Some soldiers might be admitted more than once during a calendar year for the same or different venereal disease, and a man might be readmitted for a new flare-up of a venereal disease contracted previously.

5. Data on Philippine posts taken from the surgeon general to the adjutant general, "Rates for Venereal Disease in the Second Division," letter dated November 19, 1914, AGO Docfile #2230647, filed with AGO Docfile #1045985, NARA. Data on U.S. domestic posts taken from the surgeon general to the adjutant general, "Venereal Disease in the Army," table A, letter dated September 30, 1915, AGO Docfile #2225425, filed with AGO Docfile #1045985, NARA.

6. Quoted in Brandt, *No Magic Bullet*, 98.

7. Brandt, *No Magic Bullet*, 97–98.

8. K-Packets were first introduced in the Philippines in 1910 on a small scale, and while they appeared to reduce the overall venereal disease rate briefly, they had no long-term effects. The army's surgeon general attributed this inefficacy to noncompliance with medical instructions. The standard venereal treatments during this period relied primarily on injections of salicylic mercury, both subcutaneously and urethrally, but were not particularly effective and often caused serious side effects. Wintermute, *Public Health*, 208; Brandt, *No Magic Bullet*, 11–12, 114.

9. Young, *Hugh Young*, 264–71; Walker, *Venereal Disease*, 1, 46–47.

10. General Orders, Number 6, Headquarters, AEF, July 2, 1917, reproduced in *United States Army in the World War, Vol. 16: General Orders*, 11–12.

11. Chamberlain and Weed, *Medical Department*, 938–49.

12. Pershing, *AEF Bulletin*, 17:82. Here, under the section "Facts about Venereal Disease," it is stated that "the greatest source of venereal infection is the regulated and inspected house of prostitution," and that "venereal infection is highly prevalent among unregistered 'clandestine' prostitutes, and exists to-day to an increasing degree in social classes hitherto little suspected. The practice of illicit indulgence in sexual intercourse will almost inevitably lead to venereal infection sooner or later."

13. Walker, *Venereal Disease*, 77–81; Chamberlain and Weed, *Medical Department*, 908.

14. Brandt, *No Magic Bullet*, 116.

15. U.S. Department of War, *Regulations*; Goldman, "Trends in Family Patterns"; U.S. Army, *Army Family*, 2.

16. Office of the Chief of Staff, "Army as a Life Occupation," 78.

17. *Army and Navy Journal*, January 3, 1903; October 8, 1904; October 29, 1904; and August 26, 1905.

18. *Army and Navy Journal*, April 24, 1915.

19. Noncommissioned officers existed in a space midway between these worlds, enjoying some privileges over junior enlisted soldiers, but never treated as social equals by commissioned officers.

20. U.S. Department of War, *Manual for Courts-Martial.*

21. U.S. Department of War, *Manual for Courts-Martial.*

22. Canaday, *Straight State*; Frank, *Unfriendly Fire.*

23. Bérubé, *Coming Out under Fire*, 12–14.

24. Engel, *American Therapy*; Terry, *American Obsession*; Demos, "Oedipus and America," 63–78.

25. Foucault, *History of Sexuality*, 43.

26. Engel, *American Therapy*, 7, 298; Bayer, *Homosexuality and American Psychiatry*, 21–27.

27. Freud, *Three Essays*, 133.

28. Chauncey, *Gay New York*; Chauncey, "Christian Brotherhood or Sexual Perversion?" The army's perspective on same-sex acts during this period is in sharp contrast with the U.S. military's actions toward alleged homosexuals during World War II, as chronicled by historian Allan Bérubé, who describes the military's inadvertent role in helping to create a homosexual identity and, postwar, a coherent community.

29. Rotundo, *American Manhood*; Bederman, *Manliness and Civilization*; Greenberg, *Manifest Manhood.*

Bibliography

Archives and Manuscript Materials

NARA. RG 94, Papers of the Adjutant General's Office (AGO). National Archives and Records Administration, Washington DC.

Published Works

Bayer, Ronald. *Homosexuality and American Psychiatry: The Politics of Diagnosis.* Princeton NJ: Princeton University Press, 1987.

Bederman, Gail. *Manliness and Civilization: A Cultural History of Gender and Race in the United States, 1880–1917.* Chicago: University of Chicago Press, 1995.

Bérubé, Allan. *Coming Out under Fire: The History of Gay Men and Women in World War Two.* New York: Plume, 1990.

Brandt, Allan M. *No Magic Bullet: A Social History of Venereal Disease in the United States since 1880.* New York: Oxford University Press, 1985.

Byers, Andrew. *The Sexual Economy of War: Discipline and Desire in the U.S. Army.* Ithaca NY: Cornell University Press, 2019.

Canaday, Margot. *The Straight State: Sexuality and Citizenship in Twentieth-Century America.* Princeton NJ: Princeton University Press, 2009.

Chamberlain, Weston P., and Frank W. Weed. *The Medical Department of the United States Army in the World War, Vol. 6: Sanitation.* Edited by M. W. Ireland. Washington DC: Government Printing Office, 1926.

Chauncey, George, Jr. "Christian Brotherhood or Sexual Perversion? Homosexual Identities and the Construction of Sexual Boundaries in the World War I Era." In *Hidden from History: Reclaiming the Gay and Lesbian Past*, edited by

Martin Bauml Duberman, Martha Vicinus, and George Chauncey Jr., 294–317. New York: New American Library, 1989.

———. *Gay New York: Gender, Urban Culture, and the Making of the Gay Male World, 1890–1940*. New York: Basic Books, 1994.

Coffman, Edward M. *The Regulars: The American Army, 1898–1941*. Cambridge MA: Belknap Press of Harvard University Press, 2004.

Demos, John. "Oedipus and America: Historical Perspectives on the Reception of Psychoanalysis in the United States." In *Inventing the Psychological: Toward a Cultural History of Emotional Life in America*, edited by Joel Pfister and Nancy Schnog, 63–78. New Haven CT: Yale University Press, 1997.

Engel, Jonathan. *American Therapy: The Rise of Psychotherapy in the United States*. New York: Gotham, 2008.

Enloe, Cynthia H. *Maneuvers: The International Politics of Militarizing Women's Lives*. Berkeley: University of California Press, 2000.

Foucault, Michel. *The History of Sexuality, Vol. 1: An Introduction*. New York: Vintage, 1990.

Frank, Nathaniel. *Unfriendly Fire: How the Gay Ban Undermines the Military and Weakens America*. New York: Thomas Dunne, 2009.

Freud, Sigmund. *Three Essays on the Theory of Sexuality*. Translated by James Strachey. New York: Basic Books, 1962.

Goldman, Nancy L. "Trends in Family Patterns of U.S. Military Personnel during the 20th Century." In *The Social Psychology of Military Service*, edited by Nancy L. Goldman and David R. Segal. Beverly Hills CA: SAGE, 1976.

Greenberg, Amy S. *Manifest Manhood and the Antebellum American Empire*. Cambridge: Cambridge University Press, 2005.

Höhn, Maria, and Seungsook Moon, eds. *Over There: Living with the U.S. Military Empire from World War Two to the Present*. Durham NC: Duke University Press, 2010.

Lutz, Catherine, ed. *The Bases of Empire: The Global Struggle against U.S. Military Posts*. New York: New York University Press, 2009.

Office of the Chief of Staff. "The Army as a Life Occupation for Enlisted Men." In *Annual Report of the Secretary of War, 1907*, appendix B. Washington DC: War Department, 1907.

Pershing, John J. *AEF Bulletin* 54, August 7, 1918. In *United States Army in the World War, Vol. 17*. Washington DC: U.S. Army Center of Military History, 1988.

Rotundo, Anthony. *American Manhood: Transformations in Masculinity from the Revolution to the Modern Era*. New York: Basic Books, 1993.

Terry, Jennifer. *An American Obsession: Science, Medicine, and Homosexuality in Modern Society*. Chicago: University of Chicago Press, 1999.

United States Army in the World War, 1917–1919, Vol. 16: General Orders, GHQ, AEF. Washington DC: U.S. Army Center of Military History, 1992.

U.S. Army. *The Army Family*. Washington DC: Chief of Staff, U.S. Army, 1983.

U.S. Department of War. *Regulations for the Army of the United States, 1913 Corrected to 1917*. Washington DC: Government Printing Office, 1917.

U.S. Department of War, Office of the Judge Advocate General. *A Manual for Courts-Martial*, approved by the U.S. Congress on June 4, 1920, and effective February 4, 1921. Washington DC: Government Printing Office, 1920.

Walker, George. *Venereal Disease in the American Expeditionary Forces*. Baltimore MD: Medical Standard, 1922.

"Who's in the Army Now?" *Fortune*, September 1935, 136.

Wintermute, Bobby A. *Public Health and the U.S. Military: A History of the Army Medical Department, 1818–1917*. New York: Routledge, 2011.

Young, Hugh H. *Hugh Young: A Surgeon's Autobiography*. New York: Harcourt, Brace & Company, 1940.

TWO

Compensation, Commerce, and Conjugality

*Managing Male Heterosexuality in the U.S. Military
from World War II to the War on Terror*

SUSAN L. CARRUTHERS

Sex in the military is "rarely pure and never simple," to borrow Oscar Wilde's aphorism about the truth. It is variously, and sometimes simultaneously, a matter of private pleasure and official prescription; a perceived entitlement and form of violent domination; an issue of public health and a matter of public relations; a recreational pursuit and the genesis of procreation; a commercialized transaction or conjugal affirmation. Questions about who sleeps with whom—where, when, how, and with what consequences—inform issues of command, reputation, and discipline. Not surprisingly, then, sexual intercourse is more highly charged and more intensely policed within military institutions than in American society at large. Different rules apply, such as the military's ongoing criminalization of adultery and its persistent efforts to prohibit "sodomy," "turpitude," "solicitation," and "pandering," often long after these terms and the actions they denoted had become anachronistic in civilian life. But despite attempts to uphold separate sexual standards for service personnel, military prohibitions were often flouted, with forbidden practices persisting in the face of efforts to eliminate them. "War is Hell," quipped a *New York Times* reporter in 1996. "So is regulating sex."[1]

This chapter explores the various ways in which military commanders perceived male heterosexuality to be simultaneously constitutive of and destructive to martial esprit, and how they attempted to manage sexual encounters between men in uniform and their female partners. To be clear, the exclusive focus of this essay on male soldiers and on heterosexuality stems from this volume's analytic division of labor. Other authors tackle the military's management of male homosexuality and the sexual identities and behaviors of women in the armed forces. Male heterosexuality has certainly not monopolized the attention of military commanders as the sole site of sexual desire and activity in need of disciplinary control, as other contributors to this collection make explicit. The goal of this chapter, then, is to make clear how male heterosexuality has posed not only some of the same challenges that military commanders have perceived in homosexuality—including issues of indiscipline, infection, and reputation—but also its own distinct conundrums.

This essay covers an expansive sweep of time, from World War II to the present. These eight decades saw immense changes not only in how American armed forces recruited personnel, organized themselves institutionally, and conducted operations in war and peacetime but also in normative attitudes toward sex in U.S. society more broadly. Over successive decades more liberal attitudes came to prevail toward who could marry whom, including same-sex partners. While the parameters of marriage broadened, however, the once-pervasive social expectation that adult Americans ought to be married contracted. Divorce lost its sting, and remarriage became commonplace. Adultery ceased to be such a scandalous source of stigma and shame as it had been in the nineteenth and early twentieth centuries. Arguably, by the start of the twenty-first century, many American civilians had stopped thinking about sex as posing problems in need of solution.[2]

Not so in the armed forces, though. Sex posed, and continues to pose, many and varied challenges to military commanders. The nub of the issue can be expressed succinctly: How to gratify male desire while circumscribing the kinds of intercourse that could be had? And how to orchestrate or suppress the potent sentiments that invariably swirl around sex: not simply between individuals involved in intimate acts, but also among other "external" parties who take a keen interest—whether anxious, appalled, or affronted—in these encounters? Although this chapter's remit is to analyze men's heterosexual activity, a key contention advanced here is that behavior and *emotions* are inescapably entwined. In other words, we should conceptualize sex less as purely embodied carnality, and more as an electrified field of human interaction charged with peculiarly intense feelings, not only between intimate partners themselves but wider civilian communities with their own stakes in the question of who sleeps with whom.

This essay focuses on three core issues and the intersections between them. Its goal is to highlight the entangled nature of the various manifestations and ramifications of male heterosexuality in, and for, the U.S. military: sex as a reward; sex as a commercial transaction; and sex within (and outside) marriage. These overlapping topics illustrate the thesis that sexual activity has presented irresolvable challenges for the military. Why management strategies have commonly failed to meet their architects' aspirations owes a good deal to deep-seated, durable contradictions that beset military thinking about masculinity, morality, and morale, to say nothing of the fact that managing male soldiers' heterosexual encounters necessarily involves attempts to control the behavior of their female partners. Needless to say, the military can't hope to achieve authority over civilian women, whether U.S. citizens or foreign nationals. But "managing sex" is, in any case, never so simple as merely issuing orders and eliciting compliance. Failure is surely inherent in any attempt to discipline desire and to constrain the transgressive impulses that drive human sexuality.

Compensation

The idea that men in uniform deserve—or more fundamentally *require*—heterosexual intercourse has a very long history, dating back considerably before World War II. Conceptions of entitlement have varied somewhat. Where some military commanders saw sex as a reward for soldierly service, others regarded it less as a fringe benefit—welcome, but nonessential—than as an intrinsic need of red-blooded soldiers; hence General George S. Patton's much-quoted aphorism "If they don't fuck, they don't fight." In this formulation a strong libido was an essential attribute of martial masculinity: an expression of red-blooded virility linked with fighting élan. Deprived of opportunities for gratification, soldiers' will to fight and staying power in battle would dwindle.[3]

Whether soldiers needed sex in order to perform satisfactorily as soldiers, or were owed it as compensation for services rendered, the bottom line remained the same. But if most men in uniform were unmarried, or stationed far from their spouses for protracted periods, the logistics of balancing demand with supply were complex. During World War II senior U.S. commanders confronted the challenge of how to provide their men with intimate access to women's bodies, since the conviction that soldiers required regular sex was matched by equally strong objections to any kind of sexual activity other than heterosexual intercourse. Military commanders feared the degenerative potential for "perversion" in all-male societies largely bereft of women. Draft boards and medical examinations duly sought to keep "perverts" out: an exclusionary effort that, needless to say, did not entirely succeed. Potential draftees were routinely asked whether they "liked girls" and (in more or less coded ways) whether they engaged in "self-abuse." Masturbation was widely held to be a "perverted" practice: a telltale sign of homosexuality or evidence of a proclivity in that direction. With that stigmatizing notion a fixed point of much military (and civilian) thought in the 1940s, it was unthinkable that soldiers might satisfy their sexual needs through masturbation.[4]

How and where, then, were soldiers to find women with whom to have sex? This formed a recurrent quandary for the U.S. military. In various settings, and in different eras, military commanders surreptitiously involved themselves in the business of brothels, as they had in the Philippines at the turn of the twentieth century; the next section of this chapter discusses commercial prostitution and the military's relationship with it at greater length. It's also apparent that, in the realm of sexual activity, soldiers rarely heeded their officers' instructions to the letter or waited for the military establishment to devise arrangements that would guarantee ready access to women. Having sex is, in the words of historian Mary Louise Roberts, "what soldiers do."[5]

It was certainly what they did in Europe as, and after, the continent was liberated from German occupation between the allied invasion of Sicily in July 1943 and the Third Reich's collapse in May 1945. Everywhere American troops set foot—in Allied nations and then in Wehrmacht-held territory—they lost little time in sleeping with the women they encountered. Commanders adjusted policy to accommodate, and sometimes facilitate, these ad hoc liaisons. In Germany, however, the situation was meant to be different. As a matter of official policy, decreed in Washington DC and enunciated by General Dwight D. Eisenhower, commander of the Supreme Headquarters Allied Expeditionary Force (SHAEF), American personnel were prohibited from engaging in any social exchange with the defeated German population beyond the bare minimum required for purposes of governance. The Allies agreed that the German population as a whole shared responsibility for the criminal Nazi regime, and Washington was especially fervent in its commitment to the doctrine of "collective guilt." American officials didn't restrict denazification to the ejection of Nazi party members from public office. Rather, individual Germans had to own their share of personal responsibility for the murderous regime they had either actively elected or passively endured. And the first nudge toward proper acknowledgement of guilt would come in the form of complete ostracism by Americans in uniform. No German hand would be shaken, no pleasantries would be exchanged; an aloof formality would govern all U.S. encounters with the defeated people over whom they presided.[6]

That, at any rate, was the theory behind the "fraternization ban" promulgated by SHAEF in September 1944. And it was drummed into GIs at every turn. The orientation film *Your Job in Germany*, along with the army's *Pocket Guide to Germany*, cautioned soldiers that they mustn't trust the German pretenses of friendliness that had suckered an earlier generation of U.S. occupation troops after World War I. Roadside billboards warned GIs as they entered German territory that they were *not* to fraternize, while posters employed photographic imagery from newly liberated Nazi concentration camps to underscore the message that Americans should steer clear of the people responsible for these appalling mounds of skeletal corpses. All to no avail.[7]

Despite inescapable reminders that any kind of intercourse with Germans was strictly prohibited, and despite an accompanying $65 fine for violations of the fraternization ban, American soldiers continued to have sex with German women. These encounters weren't few or furtive. They were sufficiently public and commonplace as to form a staple of photographic reports from newly defeated Germany in illustrated magazines like *Life*, which ran several stories in the spring and summer of 1945, showing readers just how pervasive "fratting" was between American men and German "furlines." Although some soldiers were aghast at their peers' behavior, it proved impossible for Eisenhower to enforce the ban. Men caught in the act typically insisted that the women in question were not, in fact, German but displaced persons from elsewhere in Europe, and hence not "verboten" at all. But many officers didn't even attempt to enforce the ban, either because they conceded the futility of any such effort from the outset or because, as enlisted men liked to point out, they themselves had German girlfriends.[8]

The rampant sexualization of postwar Germany was a substantial public embarrassment to SHAEF, fearful that inability to control its own men would be a source of schadenfreude to Germans, who might in turn prove equally ungovernable. Over the summer of 1945 Eisenhower gradually retreated, first permitting U.S. personnel to interact amicably with German children, and then with the population as a whole in October 1945. SHAEF's tactical retreat on fraternization was followed fourteen months later by the authorization of marriage between American men (in their final month of duty) and German women—a scenario that had been anathema to many senior commanders in 1945. But in this domain, too, enlisted men had proven unmindful of their superiors' orders, marrying German women in local civic ceremonies even when such unions were expressly forbidden by SHAEF.[9]

Postwar Germany offers a vivid illustration of how hard military commanders found it to revoke, or even temporarily suspend, male sexual privilege. Their attempt to outlaw intimate contact between GIs and Germans proved all the more unworkable since so many prompts prior to the fraternization ban—such as the pick-up lines in foreign languages included in army "pocket guides" to the countries U.S. forces were poised to occupy—encouraged American soldiers to regard sex as a routine entitlement: one that victory would surely cement into an unassailable prerogative. The fact that German women were *German* was evidently immaterial to many men, immune to the argument that their new sexual partners had recently been the wives, girlfriends, and fiancées of Wehrmacht soldiers and Nazi party functionaries. However, the fact that hundreds, and soon thousands, of GIs sought to marry

German women suggests that not *all* American men viewed physical intimacy as a form of carnal compensation for wartime service. Sex in ruined and dislocated postwar Germany could easily be acquired in exchange for C-rations or the many other material goods to which GIs enjoyed unprecedented access courtesy of the world's most generous military establishment. German women could be "commercially amorous," as Corporal Horace Evans (a Black tank gunner from Detroit) put it. But for some men, at least, sex wasn't just a transactional perk enjoyed thanks to asymmetries of political power and economic advantage. Physical intimacy was, or might be, about love. And emotional attachment resisted confinement along racialized lines. In an oral history interview in 1946, Evans pointed out that "love developed among some of the couples." Black GIs also petitioned for the right to marry German women in a country that, despite its recent Nazi past, proved more amenable to biracial marriage than did many parts of the United States.[10]

Commerce

SHAEF's attempt to bar fraternization was unusually far-reaching: an ideological intervention that tried (and failed) to make the personal political. Since 1945 the U.S. military has made various attempts to stamp out the solicitation of sex by uniformed personnel overseas. For instance, the military publicized its strict prohibition against sex between uniformed American men and Saudi women during "Operation Desert Shield," the months-long build up of U.S.-led coalition forces in Saudi Arabia prior to the invasion of Kuwait in January 1991. More recently, defense officials made an analogous boast of the Pentagon's zero-tolerance attitude toward prostitution in the so-called war on terror. "If there was an effort to visit prostitutes in Afghanistan, we would come down hard," claimed Senator Lindsey Graham (a former U.S. Air Force lawyer), adding, "Simply because it's a cultural no-no in Afghanistan, it would bring wrath upon us."[11]

That military spokesmen should have drawn attention to soldiers' sexual abstemiousness in predominantly Muslim countries is striking. Patronizing prostitutes, along with "pandering," has been unlawful in the military for decades, instantiated as crimes under articles 133 and 134 of the Uniform Code of Military Justice in 1950, with rules tightened further in 2005 when President George W. Bush signed an executive order that included buying sex-workers' services as a punishable offense in the *Manual for Courts-Martial.*[12] Why, then, make a boast of following one's own rules? Strategic protestations of virtue hint at how routinely the military failed to curb prostitution in many parts of the postwar world. Indeed, far from outlawing commercialized sex, U.S. commanders overseas regularly sought to channel their men's sexual activity into tacitly (or more actively) approved "contact zones." In and after World War II prostitution flourished everywhere U.S. troops occupied, from North Africa to Italy and France, as well as Japan, Korea, the Philippines, and a string of Pacific islands. Many of these sites subsequently served as key nodal points in an expanded global network of American military power, with significant numbers of troops remaining on a semipermanent basis as Cold War geopolitics rationalized long-term garrison arrangements.[13]

In newly defeated Japan the remnants of the imperial state and business interests formed the Recreation and Amusement Association (RAA) and established brothels for the victorious occupying forces: a "gift" the Eighth Army initially accepted. The shifting stance of General Eichelberger and other senior U.S. commanders vis-à-vis this Japanese gesture is instructive more broadly of attitudes toward prostitution as both a convenient solution to the logistical challenge of male heterosexual entitlement and a source of inconvenient command complications.[14]

At first the senior echelon of the Eighth Army seemed quite appreciative of the Japanese efforts to provide U.S. personnel with ready-made "entertainment" centers. Commanding officer Eichelberger noted in his diary on September 11, 1945, that, while the army couldn't become *directly* involved in running brothels, it could and would exert "strong pressure" on the Japanese police to "maintain cleanliness and order." Anecdotal accounts of the occupation, including material contained in servicemen's letters home, reveal that some U.S. officers themselves lost little time in making use of these RAA establishments.[15] Whether or not they personally patronized brothels, senior U.S. commanders saw advantages to soldiers visiting licensed sex workers rather than procuring sex through other channels. Confining, or attempting to confine, GIS' sexual encounters to sites monitored by local authorities and patrolled by American military police held out various advantages from the perspective of senior commanders. Keen to erect and maintain a color line between white and Black soldiers in their off-duty hours, officers often tried to turn houses of prostitution into racially segregated institutions, making some brothels "off-limits" to African American troops either all the time or during certain hours of the week.

But the single most compelling reason to favor the commercial sex industry, as the senior echelon of U.S. military men saw it, was the prospect of checking the spread of sexually transmitted diseases. This aspiration was predicated on an implicit (and, of course, erroneous) assumption that "unclean" women, not contagion-bearing GIS, were responsible for the soaring rates of venereal infection that had afflicted American servicemen everywhere they went overseas. Any arrangement that promised to make women's bodies accessible to military medical authority was thus welcomed primarily as a mechanism to protect American soldiers' health. In Japan RAA workers' sexual health would, at least in theory, be closely monitored by doctors. Only women certified as disease-free would be permitted to work in RAA establishments. American men would thus be better protected against sexually transmitted disease than if they patronized unregulated streetwalkers or slept with Japanese women who weren't professional prostitutes but who, by virtue of entering into sexual relationships with Americans, were presumed to be loose in their morals and hence a potent source of venereal infection.[16]

The presumption that respectable Japanese women would not consort with U.S. servicemen was an idée fixe shared by American commanders and Japanese officials, who converged in the view that another advantage offered by the RAA system was the "floodwall" function it would serve. Treating sex workers as an expendable underclass, they imagined that the ready commercial availability of their bodies to U.S. servicemen would spare other, "better" Japanese women from sexual predation. The logic of this "buffer" or floodwall thesis presumed that American soldiers would resort to rape if female sexual partners weren't easily found in postwar Japan. If sex couldn't be bought, then it would be taken by force—so senior U.S. officers and Japanese officialdom agreed.[17]

The logics underpinning military-sponsored prostitution were, however, dangerously fallacious. Risk-free sex was a chimera that rested on flawed assumptions about both viral infection and human motivation. Neither health care professionals nor sex workers always meekly submitted to mandatory gynecological inspections and STD treatment regimens. In postwar Japan women sometimes escaped confinement in hospital wards designated for the treatment of venereal infection, or used their period of hospitalization to expand their commercial networks. Meanwhile, some doctors accepted bribes to forego inspections and simply issue clean bills of health. Even where U.S. military police conducted strict checks on sex workers' licenses, closing down or placing off-limits brothels in which employees weren't all certified as disease-free, the idea that American military patrons would thereby suffer no risk of disease rested on flimsy epidemiological knowledge. With incubation periods of several days or even months, gonorrhea and syphilis could remain undetected for some time, an interlude during which sex workers certified as clean might infect numerous clients.[18]

If the idea that brothels would eliminate the risk of sexually transmitted diseases was misplaced, so too was the supposition that men who could readily patronize brothels would not need to commit crimes of a sexually violent nature. In the Republic of Vietnam, for instance, with a sex-worker population estimated at between three hundred thousand and five hundred thousand in 1973, American troops nevertheless perpetrated rape and sexual assault on a wide scale.[19] Less well-remembered in the United States than the massacre of Vietnamese peasants at My Lai on March 16, 1968, were the mass rapes that members of the Americal Division committed as they laid waste to the hamlet. The rape of Vietnamese women by grunts out on patrol was so routine as not to appear newsworthy, or so suggested Dan Rather, who blithely related that "grab[bing] a quick piece of ass" was just what "everyone who was passing through a village" did, along with stealing chickens.[20]

In postwar Japan U.S. and Japanese officials put their faith in the RAA's female "floodwall" to deter the rape of "respectable"

Japanese women by American personnel. That stratagem failed. Despite the existence of regulated brothels, U.S. troops continued to commit crimes of sexual violence. Within months U.S. occupation authorities retreated from the RAA arrangements. They did so not because the assumptions behind the floodwall thesis were dangerously misguided but rather because General Douglas MacArthur, supreme commander of the Allied Powers, and his colleagues feared that Americans back home might get wind of official collusion between U.S. and Japanese authorities to provide sexual services to American men in uniform.[21] Public outrage loomed in November 1945, when naval chaplain Lieutenant Lawrence Lacour sent his hometown newspaper a lurid account of prostitution in Japan on an industrial assembly-line scale, with MPs keeping order among queues of men "four abreast almost a block long."[22]

Skittishness over potential exposure of official involvement in prostitution points to another enduring tension in American thinking about soldiers and sex. Although the idea that martial masculinity required regular heterosexual sex was widely endorsed in twentieth-century America, so too was a belief that the military was, or ought to be, a *moral* force. "Social purity" activists warned that enlistment into a rugged all-male society threatened to induct young men into habits of vice: gambling, drinking, and whoring. In this anxious projection, a disciplinary institution that claimed to *make* men—valiant and valorous men—risked undoing them instead. Campaigners against immorality won a victory with the May Act of 1941, legislation that made prostitution a federal offense in areas around military and naval bases in the United States. (In practice, however, this did more to stigmatize women who had, or were believed to be having, sex with soldiers than to eliminate "vice" around camps.)[23]

Postwar sexual mores relaxed over time, particularly with regard to pre- and extramarital intercourse. Yet Americans still struggled to reconcile the seemingly incompatible dictates of morality and morale—one pointing to abstention, the other to gratification—in military life. In May 1966 Democratic senator William Fulbright provoked a furor when he announced that, "both literally and figuratively," Saigon had "become an American brothel." In support of this claim, he cited reports about the number of Vietnamese women who had been forced to work as "bar girls" to finance impoverished households, adding that some Vietnamese soldiers had committed suicide because their wives had dishonored the very families they'd sought to support. Tellingly, just a few days after delivering his headline-grabbing denunciation of the "arrogance of power," Fulbright attempted to backtrack. He had been attacked by critics adamant that GIs spent their downtime assisting at orphanages and performing other good deeds calculated to capture Vietnamese "hearts and minds." To mollify his assailants, the senator insisted he had never intended to "malign brave young Americans" serving in Vietnam, who were merely "behaving in the way that is to be expected of men at war." Rather, he wanted to highlight the cultural corrosion suffered by a "fragile Asian society" as a result of Americans' presence en masse. If his critics' fantasy of squeaky-clean GIs visiting only orphanages when off-duty strained credulity, Fulbright's line was equally tenuous: that prostitution damaged Vietnam's social fabric, but U.S. soldiers who frequented the bars and brothels of Saigon bore no personal responsibility.[24]

Not everyone adopted such an indulgent attitude. Some morally indignant soldiers themselves wrote to stateside newspapers to decry the way their peers treated Vietnamese women as disposable playthings. The fact that some brothels were located *inside* U.S. bases, and the freedom with which Vietnamese prostitutes could roam around these facilities, were topics intermittently revisited by American journalists throughout the war, typically focused less on ethics and more on the security risks posed by sex workers who might be surreptitiously spying for the National Liberation Front. Yet, despite MACV's ongoing anxiety that they *might*, stories about pervasive prostitution never inflicted substantial reputational damage on the military. Even when a Senate committee investigated "fraud and corruption" in Vietnam in March 1971, trying to ascertain how a "massage parlor" (with four hundred employees) had sprung up yards from an army compound, newspapers paid little attention. To the extent that a retired colonel's testimony on the subject received media coverage at all, it was because he conjured an opéra bouffe encounter between doughty

U.S. commanders and a "voluptuous Dragon Lady" who'd deviously established a brothel at Long Binh and was thwarted only by the removal of interior doors from her "steambath" that made illicit activity impossibly public. Testimony that attracted "gales of laughter" when recounted on the Hill didn't even merit coverage by the national paper of record. Many American civilians doubtless shared the view that soldiers required heterosexual intercourse, as Fulbright had conceded. But the circumstances in which these liaisons happened—and whether U.S. taxpayers' dollars covertly subsidized them—were things about which they apparently preferred to remain ignorant.[25]

Inhabitants of areas around American bases abroad, however, rarely enjoyed the luxury of turning a blind eye to soldiers' recreational pastimes. Prostitution was (and remains) an irritant to harmonious relations between the military overseas and communities that have, often reluctantly, accommodated an intrusive foreign presence. Particularly in Asia and the Philippines, where asymmetries of national power enabled the Pentagon to extract more permissive status of forces agreements—and Americans' "othering" of racialized populations served to naturalize arrangements less thinkable around U.S. bases in Europe—"entertainment districts" sprang up, tightly packed with bars, clubs, saunas, massage parlors, and brothels catering primarily to a U.S. military clientele. While some local entrepreneurs seized lucrative opportunities afforded by cash-flush Americans' presence in their midst, other residents protested the tawdry eroticization of their neighborhoods, pointing out that sexual violence tended to *increase*, rather than diminish, in areas given over to servicemen's entertainment.[26]

Among the many questionable predicates of the floodwall thesis is its insinuation that sex workers are, in effect, "unrapeable." Yet women who sell sexual services may be, and not infrequently are, raped. Buried among files of heavily redacted "serious incident" investigations from Vietnam housed at the National Archives, one particularly chilling report from April 1971 documents the case of a Vietnamese woman discovered "naked and bleeding from the vagina and rectum" near a base occupied by the 534th Quartermaster Company. A medical examination revealed that she been penetrated by between twenty and thirty men. These soldiers had agreed to pay her 50,000 piastres to participate in gang sex, promising she would be given the same again if she stayed for a second night. She did, but her wages were stolen, prompting the woman to lodge a charge of rape against her robber-assailants. Without this crime ever becoming public knowledge, the woman was quietly paid off, her rape claim recorded on file as a mendacious allegation.[27]

The proposition that the availability of women's sexual services for purchase would decrease the incidence of sexual violence rested on flawed and dangerous misconceptions about the nature of rape. Feminist scholars and activists have made this argument since the 1970s. Rather than drawing a clear distinction between "respectable" women and prostitutes—a boundary that men would supposedly recognize and respect—the commercialized sex trade tended instead to objectify female bodies in general, encouraging a belief that women and girls were universally available to gratify male desire, either for a price or not.[28] In a notorious incident in Okinawa in 1995, when three U.S. servicemen were tried for the rape of a twelve-year-old Okinawan girl, one defense attorney reported that the trio had discussed hiring prostitutes but, short of money, decided to kidnap and rape the victim instead.[29]

This shocking incident galvanized local resistance that had simmered not far from the surface almost since American forces first wrested Okinawa from Japanese control in the summer of 1945. Elsewhere, too, sexual violence perpetrated by U.S. personnel provided antibase activists with a rallying point for protest, while pervasive prostitution exposed the threadbare state of national sovereignty in several Asian countries, such as the Philippines, Thailand, and South Korea, where the sex trade was illegal yet flourishing thanks to U.S. military patronage. In South Korea prostitution was outlawed at the insistence of the American occupation regime in 1947. But for decades Korean prohibitions on prostitution—along with those enshrined in the Uniform Code of Military Justice (UCMJ)—were flouted by U.S. personnel around whom bustling "camptowns" flourished.[30] Korea's sex trade, like that of Thailand, was invigorated in the 1960s by visiting GIs on week-long, subsidized Rest and Recuperation (R&R) interludes away from active duty in Vietnam. As MACV attempted to mitigate the Saigon regime's discontent with wholesale prostitution in the Republic of Vietnam, it turned to "off-shore" solutions. For around $300, GIs could spend a week in an array of destinations across the Asia-Pacific region, including Hawaii, Australia, Hong Kong, Malaysia, Thailand, and Okinawa: destinations brimming with opportunities for "Inebriation and Intercourse," as soldiers revealingly rebranded R&R.[31]

In Asia the sex trade's proliferation provided combustible tinder for anti-American sentiment and activism aimed at reducing, or altogether removing, U.S. forces. Organized political protest sometimes occurred alongside individual acts of vigilantism, as local men in the vicinity of bases responded aggressively toward uniformed Americans they presumed to be encroaching on *their* sexual turf: sleeping with their women, and taking advantage of superior spending power to "steal" women they had cheaply bought. In other words, the rampant sexualization of U.S. military locations overseas engendered not only violence against women but also friction between men.

Conjugality

This chapter has foregrounded the ways in which the postwar U.S. military treated heterosexual intercourse as a male prerogative that required accommodation: a boon to morale not so dissimilar from other perks (like subsidized tourist trips) awarded to soldiers in recognition of their service. But while commanders may have wanted to imagine heterosexual intercourse as a discrete kind of leisure activity, ideally pursued in controlled settings, sexual encounters between male American military personnel and their female partners constantly exceeded attempts at containment. The final section of this chapter begins by considering one predictable consequence of heterosexual intercourse that the military establishment often tried to ignore until turning a blind eye became untenable—namely, pregnancy. Babies fathered by American soldiers serving overseas raised a host of thorny questions about paternity and responsibility, and also about binational marriage, immigration, and citizenship. Servicemen's sexual encounters with women invariably broached larger issues regarding what sorts of male-female relationships, other than purely transactional sexual encounters, the military was willing to countenance. While some commanding officers preferred to consider sex purely a matter of recreation, the military establishment also had to reckon with the reproductive outcomes of heterosexual intercourse. In short, it had to consider how sex, marriage, and paternity fit together—or whether (and if) they could be teased apart.

A return visit to Germany immediately after World War II highlights some telling contradictions in military attitudes toward marriage and fatherhood. One predictable consequence of the prodigious amount of sex that American GIs had in postwar Germany was a binational baby boom, with an estimated thirty thousand to ninety-four thousand infants fathered by U.S. personnel during the occupation.[32] The military's initial position was clear. Neither the American military government nor individual servicemen who fathered babies would take responsibility for them. But not every GI was willing to acquiesce in this disavowal of paternal obligation. Just as many enlisted men ignored the fraternization ban, so a substantial number determined to marry their German girlfriends, heedless of military strictures against such unions. In 1945 and 1946 hundreds of GIs married local women in civil ceremonies, although they were not officially permitted to marry Germans until December 1946, and then only in their final month of service.[33]

Official reluctance to sanction these marriages—a position staked with greater tenacity in postwar Japan, where most binational marriages involved crossing a color line, unless the serviceman husband was Japanese American—highlights the schism between the military's projection of figurative "paternalism" and its rejection of flesh-and-blood fatherhood.[34] In much the same way that the U.S. military regarded sexually transmitted diseases as borne exclusively by women, it also viewed women as solely responsible for babies, not just in utero but in the world outside the womb. As a result, in Germany, Japan, Korea, the Philippines, and Vietnam, substantial numbers of U.S.-fathered children, unclaimed by servicemen who followed rather than flouted official rules, formed another deep wellspring of conflict between the American military establishment and host communities. Many such children faced social stigma as the product of encounters between sex workers and servicemen, or of other liaisons local communities considered illicit. Babies fathered by African American servicemen commonly encountered the most severely prejudicial responses, their skin tone read as a marker of misbegotten paternity.[35]

Given the U.S. military establishment's desire to avoid STDS and to repudiate paternity, one might wonder why the services did not devote more resources to sex education. At different times, and with rather different messages, they did in fact make attempts to educate men about the dangers of sexually transmitted disease. During World War II, films and posters—variously lurid or ludic—warned men against the dangers of consorting with "loaded" women, potentially as deadly as a pistol, or against being "dumb bunnies" if they didn't hop to the nearest "pro station." In wartime Hawaii, as in postwar Germany and Japan, "prophylaxis stations" dotted the landscape. These were places where servicemen could go to "clean up" after they'd had intercourse. Like other aspects of military management of male sexuality, the provision of pro stations was informed both by white officers' racialized assumptions about Black male hypersexuality and the segregation of military facilities. African American GIs serving overseas during and after World War II noted that, although medical personnel often decried elevated rates of venereal infection among Black troops, they simultaneously limited Black troops' access to medical facilities. Captain Ralph Latimer, a Black officer stationed in Kobe, Japan, lamented that "little of a preventative nature is done; that only after rates become alarmingly high are the prophylactic stations set up, and then one has to fight for them."[36]

Two decades later, for men serving in Vietnam, the military produced films like *Where the Girls Are* that dramatized the slow-burn effects of syphilis that might go undetected for years, jeopardizing the as-yet-unborn children of GIs who frequented Asian brothels, but would later marry and try to start families back in the States. Often these initiatives conveyed decidedly mixed signals about which dangers of unprotected sex were to be guarded against. Were men to avoid intercourse altogether, or simply be more mindful of safeguarding themselves against the risk of infection? Some educational programs implied that men's health could be ensured after the fact of sex—the intended function of pro stations—without the need for any concomitant protection against unintended pregnancy.[37]

Indoctrination aimed at promoting sexual abstinence played second fiddle to ventures aimed at making intercourse a lower-risk activity for men in uniform. Avoiding intercourse altogether while away from home would seem the most obvious way to eliminate the many undesirable consequences of sex for the military, yet this zero option was less frequently prioritized. The idea of a chaste soldier, after all, defies heteronormative understandings about what makes men manly in general, and what makes men martial in particular. An evangelical-sponsored chastity campaign seemed sufficiently anomalous as to form the subject of a rather tongue-in-cheek *New York Times* story in 2005. This particular project perhaps caught the reporter's eye because it exceeded the military's efforts to ban soldiers from buying sexual services, instead warning soldiers away from *any* sexually pleasurable activity, with masturbation branded a worrisome form of "flying solo."[38]

Attempts to discourage men from engaging in pre- or extra-marital sex, on moral rather than health grounds, generally fell to the chaplaincy: the branch responsible (inter alia) for relationship counseling and "character guidance." For instance, indoctrination pamphlets produced in the 1950s under the rubric *Duty, Honor, Country* devoted a chapter to the promotion of chastity. The chaplaincy also played an important, but not unidirectional, role in shaping military marital policy. Sex and marriage were entangled issues, all the more vexingly so when they occurred (as many chaplains saw it) in the wrong sequence. In the 1940s the Office of the Chief of Chaplains objected to policies that prevented or deterred uniformed Americans from marrying women whom they had impregnated, whether the women in question were U.S. citizens or foreigners. Despite some misgivings about wedding ceremonies being conducted in unorthodox ways—via the telephone, say, with stand-in husbands—the chaplaincy prodded the War Department to sanction proxy marriages, most of them impelled by servicemen's desire to legitimate unborn babies. Similarly, in postwar occupied territories, chaplains urged U.S. military government authorities to soften their stance against marriages between local women and American men. While the sexual encounters that preceded these unions may have been illicit according to the precepts of their faith, chaplains of many denominations agreed that illegitimate children should not have to suffer for the sins of their fathers.[39]

At the same time, however, the chaplaincy was (and is) committed to the sanctity of marriage as a divinely ordained institution. Marriages contracted in order to legitimate "preconceived" children were thus a necessary evil, but far from ideal. More often, where issues of paternity were not at stake, the chaplaincy duly cautioned *against* soldiers and sailors entering into what in the 1940s were dubbed "war hysteria marriages." Here the Office of the Chief of Chaplains found itself in greater accord with secular branches of the armed services, which shared abiding concerns about enlisted men hurtling into ill-considered and impetuous marriages.[40]

A well-worn military adage points out that if the army wanted soldiers to have wives, it would issue men with them. During much of the twentieth century, however, the army and its sibling services typically preferred that servicemen *not* possess spouses. Objections against conjugality were manifold. Scruples did not apply exclusively to German and Japanese women because they were citizens of enemy (or recently defeated) nations, and not only because some U.S. states continued to have anti-miscegenation statutes on their books until 1967, making it impossible for uniformed American men to return home to those states with spouses of another race whom they'd lawfully wed overseas.[41] More sweepingly, the military struggled to square the institution of marriage with its own institutional imperatives, suspecting wives as a potential distraction to men whose attention needed to be unwaveringly focused on duty and deference to a single chain of command.

In the 1940s, while the army considered it preferable for senior officers to be married, it took a different view altogether of marriage for enlisted men. In the early months of U.S. involvement in World War II, single enlisted men in the lowest three grades were discouraged from marrying, and any man who wished to marry had to secure his regimental commander's consent. Not a mere formality, permission to wed was sometimes denied. Restrictions within the continental United States eased during the war, providing that the prospective wife was a U.S. citizen. Rules debarring marriage with foreign women remained in place rather longer, varying from one national location to the next. Yet even when and where such unions were technically permitted, with prior consent, the path to marriage could be so strewn in red tape as to deter all but the most persistent suitors.[42]

In the postwar era, with tens of thousands of U.S. personnel stationed overseas, the question of marriage to foreign nationals didn't evaporate as a wartime problem solved by peace. Soldiers continued to petition for the right to wed the women of their choice, regardless of the man's rank and the woman's nationality. Although the Universal Declaration of Human Rights (1948) hailed freedom to select a marital partner as a universal right, the military continued to imagine that it knew better than its youthful personnel who would make a suitable spouse, just as it harbored persistent doubts about whether married men made the best soldiers. The services feared that wives would divert husbands' focus from professional responsibilities. Worse yet, grasping "gold diggers"—a common characterization of women who dated GIs overseas— were liable to entrap naïve young Americans into marriage for monetary gain or an accelerated route to U.S. citizenship, or so commanders feared. Having attained their material goals, these women were seen as "flight risks" who would soon run off, leaving behind a mountain of debt and a heap of emotional wreckage. And a heartbroken soldier was a menace to both himself and the men around him.[43]

Military Assistance Command, Vietnam (MACV) took particular pains to deter GIs—of every ethnicity—from marrying Asian women, while stopping short of an all-out ban. To gain commanders' permission, servicemen had to spend months securing character references, filling out forms, gathering certificates, and subjecting fiancées to security checks and invasive medical inspections that appraised the state of their virginity. This bureaucratic obstacle course was designed to create a cooling-off period so that young men, blinded by sexual infatuation, might see clearly again before plunging into wedlock.[44] Heavy-handed efforts to discourage men in uniform from marrying may now appear antediluvian. But as recently as 1993 the Marine Corps attempted to block the recruitment of married marines, doing so for much the same reason that MACV had hoped to prevent besotted soldiers from rushing into unions with inappropriate Vietnamese women.[45]

Yet martial hostility toward the marital state is far from the whole story. Despite skepticism about spouses, the services also appreciated that dutiful, *appropriate* wives could be important adjuncts to the military: a valuable reservoir of emotional support for individual spouses, and a battalion of unpaid volunteers whose presence on-base or off might prove salutary. Mere months after World War II ended, Eisenhower petitioned the Truman administration to let wives of both officers and enlisted men stationed in occupied Germany sail over and join them. The arrival of spouses and offspring would, Ike hoped, exert a chastening influence over not just particular husbands and fathers but the U.S. occupation force as a whole. With American women and children around, men would think twice about fraternizing with German women—or would do so less publicly and less promiscuously. That, at any rate, was the aspiration underpinning the "domestication" of Germany's occupation, a move soon replicated in postwar Japan.[46]

With the shift to an all-volunteer force after 1973, the army adopted a more avowedly pro-marriage and pro-family posture. One way to recruit and retain a higher-skilled and more reliable workforce was to offer attractive benefits for spouses and dependents, turning the rhetorical conceit of an "army family" into a more practical set of entitlements.[47] From a naïve perspective, marriage also promised to eliminate the military's supply-side problem with sex, with the conjugal bedroom satisfying male soldiers' libidinous needs. But needless to say, married soldiers were no more invariably monogamous than their civilian counterparts, and perhaps less so. In part because soldiers deployed away from home enjoyed wider opportunities for infidelity, or were commonly thought to, the military policed (and continues to police) marriage much more intensively than does civilian society. Although the forces largely abandoned the attempt to constrain the spousal choices of their personnel, other than through premarital counseling programs, they still insisted that married soldiers should have sex only with their own spouses. Adultery was, and remains, a punishable offense. Strikingly, while American society broadly became more tolerant of extramarital intercourse in the final quarter of the twentieth century, the military grew more censorious. In 1984 adultery entered the *Manual for Courts-Martial* as a misdemeanor that could incur a maximum punishment of dishonorable discharge and confinement for a year. Rarely prosecuted before then, adultery charges gave rise to nearly nine hundred courts-martial from 1992 to 1997.[48]

How do we explain this seemingly counterintuitive trend? The answer has a good deal to do with the higher proportion of women who joined up in and after the 1970s. With more women enlisting and serving in frontline capacities, the military worried not only about men in uniform sleeping with civilian women but also about the increased likelihood of sexual liaisons between male and female soldiers serving alongside one another. A widely publicized survey undertaken in 1992 of 272 veterans of Operation Desert Storm found most respondents reporting that troops in their units had *more* sex in Saudi Arabia than they did at home.[49] Fears of female infidelity, ever-present among male soldiers, were matched with military wives' growing concerns over the sexual loyalty of spouses who might be tempted into affairs with female colleagues, particularly when deployed far from home. Opponents—of both sexes—of women's greater inclusion in combat capacities regularly invoked the specter of promiscuous "fraternization" within the forces to buttress their case. Kelly Flinn, a B-52 pilot dishonorably discharged in 1997 for adultery, speculated that her affairs with two married airmen had been luridly spot-lit by a military establishment keen to demonstrate that "women have no place in the military; let them in and all hell breaks loose."[50]

Critics of the military's punitive, but also capricious, stance on adultery have similarly argued that charges of sexual misconduct commonly constitute a form of payback by male personnel to punish women who have complained about sexual assault and deter those who might be minded to do so. Flipping the narrative around, these male soldiers cast women colleagues as adulterers who, having repented their marital transgressions, bring malicious charges against former lovers to degrade them and damage their careers. More frequent prosecutions for adultery, disproportionately targeting female personnel, need to be understood in tandem with the forces' escalating problem of sexual harassment and assault. Masquerading as a defense of marital morality and institutional reputation, escalating prosecutions for adultery in fact represent a misogynistic backlash against women in uniform.[51]

Conclusion

Anxieties over sexual disloyalty have played important, but largely overlooked, roles in both bolstering and undermining esprit in military ranks. Female infidelity has been a prospect calculatedly dangled before new U.S. Army and Marine Corps recruits for decades. Since World War II men undergoing basic training have made the parade-ground acquaintance of "Jody" in drill calls that showcase his imaginary exploits. He's the wily "backdoor man" poised to steal the soldier's job, home, car, and girl. The ubiquity of this trope in U.S. Army and Marine Corps cadences hints that, in the view of drill instructors at least, male ranks can be closed in shared mistrust of women whose disloyalty alone can be relied upon. Meanwhile, invocations of women's sexual promiscuity—and the supposedly irresistible temptation to the male libido posed by the mere presence of females in the military—have loomed large in deliberations over women's inclusion in combat roles and in the special forces. In other words, it has mattered profoundly in the armed forces not just who has sex with whom, but who might sexually betray whom, with purportedly dangerous consequences for unit cohesion and combat effectiveness.[52]

Yet, for as long as "Jody" has alerted men in uniform to the apparent inevitability of their betrayal, the military has also been roiled by the *disintegrative* effects of broken romantic relationships. A whole array of maladies—from elevated rates of absence without leave to the commission of atrocities and incidences of suicide—have been laid at the door of emotional abandonment's pernicious harbinger, the "Dear John" letter. Far from making men and the bonds between them stronger, the bitter reality of romantic rupture tends to tug in the opposite direction.

Over the past decade, having identified relationship failure as a common precipitant of suicide, the army has introduced various initiatives intended to shore up marriages strained by the demands of serial redeployment in an age of permanent war. But as this chapter has suggested, nothing about love, sex, or marriage in the military can be readily mustered into alignment. A field of human interaction fraught under any circumstances becomes yet more fissiparous in an institution that places its members under extreme physical and psychological stress, subjecting them to a battery of contradictory messages about "what soldiers do" and what they ought to be. In short, there has been—and remains—no easy way to make love and war simultaneously.

Notes

1. Eric Schmitt, "War Is Hell. So Is Regulating Sex," *New York Times*, November 17, 1996.

2. Cott, *Public Vows*; Lefkovitz, *Strange Bedfellows*.

3. Patton quoted in Roberts, *What Soldiers Do*, 160. On martial masculinity, see Belkin, *Bring Me Men*; Enloe, *Maneuvers*; and Goldstein, *War and Gender*.

4. Bérubé, *Coming Out*; Canaday, *Straight State*.

5. On the Philippines, see Kramer, "Darkness That Enters the Home"; on wartime Hawaii, see Bailey and Farber, *First Strange Place*; and on France, see Roberts, *What Soldiers Do*.

6. Carruthers, *Good Occupation*, 53–55; Goedde, GIs and Germans.

7. Carruthers, *Good Occupation*, 112–26.

8. Percy Knauth, "Fraternization: The Word Takes on a Brand-New Meaning in Germany," *Life*, July 2, 1945; Carruthers, *Good Occupation*, 123–24.

9. Carruthers, *Good Occupation*, 295–97.

10. Corporal Horace Evans, interview with Lawrence Reddick, 1946, Folder 8, Box 1, SCRBC; Fehrenbach, *Race after Hitler*; Höhn and Klimke, *Breath of Freedom*, 39–62.

11. Enloe, *Maneuvers*, 72; Graham quoted in "U.S. Military Faces Scrutiny over Its Prostitution Policies," Reuters, April 29, 2012, https://www.reuters.com/article/us-usa-agents-military/u-s-military-faces-scrutiny-over-its-prostitution-policies-idUSBRE83S09620120429.

12. Wilson-Buford, *Policing Sex*, 184; "U.S. Military Faces Scrutiny."

13. Cheng, *On the Move for Love*; Höhn and Moon, *Over There*; Moon, *Sex among Allies*; Sturdevant and Stoltzfus, *Let the Good Times Roll*.

14. Kovner, *Occupying Power*; Kramm, *Sanitized Sex*, 29–77.

15. Carruthers, *Good Occupation*, 136–37.

16. Kovner, *Occupying Power*; Kramm, *Sanitized Sex*; Sanders, "Panpan."

17. Carruthers, *Good Occupation*, 136; Kovner, *Occupying Power*, 22; Kramm, *Sanitized Sex*, 25.

18. Chang, "Engagement Abroad," 635.

19. Goldstein, *War and Gender*, 346.

20. Stur, *Beyond Combat*, 168–69; Rather quoted in Brownmiller, *Against Our Will*, 91.

21. Kramm, "Sexual Violence."

22. Lacour quoted in Carruthers, *Good Occupation*, 139.

23. Bristow, *Making Men Moral*; Meyer, *Creating GI Jane*, 102–3; Hegarty, *Victory Girls*, 37–40.

24. E. W. Kenworthy, "Fulbright Issues a Warning to U.S.," *New York Times*, May 6, 1966; Associated Press, "Saigon No Brothel, Mrs. Lord Asserts," *New York Times*, May 7, 1966; "Fulbright Declares He Regrets Charge of U.S. 'Arrogance,'" *New York Times*, May 18, 1966; Stur, *Beyond Combat*, 58–59.

25. Vincent E. Feeney, "Morality of the War," *New York Times*, March 29, 1969; United Press International, "U.S. Now Admitting Prostitutes to Some of Its Vietnam Bases," *New York Times*, January 25, 1972; David Hoffman, "Brothel Sorties Recounted: Colonel Bested Viet Madame," *Washington Post*, March 5, 1971; Stur, *Beyond Combat*, 171–76.

26. Höhn and Moon, *Over There*; Moon, *Sex among Allies*; Sturdevant and Stoltzfus, *Let the Good Times Roll*.

27. Serious Incident Report, Rape (Alleged), April 20, 1971, Entry A1 749, General Records, 1968–72, Box 4, NARA.

28. Brownmiller, *Against Our Will*.

29. Johnson, *Blowback*; Angst, "Sacrifice."

30. Moon, *Sex among Allies*, 46–47.

31. Lair, *Armed with Abundance*, 110–16.

32. Höhn, "You Can't Pin Sergeant's Stripes," 124.

33. Carruthers, *Good Occupation*, 296.

34. Carruthers, *Good Occupation*, 297–98; Zeiger, *Entangling Alliances*, 181.

35. Fehrenbach, *Race after Hitler*.

36. Mungia, *Protect Yourself*; Pfau, *Miss Yourlovin*; Costello, *Love, Sex, and War*, 126–31. Quote from Captain Ralph Latimer, interview with Lawrence Reddick, 1946, Folder 10, Box 1, SCRBC.

37. Sun, "Where the Girls Are."

38. John Leland, "Sex and the Faithful Soldier," *New York Times*, October 30, 2005.

39. Stahl, *Enlisting Faith*, 122–31, 148–55.

40. Stahl, *Enlisting Faith*, 123.

41. Johns, "Right to Marry"; Zeiger, *Entangling Alliances*, 166.

42. Branstetter, "Military Constraints"; Johns, "Right to Marry."

43. Wilson-Buford, *Policing Sex*, 47–77.

44. Zeiger, *Entangling Alliances*, 214–28; Gloria Emerson, "More Americans Are Marrying Vietnamese Despite the Obstacles," *New York Times*, September 12, 1970.

45. Stahl, *Enlisting Faith*, 129.

46. Carruthers, *Good Occupation*, 263–98; Alvah, *Unofficial Ambassadors*.

47. Bailey, *America's Army*; Mittelstadt, *Rise of the Military Welfare State*.

48. Rhode, *Adultery*, 90–92; Wilson-Buford, *Policing Sex*, 215–17; Annuschat, "Affair to Remember."

49. Schmitt, "War Is Hell," E1.

50. Rhode, *Adultery*, 90.

51. Rhode, *Adultery*; Annuschat, "Affair to Remember."

52. Johnson, *Cadences*; Burns, "Where Is Jody Now?"

Bibliography

Archives and Manuscript Materials

NARA. RG 472, Records of U.S. Forces in Southeast Asia. National Archives and Records Administration, College Park MD.

SCRBC. SC MG 490, Lawrence D. Reddick World War II Project. Schomburg Center for Research in Black Culture, New York Public Library.

Published Works

Alvah, Donna. *Unofficial Ambassadors: American Military Families Overseas and the Cold War, 1946–1965.* New York: New York University Press, 2007.

Angst, Linda Isako. "The Sacrifice of a Schoolgirl: The 1995 Rape Case, Discourses of Power, and Women's Lives in Okinawa." *Critical Asian Studies* 33, no. 2 (2001): 243–66.

Annuschat, Katherine. "An Affair to Remember: The State of the Crime of Adultery in the Military." *San Diego Law Review* 47 (2010): 1161–204.

Bailey, Beth L. *America's Army: Making the All-Volunteer Force.* Cambridge MA: Harvard University Press, 2009.

Bailey, Beth L., and David Farber. *The First Strange Place: Race and Sex in World War II Hawaii.* Baltimore MD: Johns Hopkins University Press, 1994.

Belkin, Aaron. *Bring Me Men: Military Masculinity and the Benign Facade of American Empire, 1898–2001.* New York: Columbia University Press, 2012.

Bérubé, Allan. *Coming Out under Fire: The History of Gay Men and Women in World War Two.* New York: Free Press, 1990.

Branstetter, Captain Ross W. "Military Constraints upon Marriages of Service Members Overseas, Or, If the Army Had Wanted You to Have a Wife." *Military Law Review* 102 (Fall 1983): 5–22.

Bristow, Nancy K. *Making Men Moral: Social Engineering during the Great War.* New York: New York University Press, 1996.

Brownmiller, Susan. *Against Our Will: Men, Women, and Rape.* New York: Simon & Schuster, 1975.

Burns, Richard Allen. "Where Is Jody Now? Reconsidering Military Marching Chants." In *Warrior Ways: Explorations in Modern Military Folklore,* edited by Eric A. Eliason and Tad Tuleja, 79–98. Logan: Utah State University Press, 2012.

Canaday, Margot. *The Straight State: Sexuality and Citizenship in Twentieth-Century America.* Princeton NJ: Princeton University Press, 2009.

Carruthers, Susan L. *The Good Occupation: American Soldiers and the Hazards of Peace.* Cambridge MA: Harvard University Press, 2016.

Chang, Emily Nyen. "Engagement Abroad: Enlisted Men, U.S. Military Policy, and the Sex Industry." *Notre Dame Journal of Law, Ethics, and Public Policy* 15, no. 2 (2001): 621–53.

Cheng, Sealing. *On the Move for Love: Migrant Entertainers and the U.S. Military in South Korea.* Philadelphia: University of Pennsylvania Press, 2010.

Costello, John. *Love, Sex, and War: Changing Values, 1939–45.* London: Collins, 1985.

Cott, Nancy F. *Public Vows: A History of Marriage and the Nation*. Cambridge MA: Harvard University Press, 2000.

Enloe, Cynthia H. *Maneuvers: The International Politics of Militarizing Women's Lives*. Berkeley: University of California Press, 2000.

Fehrenbach, Heide. *Race after Hitler: Black Occupation Children in Postwar Germany and America*. Princeton NJ: Princeton University Press, 2005.

Goedde, Petra. GIS *and Germans: Culture, Gender, and Foreign Relations, 1945–1949*. New Haven CT: Yale University Press, 2003.

Goldstein, Joshua S. *War and Gender: How Gender Shapes the War System and Vice Versa*. Cambridge: Cambridge University Press, 2001.

Gottman, John M., Julie S. Gottman, and Christopher L. Atkins. "The Comprehensive Soldier Fitness Program." *American Psychologist* 66, no. 1 (January 2011): 52–57.

Höhn, Maria. "You Can't Pin Sergeant's Stripes on an Archangel: Soldiering, Sexuality, and U.S. Army Policies in Germany." In *Over There: Living with the U.S. Military Empire from World War Two to the Present*, edited by Maria Höhn and Seungsook Moon, 109–45. Durham NC: Duke University Press, 2010.

Höhn, Maria, and Martin Klimke. *A Breath of Freedom: The Civil Rights Struggle, African American* GIS, *and Germany*. New York: Palgrave Macmillan, 2010.

Höhn, Maria, and Seungsook Moon, eds. *Over There: Living with the U.S. Military Empire from World War Two to the Present*. Durham NC: Duke University Press, 2010.

Johns, Richard B. "The Right to Marry: Infringement by the Armed Forces." *Family Law Quarterly* 10, no. 4 (1977): 357–87.

Johnson, Chalmers. *Blowback: The Costs and Consequences of American Empire*. New York: Metropolitan, 2010.

Johnson, Sandee Shaffer. *Cadences: The Jody Call Book, No. 1*. Canton OH: Daring, 1983.

Kovner, Sarah. *Occupying Power: Sex Workers and Servicemen in Postwar Japan*. Stanford CA: Stanford University Press, 2012.

Kramer, Paul. "The Darkness That Enters the Home: The Politics of Prostitution during the Philippine-American War." In *Haunted by Empire: Geographies of Intimacy in North American History*, edited by Laura Ann Stoler, 366–404. Durham NC: Duke University Press, 2006.

Kramm, Robert. *Sanitized Sex: Regulating Prostitution, Venereal Disease, and Intimacy in Occupied Japan, 1945–1952*. Berkeley: University of California Press, 2017.

———. "Sexual Violence, Masculinity, and Agency in Post-Surrender Japan, 1945." *Journal of Women's History* 31, no. 1 (Spring 2019): 62–85.

Lefkovitz, Alison. *Strange Bedfellows: Marriage in the Age of Women's Liberation*. Philadelphia: University of Pennsylvania Press, 2018.

MacLeish, Kenneth T. *Making War at Fort Hood: Life and Uncertainty in a Military Community*. Princeton NJ: Princeton University Press, 2013.

Meyer, Leisa D. *Creating* GI *Jane: Sexuality and Power in the Women's Army Corps during World War II*. New York: Columbia University Press, 1996.

Mittelstadt, Jennifer. *The Rise of the Military Welfare State*. Cambridge MA: Harvard University Press, 2015.

Moon, Katharine H. S. *Sex among Allies: Military Prostitution in U.S.-Korea Relations*. New York: Columbia University Press, 1997.

Mungia, Ryan. *Protect Yourself: Venereal Disease Posters of World War II*. Los Angeles: Boyo, 2014.

Pfau, Ann Elizabeth. *Miss Yourlovin: GIs, Gender, and Domesticity during World War II*. New York: Columbia University Press, 2008.

Rhode, Deborah. *Adultery: Infidelity and the Law*. Cambridge MA: Harvard University Press, 2016.

Roberts, Mary Louise. *What Soldiers Do: Sex and the American GI in World War II France*. Chicago: University of Chicago Press, 2013.

Sanders, Holly. "Panpan: Streetwalking in Occupied Japan." *Pacific Historical Review* 81, no. 3 (2012): 404–31.

Stahl, Ronit. *Enlisting Faith: How the Military Chaplaincy Shaped Religion and State in Modern America*. Cambridge MA: Harvard University Press, 2017.

Stur, Heather Marie. *Beyond Combat: Women and Gender in the Vietnam War Era*. New York: Cambridge University Press, 2011.

Sturdevant, Saundra Pollack, and Brenda Stoltzfus. *Let the Good Times Roll: Prostitution and the U.S. Military in Asia*. New York: New Press, 1993.

Sun, Sue. "*Where the Girls Are*: The Management of Venereal Disease by United States Military Forces in Vietnam." *Literature and Medicine* 23, no. 1 (Spring 2004): 66–87.

Wilson-Buford, Kellie. *Policing Sex and Marriage in the American Military: The Court-Martial and the Construction of Gender and Sexual Deviance, 1950–2000*. Lincoln: University of Nebraska Press, 2018.

Zeiger, Susan. *Entangling Alliances: Foreign War Brides and American Soldiers in the Twentieth Century*. New York: New York University Press, 2010.

THREE

"A Higher Moral Character"

Respectability and the Women's Army Corps

BETH BAILEY

"As I am writing this column," an army recruiter in Altoona, Pennsylvania, told readers of the *Tyrone Daily Herald* one October day in 1972, "one of my men is conducting an interview with a young lady." The young lady in question was resisting the recruiter's sales pitch, expressing some reluctance to join the Women's Army Corps (WAC). "Her main objection," wrote Sergeant First Class Joe Gaglione, "is that she feels her reputation may be damaged if she joins the WAC." Gaglione continued: "In this county there are quite a few former members of the WAC. I have met a few of them, none of whom were tramps. Yet I have met some tramps in the county." "How, then," he asked, "do the WAC attain a reputation as being tramps?"[1]

Ouch.

It was, admittedly, a difficult moment in the history of the U.S. Army. As the United States was moving ground troops out of Vietnam, it was also moving to end the draft. The coming all-volunteer force was not initially welcomed by the military, and the army, which was quite seriously occupied with other things at that moment, had just come to understand that it was going to have to recruit somewhere between twenty thousand and thirty thousand soldiers a month. (At the height of the U.S. wars in Iraq and Afghanistan, the army struggled to meet accession goals of seventy thousand a *year*.) In other words, without being able to rely on the draft or on draft-induced volunteers, army recruiters were going to have to convince tens of thousands of young Americans every month—at end of a difficult and unpopular war and at a moment when public respect for the military was at an all-time low—to join an institution that even its most devoted leaders believed was struggling and near broken.[2]

Army planners soon realized that, if they meant to fill the ranks, they had to broaden their appeal. Eventually that approach would translate into recruiting ads that insisted, "Some of our best men are women." But in the meantime, a command that would eventually specify not only the color but the brand of paint for recruiting office walls gave its recruiters a fair amount of latitude in their attempts to fill those boots. Sergeant Gaglione's discussion of the WAC "reputation as being tramps" was most definitely not a recruiting command talking point; nor was his reassurance on that point ("There is no more immorality in the Armed Forces than in civilian life. Maybe less. We do have some controls and regulations").[3] But whatever effect Gaglione's column had on his office's recruiting mission, his . . . shall we call it forthrightness? . . . lays bare a central fact about the WAC, from its 1941 origins to its dissolution in 1978: "managing sex" was always critical.

And the "sex" to be managed was not only the sexual behavior of servicewomen. That behavior would be the subject of "controls and regulations," often different in both scope and intent from those applied to servicemen. The WAC had to go beyond behavior to manage the sexual *reputation* of the WAC. Throughout its entire history, WAC leaders took extraordinary steps to guarantee that the corps was—and was perceived to be—a "respectable" institution that neither harmed its members' reputations nor undermined their femininity. Leaders focused on managing sex partly because they themselves believed in the importance of respectability and unblemished reputation, both for the individual and for the corps. But they also tried to manage sex because they were highly aware that the corps's continued existence was uncertain and its standing often fragile.

Through much of its history, the WAC faced both external suspicion and internal (army) hostility. Created grudgingly by Congress in 1942, and only as an auxiliary force until it was granted full military status in July 1943, the WAC suffered through what it dubbed a "scandal campaign"—widespread rumors that its members were prostitutes, "loose" women, or predatory lesbians—through much of the war. Both the reputation as a "tramp" and the fact of homosexuality had vastly different implications then than now. These rumors deterred potential volunteers during World War II (unlike men, women were not subject to the draft); the WAC never reached its allotted strength. And they created difficulties for the institutions and its members over the course of the WAC's existence. Thus, even as the U.S. Army struggled over the place of women, WAC leaders had the additional task of managing sex.

The origins of the Women's Army Auxiliary Corps (WAAC) lay in a bill introduced by Representative Edith Nourse Rogers in late May 1941—eight months after the United States had instituted the first peacetime draft in its history. Based on her accurate reading of the temper of the times (even as it violated her own sense of efficiency and fairness), Rogers proposed an "auxiliary" corps, one that would serve "with" the U.S. Army rather than within it. Members of the WAAC, it specified, would be noncombatants, a small organization comprised of well-educated, skilled workers, intended to "attain the highest reputation for both character and professional excellence."[4]

The bill got little traction until General George C. Marshall, the U.S. Army chief of staff, embraced Nourse's plan. Marshall, facing the rising inevitability that the United States would be pulled into the ongoing war, worried about future shortages of "manpower." He wanted authorization for a women's corps, and in the fall of 1941 he enlisted the aid of Oveta Culp Hobby, a strikingly accomplished thirty-seven-year-old currently serving as head of the Women's Interests Section of the War Department's Bureau of Public Relations, to shepherd the bill through the remaining obstacles. The Japanese attack on Pearl Harbor likely had more to do with authorization of the WAAC than Hobby's many talents, but HR 6293 made it to the floor of the House of Representatives in March 1942.[5]

Historians who write about the debate over this bill always quote—most commonly without attribution—from the comments of Clare E. Hoffman (R-MI). "Who then," Hoffman asked, "will maintain the home fires; who will do the cooking, the washing, the mending, the humble, homey tasks to which every woman has devoted herself; who will rear and nurture the children; who will teach them patriotism and loyalty; who will make men of them, so that, when their day comes, they too, may march away to war?" In some ways Hoffman's sputterings were a sideshow; he was marginalized in Congress, viewed with suspicion by Democrats and Republicans alike, widely suspected of fascist ties, and undeniably obnoxious. The historian who chronicled Hoffman's career noted that "it must have been difficult for some of his colleagues to abide him."[6]

Hoffman, however, was not the only member to oppose the corps on such grounds. As debate drew to a close, a handful of men who'd hoped the matter would never come to a vote grew vociferous in opposition. Andrew Somers (D-NY) condemned this "silliest piece of legislation" as "so revolting to me, to my sense of Americanism, to my sense of decency" that it defied discussion in a manner appropriate to the floor of the House. Butler Black Hare (D-SC) condemned the plan as "a reflection on the courageous manhood of the country." Jennings Randolph (D-WV), a man who would, in 1970, describe advocates of women's rights as "braless bubbleheads," offered an homage to the mothers of the nation who sent their *sons* off to war.[7]

Most members, however, dealt with practical questions, often those with financial implications. Would women who served be entitled to expensive benefits following the war? Would they be covered by military insurance? But a telling exchange came between Edith Nourse Rogers, who had sponsored the bill, and Winder R. Harris (D-VA). Harris asked a different sort of practical question: If members of the WAAC were sent abroad, where would they be quartered? They would have their own quarters, replied Rogers, and be well taken care of. Would they, Harris asked, be quartered in the same general location as the combat troops? And Rogers, hearing a pressing subtext, replied, "I know they would be protected. I trust the Army in that respect, and I trust the women thoroughly. It is not where you are, but what you are."[8] In other words, the women of the WAAC would be respectable, and respectable women could be trusted in any place, in any circumstance, even if men could not be.

The bill passed the House with a vote of 249 to 83; 96 members abstained.[9] And if the tone of discussions in the House, unusually divided for those early wartime months, was not sufficient to raise concern, warning signs had already come from other directions. Even before the bill authorizing the WAAC was signed into law, Hobby, functioning at the request of General Marshall as (in the words of an army historian) the "unannounced head of a nonexistent office," took caution from the experience of the British women's services. They had not only faced the challenges of rapid mobilization and unclear processes; they had also been subject to allegations that the service was rife with promiscuity, drunkenness, and "illegitimate" pregnancy. Rumors were so widespread that Parliament ordered an investigation, and while the parliamentary committee concluded that the rumors were without merit, it also recognized that they had undermined recruiting and damaged the morale of women members and their families. Forewarned, Hobby meant to do a better job managing the WAAC's public reception.[10]

From its beginnings, then, the leaders of the WAAC tried to manage sex. For it was sex—whether by "sex" one meant "appropriate" gender roles, sexual reputations and respectability, or the actual sexual behavior of women—that prompted opposition and that offered opponents points of attack. Hobby and her staff considered all plans in light of their potential effect on what they generally called "public sentiment," doing everything in their power to avoid actions and choices that might set off the rumor mill.

As Oveta Culp Hobby planned the rollout of the WAAC, she focused on circumventing the anticipated circus. While some journalists were likely to accept the WAAC as part of the nation's critical war effort—and in spring 1942, the Axis was steadily triumphant—she was confident that others would try to sensationalize the story. The night before her first press conference, Hobby and the WAAC's public relations consultant sat up late together listing and then rehearsing responses to possible questions, attempting to develop answers that would downplay the salacious and stress the serious. The following day Hobby fielded questions about girdles and makeup with strikingly brief and factual answers, and in response to a query about "illegitimate babies" noted simply that any pregnant woman would be discharged.[11]

As anticipated, coverage of the press conference varied. "Petticoat army" appeared in plenty of headlines, and much space was devoted to the feminine attributes of "Mrs. Hobby" herself. Despite one local columnist's judgement that "the naked Amazons who fought with the French Foreign Legion" and the "queer damosels of the isle of Lesbos" were not sufficient precedent for women's military service, Hobby and her staff believed they'd skirted the most obvious land mines.[12]

The next step was to select the initial class of women for officer training. There was an initial deluge of interest. Seventeen thousand women waited in line for application forms in Washington DC, even though only eight positions were allocated to the city. More than five thousand women secured applications in New York City, although the entire state, along with New Jersey and Delaware, could select a mere thirty women. Initial interest outran follow-through; of 140,000 applications requested, 30,000 were returned. But there were only 360 initial spaces. The War Department had allocated up to 10 percent of WAAC slots—for officers and "auxiliaries"—to "Negro" women, who would serve in segregated units.[13]

The stringent selection process for officer candidates emphasized respectability. Local selection boards were advised to consider whether they would "want my daughter to come under the influence of this woman" as they made their determinations, and a board of eleven "prominent psychiatrists" evaluated the records of applicants sent forward. Women who appeared "mannish" or not sufficiently feminine raised cautions. In the end Hobby, as WAAC director, read each and every application. She believed that careful selection would be key to the corps's success, and she never lost faith in that premise, later attributing the WAC's "good conduct record" to its "rigid selection process" and "severe screening." "The IQs of the women going overseas," she subsequently claimed, "would please a college dean."[14]

From the WAAC's earliest days, leaders of the women's corps struggled with the male army hierarchy over the role of the WAAC. Some of those struggles, without doubt, were due to simple sexism. But many were also due to the poorly defined status and organization of the corps. The WAAC's uncertain status frustrated army desires for efficiency. As the army head of personnel testified to Congress in support of ending the WAAC's auxiliary status, "The Army Regulations are not applicable to the Waacs. The Army Regulations are contained in a set of books as long as this table. It took years to develop them. Now we are faced with having to develop almost a parallel set of regulations to govern another part of the Army. . . . It just simplifies the whole operation . . . to have them all alike. In other words, in the Army we want one category of people."[15]

WAAC leadership powerfully—if privately—disagreed. Not on full military status; Hobby had fought for that from the beginning. Hobby and her staff, however, did not see, or desire, "one category of people." The women they led, most WAAC leaders strongly believed (and with reason), were drawn from a different pool than the male army. Unlike the men, who had been swept up in mass conscription, women of the WAAC were all volunteers, selected for aptitude, accomplishment, and "moral character." In the words of Edith Nourse Rogers, it was "what you are" that mattered. Thus, WAAC leaders believed, regulations designed to manage the sexual behavior of young men were not only inappropriate but insulting to women of the caliber who had joined the WAAC. In the words of historian Leisa Meyer, the "male military hierarchy's desire for uniformity collided with the female WAC director's firm belief in different moral standards for women, and her insistence that this difference be reflected in Army regulations."[16]

Hobby and her staff had created a set of regulations to govern the WAAC; they remained in effect until the organization was given full military status in July 1943. While in most cases patterned after army regulations, they included a separate code of conduct. WAACS were prohibited from "conduct of a nature to bring discredit upon the WAAC"; "discredit" here was presumed to come from women who violated the boundaries of the respectable middle class, most particularly in cases of public drunkenness and sexual impropriety.[17] But conflict over how to handle issues of morality and sexual behavior arose from the beginning and only intensified with the end of auxiliary status in mid-1943. As WAACS became WACS, they fell under army regulations. Yet WAC leadership, committed to maintaining the respectability of the corps, pushed through an addition to army regulations: any woman who showed "habits or traits of character which clearly indicate that the individual is not a suitable person to associate with enlisted women" could be discharged from service.[18]

Conflict between WAC leaders and the male army hierarchy would develop, specifically, over the issue of sexually transmitted disease. Venereal disease was of enormous concern to military leaders, most particularly before penicillin became available toward the end of the war. During World War I, it was estimated, VD had cost the U.S. military seven million "person days" (translating to eighteen thousand men incapacitated on a given day). Avoiding such losses was essential in a war of the current scope. Thus, unlike World War I, during which military leaders had promoted abstinence and good character as means to avoid infection, the World War II Army Medical Corps endorsed not only "will power and control" but also "rubbers" and "prophylaxis." A sixteen-page leaflet, *Sex Hygiene and Venereal Diseases*, was distributed to all men in uniform. Soldiers were issued condoms and "pro kits," which contained an ointment supposedly effective against both syphilis and gonorrhea; "pro stations" were distributed among the bars and alleys of towns in which soldiers had leave. To monitor the rates of sexually transmitted disease, army medical staff were required to prepare monthly VD reports for their units.[19]

The army's surgeon general meant to implement VD programs throughout the institution, and he began planning a venereal disease prevention program for WAACs even before the women's corps was formally made part of the army. Without first consulting—or even notifying—Colonel Hobby, he convened scientists from the National Research Council to discuss a potential sexual hygiene program for women. Based on the results of that meeting, the army surgeon general had charted out a VD prevention program that included detailed instruction in sex education and the universal distribution of condoms.[20]

Hobby was confident that some members of the press would portray such a program as evidence that the women's corps was morally suspect, that the women's true purpose was to "entertain" officers, that "morally upright" young women might be ruined by their experiences in the WAAC. Here, as always, Hobby meant to protect the reputations of her WAACs and her corps, and she found support in the War Office. Emily Newell Blair, chief of the War Department's Women's Interests Section, argued that the surgeon general's program, if implemented, would "reflect an attitude toward [women's] sexual promiscuity that whatever the practice, is not held by the majority of Americans. The Army . . . is no place to propagandize new social attitudes." In the end that position won out, and the surgeon general stepped back from the consultants' recommendations.[21]

Conflicts continued to arise after the WAAC became the WAC, often because male officers forgot that "all military personnel" included WACs. After a 1944 army circular prescribed VD-prevention instruction for "all military personnel," Hobby persuaded the War Department to publish a circular making clear that VD prophylaxis programs were for male personnel only.[22] Nonetheless, male army officers sometimes provided WACs with VD education; at Fort Polk the instructor encouraged WACs to carry their own "protection" in case "the boys" didn't have any. And at some army posts, medical officers subjected all WACs to monthly pelvic exams. They were observing army regulations that required monthly exams of personnel for evidence of venereal disease. In the case of women, these officers explained, they could not verify either infection or its absence without conducting such exams. Letters to WAC leadership complained not only of "inexpert doctors" conducting "rough and painful" exams but of "indignity" and "humiliation."[23]

Why did the "one category of people" approach to managing venereal disease provoke such reactions on the part of the WAC? Many WACs were embarrassed and angry to be subject to a program—whether education about VD prevention or mandatory pelvic exams—that seemed to presume that they were sexually promiscuous. Women's sexual reputations were immensely important during that era. The woman who, whether through her actions or her associations, lost her good reputation might well lose her middle class standing, her chance at a "good" marriage, even her friends and family. There were certainly many women during the course of World War II who enjoyed new sexual freedoms or pushed against the double standard, but few of these women did so publicly. The stakes were too high.

As for Colonel Hobby, she had faith in the morality of her WACs. But Hobby also desperately hoped to avoid bad press, and she knew that stories about programs to prevent VD would almost certainly draw public attention. Significantly, Hobby was right in her assumptions about WAC behavior. Despite the lack of VD-prevention instruction and with no mechanical aids, the WAC showed markedly low rates of venereal infection. Rates were dramatically lower than for civilian women of comparable age; in the corps's first year, only ten cases of VD were recorded among its six thousand members.[24]

The issue of pregnancy presented a different challenge. Unlike VD, which could be contracted by male and female alike, pregnancy was not a universal possibility. There was no "one category of people" approach possible. But as in the case of sexually transmitted diseases, WAC instruction offered women service members little: no information about or access to contraceptives (even as the corps contained married women whose "womanpower" it presumably was reluctant to lose). Any discussion of contraceptives, WAC leaders believed, risked public attention and accompanying condemnation.

Assumptions about public attitudes toward women's sexual behavior had likewise shaped the initial regulations governing the WAAC. In the wartime WAC, any pregnancy warranted discharge, but the initial 1942 draft of regulations for the WAAC specified that discharges for unmarried pregnant women would be "other than honorable" (OTH). Once again, however, the WAACs' ambiguous status created problems. According to military law, OTH discharges were only given for violations of either military or civil law. And neither sexual intercourse nor pregnancy outside wedlock was illegal. As the person charged with negotiating WAAC status and regulations, Hobby successfully pushed to define pregnancy, of whatever "legitimacy," as grounds for an honorable discharge. Here, Hobby again was focused on public perceptions of the corps. She believed that any OTH discharge would draw public attention and so harm the reputation of the corps as a whole. Despite official policies, however, before the WAAC gained full army status, its code of conduct (which prohibited actions that brought "discredit" on the WAAC) was cited as basis for OTH discharges of unmarried pregnant women.[25] And unmarried women did become pregnant—but as I'm sure Oveta Culp Hobby would insist I note, at rates much lower than unmarried civilian women of the same age cohort.

Leaders of the women's corps spent a disproportionate amount of time trying to manage public perceptions of the WAC, highly aware that attacks on the respectability of the corps and its members would make recruiting more difficult and harm the morale of women already in uniform. All decisions were made with an eye to public perception. WAC leaders, for example, worried about the recruiting slogan devised by advertising agency N. W. Ayer, not only because "Release a man for combat" didn't necessarily endear the corps to those who cared about the men who would be freed for combat but also because of the sexual connotation of "release."[26] WAC headquarters was likewise unhappy about cartoons in camp newspapers that focused obsessively on bras and breasts. One cartoon portrayed a male GI staring fixedly at a WAC's chest as she asks, "What's the matter?? Haven't you ever seen a soldier before?" In another, the frequently portrayed character of "Winnie the WAC" stands, breasts at attention, as a cartoon general struggles to figure out where he can pin a military decoration without touching her bosom.[27]

But a very real conflict emerged during the WAACs' first summer. In mid-August 1942, the *Morning Post* of Camden, New Jersey, announced that "Negro WAACS" would be sent to Britain. According to the news report, General Eisenhower, commander of U.S. forces in Europe, had "announced" that the women would (in the *Post*'s paraphrase) "perform duties such as car driving and secretarial work and also . . . provide companionship for the thousands of Negro troops here." Emphasizing the need for such companionship, Eisenhower had suggested that African American soldiers tend to "wander disconsolately" when on leave in large cities; for verification, the reporter quoted one African American GI: "'There's no hot music and none of our girls.'"[28]

The story provoked an identically worded denial from both Hobby and the War Department: "No members of the WAAC are being sent anywhere to provide companionship for soldiers," each insisted, and the *Baltimore African American*'s headline read: "Women's Army Auxiliary Corps Not Play Girls, Says War Department: WAAC's Not Entertainers for Troops." The story got little play outside the African American press, which may be why it raised few alarms among the exclusively white WAAC leadership. But it did reinforce concerns about the status of African American WAACS. In the *Amsterdam News*, journalist Ellen Tarry offered the story about Eisenhower and the WAACS under the headline "WAACS Segregated, Trained to 'Entertain.'" Eisenhower's misapprehension was scarcely the worst revelation in an article that described African American officer candidates being called "WAAC-coons."[29]

Despite such conflict (and perhaps because it was largely focused on African Americans), WAAC leaders thought that perhaps they'd avoided the worst of the anticipated problems. But by spring 1943, as the War Department began to consider using more women to "release" men for combat, the public reputation of the WAAC, and of WAACS, had come more generally under fire.

Letters had begun to trickle into the offices of senators and congressmen, to the mailboxes of newspaper editors, to the office of the secretary of war. An army nurse wrote a radio evangelist in Arkansas, appealing to their shared Christian concern about sin and alerting him to the moral peril in which WAACS were placed. Inductees were forced to line up naked as they waited to be examined by male medical officers, she wrote, and had been shown photographs of naked men. Understandably concerned, the man of God turned to the political realm, forwarding her letter to the press, to a state senator, to the governor of Arkansas, and to the secretary of war. The resulting investigation showed that none of the charges were true. The letter's author, in fact, was hospitalized with a diagnosis of "mild psychoneurosis."[30] But many in the public were willing to believe that women who challenged their proper, God-ordained roles had put themselves at risk. Or perhaps it was that they were not godly in the first place.

Rumors began to circulate. In Camp Lee, Virginia, it seemed that GIs had come to believe that any soldier seen dating a WAAC would be seized by military authorities and treated for exposure to venereal disease. Also in Virginia, at Hampton Roads, rumor had it that 90 percent of WAACS had been shown to be prostitutes, and that 40 percent of them were currently pregnant. In the Midwest the story was that army medical officers rejected all virgins who attempted to join the WAAC. Philadelphia was the origin of a fake "War Department Circular" for WAACS that contained "obscene anatomical 'specifications'"; soldiers carried it all the way to New

Guinea. And outside the military, in civilian society, gossip confirmed that shiploads of WAACs were being returned from their overseas postings, pregnant and unmarried.[31]

Leaders of the women's corps understood what was happening; as one noted after the war, "Men have for centuries used slander against morals as a weapon to keep women out of public life." They believed it better to ignore the rumors, while attempting to get the press to chronicle the various accomplishments of the women's corps and the praise its members had drawn from army command. But in June 1943, a charge so outrageous surfaced that WAAC leadership could not let it go unaddressed. That month a *New York Daily News* columnist charged that Colonel Hobby, the "Waac chieftain," had entered into a "super secret agreement" with the War Department to furnish members of the WAAC with contraceptives and prophylactic equipment. In response Henry L. Stimson, the secretary of war, condemned the "sinister rumors aimed at destroying the reputation of the Waac": "I have made a thorough investigation of these rumors," he stated, and "they are completely false." Supporting the WAAC were the president and first lady (who believed the charges stemmed from a Nazi plot), members of Congress, representatives of religious organizations, and the army's chief of staff, George Marshall, who condemned the "vicious slander."[32]

But the charges hit hard. Colonel Hobby broke down as she tried to tell her staff about them; she was unable to continue speaking. Parents called army posts, demanding that their daughters come home; women were in tears. Shortly after the end of the war, an enlisted woman recalled her reaction: "I went home on leave to tell my family it wasn't true. When I went through the streets, I held up my head because I imagined everybody was talking about me, but when I was at last safe inside our front door, I couldn't say a word to them, I was so humiliated—I just burst out crying, and my people ran and put their arms around me and cried with me. I couldn't understand how my eagerness to serve our country could have brought such shame on us all."[33]

It is difficult, from a current perspective, to see the claim that WAACs were provided with contraceptives as a "vicious" attack and a source of "shame." But that claim tied into a network of gossip, most originating from enlisted men and officers and then spread through civilian society. Investigation showed, for example, that in one midwestern city the rumors had begun in bars, with both officers and enlisted men calling WAACS "a bunch of tramps." Officers' wives picked up the story, confiding in friends that WAACS' "service" was to the sexual needs of men in uniform. An army chaplain, alarmed by the rumors, advised WAACS not to reenlist (reenlistment was necessary to continue to serve as the WAAC dropped auxiliary status and became the WAC). Protestant and Catholic clergy joined in, urging WAACS to remove themselves from such unsavory associations.[34] And while the claim about contraceptives was more powerful because of these claims about WAACS' individual behavior, it also suggested that the corps itself endorsed what a vast majority of Americans perceived as "sin" or immorality. Male service members—who were provided with condoms—faced no such scrutiny.

In the wake of this crisis, the corps struggled. A formal investigation found "morals" high (and no evidence of a Nazi plot), but recruiting suffered along with reputation, and over the course of the war WAC leadership continued their efforts to manage sex. Somewhat paradoxically, however, leaders' continuing concerns about the WAC's public reputation offered some women in the corps greater sexual latitude. In the interest of minimizing bad publicity, WAC officers were told to handle cases of sexual misconduct through informal measures, avoiding both publicity and the discharge of individual WACS. A pamphlet created to guide WAC officers through the potential minefield of sexual offenses, for example, urged them to address cases of homosexuality with "fairness and tolerance"; directives specifically prohibited "witch-hunting." Such "tolerance" of homosexuality, as Leisa Meyer points out, was actually a desire to avoid bad publicity, and below-the-radar witch hunts were not uncommon.[35]

Perhaps most significant, however, is that for any who found and enjoyed new sexual freedom during their wartime service, many more absorbed a caution. The very existence of the women's services depended on their perceived respectability, on their reputation. And that reputation required the careful management of sex.

Such were the challenges that shaped the WAC from the end of World War II through the mid-1970s. WAC leadership believed it was essential to guard against charges of immorality, important to emphasize the femininity and respectability of the WAC and its members. Colonel Mary Agnes Hallaren, director of the WAC from 1947 through early 1953, shepherded the corps through full integration into the regular army in 1948, led the process of racial integration, and managed the WAC role in the Korean War. But Hallaren, who had graduated in the first WAAC officer candidate school class, saw protecting the reputation of the WAC as her fundamental task. In April 1951, as American servicemen pushed north from Seoul in the tenth month of the Korean War, Hallaren sent a blistering message to WAC officers. Even as most WACs were living up to high standards, she wrote, there are "a few women who are a disgrace to the uniform they wear and to the country they are failing to serve." These women, she insisted, put the entire corps in "jeopardy." Law doesn't guarantee survival, she insisted, referring to the controversial 1948 act that had joined the WAC to the regular army. "The Corps cannot carry you," she wrote. "You must carry it."[36]

Over the continuing decades, WAC senior leadership came from those who had served during World War II. And that experience—the slander, the attacks, the public suspicion of the WAC—shaped their sense of mission. All believed that their essential task was to maintain the irreproachable reputation of the WAC. During the 1950s and 1960s, that meant emphasizing not only middle-class respectability but also the femininity—and marriageability—of those who served. A promotional pamphlet from the 1950s portrays military service as *The Fashionable Choice*, offering "smart, feminine uniforms" and respectable living arrangements "similar to those in a college dormitory." In 1968 a training film cautioned WACs not to lose their femininity; as warning it offered the story of a woman who becomes a "hard-bitten soldier" and "forgets to use lipstick." WAC basic training in 1969 included an instruction block on "Personal Standards and Social Concepts"; "personal standards" was the contemporary term for sexual abstinence. A recruiting ad in 1970 dispelled "great myths" about the WAC. "The Corps wouldn't dream of cramping a girl's style in such an important thing as marriage," read the text. "After all, we're women, too!" And in 1972—even as Sergeant Gaglione was assuring his readers that WACs weren't "tramps"—army chaplains were advised to counsel WACs against adopting "masculine traits."[37]

In such efforts leaders of the WAC attempted to reinforce the sorts of behavior, appearance, and reputation that made joining the corps a reasonable choice for a respectable young woman, whether in the eyes of her peers or her parents. But by the early 1970s, as it became clear that the coming all-volunteer army would increasingly rely on women to fill its ranks, and as the effects of the women's movement reverberated through American politics, WAC leaders faced more practical challenges. In May 1970 the head of the Army Recruiting Command (USAREC) directly confronted the problem of dual regulations based on sex. How could USAREC, in the midst of a social "movement for more liberal moral standards" and a "rising emphasis toward equality of the sexes," defend the vastly different admissions standards for men and women? Was it possible, he asked the deputy chief of staff for personnel, for the army to at least offer moral waivers for women who had an "illegitimate" child or a record of venereal disease, given that neither barred men from admission—or even required a waiver? The commander of USAREC was right to anticipate problems: by August the army was fielding complaints from members of Congress.[38]

The director of the WAC, Elizabeth Hoisington, was appalled. Hoisington, who had joined the WAAC in 1942, directly rejected the proposed moral waivers. American society, she insisted, demands "higher moral character in women" than in men. History of venereal disease or unwed pregnancy should disqualify individual women, she argued, for in women those are a clear "indication of lack of discipline and maturity." But such moral waivers, to Hoisington's mind, had implications that reached beyond the individual woman. The WAC, she wrote, has an obligation "to parents who have entrusted their daughters in our keeping, and to itself, to advance the standards of morality." Enlistment standards, insisted the director who had weathered the 1943 "scandal campaign," must continue to reflect "the necessity to maintain an impeccable public image."[39]

Hoisington lost her battle to maintain different "moral" standards for women—not because army leaders universally opposed her understandings, but because legal challenges rendered them untenable. In August 1970 U.S. Navy Seaman Anna Flores filed a class action suit on behalf of all women serving in the armed forces. Her suit, crafted by the American Civil Liberties Union (ACLU), petitioned the U.S. District Court in Pensacola, Florida, to end all military regulations based on sex. Seaman Flores, who with her fiancé—a navy enlisted man—was expecting a baby, had miscarried in the base dispensary on their planned wedding day. Her commanding officer then initiated her discharge from service. "To do otherwise," he stated, "would imply that unwed pregnancy is condoned and would eventually result in a dilution of the moral standards set for women in the Navy." Flores's suit made the incontrovertible case that male members of the U.S. Navy had had sexual intercourse and fathered children with women to whom they were not married, but had not faced discharge for such actions. On such grounds Flores asserted that she, along with all female members of the military, were deprived of equal protection of the law. "Pregnant Wave Wins," proclaimed the *Pacific Stars & Stripes* the following month, though the adjacent headline offered cautionary context for those who saw a clear victory for women's rights: "A Helping of Gal's Lib on Nixon Menu."[40]

In March 1973 the U.S. Army announced that it would drop a series of restrictions on the "moral character" of servicewomen and prospective enlistees; as of April 20, when the new regulations were to be published, applicants for enlistment no longer had to provide three character references or apply for a waiver if they had been pregnant outside marriage. In its coverage, the *New York Times* linked this decision to an ongoing set of cases supported by the ACLU, and tied it directly it to a lawsuit filed the previous week. In a complaint joined by the National Organization for Women, Kaye Hasson of Oakland, California, had asserted that she had been prevented from enlisting in the WAC solely because she had a seven-year-old daughter who was "born out of wedlock"—a criterion that does not apply to male applicants. The WAC director insisted that the changes "were unrelated to Miss Hasson's suit," as they'd been in process for several months.[41] But the broader connections were clear.

As U.S. women claimed broader rights in the late 1960s and early 1970s—the right to serve on a jury; the right for married women to hold credit in their own names; the right to compete for all jobs, not just those designated "female" in sex-segregated want ads; the right of unmarried women to have access to birth control; the right to abortion; the right to equal opportunity in admission to schools of law and medicine—women in the military were part of that movement. Hoisington's successor, General Mildred Bailey, fought to open more military occupational specialties to women and encouraged WACs to embrace nontraditional assignments and commit to "work and a career," even as she insisted that the civilian women's liberation movement was largely irrelevant to women under her command. But as more and more specialties opened to women, the army claimed that "today's Army may be your most equal opportunity."[42]

But even as WAC leaders spearheaded this expansion of opportunity, they remained sensitive to the "moral" reputation of the corps. All had joined the WAAC during World War II; all had weathered the "scandals" and the struggles to redeem the corps's reputation. But it was not only the weight of that experience that shaped their concerns. Although the women's movement and ongoing sexual revolution had challenged traditional gender roles and sexual mores, those challenges were hotly contested. It was not at all clear what the outcome of the revolutions would be, and even as society changed, parents continued to worry about their daughters' reputations, and "marriageability" remained key to most young American women. As late as 1976, "SGT Judy" told the army recruiting journal that parents were her biggest recruiting challenge. "Some parents," she explained, "have the impression their daughters will 'morally decline' if they join the Army." And in 1974, when *The Today Show* scheduled a special on the WAC, NBC submitted a list of questions to the office of the WAC director. Of eighteen questions, ten concerned sex. Viewers were evidently eager to learn how many WACs had been released "for homosexuality" during the past year, about the army budget for birth control, "to include pills," whether WACs were required to wear bras. The final question: "Are all married men who serve as supervisory or Cadre personnel with WACs required to have written consent from wives?"[43]

The WAC survived, within the U.S. Army, for four more years. Its 1978 demise stemmed, in great part, from the broader social movement for women's equal rights and responsibilities. To the end WAC senior leadership did all in their power to guard the reputation of their corps and its women. But once women were fully integrated into the army, they were no longer subject to separate regulations managing sex.

What lessons can we draw from this history of managing sex? First, and most obvious, is that gender presented a challenge to an institution that sought to impose universal regulations ("one category of people," as army leaders put it during World War II) but that had to function in a society with a sexual double standard and a strong belief that men and women were fundamentally different creatures. The internal process of managing sex reveals some of the tensions that emerged as this massive institution attempted to cope with the demands of difference.

Second, this history illustrates how important external perceptions are to the function of the military in a democracy, most particularly to a military that relies on volunteers (as it always has in the case of women). Enlistment in the WAC did, indeed, rise and fall with its reputation as a respectable institution. And the challenge of managing sex was, from the beginning, less about managing the behavior of the highly screened women who joined the WAC than about managing the public reputation of the institution.

Finally, this history emphasizes the critical connections between the military and civilian authority. For all the regulations and directives and instructions issued within the military, it was civilian power that defined the WAC's possibilities and limits, that determined what could and could not be done when it came to the ever-shifting challenge of "managing sex."

Notes

1. Sergeant First Class Joe Gaglione, "About the Army," *Tyrone (PA) Daily Herald*, October 18, 1972, 10.

2. Bailey, "Soldiering as Work," 581, 588.

3. Bailey, *America's Army*, 210, 242; Gaglione, "About the Army."

4. My discussion of the WAAC/WAC during World War II is heavily indebted to the voluminous research conducted by Mattie Treadwell for the official army history *Women's Army Corps*; quote from Treadwell, 19.

5. Treadwell, *Women's Army Corps*, chaps. 1–2; for a description of Hobby, see "Head of Women's Army Auxiliary Is Mother of 2 Young Children," *Tampa Morning Tribune*, May 16, 1942, 1.

6. Clare Hoffman, speaking on HR 6293, March 17, 1942, 77th Cong., 2nd sess., *Congressional Record 88*, H 2593; Walker, "Congressional Career," 100.

7. Comments on HR 6293, H 2606-07. On Randolph, see David Stout, "Senator Jenning Randolph of West Virginia Dies at 96," *New York Times*, May 9, 1998, A12.

8. Comments on HR 6293, H 2603, H 2605.

9. Comments on HR 6293, H 2608.

10. Treadwell, *Women's Army Corps*, 30, 32–33.

11. Ruth Cowan, "Mrs. Hobby to Head WAAC," *Statesman Journal* (Salem OR), May 16, 1942, 2; Treadwell, *Women's Army Corps*, 48.

12. Sander S. Klein, "Petticoat Army Can Wear Lipstick, BUT—," *Oakland Tribune*, May 17, 1942, 3; "Mrs. Hobby Heads Corps," *Daily Record* (Long Branch NJ), May 16, 1942, 2; Jack Kofoed, "Miami Story," *Miami News*, May 20, 1942, 9; Treadwell, *Women's Army Corps*, 49.

13. Treadwell, *Women's Army Corps*, 55, 58.

14. Treadwell, *Women's Army Corps*, 54–58; "Col. Hobby Says Army Has No Hush Policy Regarding WACS," *Star Press* (Muncie IN), February 28, 1945, 6.

15. Treadwell, *Women's Army Corps*, 113–17, 120, 98.

16. Meyer, *Creating GI Jane*, 101.

17. The WAAC code of conduct is reprinted in Shea, *Waacs*, 232–34; see also Morden, *Women's Army Corps*, 21; and Meyer, *Creating GI Jane*, 69.

18. Meyer, *Creating GI Jane*, 69.

19. Army VD film, n.d., Periscope Film Archives, https://archive.org/details/21484AAFHealthHygene (accessed July 8, 2021); Treadwell, *Women's Army Corps*, 203; Hegarty, *Victory Girls*, 103; Bailey and Farber, *First Strange Place*, chap. 3; Meyer, *Creating GI Jane*, 106.

20. Information drawn from Treadwell, *Women's Army Corps*, 617–18; Meyer, *Creating GI Jane*, 104–6.

21. Meyer, *Creating GI Jane*, 104, 105.

22. Treadwell, *Women's Army Corps*, 618.

23. Meyer, *Creating GI Jane*, 107; Treadwell, *Women's Army Corps*, 608–9.

24. See Meyer's account of instruction and monthly exams, *Creating GI Jane*, 106–7; VD rates from Treadwell, *Women's Army Corps*, 619, 398.

25. Meyer, *Creating GI Jane*, 108–11; Treadwell, *Women's Army Corps*, 620.

26. Treadwell, *Women's Army Corps*, 184.

27. Knaff, *Beyond Rosie the Riveter*, especially 88.

28. "Negro WAACS Due to Serve in Britain," *Morning Post* (Camden NJ), August 19, 1942, 7.

29. Lula Garrett, "Women's Army Auxiliary Corps Not Play Girls, Says War Department: WAAC's Not Entertainers for Troops," *Baltimore Afro-American*, September 5, 1942, 16; Ellen Tarry, "WAACS Segregated, Trained to 'Entertain,'" *Amsterdam News*, August 29, 1942, 1.

30. Treadwell, *Women's Army Corps*, 197.

31. Treadwell, *Women's Army Corps*, 201.

32. Treadwell, *Women's Army Corps*, 218; "Stimson Condemns Gossip About WAAC," *New York Times*, June 11, 1943, 6; Eleanor Darnton Washington, "WAACS Fight Back: 'Sinister Rumors, Aimed at Destroying Their Reputation' Are Denounced," *New York Times*, June 27, 1943, x9; Treadwell, *Women's Army Corps*, 203–4.

33. Treadwell, *Women's Army Corps*, 204; Treadwell cites "Sgt. Amelia Madrak, Hist Div SSUSA, secy of author, 1947."

34. Treadwell, *Women's Army Corps*, 206–7.

35. Meyer, *Creating GI Jane*, 158–59.

36. Memo from Colonel Hallaren, April 4, 1951, no folder label, Box 86, NARA.

37. *The Fashionable Choice*, Folder 82, Box 12, NARA; Department of the Army, *Duty, Honor, Country*, pamphlet 16-13 (which includes a synopsis of *The Lady in Military Service*, training film 16-3415) (Washington DC: U.S. Government Printing Office, 1968); Richard A. Dey Jr., "Training for Army Service," *Army Digest*, n.d. [ca. 1969?], 41–42, in Magazine/Newspaper Articles file, Box 38, NARA; "Great Myths about the Women's Army Corps" advertisement, N. W. Ayer for *Sr. Scholastic* magazine, April 20, 1970, N. W. Ayer Advertising Collection; Department of the Army, *Human Self Development: Our Moral Heritage*, pamphlet 165-10 (Washington DC: U.S. Government Printing Office, 1972).

38. Morden, *Women's Army Corps*, 232–35.

39. "Elizabeth Hoisington," *Kansapedia*, Kansas Historical Society, https://www.kshs.org/kansapedia/elizabeth-hoisington/17816 (accessed July 8, 2021); Morden, *Women's Army Corps*, 232–35.

40. "A Double Standard in the Navy?" *Washington Post*, August 25, 1970, B2; James T. Wooten, "Enlisted Woman, 23, Sues Navy Over Sexual Rights," *New York Times*, August 26, 1970, 44; Kenneth Reich, "Unwed WAVE Sues to Stay in Navy after a Miscarriage," *Los Angeles Times*, August 25, 1970, 1; "Wave Fights Discharge," *Afro-American*, September 5, 1970, 10; "Pregnant Wave Wins," *Pacific Stars and Stripes*, September 4, 1970, 3.

41. "Marriage and Pregnancy Curbs on WAC Enlistees Are Eased," *New York Times*, March 27, 1973, 26.

42. On recruiting campaigns, see Bailey, *America's Army*, 152–53, 161–63.

43. "Tom Pettit, NBC, for WAC Show on Friday, 1 Mar 74," in Magazine/Newspaper Articles file, Box 38, NARA. For a complete discussion, see Bailey, *America's Army*, chap. 5.

Bibliography

Archives and Manuscript Materials

NARA. RG 319, Women's Army Corps, 1945–78. National Archives and Records Administration, College Park MD.

N. W. Ayer Advertising Collection. Archives Center, National Museum of American History, Smithsonian Institution, Washington DC.

Published Works

Bailey, Beth. *America's Army: Making the All-Volunteer Force.* Cambridge MA: Harvard University Press, 2009.

——. "Soldiering as Work." In *Fighting for a Living: A Comparative History of Military Labour, 1500-2000,* edited by Erik-Jan Zurcher, 581–612. Amsterdam: Amsterdam University Press, 2013.

Bailey, Beth, and David Farber. *The First Strange Place: The Alchemy of Race and Sex in World War II Hawaii.* New York: Free Press, 1992.

Hegarty, Marilyn E. *Victory Girls, Khaki-Wackies, and Patriotutes: The Regulation of Female Sexuality during World War II.* New York: New York University Press, 2008.

Holm, Jeanne. *Women in the Military: An Unfinished Revolution.* Novato CA: Presidio, 1992.

Knaff, Donna B. *Beyond Rosie the Riveter: Women of World War II in American Popular Graphic Art.* Lawrence: University Press of Kansas, 2012.

Meyer, Leisa D. *Creating GI Jane: Sexuality and Power in the Women's Army Corps during World War II.* New York: Columbia University Press, 1996.

Morden, Bettie J. *The Women's Army Corps, 1945–1978.* Washington DC: U.S. Army Center of Military History, 1990.

Murnane, Linda Strite. "Legal Impediments to Service: Women in the Military and the Rule of Law." *Duke Journal of Gender Law and Policy* 14 (2007): 1061–96.

Shea, Nancy. *The Waacs.* New York: Harper & Brothers, 1943.

Treadwell, Mattie E. *The Women's Army Corps.* Washington DC: Center of Military History, [1953] 1991.

Walker, Donald Edwin. "The Congressional Career of Clare E. Hoffman, 1935–63." PhD diss., Michigan State University, 1982.

PART 2

Family and Reproduction

FOUR

"We Recruit Individuals but Retain Families"

Managing Marriage and Family in the All-Volunteer Force,
1973–2001

JOHN WORSENCROFT

"We recruit individuals but retain families." It's a phrase often attributed to Chief of Staff of the Army John A. Wickham Jr. in his landmark 1983 white paper, *The Army Family*, and it has since become a mantra among policymakers and military leaders.[1] In a 2019 speech, undersecretary of the U.S. Air Force Matthew Donovan told an audience that families were essential to the mission. As the air force continued to face a massive pilot shortage, Donovan reminded everyone that "we recruit individuals but we retain families."[2] That very same year, Senator Susan Collins of Maine uttered that exact phrase on the floor of the Senate as she introduced legislation to cut taxes on military spouses' benefits, adding, "We have an obligation to make sure that we are taking care of our military families who have sacrificed so much for our country."[3]

We live in a time when Americans thank military families in the same breath as men and women in uniform. But for most of American history, the old saying "If the military wanted you to have a wife, it would have issued one to you" was a truism of military life—not just as a matter of tradition but also one inscribed in defense manpower policy and in military regulations. As the United States fought wars abroad, from World War I through the Vietnam War, manpower officials worked hard to keep family men out of the enlisted ranks. Occasionally policymakers would fail to meet this goal—men with families were drafted in World War II, Korea, and for part of the Vietnam War—but Americans in and out of uniform believed firmly that military service was for the young and single. This belief continued even after the United States stopped drafting men, and Americans stopped thinking of military service as an obligation of male citizenship. In the words of Captain Paula Scott, who in 1979 was serving as a personnel officer in Baumholder, Germany, "The Army is not in the baby business; it is not in the marriage business."[4]

Yet today military policymakers talk about families as "force multipliers," as a positive and essential component of mission readiness. Inside and out of the military community, families are a focal point. As First Lady Michelle Obama unveiled as one of her signature issues "Joining Forces," a nationwide effort to encourage "companies, schools, philanthropic and religious groups, and local communities to recognize the unusual stress that is endured by families of active-duty personnel, reservists and veterans, and to strive to meet their needs."[5] Every year on a military base, some commanding officer decrees to his or her subordinates that this year is "The Year of the Family."

So what changed? How did the military get its family-friendly reputation? When did military officials begin to see families as an essential component of the overall mission? When did senators and first ladies start caring about the needs of families on far-flung military bases? And how did Americans come to view families as sacrificing for the nation, as needing benefits usually reserved for uniformed service members, and as worthy of the nation's gratitude?

The simplest answer to these questions is that more military personnel started getting married, a trend that began in the decade after World War II, when the United States chose to maintain a large peacetime military during the Cold War. Looking across the services, during the 1950s marriages crept above 40 percent for the first time, then dipped following the massive initial draft call-ups of the Vietnam War in 1965–66, but resumed their rise as deferments tightened. In 1973 the United States transitioned to the all-volunteer force (AVF), effectively ending the practice of conscripting young, mostly single men, and within a year, more than half of the military was married.

But more marriages was only the beginning. More important is exactly *who* was getting married. The army—which relied most heavily upon those young, unmarried draftees prior to 1973—saw marriages spike and continue to rise during the 1970s, so that by the end of the decade nearly 60 percent of soldiers were married. The main driver of this surge was junior enlisted soldiers, whose families, at the time, were barred from enjoying the on-base privileges afforded to officers' families.[6]

Because of the army's size (historically, the army has comprised roughly 40 percent of the total force), what happened in its ranks affected the other services. For comparison, in 1975 the army had about 785,000 soldiers, while the Marine Corps only had about 196,000 members in uniform. As army marriages crept toward 60 percent in the 1970s, marines got married at roughly half that rate. In the 1980s the army began offering more benefits to families, and the Department of Defense (DOD) started to defer more and more to its largest service on family policy. As marines complied with new DOD policies, family rates in the corps began to rise, so that by the 1990s, half of the Marine Corps had families.

The story of how policymakers managed families is enmeshed in the military's efforts to rebuild itself after the disastrous war in Vietnam. After losing the ability to draft young men, the military, especially the army, had to learn to recruit qualified and motivated people in the marketplace.[7] Policymakers did not want to make changes at first, and those they did make were adopted as stopgap measures to manage acute crises in recruitment and retention. More and more those qualified young people were women, but senior military officers, who, until the twenty-first century, were almost exclusively men, saw issues like marriage, children, and families as problems that existed outside of the scope of the mission to train for and fight the nations' wars. Importantly, these men frequently, and wrongly, conflated family problems with more women entering the ranks. In the initial years of the AVF, many policymakers believed that the draft would eventually be reinstated, especially if a major war broke out, and all of these other problems—demanding volunteers, needy families, even women— would simply go away.[8]

Families did not simply wait around for the military to figure it out, and increasingly, military families turned to activism. The U.S. Army and Marine Corps were not immune to outside forces at work in society. As younger Americans, who had grown up in the civil rights era and witnessed a growing national women's movement, started entering the military, policymakers increasingly confronted activist women (both civilian wives and women in uniform) who were willing to organize, petition, and advocate for the growing needs of their families in an era of economic uncertainty. National women's groups and their allies in Congress also saw the military as a site for pursuing the aspirational goals of feminism to secure women's equality and full citizenship. These groups fought to dismantle barriers to women's full participation in the military and advocated for services such as childcare and career services to balance the competing demands of work and family.

Each of the services took the slow march toward accommodating families—but some marched faster, and more willingly, than others. When we think about the military as a singular institution, as opposed to distinct branches with internal goals, needs, and cultures, we miss important developments in the history of the AVF and the role of families in its development. To illustrate these tensions, this essay compares the experiences of the U.S. Army and Marine Corps. Indeed, it was not the army but the Marine Corps—the least family-friendly branch and the one most concerned about all of the "problems" ushered in by the AVF—that ensured the viability of a voluntary military by figuring out how to put families to work for it, effectively ending the equation of benefits for families with social welfare programs.

The Revolution in Military Life

In the 1970s the military as a whole transformed from a majority-single institution to majority-married. Although marriages had been on the rise since the end of World War II, the use of the draft during the early years of the Cold War through the 1960s kept rising marriage rates in check by providing the military a steady stream of young, unwed draftees. From 1963 until 1966 married men were assigned a lower draft priority than single men, and up until 1970 married men with children were categorized 3-A, meaning they were draft exempt. But when Richard Nixon ended deferments for family men in April 1970 and then moved to the AVF in 1973, marriage rates grew to 56 percent. By the beginning of the 1980s, over 60 percent of servicemen and -women were married. Importantly, the army and the Marine Corps did not experience these changes concurrently. Keeping in mind the relative size of each branch, in 1980 army marriages set the trend for the rise in marriages in the overall force, even though only 34 percent of marines were married at the time.[9]

For the army the more serious problem was who was getting married. The army in the 1970s saw a dramatic increase in marriage among the junior enlisted ranks, or those soldiers in pay grades E-4 and below.[10] The increase in married junior enlisted soldiers resulted from ending the draft (most draftees were in the lower ranks), coupled with a decision by the army to loosen marriage and dependent children restrictions on incoming recruits—in order to meet very serious recruiting shortfalls in the years after the Vietnam War. During the transition years to the AVF, E-4s and below had almost five hundred thousand dependent children living under their care. From 1975 to 1977, the percentage of married E-3s in the army went from 25 percent to 38 percent; for E-4s rates went up from 43 percent to 54 percent during the same period.[11]

But the army did not recognize these marriages at the time. In the 1970s married junior enlisted personnel were not entitled to on-base family housing, subsidized off-base housing, commissary privileges for families, family medical care, or defrayed moving costs. This presented myriad difficulties for these young, unsanctioned families. In Europe families organized "under four" clubs (for E-4-and-below families) to pool money to buy cooking utensils, pots and pans, and other durable household items, passing the used goods along to the next family once they rotated back to the states.[12]

More military families became dual-income families as family work patterns in the United States changed in the 1960s and 1970s, especially for working-class and lower-middle-class families. For these Americans a "family wage" was only possible if two earners were bringing in an income—and for women, this meant pulling double duty at work and at home. By the early 1970s, more than half of all civilian women between eighteen and sixty-four engaged in work for pay. One in three married women worked—and half of all African American women worked. At the beginning of the decade, military wives were less likely to be working than wives in civilian society, 30.5 percent and 41 percent, respectively, but they quickly joined their civilian counterparts in the workforce. By 1979 military wives had surpassed civilian wives in labor participation, at 50.2 percent and 49.4 percent, respectively.[13]

The growth in military wives' labor participation is remarkable, given the number of unique obstacles military life created when compared to civilian life. Military wives had to move when their husbands changed duty stations, commonly every couple of years. These working wives had spotty employment records, and they often could not keep a position long enough to get promoted. They usually worked in jobs that did not have retirement benefits or pensions, but even if they did, they could not stay with a company long enough to ever enjoy them.

Junior enlisted families turned to government assistance programs for relief. In March 1970 the military began allowing personnel to use food stamps at its more than three hundred base commissaries. The DOD had to issue this order because there was a lot of confusion about whether military personnel could even legally apply for food stamps. Legal or not, that year over twelve thousand military families were using food stamps, and the DOD estimated that as many as thirty-two thousand families were eligible. Until 1973 sympathetic stories about draftees supporting their families on food stamps were a mainstay in the press, but what was once reported on as a moral outrage quickly became an outrage of a different kind in the AVF era. In 1975 a headline in the *Chicago Tribune* asked, "GIs Licking System with Food Stamps?" and quoted a Republican congressman, Paul Findley, who said, "It is ridiculous for one agency of the federal government to pass out welfare benefits to persons employed full-time by another agency of the same government." Democratic senator John Stenos "expressed amazement" that people who got paid so well "should turn to 'welfare.'" In a general response to such charges, an army counselor at Fort Meyer pointed out that "a typical food stamp user is a private [E-1] with a wife and two children." An E-1s pay would bring in about $384 a month. In 2019 dollars that's roughly $1,700 a month that a young private would have to support his or her family of four. Recall that the families of E-4s and below were not eligible for housing, medical care, moving expenses, or on-base shopping privileges. To Congressman Findley and other critics, military families on welfare represented "a dramatic example of the extent to which the food stamp program has moved from its original objective." But to those families, it demonstrated that the military was failing to take care of its own.[14]

If marriage was difficult in the army, it was nearly impossible in the marines. The Marine Corps had a much higher tolerance for attrition than the army—most junior marines finished their initial enlistments, and then went back to the civilian world. Less concerned about enticing people to reenlist, the corps pursued concrete policies that made marriage and having a family difficult, especially for women. As the army incrementally eased its policy of forcing women who became pregnant out of the service in the 1970s, the marines aggressively forced out pregnant women and single parents (men and women) on the grounds that parental obligations conflicted with the demands of the corps. Indeed, the Marine Corps was the last branch to stop involuntarily discharging pregnant women, and it only stopped this practice when the courts ruled it unconstitutional in 1976.[15] Still, every commandant to serve after 1973 reaffirmed the corps's hardline position, through written orders, that a marine's commitment to the Marine Corps came before any family obligations. And those policies had their desired effect: in the 1970s the combination of a grueling deployment schedule—first-term marines spent over half of their enlistment overseas, usually aboard naval ships—and antifamily policies worked to keep marriage rates at around 30 percent, or roughly half the rate the army was experiencing.

Although married soldiers and soldiers with children became more common in the post–World War II era, officials did not think that marriage was a "problem" to manage until the 1970s. Post–World War II policies that governed military life were written assuming that men wore uniforms, and that if a serviceman had a family, his wife would be a homemaker, capable of taking care of the kids and managing the household while he was away on maneuvers.[16] But in the 1970s, more women began serving, and junior enlistees overall were starting families with greater frequency. These young families could not survive on a single income, so more spouses entered the workforce, and the gendered assumptions that had shaped military policy no longer reflected reality. Policymakers, who were overwhelmingly men, believed that women were to blame for family problems even though men were far more likely to get married while in uniform and far more likely to have dependent children. For example, in the late 1970s nearly 60 percent of men in uniform had dependent children, compared to only 22 percent of women.

These attitudes were widespread among both officers and enlisted personnel. In 1978 Congressman Robin Beard commissioned an opinion study of service members. Beard reported to a Senate Armed Services Committee hearing that "the effects of pregnancy and the disposition of children" topped the list of concerns that men had about women in the military. Men in the military believed that pregnancy was a woman's problem that affected operational readiness, and "coupled with the radical increase in the number of junior enlisted persons who are now married," pregnancy and marriage "are causing commanders to ask philosophical questions about whether the Army is a fighting machine or a social welfare institution." Beard concluded, "Collectively, commanders and NCOs [noncommissioned officers] agree that too much of their time is being drained by social welfare and reform activities to the point that operational readiness is being impacted."[17] Beard's study revealed a pattern of belief among commanders and NCOs that army policies were creating a spiraling cycle in which more women required more social welfare benefits, and more social welfare benefits attracted more women.[18]

Commanders conflated the question of female pregnancy and single-parent dependent care. Without referencing any concrete numbers, the report stated that service members believed "there is a high incidence of pregnancy among women serving in the Army. Many single women are having children while on active duty." Without stopping to ask who these women might be having sex with, or whether their male partners bore any responsibility for these children, the report blamed women for the rise in single parenthood, as well as its threat to unit readiness: "As social mores have changed and women feel free to act as single parents the unit commander is frequently faced with finding a replacement for the female soldier during the period of maternal leave and, of greater significance, worrying about the care of the child during alerts, mobilization and training." The reality was quite the opposite: of the 24,400 single parents in the army in 1980, 80 percent were men; for the military as a whole, 75 percent of single parents were men.[19] And even if one factored in lost time due to pregnancy, men still missed more on-duty days per year, on average, because men were far more likely to desert or go absent without leave (AWOL), more likely to abuse alcohol, and more likely to use drugs than women.[20] Commanders believed family problems were women's problems even when both parents wore the uniform, concluding, "In some cases the female soldier is married to another soldier and during alerts the couple shows up with their children."[21]

Army Families Fight Back

Within this hostile environment, military families struggled to make ends meet. Military compensation was always a complicated mixture of monthly wages and "fringe benefits," or the ways the military compensated personnel with access to health care, discounted goods at the PX and commissary, allowances for housing, and the GI Bill. But the economic turmoil and inflation of the 1970s meant that a service member's total compensation declined in value as the decade wore on.[22]

Wives' frustration had reached a boiling point by the end of the 1970s, particularly in the army. Army wives' clubs—which had existed for decades at larger bases—became key sites for women's activism in the military community. According to a 1979 *Army Times* family manual, "Traditionally, wives clubs hold regular social events—monthly luncheons and business meetings, weekly bridge sessions, bowling leagues and golf teams, sometimes formal dances with the husbands."[23] For senior officers' wives, these clubs recaptured "a little of the grandeur of past tradition with an occasional fancy dress ball or dinner tables aglitter in crystal and silver." But for the wives of more junior officers, this was an infuriating waste of time. As Bonnie Stone and Betty Alt, two former military wives who write about family life in the military, recall, "The double whammy of feminism and the uneasy economy . . . effected catastrophic changes in wives' club participation."[24]

Some wives and women in uniform found allies in the women's movement, both through national women's organizations like the National Organization for Women (NOW) and the Women's Equity Action League (WEAL), or with members of Congress allied with those groups. Congresswomen like Patricia Schroeder, Patsy Mink, Shirley Chisolm, and Bella Abzug took up the mantle of military families in the 1970s, seeing them as part of the fundamental struggle of second-wave feminism: reshaping the public sphere to accommodate the needs of women. Groups interested in advancing civil rights and liberties, such as the American Civil Liberties Union (ACLU), also fought for equality in the military through the courts. When the ACLU began its Women's Rights Project in 1971, it made the subject of women in the military a focal point. The Women's Rights Project sought to eliminate gender-based discrimination through legal action, and the ACLU helped with several landmark court cases involving the military during the 1970s and 1980s. Women's rights activists saw the military as an essential venue for advocating for women's equality, opening up women's access to the workplace, and enacting labor laws that addressed the specific needs of women.[25]

One particularly active wives' group was the Army Officers' Wives Club of the Greater Washington Area, many members of which tended to be younger, more educated, and more active in the women's movement. For example, club member Carolyn Becraft worked for WEAL, managing its "Women in the Military" project. Talk of putting together a symposium to discuss families had been going on since the mid-1970s, and in the spring of 1980, the Washington Area Wives Club held a small planning workshop to establish an agenda for a symposium in October. Although many women spoke at the workshop, one army wife named Joyce Ott made recommendations that would set the tone for the upcoming symposium. Ott had a master's degree in counseling and worked at a women's center in Washington. She asked three important questions at the workshop that delegates would grapple with later that year: "What is going to happen to the concept of the military family? What can we do to help both husband and wife blend their careers? How can we help those who want to use volunteerism as a stepping stone to help her career?" Her preliminary answers called for building stronger communities, promoting "wellness," and working toward partnership between families and the military.[26]

When the Washington Area Wives Club held its symposium in October 1980, nearly two hundred women registered as delegates and showed up to discuss improving army life. Delegates asked for lines of communication between families and the chain of command to be more uniform and reciprocal. While they conceded that mobility was a necessary part of life in the military, wives proposed that the army give them a six-month notice prior to relocation, and a modest increase in financial compensation for moving expenses. Nearly 60 percent of military wives were working (71 percent among junior enlisted wives), but the transient nature of military life meant that they frequently had to terminate employment, pull their kids out of school, and sever already tenuous ties to local community networks each time their husbands changed duty stations. To assist with these regular transfers, wives proposed the creation of "job opportunity centers" to provide job counseling, and the creation of an on-base liaison who could cultivate career opportunities in the surrounding community.[27]

The delegates devoted a considerable amount of their attention to quality of life issues. They requested improvements to the Civilian Health and Medical Program of the Uniformed Services (CHAMPUS), a hybridized health care system in which military families utilized both military medical facilities and subcontracted private-sector health services for their health care needs. They requested improvements to on-base housing and higher allowances for those who lived off base and overseas. Finally, the delegates wanted improvements to on-base childcare facilities. Citing the increase in single parents, dual-military families, and families in which both parents were employed, they requested army-wide uniformity in childcare services and facilities and subsidies for low-income families.[28]

At the symposium delegates confronted a system that required women to sacrifice their needs and desires for the demands of the army. They rejected the entrenched notion that a wife's identity in the military community was an extension of her husband's rank. This paternalistic belief reinforced policies that made them feel like second-class citizens, and the delegates explicitly demanded more control over their lives. Echoing the social transformations of the 1970s, specifically for women, they declared, "As social, economic and educational roles change for the American woman, there is an expectation by women that institutions will recognize those changes and address them in a manner which is constructive to both the individual woman and the organization."[29] Determined to carve out an identity separate from their husbands, the wives demanded that the army stop referring to them as "dependents" and work towards "increased recognition . . . that the Army spouse is an individual [and] not an extension of the service member." Finally, they wanted the army to eliminate the pressure on wives to volunteer for on-base functions.[30]

In 1979 and 1980 the DOD and Congress took significant steps to address quality of life and compensation issues for service members and their families, especially in the junior ranks. The Defense Authorization Bill for FY 1981 resulted in an 11.7 percent pay raise for service members and changed the housing allowance from a flat rate to one that varied based upon local rent costs. The Nunn-Warner Amendment also authorized E-1s through E-4s to begin receiving family separation pay. These increases in compensation and benefits were certainly welcome relief, but they fell far short of the mark. Most families in the junior ranks still needed two incomes to get by, and the military had done nothing to address the issues that dual-income families faced.[31]

Army wives held symposia each year between 1980 and 1983, and through these annual meetings, they laid the groundwork for institutional change. Army family policies reflected traditional notions of gender roles and family life that were unworkable in the economic and social realities of 1980s America. Wives wanted more control over their lives and, in particular, resources for seeking meaningful employment and for childcare. When the army decided it was time for a family to move, wives wanted to know when, where, and for how long. They wanted to be treated as partners, not dependents. These demands, firmly within the mainstream of second-wave feminism, were not radical: the wives wanted a stake in the system.

The Services Respond

Meanwhile, the army as an institution was at its historical nadir. After several years of budget cuts and recruiting shortfalls, six of the army's ten divisions were understaffed and ill equipped. The outgoing army chief of staff, General Edward "Shy" Meyer, warned his superiors that he was in charge of a "hollow Army." In 1983 President Reagan appointed General John A. Wickham Jr. to be his new chief of staff. Despite the serious problems facing the army, General Wickham was viewed as the safe choice for Reagan. Those close to Wickham believed he was an unassuming Boy Scout—and a bit of a prude: Wickham would scold subordinates if they uttered a swear word in his presence. In these tumultuous times for the army, many believed General Wickham would chart a steady course.

But immediately after assuming command in the summer of 1983, Wickham went to work reviewing the army's family policies, publishing a white paper called *The Army Family* in August. "Once a private matter," he began, the family "is now an organizational concern." Wickham saw "geographic mobility, changing family structures and the recognition that competition between family and organizational needs can be destructive to both parties," and that this new reality required action.[32]

Wickham recognized that society was changing, and that the army needed to adapt in order to survive. He credited wives' activism for creating urgency, noting the "political sophistication of Army families that organize at the grassroots level to form self-help and advocacy groups." He also recognized that wives' activism was taking place within the broader context of the women's movement: "Today's families are also a product of the social movements of the 1960s and 1970s" and had "internalized the questioning, activist nature of these movements."[33] American values were shifting, and General Wickham knew that an all-volunteer military, which relied solely upon recruiting to fill its ranks, could not survive without adapting. Wickham saw that, "when a tug-of-war occurs between a military family and a military organization, the family usually wins."[34]

While General Wickham saw the need to adapt with a changing society, *The Army Family* also reflected the national mood over a perceived weakening of the family in America. To the "values voters" who elected Ronald Reagan, families were the building blocks of a healthy nation. By 1983 the New Right had successfully halted, and even reversed, many of the gains made by women's rights advocates during the 1970s. The effort to ratify the Equal Rights Amendment was effectively dead, and evangelical Christians, who advocated a return to "traditional" gender roles in the family and the wider society, found allies in institutions at every level of government. Indeed, Wickham considered himself a born-again Christian and frequently called upon the council of his personal friend Dr. James Dobson, the leader of the fundamentalist political lobbying group Focus on the Family.[35]

Americans often cast their imagined national community and its institutions in terms of family. But in the early 1980s, the metaphors of family and nation took on a different meaning. The loss in Vietnam, the social and cultural upheavals of the 1960s and 1970s, economic decline, the Iran hostage crisis, and challenges to traditional mores all evoked expressions of American identity as a family in crisis.[36] To many the very survival of the nation required action, and in *The Army Family* General Wickham took up that cause. Fusing the language of family with national institutions, he wrote, "Soldiers and their families gain through the Army a sense of common identity. They come to view the Army as providing for their total basic needs in exchange for total commitment."[37] The reciprocity of that statement was implied, although earlier Wickham made the connection explicitly: "In fostering interdependence between the family and the Army, we are again looking at the Army as an institution. . . . It is not a we/they situation, it is us—US as in U.S. Army."[38] These discursive nuances elevated the white paper's significance in this context. The army was a family, and its foundation, Wickham concluded, rested on guaranteeing wellness and nurturing a sense of community.

The Army Family embodied the phrase "The Army recruits individuals but retains families," and in 1984 Wickham declared the first "Year of the Army Family," ordering his subordinate commanders around the globe to focus on strengthening the bonds between families and the army. And Wickham was serious about making concrete changes—so serious that he turned to the same women who started the family symposiums, charging them with writing a plan for the future of the army family. Sitting around the kitchen table of Carolyn Becraft—the military wife, WEAL worker, and future deputy secretary of defense for community support—the wives took the lessons of the symposiums and made them army doctrine.[39]

Almost immediately the DOD began adopting many of the programs the army pioneered under General Wickham. In 1988 the DOD issued guidance to safeguard the rights and autonomy of families in all policy decisions. Military families deserved, according to the new guidelines, "a quality of life that reflects the high standards and pride of the nation they defend." Building upon the commitments made by the army four years earlier, the Pentagon now recognized that it had a primary responsibility for the welfare of its members' families. The DOD directive included childcare, private and public sector employment assistance for spouses, education support for families, substance abuse prevention programs, and resources for "spiritual growth and development." Family wellbeing was now DOD policy, and the secretary of defense began demanding accountability from each of the services.[40]

Over at the commandant's office, marine policymakers watched what the army was doing with increasing alarm. Ever since the beginning of the AVF, the Marine Corps pursued deliberate policies that made marriage and having a family difficult, especially for women. But the marines also had to compete for recruits in the marketplace, and as the DOD embraced the army's approach to quality of life for families, the Marine Corps had no choice but to offer higher pay and more benefits to married marines. Over time this had a clear effect on the marriage rate in the marines, which had historically been roughly half that of the army. By the 1990s fully half of the Marine Corps was married, had dependent children, or both.

Buried in a report on the progress of women in the Marine Corps, policymakers expressed concern that the growing number of families, women marines, working spouses, and single parents were forcing base and installation commanders to devote too much time to childcare issues. Some believed that recruitment and retention required the marines to adopt more policies like the army, but others argued that the marines should not be in the family business, concluding that the Marine Corps "is not responsible for providing child care at all."[41] "Family readiness," according to an article in the *Marine Corps Gazette*, published shortly after

Operation Desert Shield/Storm, "appears to have priority over military readiness in many areas. Particularly in a time of shrinking budgets, the family support requirements placed on the Marine Corps, the Marine, and the families themselves are costs out of proportion to the benefits received." This was a familiar claim: the Marine Corps was in the business of warfighting, and families were an unwanted distraction.[42]

The context for this debate is important. With the collapse of the Soviet Union and the Warsaw Pact, between 1990 and 1995 the U.S. armed forces shed about 22 percent of its uniformed members. The DOD closed 330 military installations and consolidated 130 more. In the 1970s the defense budget accounted for roughly twenty-five cents per every dollar the government spent; by 1995 the DOD spent about thirteen cents on the dollar.[43] The rising cost of providing benefits to families became a budgetary concern, but one that was expressed in gendered terms that reflected the deeply held beliefs of male policymakers that women and families had no business in the military. According to Jim Webb, the former marine and secretary of the navy under Reagan, the post–Cold War military needed to be more cost-effective. In Webb's gendered logic, budget priorities could be expressed in stark binaries: "If offered the choice between two people of equal talent, one of which needs only a bunk while the other requires full family benefits," who should the Marine Corps pick? "To put it another way," he continued, "if one is given the awesome task of providing the best defense a specific sum can buy, should he be faulted for wanting to put the money into troops and weapons rather than into dependents and day care centers?"[44]

Right around the Marine Corps's 217th birthday celebration in November 1992, the director of Human Resources at Headquarters, Marine Corps (HQMC), began asking senior marine officers for input on a plan to ban marriages among first-term marines—or the most junior enlistees, those on their first enlistment. Despite significant pushback from Judge Advocate General's Corps lawyers, who worried that such a ban would be challenged in court on constitutional grounds, the plan found enthusiastic support among the senior staff at HQMC.

In the winter of 1993, the recently appointed commandant, General Carl Mundy, authorized "Operation Gold Band," which would "reduce, then eliminate sponsored dependents among Corporals [E-4s] and below" over a two-year period.[45] For the next six months, Operation Gold Band remained a secret among policymakers in the Marine Corps, as they busily drafted new training programs for junior marines and their commanders. These programs included instructional videos, warning young recruits about the dangers of marriage. All of the policymakers being men who held entrenched beliefs about gender roles, the marine was always cast as a man, and the potential spouse as a woman. Until marriages among first-term enlistees were entirely phased out, the training material would teach three core lessons: first, "Don't Rush it!" urged marines to put the brakes on serious relationships and cast women as trouble. "Many Marines are tempted to marry to have a regular sex partner, to escape from barracks or shipboard life, with the illusion that they'll make more money, or perhaps because they got someone pregnant. However, most Marines who marry for these reasons end up as 'statistics.'" Second, those who wanted to get married before the ban took effect should "consider the advantages of a religious marriage," pointing out that while half of American marriages end in divorce, that number dropped to 20 percent among those who "worship together regularly." And third, policymakers urged Marines to enroll in a marriage preparation program, which HQMC would begin developing later that year.[46]

But when the commandant's plan went public in August 1993, it didn't last twelve hours after it was broadcast on the nightly news. As word reached Secretary of Defense Les Aspin, he remarked in his diary that he would have to "swat that one down," and the very next day, he publicly chastised General Mundy for "blindsiding" the president of the United States at a Pentagon news conference. Mundy was forced to apologize in front of the cameras, stating, "I did not adequately inform my civilian superiors of the policy that I was putting forth. . . . It's not one of my prouder moments in history here. I would . . . try not to do it again."[47]

Conclusion

Thoroughly rebuffed, Mundy still needed to bring the needs of the Marine Corps, and its institutional culture that was hostile to families, into line with the now-entrenched family-friendly posture of the wider DOD. His actions shaped how the entire military would manage families in the future. In the September 1993 issue of the *Marine Corps Gazette*, the commandant published his own "white paper" of sorts. The article, titled "FOCUS on the Military Family: The Fifth Leg of the MAGTF," at once borrowed from the religious right's rallying cry of the previous decade and also signaled the Marine Corps's new way forward. The MAGTF—or Marine Air Ground Task Force—is the basic organizational structure for any Marine Corps unit tasked with a mission. To manage marine marriages, Mundy essentially embedded families into the corps's warfighting doctrine. He cast families as "any one of the other four elements that comprise our combined arms teams" and charged them with needing to "contribute to the overall effectiveness of the Corps." Whereas the army's General Wickham would have agreed that families and the military had mutual obligations to provide wellbeing in exchange for support, the marines were integrating families into the force structure. "Today," Mundy wrote, "family members outnumber those of us in uniform. The tremendous responsibilities military spouses shoulder, and the immeasurable contribution many make relate directly to our operational effectiveness. The Marines and Sailors of our Corps are able to respond to whenever and wherever needed largely because of the support structure at home."[48]

To take family well-being and support and make them about readiness and mission accomplishment also allowed the Marine Corps to mitigate growing concerns in the military and the wider society about the relationship between social welfare and dependence. Republicans, for instance, were about to ride a wave of conservative backlash in the upcoming midterms, allowing Newt Gingrich to pursue his "Contract with America." Amid all this, and in contrast with the army's position on entitlements and benefits, Mundy flipped the logic of dependency: "Over time, I've come to realize that if there is a state of 'dependency' in the Corps, it comes from those of us who wear the uniform who are dependent on those who don't. . . . The dedication of Marine Corps spouses, their ability to maintain themselves when we deploy while picking up many of the responsibilities normally carried by us, and their increasing efforts and readiness to sustain each other during our deployments, are a mainstay in enabling the Corps to function effectively." General Mundy was attuned to the political climate, and his appeals to "readiness" worked to assuage simmering fears about dependency.[49]

The speed with which the marines did an about-face on marriage, charging into a future that embraced families, clearly demonstrates just how transformative those family policies were to the military in the 1980s. And by the year 2000, it was the army that joined the Marine Corps in defining family support as an essential component of readiness. Army planners identified quality of life for families and soldiers as one of their top three priorities (behind readiness and modernization) for the future.[50] Army Family Support Groups became Family Readiness Groups (FRGS), and the army began thinking about holistic approaches to quality of life, which they defined as encompassing the physical, mental, material, and spiritual needs of soldiers and their families—all in the name of readiness. As the AVF entered a new millennium, family life was not only compatible with military life; families had also become an essential component to the way the AVF functioned.

Notes

1. Wickham, *Army Family*, 1. Wickham's predecessor, General Edward C. "Shy" Meyer, actually said it first at a symposium on the army family in October 1980, but nobody saw the connection between families and retention more clearly than Wickham.

2. Quoted in James Neal, "Air Force Under Secretary Tells Vance Airmen to Prepare for New Conflicts," *Military*, February 19, 2019, https://www.military.com /daily-news/2019/02/17/air-force-under-secretary-tells-vance-airmen-prepare-new -conflicts.html.

3. "Collins, Jones Lead Effort to Bring Military Widow's Tax Elimination Act to a Vote in the Senate," Office of Senator Susan Collins, June 23, 2019, https://www .collins. senate.gov/newsroom/collins-jones-lead-effort-bring-military-widow%E2 %80%99s-tax-elimination-act-vote-senate.

4. Bernard Weinraub, "Army in Europe has Family and Housing Problems," *New York Times*, July 6, 1979, https://www.nytimes.com/1979/07/06/archives/army-in -europe-has-family-and-housing-problems-unable-to-pack-up.html.

5. Thom Shanker, "Obama Asks McChrystal to Return in New Role," *New York Times*, April 11, 2011, 15.

6. Unless otherwise noted, the marriage percentages discussed in this essay include both officer and enlisted, but because enlisted personnel far outnumber officers, it has been the enlisted folks driving marriage trends since World War II.

7. Bailey, *America's Army*.

8. See, for example, U.S. Senate, Committee on Armed Services, *Status of the All-Volunteer Armed Force*, 95th Cong., 2nd sess., June 20, 1978. The tone of the hearing was reflected in the testimony of Congressman Robin Beard, who asked, "Is the Army a fighting machine or a social institution?" Beard saw the expanded role of women as a harbinger for the military's "social welfare" problems.

9. "Classifications," Selective Service System, accessed July 5, 2019, https://www .sss.gov/Classifications. On marriage and dependent statistics, see Hunter and Cheng, *Report on the Military Family*; and Morrison et al., *Families in the Army*.

10. Each service has different names for each rank, but they all use the same pay grades. For example, an E-3 in the army holds the rank of private first class, but an E-3 in the Marine Corps is called a lance corporal. All E-3s, regardless of which service, are paid the same base pay.

11. Hunter and Cheng, *Report on the Military Family*.

12. "Making Ends Meet in Europe Is Tough for GIs," *Stars and Stripes*, March 1, 1971, 10.

13. Allyson Sherman Grossman, "The Employment Situation for Military Wives," *Monthly Labor Review*, February 1981, Box 78, Folder 6, WEAL.

14. Arthur Siddon, "GIs Licking System with Food Stamps?" *Chicago Tribune*, November 25, 1975, 4; for comparison in language and tone to the draft era, see Robert Dobkin, "GI Families on Welfare Rolls," *Boston Globe*, October 14, 1969, 29; and "Needy GI Families to Use Food Stamps at Commissaries," *New York Times*, March 7, 1970, 30.

15. Vuic, "Mobilizing Marriage and Motherhood," 177–78.

16. This belief, and the policies it has shaped, has had a profound impact on military husbands, but in large part due to how those beliefs construct archives, their voices are largely missing from the record. Anthropologists working in the field of critical war studies have written on the subject of male spouses in the military. See MacLeish, *Making War at Fort Hood*; and Wool, *After War*.

17. "An Analysis and Evaluation of the United States Army: The Beard Study," prepared by Jerry Reed, U.S. Senate, Committee on Armed Services, in *Status of the All-Volunteer Armed Force: Hearing before the Subcommittee on Manpower and Personnel*, 95th Cong., 2nd sess., June 20, 1978, 140–41, hereafter referred to as "Beard Study." For an insightful analysis of the history of questioning the military's role as social experiment, see Whitt and Perazzo, "Military as Social Experiment."

18. "Beard Study," 255.

19. "Fact Sheet: Single Parents and the Military," Box 78, Folder 14, WEAL.

20. Binkin and Bach, *Women and the Military*.

21. "Beard Study," 255.

22. Tom Morganthau, David C. Martin, and Michael Reese, "GI Joe Can't Make Ends Meet," *Newsweek*, March 31, 1980, 31. For year-by-year comparisons

of military base pay scales (including Basic Allowances for Housing, or BAH) for married and unmarried service members, see "Military Pay Charts," Defense Financial and Accounting Services, updated February 7, 2017, https://www.dfas.mil /militarymembers/payentitlements/military-pay-charts.html.

23. "Handbook for Military Families," supplement to *Army Times*, June 18, 1979.

24. Stone and Alt, *Uncle Sam's Brides*, 42–44.

25. See, for example, "Weal Budget 1984," Box 3, Folder 32, WEAL.

26. "The Army Wife—Her Career: Hers—Or His & Hers!," Joyce Ott, MFC.

27. "1st Symposium, 1980," MFC; employment figures from "Families in Blue Study," Box 78, Folder 6, WEAL.

28. "1st Symposium," 14–17.

29. "1st Symposium," 14–17.

30. "1st Symposium," 10–11.

31. "Department of the Army Historical Summary, 1980," DAHSUM. See also Mittelstadt, *Rise of the Military Welfare State*, 71; Rostker, *I WANT YOU!*, 502–3.

32. Wickham, *Army Family*, 1.

33. Wickham, *Army Family*, 10.

34. Wickham, *Army Family*, 14.

35. For more on the nature of Wickham's relationship to Dobson, see Correspondence 1982–86, Box 3, Folder D, JAW.

36. See Zaretsky, *No Direction Home*.

37. Wickham, *Army Family*, 13.

38. Wickham, *Army Family*, iii.

39. Carolyn Becraft, interview with the author, December 8, 2016.

40. "Department of Defense Directive, Family Policy, Number 1342.17," December 30, 1988, MFC.

41. U.S. Marine Corps, "Report on the Progress of Women in the Marine Corps," 1988, Box 253, SRC.

42. Major Laura J. Brush, "Another Case of Less Is More," *Marine Corps Gazette*, April 1991, 82–83, MFC.

43. U.S. Department of Defense, *Base Closure and Realignment Report*, 15; Rostker, *I WANT YOU!*, 639–44, Sorenson, *Shutting Down*, 1.

44. James Webb, "The Military Is Not a Social Program," *New York Times*, August 18, 1993, https://www.nytimes.com/1993/08/18/opinion/the-military-is-not -a-social-program.html.

45. "Operation Gold Band," ca. January 1993, Box 40, MRAC.

46. E. T. Gomulka, "Marriage and the First Term Marine" (script), in "Lesson: Marriage and the First Term Marine" (Washington DC: Marine Corps Human Resources Division, 1993), Box 40, MRAC.

47. "Personal Daily Records, 1993 June–December," Les Aspin, Box 62, LAP; Art Pine, "Top Marine Says He 'Blindsided' the President," *Los Angeles Times*, August 13, 1993, A1. For more press coverage, see the Clippings folder in Box 40, MRAC.

48. Carl E. Mundy Jr., "FOCUS on the Military Family: The Fifth Leg of the MAGTF," *Marine Corps Gazette*, September 1993, 22–23, MFC.

49. Mundy, "FOCUS on the Military Family." For more on fears of dependency and military welfare, see Mittelstadt, *Rise of the Military Welfare State.*

50. Department of the Army Historical Summary, 1996, DAHSUM.

Bibliography

Archives and Manuscript Materials

CEM. Papers of Carl E. Mundy. Marine Corps Archive/Marine Corps History Division, Quantico VA.

DAHSUM. Department of the Army Historical Summaries, 1969–2010. Center of Military History, Fort McNair, Washington DC.

JAW. Papers of John A. Wickham Jr. U.S. Army Military History Institute, Carlisle Barracks, Carlisle PA.

LAP. Les Aspin Papers. Wisconsin Historical Society, Madison.

MFC. Military Family Collection. Center of Military History, Fort McNair, Washington DC.

MRAC. Manpower and Reserve Affairs Collection. Marine Corps Archive/Marine Corps History Division, Quantico VA.

NOW. National Organization for Women Records, 1959–2002. Arthur and Elizabeth Schlesinger Library on the History of Women in America, Radcliffe Institute, Harvard University, Cambridge MA.

SRC. Studies and Reports Collection. Marine Corps Archives/Marine Corps History Division, Quantico VA.

WEAL. Women's Equity Action League Records, 1967–1990. Arthur and Elizabeth Schlesinger Library on the History of Women in America, Radcliffe Institute, Harvard University, Cambridge MA.

Published Works

Alt, Betty Sowers, and Bonnie Domrose Stone. *Uncle Sam's Brides: The World of Military Wives.* New York: Walker, 1990.

Bailey, Beth. *America's Army: Making the All-Volunteer Force.* Cambridge MA: Harvard University Press, 2009.

Hunter, Enda, and Lucile Cheng, eds. *A Report on the Military Family Research Conference: Current Trends & Directions.* San Diego CA: Family Studies Branch of the Naval Health Research Center, 1977.

Mittelstadt, Jennifer. *The Rise of the Military Welfare State.* Cambridge MA: Harvard University Press, 2015.

Morrison, Peter A., Georges Vernez, David W. Grissmer, and Kevin F. McCarthy. *Families in the Army: Looking Ahead.* Santa Monica CA: RAND, 1989.

Rostker, Bernard. *I WANT YOU! The Evolution of the All-Volunteer Force.* Santa Monica CA: RAND, 2006.

Sorenson, David S. *Shutting Down the Cold War: The Politics of Military Base Closure.* New York: St. Martin's, 1998.

U.S. Department of Defense. *Base Closure and Realignment Report.* Washington DC: Department of Defense, 1991.

Vuic, Kara Dixon. "Mobilizing Marriage and Motherhood: Military Families and Family Planning since World War II." In *Integrating the US Military: Race, Gender, and Sexual Orientation since World War II,* edited by Walter Bristol Jr. and Heather Marie Stur, 142–66. Baltimore MD: Johns Hopkins University Press, 2017.

Wickham, John A., Jr. *White Paper 1983: The Army Family.* Washington DC: Office of the Army Chief of Staff, 1983.

Whitt, Jacqueline E., and Elizabeth A. Perazzo. "The Military as Social Experiment: Challenging a Trope." *Parameters* 48, no. 2 (Summer 2018): 5–12.

Zaretsky, Natasha. *No Direction Home: The American Family and the Fear of National Decline, 1968–1980.* Chapel Hill: University of North Carolina Press, 2007.

FIVE

Reproduction in Combat Boots

KARA DIXON VUIC

In September 2015 U.S. Air Force veteran Tara Ruby posted a photograph she had taken of ten female army soldiers to her Facebook account. She did not intend to cause a stir, but as one journalist put it, the photograph caused the internet to "lose its collective mind."[1] It featured ten ordinary women wearing their camouflaged Army Combat Uniforms and was in all respects, save one, unremarkable. The photograph became a lightning rod for public debate because each servicewoman was breastfeeding her child.

Ruby had volunteered to take the photograph after hearing about the opening of a lactation room at Fort Bliss army post, created to implement a new army policy intended to help active duty women more easily combine work and parenthood.[2] The Fort Bliss Public Affairs and Garrison Command approved of the photo shoot, and women from the post's mothers' support group volunteered as models. Ruby explained that she had been motivated to take the photograph because of her own difficult experiences of trying to breastfeed her children while on active duty. In the late 1990s, the military provided no lactation rooms, so Ruby nursed in restrooms and empty offices, unprotected by any policy that assured her right to do so. She hoped that photographs of servicewomen nursing their children would empower other women like her. The soldiers were changing the public image of "military mommies," Ruby explained, proving that they could be both mothers and soldiers, and that the two roles were mutually beneficial. "Breastfeeding their babies doesn't make them less of a soldier," Ruby insisted, but "makes them a better one." Not everyone agreed. Some critics insisted that motherhood and service were incompatible, and that nursing children in uniform constituted unprofessional behavior for a soldier.[3]

Breastfeeding in combat boots—as one military mothers support group called itself—is certainly an experience specific to many female soldiers, but it points to a much broader history of the military's regulation of reproduction for all its soldiers, sailors, airmen, and marines. Throughout the twentieth century, reproductive and parenthood policies derived from a changing mix of institutional and cultural demands that have exerted varying degrees of influence. Although not an exhaustive history of the military's reproduction and parenthood policies, this chapter highlights several important themes for those interested in understanding how and why these demands have shaped the armed forces' regulation of the reproductive lives of service personnel.

First, military officials have understood reproduction both as a matter of readiness and a matter of gender, and as such, reproductive policies have often differed for servicewomen and for servicemen. Some policies reflect the specific physical needs and concerns of women who bear children. Military officials have been reluctant, for example, to assign pregnant women to dangerous assignments for fear of causing undue stress to the mother and the fetus. At the same time, reproductive policies have reflected broader social and cultural beliefs about womanhood and women's place in the military. Many policies have forbid women, but not men, from having families for reasons that have nothing to do with the physical acts of pregnancy, birth, or nursing. The military has never excluded fathers, and even public reluctance toward conscripting fathers has never outweighed military need. Conversely, despite a long history of fathers—even single fathers—serving and deploying away from their children, the military excluded mothers during the world wars and in the Korean War, including stepmothers and women whose children no longer required constant care, even as it faced serious shortages of women. Military policies that until the 1970s disqualified mothers from enlisting and called for the discharge of women who became mothers reflected most Americans' belief that a mother's place was in the home.

Second, reproductive policies have reflected complicated relationships between institutional and cultural change. Military officials have made decisions based on pragmatic personnel considerations, to be sure, but they have also responded to changing notions of appropriate gender roles to create the kind of force that would meet with public approval. Throughout the twentieth century, policy changes increasingly accommodated and supported parenthood to meet institutional personnel needs. For example, increasing demands for soldiers and nurses during the Cold War pressed officials to withdraw draft deferments for fathers and to allow some mothers to remain on duty, despite a long-standing practice of discharging women with children. Women's activism and willingness to sue for the right to serve also played a role in the military's relaxation of prohibitions against mothers serving on active duty. This balance between institutional and cultural change continued after the forces switched from a conscripted to a volunteer force in 1973 and increasingly relied on both women and men with families to meet personnel needs. These demographic changes, coming as they did when second-wave feminists were pressing for the removal of all restrictions on women's careers, persuaded officials to adopt policies that would help them recruit and retain the individuals they needed—women and men who increasingly expected that they should be able to combine a military career and a family.

Manpower and Marriage

Throughout the twentieth century, military marriage policies reflected a mix of constantly changing gender and cultural norms, and manpower needs. Generally, military policies during World War I and World War II permitted men (officers more so than enlisted personnel) to be married and have children, and regulations gradually expanded to allow married women to serve, though not women with children.[4] The pressing demands for manpower during both wars stretched these policies in ways that challenged, but did not upturn, widespread understandings of the relationships among gender, the family, and military service. Even in the face of great demands for men to serve, reproductive policies reflected public opposition to the disruption of the family, as well as government insistence that the preservation of the nuclear family unit was a central war aim. As Selective Service regulations instructed in 1940, "The maintenance of the family as a unit is of importance to the national well-being."[5] In both world wars, policies privileged men's roles as husbands and fathers when personnel demands permitted. National needs opened the doors of military service to wives, but motherhood continued to trump wartime demands until much later in the twentieth century.

Institutional and public preference for preserving the family ran so deep during the world wars that many married men and fathers received deferments based on the degree to which others, especially children, depended on them. For example, fathers with dependent children were more likely to receive a deferment than husbands whose wives who were capable of earning wages in their absence. American involvement in World War I proved brief enough to avoid drawn-out public debates about the relationship between men's familial and martial obligations, but increasing demands in World War II spawned changes in draft policies that reflected shifting balances of family and wartime needs. The Selective Service System and War Manpower Commission made the very unpopular move of expanding the pool of eligible draftees to include eighteen- and nineteen-year-old men and recruited women into wartime industry in an effort to avoid sending fathers into war. A Gallup poll administered in September 1943 even found that a "great majority" of Americans preferred drafting single women for noncombatant jobs over drafting fathers for the same positions.[6] However, there were limits to how far the military and government were willing to go to protect the conventional family with a breadwinning father at its head. When wartime needs drained the reservoir of eligible men, the government prioritized the nation and called up more married men and fathers into service.[7]

Although conscription policies minimized the chances that fathers would be drafted into service during World Wars I and II, military policies always endorsed the notion that men could combine duty to the nation and family. The military never prohibited fathers from serving as it did mothers, and it explicitly supported servicemen's families.[8] Many servicemen with wives and children received allotments, and the services gradually extended an expanding array of other benefits, including medical and dental care, commissary privileges, and housing, to even the lowest-ranking soldiers. Even more, in an era when servicewomen were prohibited from having families, the military's medical branches assigned significant numbers of physicians, nurses, and other staff to obstetrical care for servicemen's wives and to pediatric care for their children. Such policies fell in line with and reaffirmed a broader national trend to support men's role as breadwinners and to tether women to home and family.

National needs similarly pressed the military to allow wives to serve during the world wars, while having the added benefit of helping to assuage public fears about servicewomen's sexuality.[9] When Representative Edith Nourse Rogers proposed a bill to create a women's corps within the army in 1941, critics charged that military service would undermine women's femininity and lead to the decline of the family, the disruption of the home, and falling birth rates. In an effort to win over the public, military leaders responded to these charges by crafting an image of servicewomen that was in line with white, middle-class notions of sexual respectability. Thus, the military advertised service as a respectable way for a woman to find a husband, and it carefully managed women's sexuality—or at least gave the perception that it was doing so. Allowing married women to serve helped to suggest that servicewomen were not women of depraved morals or lesbians, as many feared, but respectable women serving their nation.

Although wartime demands pressed military officials to stretch their image of servicewomen to include wives, allowing mothers to serve was too radical a proposition even to be considered. Any woman who became pregnant or a parent (through adoption or marriage to a man with children) was immediately discharged, despite the significant personnel turnover that the policy created. The armed forces were willing to assume these losses because wives who left the corps to have and raise children affirmed a public image of military women as fulling their most basic gendered role. Wives could combine their duties to the nation and their husbands, but their duty to children trumped their duty to the nation.[10] Single women who became pregnant, by contrast, failed to adhere to the military's notions of ideal womanhood and received dishonorable discharges until the integration of women's corps into the military in 1943 forced a standardization of discharge policies for women and men, and they were discharged honorably. Policies prohibiting mothers from serving reflected more than just cultural notions of mothers' obligation to their children; they reflected the military's assignment of moral value and punitive consequences to women's reproduction.

The early Cold War era brought significant changes to policies regulating reproduction, though changes continued to reflect a combination of military need and cultural expectations. Postwar domestic culture attached great significance to the nuclear family, which many Americans came to see as a symbol of national strength and defense against the expansion of communism. Women and men married at record-setting young ages and began their families quickly. In this environment the military found itself balancing personnel needs and rapidly changing cultural norms.

In the first years after World War II, as the military downsized, officials prioritized women's family roles over their value to the military. Married nurses could no longer serve on active duty but only within the less career-minded reserves.[11] Other women in the services could be married at enlistment or commission, and they could marry while serving. Still the military prioritized their marriages by allowing them to request a discharge simply because they were married, even before they had completed their enlistment contract. This policy, while conforming to late 1940s and 1950s cultural norms, cost the military significantly. Throughout the 1950s 70 to 80 percent of enlisted women left the military before their first enlistment had ended, meaning that the military had to replace 40 to 50 percent of the women's corps annually.[12] This cost was not high enough, however, to force a change in policy; only wartime personnel needs outweighed the military's preference to attach greater importance to women's marriages than to their military service.

During the Korean War, a rapidly increasing need for servicemen and women led the military to change its marriage policies. To meet personnel needs, President Truman signed an executive order in September 1951 mandating that husbands without children no longer receive automatic deferments. Fathers continued to be deferred, with the understanding that they could eventually be called if circumstances required it.[13] But even with revised draft rules and the call-up of reservists (including many women), the military continued to desperately need personnel. Many officials saw women as part of the solution, and the Department of Defense (DOD) launched a massive campaign to recruit women who could fill noncombatant positions and stymie an especially problematic nursing shortage. The DOD also ended the practice of allowing wives to request discharge regardless of their contractual obligation.[14] In war national defense needs outweighed marital duties, but parenthood continued to hold priority.

As the military's need for women declined again after the Korean War, it returned to the practice of allowing married women to request a voluntary discharge, despite the significant turnover that the policy created.[15] The services only ended voluntary marriage separations in the mid-1960s after a government report concluded that the military spent $12 million annually to replace enlisted women who failed to complete their first enlistment due to marriage. Many interpreted the report as suggesting that women cost the military more than men because of their desire to marry, but the report took men's families for granted. Had the government pointed out the allowances, medical care, and housing it provided for enlisted men's dependents, readers would have drawn a different conclusion. Still the report revealed the military's preconception that servicemen would and should have families, while servicewomen should not. The costs of men's families were just part of the costs of men's service, not even a variable to be debated or considered.[16]

Even as the military began to embrace the idea that wives could serve on active duty, their husbands were treated very differently than were servicemen's wives. The 1948 Women's Armed Services Integration Act defined the civilian husband of a servicewoman as her "dependent" only if he depended on her for more than 50 percent of his support. All wives of servicemen, conversely, were automatically considered dependents, regardless of their income. The practice reflected social understandings of marital gender roles, rooted in centuries of feme covert legal doctrine that defined men as breadwinners and women as homemakers. These unequal dependency policies increasingly hampered the military's recruitment of women by discriminating against them. Women married to civilian husbands, for example, were forbidden on-post housing (often a much more economical choice for families), while their husbands were ineligible for military medical and dental care and could not accompany their wives to overseas assignments. Only in 1973, when the Supreme Court ruled in favor of U.S. Air Force Lieutenant Sharron Frontiero, did the military grant dependency status to spouses and children without regard to the sex of the service member.[17]

Military officials made some effort to assign uniformed wives and husbands near each other, but only when those assignments served larger personnel demands. During the Vietnam War, some female nurses requested and received assignments to the war so that they could be near their husbands. The army granted many of their requests and thereby helped to meet its considerable demand for in-country nurses, but it did not guarantee those women an assignment near their husband, much less shared living quarters. Nevertheless, married nurses requested assignments to the war out of a commitment both to their marriage and to the army. The Women's Army Corps (WAC), which did not have the significant demand for personnel in Vietnam that the nurse corps did, granted fewer requests by women to be assigned in Vietnam near their husbands and ultimately barred female soldiers whose husbands were in Vietnam from being assigned in-country to avoid housing problems.[18]

Parenting in Uniform

As the Cold War military slowly accommodated married servicewomen, it even more slowly permitted mothers to serve. Policies excluding pregnant women and mothers from the military were rooted in policies that guaranteed the very existence of the women's corps. A significant step forward for women in the military, the 1948 Women's Armed Services Integration Act made the women's corps (like the Army and Navy Nurse Corps) permanent, not temporary, parts of the military. Yet the political compromise that allowed for women to become a permanent part of the military also required limits on the rank women could attain, capped their numbers at 2 percent, and allowed for women to be discharged "under circumstances and in accordance with regulations proscribed by the President." Executive Order 10240, signed by President Harry Truman on April 27, 1951, clarified what most military officials already understood as the intent of the act's broad discharge powers. Women could be dismissed for becoming pregnant (even if the pregnancy ended in a miscarriage), giving birth (even if they surrendered the child for adoption), or becoming the parent or guardian of a child. Although many believed the executive order *required* women's dismissal for these reasons, it was never a mandate. Women "may be terminated," the order stated, and it applied specifically to women in the regular forces, not the reserves. Thus, until the 1970s when the Supreme Court began to side with women fighting to retain their military careers after they became pregnant or mothers, military leaders had the authority both to discharge mothers and pregnant women and to retain them when needed.[19]

The military began granting exceptions to pregnancy and parenthood discharges in the 1950s, though it did so sparingly and only when driven by personnel demands. For example, when the Korean War created a serious nurse shortage that had ramifications for the corps worldwide, three pregnant U.S. Army nurses assigned to a hospital in Germany were allowed to remain on duty for several months before they were ordered out of the corps.[20] The Vietnam War's nurse shortage led to even more pregnancy and parenthood waivers. The first went to mothers who wanted to serve in the reserves and whose children were between fifteen and eighteen years old. In the late 1960s, after thousands of nurses had deployed to Vietnam, and as the corps continued to suffer a nurse shortage, the army began granting waivers to pregnant women and mothers of young children.[21] However, the WAC, which assigned fewer women to Vietnam and did not face the same kind of personnel demands as the ANC, did not grant pregnancy and motherhood waivers until 1971.[22]

Even as the military slowly began to grant waivers to women who wanted to remain on duty while they started and raised their families, policies and practices reflected the idea that mothers' first duties were to their families. As ANC chief Lillian Dunlap explained, the corps only granted a waiver to a woman who "demonstrated the ability to manage her affairs after the baby was born . . . with the understanding that if it interfered with her duty, she would have to ask to be relieved." Nurse corps leaders were particularly careful to insist that women who received waivers did not appear to be receiving any special favors. They had to continue to "pull their share of the workload."[23]

By contrast military policies did not consider whether or how men, even single fathers, would balance their families and military duties. It seems that officials only considered questions about single fatherhood when it became a matter of foreign policy—that is, when American servicemen impregnated foreign women and failed to marry the mother or provide for the child. Even American jurisprudence failed to recognize the foreign-born "illegitimate" children of servicemen as birthright citizens, unless the father met a series of criteria unrequired of mothers. Although rooted in legal traditions unrelated to service members, U.S. citizenship laws affirmed cultural understandings of the different responsibilities of fathers and mothers and thereby relieved untold numbers of servicemen of the responsibilities of parenthood when they fathered children abroad.[24]

The American military and media celebrated single fathers who combined service and responsibility for their children. Advocates for servicewomen seized on these cases to highlight the ways that discharging pregnant women and mothers reflected institutional concerns about gender, not about children. For example, the press celebrated a widowed sergeant and single father to several children for his willingness to accept an assignment to Vietnam, as well as a male chaplain who became a single father when he adopted two Vietnamese children. As the director of Women in the Air Force (WAF), Jeanne Holm, pointed out, had either of these parents been a woman, she would have been involuntarily discharged from the military, certainly not celebrated for her dedication to it. Moreover, had either of these single fathers married a servicewoman, she would have been discharged for becoming the children's stepmother.[25]

Sex-based reproductive policies became less and less defensible after the 1964 Civil Rights Act forbid discrimination based on sex, and as a new generation of women began to demand change. In the late 1960s and early 1970s, several women who had been discharged for pregnancy sued the military on the grounds that their discharge amounted to unconstitutional sex discrimination. The services granted waivers to women who took their cases to court in an attempt to avoid a ruling that would upturn the old policies. Officials also liberalized the policies in small ways, hoping that the changes would stymie a court ruling against the services, but neither of these stop-gap measures lasted for long.[26]

After Congress passed the Equal Rights Amendment in 1972, the secretary of defense expected that the military would soon have to revise any policies that differed by sex, including those that authorized the involuntary discharge of women for pregnancy and parenthood. In June 1974 he directed that all regulations permitting the discharge of women for pregnancy and parenthood be repealed. Apparently some military officials hesitated to implement a policy they opposed, and so in May 1975 the DOD issued a directive ordering the change.[27] In 1976 the Second Circuit Court confirmed the policy when it ruled in *Crawford v. Cushman* that the Fifth Amendment right to due process had been violated for a marine who was discharged for pregnancy.[28] Thereafter all servicewomen enjoyed the same right to combine military service and parenthood that their male comrades had never questioned.

But policies that permitted pregnant women and mothers to serve did not make it easy for them to do so, nor did they mean that women had the support of the upper echelons of the armed forces. One disappointed assistant secretary of the army suggested that women's equity would undermine military efficiency.[29] He was not the last official to make such a claim, but soon the military's own studies revealed that allowing women to combine motherhood and service did not have the disastrous effects that opponents had forecast. Several studies in the late 1970s and early 1980s found that, even when accounting for lost time due to pregnancy, childbirth, and maternity leave, women lost less time on duty than did men.[30]

Maneuvering around Pregnancy

Policy changes that allowed women to remain on duty as they married and had children forced the services to reconsider their policies on birth control and abortion. Again both institutional and cultural demands shaped policy discussions, which occurred in the era of the sexual revolution and the 1973 *Roe v. Wade* decision.[31] The military had, to some degree, been concerned about birth control even before the 1960s because commanders did not want servicemen impregnating women (at least those who were not their wives) during deployments. This desire—along with the perhaps even more important goal of preventing the spread of sexually transmitted infection—led to the distribution of prophylaxis devices to servicemen. When it came to women, however, the military trod much more carefully. Always conscientious of public perception, WAC leaders in World War II refused any discussion of contraceptives for servicewomen. Later, medical policies limited "surgical intervention" in women's reproduction, whether through abortion, sterilization, or contraceptives. But as the scales balancing military and cultural needs tipped in favor of women's demands for sexual equality, military policies followed and the armed forces began providing access to birth control for servicewomen and the female dependents of servicemen.[32]

The military initiated a discussion about its reproduction policies in 1966, less than a year after the Supreme Court ruling in *Griswold v. Connecticut* guaranteed married couples the right to privacy in matters of reproduction and in the same year that the DOD ruled that state law held no jurisdiction over military medical practice.[33] That fall the DOD began providing reproductive counseling, birth control devices, and the birth control pill free of charge in military medical facilities. Servicewomen and servicemen's wives noted their approval of the policy as they made more than 478,000 visits to military hospitals in under a year, mostly to obtain the pill.[34] Women serving in Vietnam also sought access to reproductive care and the pill, though they enjoyed less success than stateside women in acquiring both.

Before July 1970 each of the services determined and managed its own policies on abortion. Generally they provided women with access to abortions only when medically indicated by a review board. This practice mirrored that of the 1962 Model Penal Code recommended by the American Law Institute, and in most cases, physicians and hospital commanders adhered to the guidelines issued by the states where they practiced to determine what conditions warranted a medically indicated abortion. After the DOD ruled that state laws should not determine military medical practice, however, the services were free to instate whatever policy they wished. Seeking clear guidance, each of the services' surgeons general asked the newly appointed assistant secretary of defense for health and environment, Dr. Louis M. Rousselot, for a uniform policy. They hoped that Rousselot would clarify things by ordering military hospitals to follow the laws of the states where they were located.

Instead Rousselot surprised the surgeons general when he instated one of the nation's most liberal abortion policies in July 1970. A World War II army surgeon, Rousselot was not necessarily an advocate of liberal abortion policies, but he did believe that medical policies should be guided by the best in scientific and medical practices, and he believed that the services should follow a uniform policy. Thus he ordered that "pregnancies may be terminated in military medical facilities when medically indicated or for reasons involving mental health." Two physicians had to agree that the abortion was medically necessary, and one could be a psychiatrist who testified that the pregnant woman's mental state justified the procedure. Rousselot's policy imposed no time restriction and indicated that no personnel were required to assist in the abortion if it violated their religious, moral, or ethical beliefs.[35] In overseas medical facilities, physicians were to perform abortions in accordance with the country's "pertinent mores, the applicable laws of the nations concerned and applicable status of forces agreements."[36] Even then policies seemed to vary. Women serving in Vietnam could have an abortion at in-country army hospitals, or at an army hospital in Japan or Okinawa, depending on the year.

Pentagon officials insisted that the new policy was "not intended as a general abandonment of limitations upon the performance of abortions" nor designed to "make it easier for the wife of a serviceman to obtain an abortion."[37] Yet the policy did just that. Although reports on the number of abortions remain scattered, what data exists suggests that women quickly made use of the more liberalized policy. The number of abortions performed in the air force increased more than sixfold, from 44 in 1969 to 275 in 1970, with most of them having been performed after the policy was instated.[38] Army data suggests the pervasiveness of abortion: of the 1,560 active-duty army women who became pregnant in 1974, 1,035 ended their pregnancy through an abortion.[39]

Rousselot had not intended the policy to be controversial, but his July 1970 abortion policy unleashed a political firestorm that continues to frame military policies on reproduction today. His policy was one of the nation's most liberal; that year only four states placed fewer restrictions on women seeking abortions. That fact did not sit well with President Richard M. Nixon, who learned of the policy in December and ordered its retraction as a way to garner support among Catholic, midwestern, and southern voters in anticipation of the 1972 presidential election. Thus, in March 1971, at Nixon's direction, Secretary of Defense Melvin Laird ordered that abortions performed in military facilities must adhere to state laws. The policy change had immediate results: abortions in military facilities fell from 1,152 in the three months prior to the change, to 363 in the three months following.[40] Strictly speaking the new policy did not prevent servicewomen or female dependents from getting an abortion in a military hospital (they could travel across state lines to places with less restrictive policies), but it did make it more difficult for them to do so.

The *Roe v. Wade* decision also had significant legacies for the military's abortion policies. After states began imposing more restrictive policies in an effort to limit *Roe*'s reach, the DOD insisted that all military hospitals follow *Roe*. Beginning in 1978 it also pushed back against congressional efforts to limit the use of federal funding for abortion. Pentagon officials characterized proposed legislation to prohibit federal funding as "unduly restrictive" and explained that the prohibition would force military women to seek abortions outside the military medical system, an especially difficult proposition for women stationed outside the United States or in places where they could not otherwise access safe abortions.[41] Officials also invoked military need. The services—especially the army—depended on increasing numbers of women to meet the all-volunteer force's personnel needs, and officials argued that providing women with access to abortion was an important part of retention. Failing to provide women with access to abortion, they warned, would create undue hardships "just at the time when the armed forces are trying to encourage more women to enter operational jobs with field units."[42]

Passed over military objections, Section 863 of the 1979 Department of Defense Authorization Act began the pattern that continues today, of prohibiting the use of federal funds and facilities to facilitate servicewomen and female dependents' access to abortion, except when the mother's life is endangered, or in cases of rape or incest.[43] Although the specific restrictions imposed on military women seeking abortions have changed over time and have differed depending on whether the women were serving or living in the United States or abroad, in general, today's policies mean that military women must use civilian facilities (whose laws vary by state) and pay for the procedure. In recent years these policies have attracted scrutiny as women have deployed to countries that prohibit abortion for any reason, such as Afghanistan, and as the military faces an intractable epidemic of sexual assault.[44]

The Military Family

Since the military ended conscription in 1973, it has increasingly relied on women and families to meet personnel demands, and it has gone to great lengths to accommodate them, even as it has deployed parents and families around the world.[45] The Gulf War of 1990–91 focused public attention on parents who served in war, and particularly to the new phenomenon of dual-service parents who both deployed. Still the deployment of mothers received special attention, with press coverage especially lamenting the separation of mothers and children, despite the fact that more fathers deployed away from their children than did mothers.[46]

Some commentators continue to oppose mothers' military service—but not fathers'—as threatening families and the broader social order, but they no longer dictate the military's reproductive policies.[47] Instead, as both women and men combine their desires to have families with their military careers, the services continue to adapt to changing needs and expectations. In 2017, 38.4 percent of active-duty military personnel had children, including 4 percent who were single parents.[48] That same year the National Defense Authorization Act established a baseline parental leave policy for active-duty personnel across the services that provided six weeks of maternal convalescent care following the birth of a child, six weeks of leave for primary caregivers, and up to three weeks for secondary caregivers.[49] Military parents praised much of the policy, including its use of gender-neutral language and recognition of all kinds of families (including same-sex families, surrogate families, and adopted families), but they continue to advocate for more guaranteed leave time and additional help balancing deployments, new assignments, and childcare.

The complicated relationship between institutional readiness and gender continues to evolve. Even as military families today enjoy a range of policies and practices that would have been unheard of not that long ago, they still struggle to balance family and career goals. Women face particular challenges as they attempt to time pregnancies and births with staff assignments that are more conducive to family demands than operational assignments or overseas deployments. Even servicewomen with the fortune of good timing find their careers negatively impacted by pregnancy and parenthood, limited by missed opportunities for career advancement and deployment in ways that fathers' careers are not.[50] Military mothers today can often access well-apportioned lactation rooms and wear newly designed uniforms that facilitate nursing or pumping, yet they continue to struggle to balance postpartum care, breastfeeding, and the physical demands of their military jobs. These challenges motivate women to advocate for greater specificity in policies so that their ability to nurse is not impeded by unsupportive or uneducated commanders.[51]

Today's military leaders make decisions about reproduction in a very different culture than did their predecessors, but the need to balance institutional and cultural demands has not changed. It seems, though, that at least some of today's leaders recognize the two demands as intertwined. In July 2019, when Marine Corps Commandant David Berger announced he was considering a one-year leave of absence for new mothers, he explained the proposal as a way to meet the corps's personnel needs, while meeting marines' expectations that they should be able to combine their family and career. Describing the military's family leave policies as "inadequate" and "fail[ing] to keep pace with societal norms and modern talent management practices," Berger insisted that the corps "should never ask our Marines to choose between being the best parent possible and the best Marine possible."[52] Ray Mabus, secretary of the navy from 2009 to 2017, who had argued for longer parental leave policies, supported the recommendation. Better family policies, particularly better maternal policies, he argued, would help the Marine Corps recruit and retain women and would ultimately make the corps stronger.[53]

Today's military frequently bills itself not only as family-friendly but as a family. As military leaders look to a future in which the force will rely on men and women with families more than ever before, compassionate marriage and family policies might just be the way forward.

Notes

1. Quoted in Maressa Brown, "4 Working Moms Breastfeed Their Babies in Stunning New Photos," *Cosmopolitan*, April 14, 2016, https://www.cosmopolitan .com/lifestyle/a56803/tara-ruby-breastfeeding-on-the-job-photos/. Ruby's photograph echoed a 2012 photograph featuring two women from the U.S. Air National Guard that also sparked a public controversy about servicewomen breastfeeding in uniform. Spokesman for the Washington National Guard Captain Keith Kosik explained that while the military did not have a specific regulation about breastfeeding in uniform, service members were forbidden from using their uniforms to further a cause. See Chelsea Bannach, "Fairchild Moms in National Spotlight," *Spokesman-Review* (Spokane WA), June 1, 2012, https://www.spokesman.com/stories /2012/jun/01/fairchild-moms-in-national-spotlight/.

2. Army Directive 2015-37 (Breastfeeding and Lactation Support Policy), September 29, 2015, https://www.army.mil/e2/c/downloads/412349.pdf.

3. Dominique Mosbergen, "Stunning Photo Shows Soldiers Breastfeeding in Full Uniform," *Huffington Post*, September 14, 2015, https://www.huffpost.com /entry/soldiers-breastfeeding-photo_n_55f680ebe4b042295e36b3ca; Emanuella Grinberg, "Soldiers in Uniform Pose for Photo to 'Normalize Breastfeeding,'" CNN, September 15, 2015, https://www.cnn.com/2015/09/13/living/breastfeeding-soldiers -uniform-feat/index.html.

4. Specifically, regulations forbid women with dependents from serving, though the age of those dependents varied. "Dependents" could include children, including stepchildren, as well as anyone who depended on the woman for support, such as elderly parents or a sibling. For most women a regulation against dependents meant children.

5. Quoted in Geva, *Conscription, Family, and the Modern State*, 169.

6. George Gallop, "Draft of Fathers Opposed by Public," *New York Times*, September 15, 1943, 17. See also Flynn, *Lewis B. Hershey*, 85–87, 90–91, 108–10; and Weatherford, *American Women and World War II*, 36.

7. See Geva, *Conscription, Family, and the Modern State*, chaps. 4–5; and Flynn, *Draft*.

8. On marriage regulations for men before World War II, see Byers, *Sexual Economy of War*. The government's goal of protecting families was largely focused on protecting white, middle-class families. Black fathers were much less likely to receive deferments than were white fathers in similar situations. Geva, *Conscription, Family, and the Modern State*, 201; Keith, *Rich Man's War*, 10.

9. See Vuic, "Mobilizing Marriage and Motherhood," 171; Sarnecky, *History of the U.S. Army Nurse Corps*, 93; Dumenil, *Second Line of Defense*, 130; Jackson, *They Called Them Angels*, 4–5; Witt et al., *Defense Weapon*, 2–3.

10. During World War II, policies allowed mothers with children under fourteen to serve if the child had been placed in another's custody for eighteen months prior to enlistment. Any mother with a child in her care or dependent on her for support could not enlist. "Separation Policies," Discharge Policy—wac, Background Materials for "The wac, 1945–1978," nara. Women with minor children were initially allowed to enlist as nurses if they had childcare, yet were later disallowed from doing so if they had children under the age of fourteen. Jackson, *They Called Them Angels*, 4.

11. Vuic, *Officer, Nurse, Woman*, 115; Witt et al., *Defense Weapon*, 3.

12. Holm, *Women in the Military*, 163.

13. "Effects of Marriage and Fatherhood on Draft Eligibility," Selective Service System, accessed August 27, 2019, https://www.sss.gov/About/History-and -Records/Effects.

14. A little over a year later, in September 1951, officials reversed course and allowed enlisted wives—but not officers—to request discharge. Wives with officer rank were forbidden from marriage discharges until 1953, after the armistice. Witt et al., *Defense Weapon*, 2–3, 70–84, 90, 230; Holm, *Women in the Military*, 156.

15. Enlisted wacs had to have completed one year of service after their initial training before requesting a marriage discharge. Officers had to have completed two years, and everyone at a foreign assignment had to have completed one year at that post in addition to other requirements. Morden, *Women's Army Corps*, 138.

16. Holm, *Women in the Military*, 162–64; Morden, *Women's Army Corps*, 175, 205, 226–27.

17. Women's Armed Services Integration Act of 1948, 62 Stat. 356, Public Law 8-625, June 12, 1948; Frontiero v. Richardson, 411 U.S. 677 (1973); Vuic, *Officer, Nurse, Woman*, 121–22; Holm, *Women in the Military*, 290–91; Witt et al., *Defense Weapon*, 231–34.

18. Vuic, *Officer, Nurse, Woman*, 117–21; Morden, *Women's Army Corps*, 252.

19. Women's Armed Services Integration Act of 1948; Executive Order 10240, Code of Federal Regulations, title 3, sec. 749 (1949–53), April 27, 1951. See also Holm, *Women in the Military*, 291–92.

20. Witt et al., *Defense Weapon*, 232–33.

21. Vuic, *Officer, Nurse, Woman*, 123–28.

22. Morden, *Women's Army Corps*, 302–10.

23. Gurney, *33 Years of Army Nursing*, 278.

24. Zeiger, *Entangling Alliances*; Collins, "Illegitimate Borders."

25. Holm, *Women in the Military*, 293–94.

26. Vuic, *Officer, Nurse, Woman*, 125–27; Vuic, "Mobilizing Marriage and Motherhood," 177; Holm, *Women in the Military*, 294–99; Morden, *Women's Army Corps*, 233–40.

27. Morden, *Women's Army Corps*, 302–10; Vuic, *Officer, Nurse, Woman*, 127; Holm, *Women in the Military*, 300.

28. Crawford v. Cushman, 531 F. 2d 1114 (CA2 1976); Holm, *Women in the Military*, 300–303.

29. Quoted in Morden, *Women's Army Corps*, 308.

30. Morden, *Women's Army Corps*, 309–10; Holm, *Women in the Military*, 301–3, 388–89.

31. Roe v. Wade, 410 U.S. 113 (1973).

32. All information in this section not otherwise cited can be found in Vuic, "Mobilizing Marriage and Motherhood," 178–84.

33. Griswold v. Connecticut, 381 U.S. 479, 85 S. Ct. 1678, 14 L. Ed. 2d 510 (1965).

34. Chritchlow, *Intended Consequences*, 86–87.

35. Louis M. Rousselot, Memorandum for the Surgeons General of the Military Departments, July 16, 1970, Abortions/Family Planning, Background Materials for "The WAC, 1945–1978," NARA; "Fact Sheet: Abortions in Military Hospitals," January 18, 1971, EX WE 3 Family Planning, January 1, 1971–April 30, 1971, White House Central Files, Nixon Archive.

36. George J. Hays, Memorandum for the Assistant Secretaries of the Military Departments (M&RA), September 11, 1970, Abortions/Family Planning, Background Materials for "The WAC, 1945–1978," NARA.

37. "DOD letter to Congressman," n.d., 3, EX WE 3 Family Planning, January 1, 1971–April 30, 1971, White House Central Files, Nixon Archive; "Nixon Orders End to Eased Abortions in Armed Services," *New York Times*, April 3, 1971.

38. "President Overturns Pentagon Abortion Rule," *Washington Post*, April 3, 1971.

39. Gompf memorandum for Brotzman, April 23, 1975, Discharge/Waivers-Pregnancy, Parenthood, Dependents, 1974–1978, Background Materials for "The WAC, 1945–1978," NARA.

40. "Abortions Drop, Military Says," *Washington Post*, October 16, 1971.

41. Tom Philpott, "DOD Walks Thin Line on Abortions," *Army Times*, October 2, 1978, Abortions/Family Planning, Background Materials for "The WAC, 1945–1978," NARA.

42. "Army-Funded Abortions Out, Congress Says," *Army*, November 1978, news clipping, Abortions/Family Planning, Background Materials for "The WAC, 1945–1978," NARA.

43. Public Law 95-457, Section 863, October 13, 1978, 92 Stat. 1254.

44. 10 U.S.C. 1093; Karen Jowers, "States' Increasing Restrictions and Bans Could Put Abortions 'Out of Reach' for Some Military Women," *Military Times*, May 24, 2019, https://www.militarytimes.com/pay-benefits/2019/05/24/states -increasing-restrictions-and-bans-could-put-abortions-out-of-reach-for-some -military-women/; Camilia Domonoske, "'You're On Your Own': Servicewomen Describe Impact of Military's Abortion Policy," NPR, November 15, 2017, https:// www.npr.org/sections/thetwo-way/2017/11/15/564336406/-you-re-on-your-own -study-describes-impact-of-militarys-abortion-policy.

45. See Mittlestadt, *Rise of the Military Welfare State*.

46. Holm, *Women in the Military*, 465–69.

47. See, for example, Eberstadt, "Mothers in Combat Boots."

48. These percentages are slightly higher among the military as a whole (including the reserves and National Guard): 39.5 percent and 6 percent. Among the single parents, 64.7 percent are fathers, and 35.3 percent are mothers. See U.S. Department of Defense, "2017 Demographics," 124, 132, 142.

49. National Defense Authorization Act for Fiscal Year 2017, Public Law 114-328, December 23, 2016, https://www.congress.gov/114/plaws/publ328/PLAW -114publ328.pdf.

50. See Meghann Myers, "He Said, She Said: The Battle over Maternity Leave at This Army Leadership School," *Army Times*, July 20, 2018, https://www.armytimes .com/news/your-army/2018/07/20/he-said-she-said-the-battle-over-maternity-leave -at-this-army-leadership-school; Oriana Pawlyk, "Military Leaders Are Confronting a New Form of Discrimination: Pregnancy Bias," *Military*, August 2, 2020, https:// www.military.com/daily-news/2020/08/02/military-leaders-are-confronting-new -form-of-discrimination-pregnancy-bias.html.

51. Thomas C. Seamands, DAPE-ZA, "Authorization for Female Soldiers to Wear an Optional 499 or Sand T-shirt during Postpartum Nursing," April 12, 2018; Shon J. Manasco, "Air Force Guidance Memorandum to AFI 36-2903, Dress and Personal Appearance of Air Force Personnel," April 15, 2019; R. P. Burke, "NAVADMIN 075/19: Navy Uniform Policy and Uniform Initiative Update," March 2019; Kevin Lilley, "New Army Breastfeeding Memo Bans Bathroom as Lactation Area," *Army Times*, December 16, 2015, https://www.armytimes.com/news/your-army/2015/12 /16/new-army-breastfeeding-memo-bans-bathroom-as-lactation-area/; Michelle Tan, "Photo of Soldiers Breastfeeding in Uniform Goes Viral," *Army Times*, September 14, 2015, https://www.armytimes.com/off-duty/2015/09/14/photo-of-soldiers -breastfeeding-in-uniform-goes-viral/.

52. David H. Berger, "Commandant's Planning Guidance," U.S. Marine Corps, accessed July 30, 2019, https://www.hqmc.marines.mil/Portals/142/Docs/%2038th %20Commandant's%20Planning%20Guidance_2019.pdf?ver=2019-07-16-200152-700.

53. Gina Harkins, "Former SecNav Applauds Marine Commandant's Call for 1-Year Maternity Leave," *Military*, July 22, 2019, https://www.military.com/daily -news/2019/07/22/former-secnav-applauds-marine-commandants-call-1-year -maternity-leave.html.

Bibliography

Archives and Manuscript Materials

NARA. RG 319, Records of the Army Staff. National Archives and Records Administration, College Park MD.

Oveta Culp Hobby Papers. Manuscript Division, Library of Congress, Washington DC.

White House Central Files. Nixon Archive, Yorba Linda CA.

Published Works

Byers, Andrew. *The Sexual Economy of War: Discipline and Desire in the U.S. Army.* Ithaca NY: Cornell University Press, 2019.

Chritchlow, Donald T. *Intended Consequences: Birth Control, Abortion, and the Federal Government in Modern America.* New York: Oxford University Press, 1999.

Collins, Kristin A. "Illegitimate Borders: *Jus Sanguinis* Citizenship and the Legal Construction of Family, Race, and Nation." *Yale Law Journal* 123, no. 7 (May 2014): 2134–67.

Dumenil, Lynn. *The Second Line of Defense: American Women and World War I.* Chapel Hill: University of North Carolina Press, 2017.

Eberstadt, Mary. "Mothers in Combat Boots." *Policy Review* 159 (February 2010): 33–44.

Flynn, George Q. *The Draft, 1940–1973.* Lawrence: University of Kansas Press, 1993.

———. *Lewis B. Hershey, Mr. Selective Service.* Chapel Hill: University of North Carolina Press, 1985.

Geva, Dorit. *Conscription, Family, and the Modern State: A Comparative Study of France and the United States.* New York: Cambridge University Press, 2013.

Gurney, Cynthia A. *33 Years of Army Nursing: An Interview with Brigadier General Lillian Dunlap.* Washington DC: United States Army Nurse Corps, 2001.

Holm, Jeanne *Women in the Military: An Unfinished Revolution.* Novato CA: Presidio, 1992.

Jackson, Kathi. *They Called Them Angels: American Military Nurses of World War II.* Lincoln: University of Nebraska Press, 2006.

Keith, Jeanette. *Rich Man's War, Poor Man's Fight: Race, Class, and Power in the Rural South during the First World War.* Chapel Hill: University of North Carolina Press, 2004.

Mittlestadt, Jennifer. *The Rise of the Military Welfare State.* Cambridge MA: Harvard University Press, 2015.

Morden, Betty J. *The Women's Army Corps, 1945–1978.* Army Historical Series. Washington DC: Center of Military History, 1990.

Sarnecky, Mary T. *A History of the U.S. Army Nurse Corps.* Philadelphia: University of Pennsylvania Press, 1999.

Treadwell, Mattie E. *The Women's Army Corps.* The U.S. Army in World War II, Special Studies. Washington DC: Office of the Chief of Military History, 1991. http://www.history.Army.mil/books/wwii/wac/index.htm.

U.S. Department of Defense, Office of the Deputy Assistant Secretary of Defense for Military Community and Family Policy. "2017 Demographics: Profile of the Military Community." Accessed July 30, 2019. https://download.militaryonesource.mil/12038/MOS/Reports/2017-demographics-report.pdf.

Vuic, Kara Dixon. "Mobilizing Marriage and Motherhood: Military Families and Family Planning since World War II." In *Integrating the U.S. Military: African Americans, Women, and Gays since World War II*, edited by Heather M. Stur and Douglas Bristol, 167–97. Baltimore MD: Johns Hopkins University Press, 2017.

———. *Officer, Nurse, Woman: The Army Nurse Corps in the Vietnam War*. Baltimore MD: Johns Hopkins University Press, 2010.

Weatherford, Doris. *American Women and World War II*. New York: Facts on File, 1990.

Witt, Linda, Judith Bellafaire, Britta Granrud, and Mary Jo Binker. *"A Defense Weapon Known to be of Value": Servicewomen of the Korean War Era*. Hanover NH: University Press of New England, 2005.

Zeiger, Susan. *Entangling Alliances: Foreign War Brides and American Soldiers in the Twentieth Century*. New York: New York University Press, 2010.

PART 3

Orientation and Identity

A Comparative Analysis of the Military Bans on Openly Serving Gays, Lesbians, and Transgender Personnel

AGNES GEREBEN SCHAEFER

Over the last seventy-five years, the U.S. military has made landmark decisions to increase diversity in its ranks based on race, gender, and sexual orientation. This chapter examines two of those decisions: (1) the decision to rescind the ban on allowing gays and lesbians to serve openly in the military; and (2) the decision to rescind the ban on allowing transgender personnel to serve openly in the military. The chapter considers the historical and political contexts of the establishment of these bans, why they were put into place, how the military managed them, why the bans were eventually repealed, and why there was an attempt to reinstate the transgender ban.

These cases are key examples of the military's evolving understanding of sexual orientation and gender identity. In both, sexual orientation and gender identity were initially considered disqualifying psychological conditions and grounds for administrative discharge. The military's concerns about allowing gays, lesbians, and transgender personnel to serve openly focused on the potential impacts on military readiness and unit cohesion. Other concerns focused on the potential impacts on recruitment and retention and, in the case of the transgender ban, the costs associated with providing transition-related health care to transgender service members.

Both bans were managed in similar ways by the military: once a service member was found to be gay, lesbian, or transgender, the service member was discharged from the military. As a result of this practice, gay, lesbian, and transgender service members often hid their sexual orientation and gender identity from others in order to avoid discharge. However, there were key differences in the ways that the bans were managed. For instance, the military services were given some latitude in implementing the ban on gays and lesbians, particularly after the Don't Ask, Don't Tell (DADT) policy went into effect in 1994, which led to inconsistent implementation of DADT across the Department of Defense (DOD).

Eventually both bans were repealed because public attitudes toward gays, lesbians, and transgender individuals evolved over time; the military was concerned that it was losing out on high quality talent by maintaining the bans, and there was little evidence to indicate that allowing gay, lesbian, and transgender personnel to serve openly would negatively impact military readiness or unit cohesion. In both cases, when the DOD was considering lifting the bans, it looked to evidence from the civilian sector and other countries' militaries to identify whether allowing gay, lesbian, and transgender personnel to serve openly might negatively impact readiness and cohesion. It found little data to substantiate those initial concerns. However, in the case of the transgender ban, a year after the Obama administration rescinded it, the Trump administration announced that it would be reinstated. The chapter examines the political context in which this decision was made, the legal battles that ensued, the way public opinion on the transgender ban continues to evolve, and the subsequent Biden administration policies reversing the Trump era policies.

Lastly, the chapter identifies cross-cutting conclusions from the two cases. These include what key factors led to the establishment of the bans, what changed to cause the military to reexamine the bans, and why the bans were eventually rescinded (and in the case of the transgender ban, reinstated and then again revoked). While these two cases of military personnel policy evolved in very different ways, their evolution has also been remarkably similar in that they were shaped by politics, broader societal changes, and an increased awareness that gay, lesbian, and transgender individuals who were already serving in the military (albeit concealing their identities in some cases) had not negatively impacted military readiness or unit cohesion.

Origins of the DOD's Don't Ask, Don't Tell Policy, Its Implementation, and Repeal

Both the ban on gays and lesbians and the ban on transgender personnel are key examples of the military's evolving understanding of sexual orientation and gender identity. This section of the chapter examines the historical context of the establishment of the ban on gays and lesbians in the U.S. military, the military's management of that ban, and the reasons the ban was eventually repealed. It highlights the role that politics and public attitudes played in the eventual repeal of the ban on allowing gays and lesbians to serve openly in the military.[1]

The origins of the ban on allowing homosexual personnel to serve in the U.S. military date back to World War II, when many psychiatrists classified homosexuality as a mental or behavioral disorder, and the military's "Mobilization Regulations" stated that "persons who habitually or occasionally engage in homosexual or other perverse sexual practices are unsuitable for military service and will be excluded."[2] After World War II, the DOD's new military policy stated that "homosexual personnel, irrespective of sex, should not be permitted to serve in any branch of the Armed Services in any capacity, and prompt separation of known homosexuals from the Armed Service is mandatory."[3]

In 1951 Article 125 of the new Uniform Code of Military Justice (UCMJ) made sodomy an act subject to court martial (10 U.S.C. 925). While the UCMJ's prohibition on sodomy was meant to apply equally to same-sex and heterosexual activity, it was a key legal basis for not allowing gays and lesbians to serve.[4] Despite the early policy mandating the separation of gay and lesbian service members, inconsistencies among the military services "resulted in substantial difficulties in responding to legal challenges in the courts."[5] In 1981 a new DOD policy made "discharge(s) mandatory for admitted homosexuals and establishes very limited grounds for retention."[6] The following year a revised policy provided a single rationale for the ban, explaining that "homosexuality is incompatible with military service" because the presence of such individuals "seriously impairs the accomplishment of the military mission."[7]

While past and competing rationales for the ban had included notions of the physical or mental unfitness of gays and lesbians in the military, the 1981 policy grounded the ban in concerns over military readiness.[8] In an effort to make enforcement of the policy more uniform, the 1981 policy also provided a standard basis for separation from military service on grounds of sexual orientation: (1) a *statement* by a member that he or she is gay; (2) engagement in or attempted engagement in same-sex sexual *acts*; and (3) *marriage* or attempted marriage to a person of the same sex.[9]

Issues regarding fair and consistent implementation of the 1981 policy persisted throughout the 1980s. These issues included improper investigations, inconsistent enforcement, and exploitation of the policy by some service members seeking to void their military commitments.[10] It was in this context that the issue of gays and lesbians serving in the military emerged onto the national political stage in the early 1990s.

The Evolution of a Political Compromise

In October 1991 presidential candidate Bill Clinton stated that, if elected president, he would sign an executive order to end discrimination in the military on the basis of sexual orientation.[11] During his first weeks in office, the president's statement was met with widespread resistance from military and congressional leaders.[12] The administration understood that Congress held the upper hand, and that, if Clinton issued an executive order, Congress would enact a reversal in response.[13] Secretary of Defense Les Aspin told National Public Radio on January 24, 1993, "At any point, Congress can overturn what Bill Clinton has determined. I mean, if Bill Clinton were to write an executive order today eliminating the ban on homosexuality in the military, Congress could, tomorrow, vote a piece of legislation that restores the ban."[14] Faced with the prospect of congressional action to codify the ban on gays and lesbians in the military, the Clinton administration struck a deal with the Joint Chiefs and the Senate leadership in which Clinton agreed to postpone issuing a new policy for six months in exchange for Congress agreeing to withdraw efforts to pass legislation concerning the issue.[15]

In January 1993 Clinton directed Secretary Aspin to draft an executive order "ending discrimination on the basis of sexual ori-

SCHAEFER

entation in determining who may serve in the Armed Forces of the United States."[16] Clinton's vision involved separating sexual orientation from conduct and creating a zone of privacy for gay and lesbian service members, such that they could serve in the military as long as their behavior was otherwise consistent with high standards of conduct. Clinton explained this vision as follows: "I want to make it very clear that this is a very narrow issue. It is whether a person, in the absence of any other disqualifying conduct, can simply say that he or she is homosexual and stay in the service." The president also announced that, with the consent of the Joint Chiefs, an interim policy would immediately take effect in which questions related to sexual orientation would be removed from military accession forms, thereby establishing the first "Don't Ask" component of the policy.[17]

On April 1, 1993, Secretary Aspin asked the RAND Corporation, a federally funded research and development center, to provide information and analysis that would be useful in helping formulate the required draft executive order.[18] The RAND study concluded that President Clinton's decision to integrate gays into the military without restriction could be accomplished through a "policy that would establish clear standards of conduct for all military personnel, to be equally and strictly enforced, in order to maintain the military discipline necessary for effective operations."[19] However, these findings were overtaken by the events described below, which ultimately resulted in a compromise between the president and Congress.

After Clinton's announcement in January 1993, it became clear that the president did not have the backing in Congress to move forward with his original goal of ending discrimination on the basis of sexual orientation in the military.[20] Explaining the political realities of the time, Clinton remarked that "those who want the ban to be lifted completely . . . must understand that such action would have faced certain and decisive reversal by Congress."[21] Instead the administration adopted an alternative policy that came to be known as Don't Ask, Don't Tell, in which service members would not be asked about their sexual orientation, and gay and lesbian service members would be required to keep that orientation private.[22] Once a gay or lesbian service member's sexual orientation became known, however, sexual orientation would become grounds for investigation and dismissal. The new policy made a distinction between sexual orientation and conduct: "Sexual orientation is considered a personal and private matter, and homosexual orientation is not a bar to service entry or continued service unless manifested by homosexual conduct."[23] Although this meant that the president was compromising on his original goal of nondiscrimination for gays and lesbians in the military, he ultimately decided that working within the confines of DADT would achieve more than lifting the ban only to have it reinstated by Congress.[24]

However, a majority of senators on the Senate Armed Services Committee (SASC) had already made clear that they did not support the president's efforts to permit gay and lesbian individuals to serve in the military, and a number argued that permitting them to serve would compromise unit cohesion and military readiness.[25] Congress eventually took matters into its own hands and passed an amendment to the National Defense Authorization Act.[26] Offering an alternative vision of DADT, Congress rejected the distinctions between sexual orientation and conduct that the Clinton administration had so carefully crafted. The law noted that gays and lesbians would pose an "unacceptable risk" to military effectiveness, and that the exposure of gay or lesbian sexual orientation, irrespective of other same-sex conduct, was enough to warrant investigation and separation.[27] The law contrasted sharply with President Clinton's original aims.

The clash between the administration and Congress highlighted the competing visions for the conditions under which gays and lesbians could serve in the military. President Clinton had initially aimed to permit gay and lesbian personnel to serve openly in the military without restrictions. When that proved politically untenable, he sought to provide greater protections for gay and lesbian service members by establishing policies that separated sexual orientation from conduct and limited the conditions under which commanders could initiate investigations.[28] But those who opposed allowing those members to serve openly pointed to the "unacceptable risk" that such a policy would pose to military readiness.[29] Few parties were satisfied with DADT. The competing visions would provide a basis for ongoing disagreements throughout the next decade. The DOD, the White House, Congress, and advocacy groups would continue to debate what the policy meant and how to interpret its ambiguities.

Implementation and Repeal of DADT

Former public officials and advocacy organizations have indicated that after the presidential transition in 2001, the new George W. Bush administration showed little interest in dealing with "social issues" in the military.[30] With ongoing combat operations in Iraq and Afghanistan, administration officials also argued that revisiting DADT was unwise in a time of war.[31] In 2007 Under Secretary of Defense for Personnel and Readiness David Chu pointed to the relatively small number of overall discharges for same-sex conduct as an additional factor diminishing "the urgency to launch this debate" at such a sensitive time.[32] When asked about the future of DADT, the Pentagon took the position that it was simply implementing the policy established by Congress, that "the Department will, of course, follow Congressional direction," and that appeals to change the law were directed to that branch of government.[33]

Given this more hands-off approach to the implementation of DADT, advocacy groups began shifting their focus from DADT's shortcomings to highlighting the need for its repeal.[34] This put Congress at the center of debates over the policy's future. The first of a series of repeal bills was introduced in 2005, and in 2008 the Military Personnel Subcommittee of the House Armed Services Committee held the first hearings on the issue in fifteen years.[35] Supporters of retaining DADT continued to argue that allowing gay and lesbian military personnel to serve openly would undermine military readiness and unit cohesion. They further asserted that changing the law during wartime would place undue stress on the troops.[36]

But public opinion regarding sexual orientation had changed somewhat since 1993. By 2010 several states had passed gay marriage provisions, gays and lesbians were more visible in the workplace and in broader society, and Americans were more favorable toward allowing them to serve openly in the military. For example, the number of adult Americans who indicated that they knew someone who is gay or lesbian grew significantly, from 42 percent in 1992 to 77 percent in 2010, with younger people reporting higher numbers than older people.[37]

The issue of gay marriage had been the primary LGBT+ issue that received national attention in the late 1990s and 2000s. By 2010 thirty states had passed constitutional amendments banning gay marriage, but public attitudes toward gay marriage were changing. For instance, public opinion changed from 35 percent of respondents expressing support and 57 percent opposed in 2001[38] to 42 percent expressing support and 48 percent opposed in 2010.[39] The 2010 poll was the first time in fifteen years of Pew Research Center polling that fewer than half of those polled opposed same-sex marriage.[40]

Public attitudes about whether gays and lesbians should be allowed to serve openly in the U.S. military also changed. For instance, since 2005 Gallup polls have consistently found that more than 60 percent of Americans favor allowing openly gay men and lesbian women to serve in the U.S. military, including majorities of the most conservative segments of the population.[41] A 2010 Gallup poll indicated that 70 percent of Americans favored allowing openly gay men and lesbian women to serve openly in the U.S. military. Support for DADT also steadily declined among service members. For instance, in a 2006 survey of Iraq and Afghanistan war veterans, respondents showed declining support for the DADT policy, which was consistent with prior surveys of military personnel (from approximately 73 percent support in 1993 to 40 percent support in the 2006 survey).[42]

Presidential candidate Barack Obama's positions on LGBT+ issues also evolved throughout the course of his political career. Early in his career, he did not support gay marriage. During his U.S. Senate campaign in 2004, he told WTTV Chicago public television that "marriage is between a man and a woman, but what I also believe is that we have an obligation to make sure that gays and lesbians have the rights of citizenship that afford them visitations to hospitals, that allow them to transfer property between partners, to make sure they're not discriminated against on the job."[43] He later became an advocate for civil unions, but still opposed gay marriage. During the July 23, 2007, CNN/YouTube debate, he stated, "We've got to make sure that everybody is equal under the law. And the civil unions that I proposed would be equivalent in terms of making sure that all the rights that are conferred by the state are equal for same-sex couples as well as for heterosexual couples."[44] In 2010 Obama told a group of liberal bloggers that "I have been to this point unwilling to sign on to same-sex marriage primarily because of my understandings of the traditional definitions of marriage. But I also think you're right that attitudes evolve, including mine."[45]

In his 2010 State of the Union address, President Barack Obama announced that he would work with Congress to repeal DADT. In early February Secretary of Defense Robert Gates announced that he would appoint a high-level working group within DOD to review the issues associated with repeal, and that he would ask the RAND Corporation to update its 1993 DADT study. The DOD's primary concerns remained focused on how the repeal of DADT might affect military readiness and effectiveness—such as recruitment and retention, unit cohesion, and the health of the force. The detailed analyses conducted by the Comprehensive Review Working Group and the RAND Corporation found that allowing gay and lesbian service members to serve openly could be accomplished without significant negative impacts to military readiness.

In December 2010 Congress passed a law repealing DADT, and President Obama signed it on December 22, 2010.[46] When Obama certified the repeal of DADT, he specifically cited concerns the ban had on losing talent: "Our military will no longer be deprived of the talents and skills of patriotic Americans just because they happen to be gay or lesbian."[47] While the repeal of DADT allowed gay and lesbian personnel to serve openly in the military, the policy that prohibited transgender individuals from serving openly remained in place.

Origins of the DOD's Ban on Transgender Personnel, Its Implementation, Repeal, and Reinstatement

The origins of the DOD ban on transgender personnel are similar to the origins of the ban on gays and lesbian personnel. Since the 1960s DOD policies have rendered both the physical and psychological aspects of "transgender conditions" as disqualifying conditions for accession and allowed for the administrative discharge of service members who fall into these categories. DOD Instruction (DODI) 6130.03 established medical standards for entry into military service, including a list of disqualifying physical and mental conditions (some of which are transgender related). During the debate over DADT in the 1990s, policymakers decided to focus the policy on gay and lesbian military personnel and to allow the transgender ban to remain in place. Therefore, while the repeal of DADT by the Obama administration allowed gay and lesbian service members to serve openly, the transgender ban remained in place.

Implementation of the Ban on Transgender Personnel

As with the ban on gays and lesbians and the DOD's DADT policy, once a service member was found to be transgender, they could be discharged from the military. As a result transgender service members often did not divulge their gender identity. In the case of transgender individuals in general, and in particular those who have gender dysphoria, this can exacerbate distress and could create barriers to receiving appropriate medical care and treatment.

During the time that the transgender ban was implemented up until its repeal in 2016, DOD policies were trying to keep up with the rapidly evolving medical understanding of gender identity issues. For example, under the established criteria and terminology outlined in the 2013 fifth edition of the *Diagnostic and Statistical Manual of Mental Disorders* (DSM-5), the American Psychiatric Association (APA) publication that provides standard language and criteria for classifying mental health conditions, transgender status alone does not constitute a medical condition.[48] Instead, under the revised diagnostic guidelines, only transgender individuals who experience significant related distress are considered to have a medical condition called "gender dysphoria." Some combination of psychosocial, pharmacologic (mainly but not exclusively hormonal), or surgical care may be medically necessary for these individuals. As a result of this change, the broader ban on transgender individuals and DOD policies have gradually evolved to focus more narrowly on gender dysphoria.

In addition, the language pertaining to transgender individuals in military accession instructions did not match that used in

DSM-5. This resulted in restrictions in DOD policies that may have been misapplied or difficult to interpret in the context of current medical treatments and diagnoses. Otherwise qualified individuals could have been excluded for conditions that were unlikely to affect their military service, and individuals with true restrictions may have been more difficult to screen for and identify.[49]

DOD policies were also trying to keep up with medical advancements that could minimize the invasiveness of treatments and allow for telemedicine or other forms of remote medical care—especially while service members are on deployments.[50] For example, DOD regulations specified that conditions requiring regular laboratory visits made service members ineligible for deployment, including all those who were receiving hormone treatments, since such treatments require laboratory monitoring every three months for the first year as hormone levels stabilize.[51] Similarly, the use of refrigerated medications was a disqualifying condition for deployment, even though nearly all hormone therapies are available in other formats that do not require refrigeration.

Repeal of the Ban on Transgender Personnel

While transgender prevalence in the U.S. general population is thought to be significantly less than 1 percent, there have been no rigorous epidemiological studies in the general population that confirm this estimate.[52] However, as the LGBT+ movement has grown over time, transgender individuals have become more commonplace and part of popular culture (e.g., Caitlyn Jenner, Laverne Cox), and transgender issues have moved more into the mainstream. Some of those issues (such as transgender bathroom bills) have become national issues. As a result public attitudes toward transgender issues have also changed. In 2019 more than six in ten (62 percent) Americans say they have become more supportive toward transgender rights compared to their views five years ago. By contrast, about one-quarter (25 percent) said their views were more opposed compared to 2014.[53]

In July 2015 Secretary of Defense Ashton Carter announced that the DOD would "create a working group to study the policy and readiness implications of welcoming transgender persons to serve openly." He additionally directed that "decision authority in all administrative discharges for those diagnosed with gender dysphoria or who identify themselves as transgender be elevated to the Under Secretary of Defense (Personnel and Readiness), who will make determinations on all potential separations."[54] The under secretary of defense (personnel and readiness) asked the RAND Corporation to conduct a study on a number of issues, including: (1) identifying the health care needs of the transgender population, transgender service members' potential health care utilization rates, and the costs associated with extending health care coverage for transition-related treatments; (2) assessing the potential readiness implications of allowing transgender service members to serve openly; and (3) reviewing the experiences of foreign militaries that permit transgender service members to serve openly. The RAND study found that the number of U.S. transgender service members who are likely to seek transition-related care is so small that a change in policy will likely have a marginal impact on health care costs and the readiness of the force.[55]

On June 30, 2016, Defense Secretary Ashton Carter announced that transgender service members in the U.S. military could openly serve their country without fear of retribution. Given the findings from the working group and the RAND study, Secretary Carter said during a Pentagon news conference that three main reasons led to the decision to lift the transgender ban: the force of the future, the existing force, and matters of principle. When announcing his decision, Secretary Carter reinforced the DOD's concern about losing talent due to the transgender ban: "[We in] the Defense Department and the military need to avail ourselves of all talent possible . . . to remain what we are now—the finest fighting force the world has ever known. Our mission is to defend this country and we don't want barriers unrelated to a person's qualifications to serve preventing us from *recruiting or retaining the Soldier, Sailor, Airman, or Marine* who can best accomplish the mission. The Defense Department must have access to 100 percent of America's population for its all-volunteer force to be able to recruit from among the most highly qualified, and to retain them."[56]

Following this announcement, transgender individuals already serving in the military were able to do so openly and were no longer able to be discharged simply because of their gender identity.

Transgender service members were also able to access all medically necessary health care and officially change their gender in Pentagon personnel systems.

Under the new policy, within ninety days of the lifting of the ban: (1) the DOD will issue medical guidance for providing transition-related care to transgender service members; (2) the Military Health System will be required to provide transgender service members with all medically necessary care related to gender transition, based on the guidance that is issued; (3) and service members will be able to begin the process to officially change their gender in personnel management systems. Importantly, the new policy also clarified that "any discrimination against a Service member based on their gender identity is sex discrimination and may be addressed through the Department's equal opportunity channels."[57]

Reinstatement of the Ban on Transgender Personnel

In January 2017, when President Donald Trump took office, there was some uncertainty as to how LGBT+ issues would factor into his political agenda. But in February 2017 President Trump swiftly rescinded protections for transgender students that had allowed them to use bathrooms corresponding with their gender identity. On July 26, 2017, President Trump tweeted that the U.S. military would no longer "accept or allow transgender individuals to serve in any capacity," and that "our military must be focused on decisive and overwhelming victory and cannot be burdened with the tremendous medical costs and disruption that transgender in the military would entail."[58] These tweets were formalized a month later in August 2017, when the White House issued a presidential memorandum in which the president directed "a return to the longstanding policy and practice on military service by transgender individuals that was in place prior to June 2016 until such time as a sufficient basis exists upon which to conclude that terminating that policy and practice would not have the negative effects discussed above" starting March 23, 2018.[59] In the memo he also reiterated the emphasis on his original tweet regarding military readiness and potential health care costs: "In my judgment, the previous Administration failed to identify a sufficient basis to conclude that terminating the Departments' longstanding policy and practice would not hinder military effectiveness and lethality, disrupt unit cohesion, or tax military resources, and there remain meaningful concerns that further study is needed to ensure that continued implementation of last year's policy change would not have those negative effects."[60]

While the memo allowed currently serving transgender service members to remain in the military, it ordered a halt to the use of DOD or Department of Homeland Security resources to "fund sex reassignment surgical procedures for military personnel, except to the extent necessary to protect the health of an individual who has already begun a course of treatment to reassign his or her sex" starting March 23, 2018. The memo also canceled the Obama order to begin recruitment of transgender individuals starting in January 2018, "until such time as the Secretary of Defense, after consulting with the Secretary of Homeland Security, provides a recommendation to the contrary that I find convincing."[61]

While Trump's memo resonated with his conservative political base, many Democrats and some Republicans came out against the proposed change in policy, including Senator John McCain, who said that any service member who meets appropriate military standards should be permitted to serve because "when less than 1 percent of Americans are volunteering to join the military, we should welcome all those who are willing and able to serve our country."[62] Fifty-six former military generals and admirals,[63] as well as fifteen attorneys general, also expressed opposition to the proposed change in policy.[64]

The president's announcement was also out of step with a large segment of the public. In July 2017 a Harris poll found that a majority (58 percent) of Americans disagreed with President Trump's decision to ban transgender people from serving, including four-in-ten current active duty service military personnel and 41 percent with past military service. And while 35 percent of Americans supported the ban, an overwhelming majority (66 percent) of Americans did not believe the ban should extend to transgender individuals currently serving in the military.[65]

In August 2017 Secretary of Defense James Mattis announced that he would carry out the president's policy direction, and that the DOD would develop a study and implementation plan. He also said he would establish a panel of experts serving within the Departments of Defense and Homeland Security to provide advice and recommendations on the implementation of the president's direction.[66] Once the panel of experts reported its recommendations, Mattis would provide his advice to the president.

Opposition to the president's proposed ban was immediate—especially in the courts. In August 2017 the first of four lawsuits were filed against the president and the secretary of defense on behalf of transgender service members.[67] Later that month three former secretaries of military services, Eric Fanning (army), Ray Mabus (navy), and Deborah Lee James (air force), submitted declarations in support of the plaintiffs. Thirty-three former national security officials also submitted a "friends of the court" brief in support of the plaintiffs.[68] In October–November 2017 preliminary injunctions were issued in all four cases blocking the implementation of the ban. On December 22, 2017, a panel of the federal appeals court in the District of Columbia rejected the Trump administration's request to prevent the recruitment of transgender military recruits beginning on January 1, 2018. On December 30, 2017, the Justice Department made clear that its proposed ban on transgender military recruits was on hold, and as a result, for the first time in history, openly transgender individuals began joining the military on January 1, 2018.

In March 2018 Secretary Mattis sent the president a memo that laid out his recommendations for a revised policy in which most individuals with a history or diagnosis of gender dysphoria and those who require or have undergone gender transition would be disqualified from serving in the military. All other transgender individuals who do not have gender dysphoria could serve in the military, as long as they serve in their birth sex, not their target gender.[69] The president approved Mattis's recommendations, which would become known as "the Mattis plan."

During this time Congress also continued to focus on this issue. For instance, when the service chiefs appeared before the SASC for budget hearings, Senator Kirsten Gillibrand (D-NY) asked whether they were aware of or if any of them had seen problems with unit cohesion, discipline, or morale resulting from open transgender service. They all indicated they had not seen any such reports in their respective service branches.[70]

Additionally, some members of Congress began to ask questions regarding the composition of Mattis's panel of experts, their qualifications, and the rigor of the study that was conducted. For instance, Senator Gillibrand said, "It appears that this report your department has issued is not based on the department's data or science, but rather on quote 'potential risks' that the authors cannot back up. In fact, this seems to me to be the same unfounded claims and unfounded concerns that led the opposition to repealing 'Don't Ask Don't Tell,' integrating women into the military, integrating African Americans into the military, and I think you need to do a lot more work on this topic to inform yourselves."[71]

The lawsuits working their way through the courts also took up the questions of whether the Mattis plan was based on analysis or whether it was rooted in discrimination. The administration's communications with external advocacy groups, as well as communications within the administration over how the Mattis plan was developed, have been subpoenaed and those legal battles have not yet been resolved.[72] In December 2019 a U.S. district judge made a ruling requiring the government to turn over about thirty-five thousand documents cited in its decision to ban transgender service members. The judge said the plaintiffs were entitled to all the documents and information used to justify the administration's restrictions on transgender service members.[73]

In January 2019 the administration asked the U.S. Supreme Court to intervene, and the court ruled 5–4 to stay lower court injunctions and allow the ban to go into effect until the four lawsuits against the administration made their way through the courts. The administration reinstated the transgender ban on April 12, 2019, and replaced the Obama-era policy that allowed transgender individuals to serve openly and receive transition-related medical care, with the Trump-Mattis policy that allows service members who received a diagnosis of gender dysphoria prior to April 2019 to continue to serve in their preferred gender. The policy also indicated that any currently serving troops diagnosed after that date must serve according to their sex as assigned at birth and are prohibited from seeking transition-related care. In addition, prospective recruits who have received a gender dysphoria diagnosis were barred from enlisting or enrolling in military academies.

The DOD insisted that the new policy was not a ban on transgender individuals because it did not ban all transgender individuals from serving in the military—only those with a history or diagnosis of gender dysphoria, those who required or had already begun the gender transition process from serving in the military, and those who did not serve in their gender assigned at birth. Opponents of the ban argued that the new policy was akin to DADT in that transgender individuals were allowed to serve as long as they were not known to be transgender and as long as they hide their gender identities.

At the heart of the tug-of-war between the lifting of the transgender ban in the Obama era and its reinstatement in the Trump era (as well as other LGBT+ issues) is a disagreement over the legal meaning of the word "sex"—and whether discrimination against transgender individuals is sex discrimination. This conflict has broader implications as well. For instance, on June 12, 2020, the Trump administration finalized a rule that would remove nondiscrimination protections for LGBT+ people regarding health care and health insurance. This was one of several Trump policies that defined "sex discrimination" as only applying when someone faces discrimination for being female or male and did not protect that person from discrimination on the basis of sexual orientation or gender identity. In 2016 Section 1557 of the Affordable Care Act clarified that protections regarding "sex" encompass those based on gender identity, which it defined as "male, female, neither, or a combination of male and female."[74] According to the revised Trump version of the policy, the Department of Health and Human Services would be "returning to the government's interpretation of sex discrimination according to the plain meaning of the word 'sex' as male or female and as determined by biology."[75]

On June 15, 2020, the Supreme Court made a landmark ruling that protects gay and transgender workers from workplace discrimination. The Supreme Court decided that a key provision of the Civil Rights Act of 1964, known as Title VII, which bars job discrimination because of sex, applies to sexual orientation and gender identity. While lower courts have found that Title VII does not apply to uniformed military personnel, this decision put increasing pressure on the Trump administration to repeal the current ban. On June 19, 2020, twelve members of Congress had already urged the DOD to rescind the transgender ban on the basis of the Supreme Court's Title VII ruling.[76]

Transgender issues continue to evolve and grow in social visibility. In 2017 a Pew poll found that 37 percent of Americans knew someone who was transgender (with millennials indicating they were most likely to know someone who is transgender).[77] An increasing number of Americans also support allowing transgender individuals to serve openly in the military. For instance, a January 2019 Quinnipiac University Poll found that 70 percent of Americans support open transgender military service,[78] and a May 2019 Gallup poll found that 71 percent of Americans support allowing openly transgender men and women to serve in the military,[79] up from 58 percent in 2017.[80] The Gallup poll also found that younger age groups supported open transgender service more than older age groups. This mirrors differences across age groups in public attitudes toward gay and lesbian military service. Support for open transgender service also appears to be growing within the military. A study funded by the DOD and published in February 2020 in the journal *Sexuality Research and Social Policy* found that about 66 percent of active-duty soldiers, sailors, airmen and marines support the idea of serving alongside transgender personnel.[81] While 37 percent of Republicans supported the idea of transgender personnel in the U.S. military in 2017, that number increased to 47 percent in 2019.[82] Another poll also indicated an increase in the number of Republicans who support allowing transgender personnel to serve openly. A Quinnipiac University poll conducted in 2017 showed 32 percent.[83] By January 2019 that number had risen to 40 percent.[84] It is unclear what kind of an impact these attitudes will have on the future course of the ban.

On January 25, 2021, President Joseph Biden signed an executive order revoking President Trump's presidential memorandum of August 27, 2017 (Military Service by Transgender Individuals) and his presidential memorandum of March 23, 2018 (Military Service by Transgender Individuals).[85] This executive order also declared that "it shall be the policy of the United States to ensure that all transgender individuals who wish to serve in the United States military and can meet the appropriate standards shall be able to do so openly and free from discrimination."[86] On March 31, 2021, the DOD published policy updates for transgender military service that resembled the 2016 policies regarding transgender military service.[87] The DOD's updated policies became effective on April 30, 2021. While President Biden's executive order reverses President Trump's policies regarding transgender military service for the near term, the future of policies pertaining to transgender military personnel remains uncertain because a future president could potentially revoke President Biden's executive order or Congress could pass legislation banning transgender military service.

Cross-Cutting Conclusions from the Two Cases

Several conclusions can be identified from the previous analysis of these two bans on military personnel: what led to the establishment of the bans, what changed to cause the military to reexamine the bans, and why the bans were eventually rescinded (and reinstated, and then reversed again, in the case of the transgender ban).

The initial concerns that led to the establishment of the bans on gay, lesbian, and transgender military personnel were similar: in both cases, sexual orientation and gender identity were seen as disqualifying conditions and grounds for administrative discharge from the military. Over time other concerns also arose, including the potential negative impacts that open service might have on military readiness and unit cohesion—for instance, in the case of DADT, about whether unit cohesion, recruiting, and retention might be negatively impacted if gay and lesbian service members were allowed to serve openly. In the case of the transgender ban, there were similar concerns about the potential negative impacts of open service on unit cohesion, as well as on military readiness due to recovery times associated with gender reassignment surgeries and other transition-related medical procedures, and about the costs associated with extending health care coverage for gender transition–related treatments. These concerns framed the main research questions that the DOD Working Groups and the RAND Corporation explored in 1993 and 2010 when the DOD was considering repealing DADT, as well as in 2016 when it was considering repealing the transgender ban. This research ultimately informed

Defense Secretary Leon Panetta's decision to repeal DADT and Defense Secretary Carter's decision to repeal the transgender ban.

In both cases politics had an enormous impact on the reason DADT and the transgender bans were rescinded. For instance, while President Clinton initially intended to outright repeal the ban on gays and lesbians serving in the military, the political environment—in particular, the power struggle between the president and Congress over military personnel policy—would not allow him to do so. That led to DADT as a compromise, one that ultimately no one was satisfied with. In the case of President Obama, he was ultimately able to work with Congress to repeal DADT fairly easily in 2010.

When Defense Secretary Carter rescinded the ban on transgender personnel serving in the military, there was not significant opposition from Congress. The repeal of the transgender ban came on the heels of two other landmark military personnel decisions during the Obama administration: the repeal of DADT in 2010 and the decision to open combat positions to women in 2015; perhaps by the time the repeal of the transgender ban occurred in 2016, it did not seem so controversial. In 2017, when President Trump announced that he would reinstate the ban on transgender military service, much of his conservative political base was pleased. The main difference with the Trump decision is that it revised a military personnel policy that a former president had instated. Up until that point, presidents had been wary to deconstruct personnel policy decisions for the DOD because it is such a large organization and such decisions can bring confusion and stress to service members as they try to navigate the changes in policy. In 2021 President Biden revoked President Trump's policy on transgender military service.

One of the biggest factors in the timing of the repeals of the bans was the way public attitudes about gays, lesbians, and transgender individuals have changed over time. In both instances the degree to which the public was accepting of gay, lesbian, and transgender military service dictated the pace of change. In 1993, for example, there was significant opposition to gay and lesbian military service across broader society, Congress, and the DOD; by the time President Obama called for the repeal of DADT in 2010, society,

Congress, and the DOD had changed dramatically since 1993. This included increases in the number of Americans who personally knew someone who was gay or lesbian, as well as in the number of Americans who supported allowing gay and lesbian military personnel to serve openly. The role of generational change is also key to understanding why both DADT and the transgender ban were repealed. Younger generations expressed more support for the changes than did older demographics.

Additionally, before the two bans were rescinded, gay, lesbian, and transgender personnel were already serving in the military, albeit some were hiding their sexual orientation or gender identity. Therefore, in both cases, the DOD was trying to manage personnel policy for hidden populations about which it knew very little, including the size of the gay, lesbian, and transgender populations in the military (because, if they self-identified, they risked being separated from the military); their health care needs; and their propensity to remain in the military. Over time more gay, lesbian, and transgender personnel came out to their fellow service members and, in some cases, to their commanders, calling into the question the argument that allowing them to serve in the military would have negative impacts. They were already serving in the military, and many were high-performing personnel serving with distinction.

In many ways this echoes the impetus for the DOD's decision to consider opening combat positions to women. During military operations in the Gulf Wars, Iraq, and Afghanistan, women were not formally assigned to these positions, but given the emerging nature of warfare in those conflicts, women often found themselves in combat nonetheless. Their performance in these situations over the long term eventually initiated DOD leaders to question whether the exclusion of women in ground combat positions should be reexamined.

Conclusions

Eventually both bans were repealed because the military was concerned that it was losing out on high-quality talent by maintaining the bans; attitudes towards gay, lesbian, and transgender individuals changed over time; there was little evidence to indicate that allowing gay, lesbian, and transgender personnel would negatively impact military readiness or unit cohesion; and the political context also changed. When the DOD was considering lifting the bans, it looked to evidence from the civilian sector and other countries' militaries to identify whether allowing gays, lesbians, and transgender personnel to serve openly might negatively impact readiness and cohesion. In both cases little evidence was found to substantiate those initial concerns.

Notes

1. For a more comprehensive history of Don't Ask, Don't Tell, see RAND, *Sexual Orientation and U.S. Military Personnel Policy*.

2. Menninger, *Psychiatry in a Troubled World*, 228.

3. RAND, *Sexual Orientation and U.S. Military Personnel Policy*, 6.

4. RAND, *Sexual Orientation and U.S. Military Personnel Policy*, 339.

5. U.S. General Accounting Office, *Defense Force Management*, 11.

6. W. Graham Claytor Jr., "Enlisted Administrative Separations Including a Completely New Enclosure 8 on Homosexuality," memorandum to secretaries of the Military Departments and chairman of the Joint Chiefs of Staff, January 16, 1981, in U.S. Department of Defense, *Report*, 20.

7. U.S. Department of Defense, Directive 1332.14, *Enlisted Administrative Separations*, 1982, in RAND, *Sexual Orientation and U.S. Military Personnel Policy*, 41.

8. RAND, *Sexual Orientation and U.S. Military Personnel Policy*, 41.

9. RAND, *Sexual Orientation and U.S. Military Personnel Policy*, 41.

10. U.S. General Accounting Office, *Defense Force Management*.

11. RAND, *Sexual Orientation and U.S. Military Personnel Policy*, 41.

12. RAND, *Sexual Orientation and U.S. Military Personnel Policy*, 42.

13. RAND, *Sexual Orientation and U.S. Military Personnel Policy*, 42.

14. RAND, *Sexual Orientation and U.S. Military Personnel Policy*, 42.

15. Stephanopolous, *All Too Human*, 126–28.

16. Bill Clinton, "Memorandum on Ending Discrimination on the Basis of Sexual Orientation in the Armed Forces," January 29, 1993, https://www.presidency.ucsb.edu/node/220128.

17. Bill Clinton, "Press Conference on Gays in the Military," January 29, 1993, https://millercenter.org/the-presidency/presidential-speeches/january-29-1993-press-conference-gays-military.

18. RAND, *Sexual Orientation and U.S. Military Personnel Policy*.

19. RAND, *Sexual Orientation and U.S. Military Personnel Policy*.

20. RAND, *Sexual Orientation and U.S. Military Personnel Policy*, 43.

21. Bill Clinton, "Remarks Announcing the New Policy on Gays and Lesbians in the Military," July 19, 1993, https://www.govinfo.gov/app/collection/cpd/1992/02.

22. The term "Don't Ask, Don't Tell" was introduced by Northwestern University professor Charles Moskos. Moskos worked closely with Senate Armed Services Committee chairman Sam Nunn and played a key role in shaping the contours of the DOD policy.

23. Les Aspin, memorandum to secretaries of the Military Departments and chairman of the Joint Chiefs of Staff, "Policy on Homosexual Conduct in the Armed Forces," July 19, 1993, https://babel.hathitrust.org/cgi/pt?id=uiug.30112104125270&view=1up&seq=3.

24. Drew, *On the Edge*, 250.

25. RAND, *Sexual Orientation and U.S. Military Personnel Policy*, 45.

26. Section 571 of FY 1994 National Defense Authorization Act, codified at 10 U.S.C. 654, Policy Concerning Homosexuality in the Armed Forces.

27. The law stated: "The presence in the armed forces of persons who demonstrate a propensity or intent to engage in homosexual acts would create an unacceptable risk to the high standards of morale, good order and discipline, and unit cohesion that are the essence of military capability" (10 U.S.C. 654). As for the "Don't Ask" component, the law included a "Sense of Congress" that individuals should not be asked questions concerning sexual orientation during the accession process, but it also gave the secretary of defense the authority to reinstate such questions (10 U.S.C. 654).

28. RAND, *Sexual Orientation and U.S. Military Personnel Policy*, 47.

29. RAND, *Sexual Orientation and U.S. Military Personnel Policy*, 47.

30. RAND, *Sexual Orientation and U.S. Military Personnel Policy*.

31. David Chu, "Revisiting Title 10, United States Code, Section 654," letter to Senator Ron Wyden, February 12, 2007.

32. Chu, "Revisiting Title 10."

33. David Chu to Ron Wyden, ABC News, February 12, 2007, https://abcnews.go.com/images/WNT/ross_dod_response_Wyden.pdf.

34. RAND, *Sexual Orientation and U.S. Military Personnel Policy*, 60.

35. RAND, *Sexual Orientation and U.S. Military Personnel Policy*, 60.

36. RAND, *Sexual Orientation and U.S. Military Personnel Policy*, 60.

37. "Views of Gays and Lesbians: May 20–24, 2010," CBS News, June 9, 2010, http://www.cbsnews.com/htdocs/pdf/poll_gays_lesbians_060910.pdf.

38. Joseph Liu, "Overview of Same-Sex Marriage in the United States," Pew Research Center, December 7, 2012, https://www.pewforum.org/2012/12/07/overview-of-same-sex-marriage-in-the-united-states/.

39. Tom Rosentiel, "Gay Marriage Gains More Acceptance: Majority Continues to Favor Gays Serving Openly in Military," Pew Research Center, October 6, 2010, https://www.pewresearch.org/2010/10/06/gay-marriage-gains-more-acceptance/.

40. Rosentiel, "Gay Marriage Gains More Acceptance."

41. Lymari Morales, "In U.S., 67% Support Repealing 'Don't Ask, Don't Tell,'" Gallup, December 9, 2010, https://news.gallup.com/poll/145130/support-repealing-dont-ask-dont-tell.aspx.

42. Moradi and Miller, "Attitudes of Iraq and Afghanistan War Veterans."

43. "Illinois Senate Debate," CSPAN, October 26, 2004, https://www.c-span.org /video/?184143-1/illinois-senate-debate#.

44. "Part 1: CNN/YouTube Democratic Presidential Debate Transcript," CNN, July 24, 2007, https://www.cnn.com/2007/POLITICS/07/23/debate.transcript/index.html.

45. Josh Gerstein, "Obama Says He's Evolving on Gay Marriage," *Politico*, October 27, 2010, https://www.politico.com/blogs/under-the-radar/2010/10/obama-says -hes-evolving-on-gay-marriage-030309.

46. Public Law 111-321, "Don't Ask, Don't Tell" Repeal Law of 2010, December 22, 2010.

47. White House, Office of the Press Secretary, "Statement by the President on Certification of Repeal of Don't Ask, Don't Tell," July 22, 2011, https:// obamawhitehouse.archives.gov/the-press-office/2011/07/22/statement-president -certification-repeal-dont-ask-dont-tell.

48. American Psychiatric Association, DSM-5.

49. Schaefer et al., *Assessing the Implications*.

50. Schaefer et al., *Assessing the Implications*.

51. Hembree et al., "Endocrine Treatment of Transsexual Persons"; Elders et al., *Report of the Transgender Military Service Commission*.

52. Gates, *How Many People*, 6; American Psychiatric Association, DSM-5, 454.

53. Daniel Greenberg, Maxine Najle, Natalie Jackson, Oyindamola Bola, and Robert P. Jones, "America's Growing Support for Transgender Rights," Public Religion Research Institute, June 11, 2019, https://www.prri.org/research/americas -growing-support-for-transgender-rights/.

54. U.S. Department of Defense, "Statement by Secretary of Defense Ash Carter on DOD Transgender Policy," press release, no. NR-272-15, July 13, 2015, http:// www.defense.gov/News/News-Releases/News-Release-View/Article/612778.

55. Schaefer et al., *Assessing the Implications*.

56. Terri Moon Cronk, "Transgender Service Members Can Now Serve Openly, Carter Announces," DOD News, June 30, 2016, https://www.defense.gov/Explore /News/Article/Article/822235/transgender-service-members-can-now-serve-openly -carter-announces/.

57. U.S. Department of Defense, "Transgender Service Member Policy Implementation Fact Sheet," 2016, https://dod.defense.gov/Portals/1/features/2016/0616 _policy/Transgender-Implementation-Fact-Sheet.pdf.

58. @realDonaldTrump: "After consultation with my Generals and military experts, please be advised that the United States Government will not accept or allow . . . Transgender individuals to serve in any capacity in the U.S. Military. Our military must be focused on decisive and overwhelming . . . Victory and cannot be burdened with the tremendous medical costs and disruption that transgender in the military would entail. Thank you" (Twitter, July 26, 2017).

59. Donald J. Trump, "Military Service by Transgender Individuals," August 25, 2017, *Federal Register* 82, no. 167 (August 30, 2017): 41319–20.

60. Trump, "Military Service by Transgender Individuals."

61. Trump, "Military Service by Transgender Individuals."

62. "Pentagon Sets Up Panel to Study Transgender Ban," Reuters, September 15, 2017, https://www.reuters.com/article/usa-military-transgender/pentagon-sets -up-panel-to-study-transgender-military-ban-idUSL2N1LW1UA.

63. "Fifty-Six Retired Generals and Admirals Warn That President Trump's Anti-Transgender Tweets, If Implemented, Would Degrade Military Readiness," Palm Center, August 1, 2017, https://www.palmcenter.org/fifty-six-retired-generals -admirals-warn-president-trumps-anti-transgender-tweets-implemented-degrade -military-readiness/.

64. "15 Attorneys General Oppose Trump Transgender Ban," Associated Press, October 17, 2017, https://apnews.com/article/27015036185a4d568dbb72a54ad6e4cf.

65. John Gerzema, "New Data Reveals Americans Disagree with the President's Ban on Transgender Military Service," Harris Poll, July 27–28, 2017, https:// theharrispoll.com/tweet-tweet-new-data-reveals-americans-disagree-with-the -presidents-ban-on-transgender-military-service-and-the-current-focus-of-his -agenda/.

66. U.S. Department of Defense, "Statement by Secretary of Defense Jim Mattis on Military Service by Transgender Individuals," August 29, 2017, https://www .defense.gov/Newsroom/Releases/Release/Article/1294351/statement-by-secretary -of-defense-jim-mattis-on-military-service-by-transgender/.

67. The four lawsuits are: *Doe v. Trump*; *Stockman v. Trump*; *Karnoski v. Trump*; and *Stone v. Trump*.

68. "Brief of Retired Military Officers and Former National Security Officials as Amici Curiae in Support of Plantiffs-Apellees," *Ryan Karnoski and State of Washington v. Donald Trump*, July 3, 2018, https://www.lambdalegal.org/sites/default/files /legal-docs/downloads/karnoski_wa_20180703-retired-military-officers-amicus -brief.pdf.

69. James Mattis, "Memorandum for the President, Subject: Military Service by Transgender Individuals," February 22, 2018, https://media.defense.gov/2018/Mar/23 /2001894037/-1/-1/0/MILITARY-SERVICE-BY-TRANSGENDER-INDIVIDUALS .PDF.

70. Tara Copp, "All 4 Service Chiefs on Record: No Harm to Units from Transgender Service," *Military Times*, April 24, 2018, https://www.militarytimes.com /news/your-military/2018/04/24/all-4-service-chiefs-on-record-no-harm-to-unit -from-transgender-service/.

71. Corey Dickstein, "Mattis Defends New Transgender Policy, Drawing Senator's Ire," *Stars and Stripes*, April 26, 2018, https://www.stripes.com/news/mattis -defends-new-transgender-policy-drawing-senator-s-ire-1.524134.

72. Marcia Coyle, "Transgender Troops Probe Conservative Groups' Contacts with Trump Administration," *Law*, April 9, 2018, https://www.law.com /nationallawjournal/2018/04/09/transgender-troops-probe-conservative-groups -contacts-with-trump-administration/?slreturn=20210112175557.

73. Dickstein, "Mattis Defends New Transgender Policy."

74. Department of Health and Human Services, Office of the Secretary, "Non-discrimination in Health Programs and Activities," *Federal Register* 81, no. 96 (May 18, 2016): 31384–85, https://www.govinfo.gov/content/pkg/FR-2016-05-18/pdf/2016-11458.pdf.

75. Health and Human Services Press Office, "HHS Finalizes Rule on Section 1557 Protecting Civil Rights in Healthcare, Restoring the Rule of Law, and Relieving Americans of Billions in Excessive Costs," June 12, 2020, https://www.hhs.gov/about/news/2020/06/12/hhs-finalizes-rule-section-1557-protecting-civil-rights-healthcare.html.

76. Gil Cisneros, "Press Release: Rep. Cisneros Urges DOD to Reverse Transgender Military Ban," *Orange County Breeze*, June 19, 2020, http://www.oc-breeze.com/2020/06/22/183795_rep-cisneros-urges-dod-to-reverse-transgender-military-ban.

77. Anna Bown, "Republicans, Democrats Have Starkly Different Views on Transgender Issues," Pew Research Center, November 8, 2017, https://www.pewresearch.org/fact-tank/2017/11/08/transgender-issues-divide-republicans-and-democrats/.

78. Quinnipiac University Poll, "U.S. Voters Trust Pelosi More than Trump on Big Issues," January 29, 2019, https://www.washingtonblade.com/content/files/2019/01/JAN-29-US-PRESBP.pdf.

79. Justin McCarthy, "In U.S., 71% Support Transgender People Serving in Military," Gallup, June 20, 2019, https://news.gallup.com/poll/258521/support-transgender-people-serving-military.aspx.

80. Chris Kahn, "Majority of Americans Support Transgender Military Service," Reuters, July 28, 2017, https://www.reuters.com/article/us-usa-military-transgender-poll/exclusive-majority-of-americans-support-transgender-military-service-idUSKBN1AD2BL.

81. Dunlap et al., "Support for Transgender Military Service."

82. Greenberg et al., "America's Growing Support."

83. Quinnipiac University Poll, "August 3, 2017—U.S. Voters Say 68–27% Let Transgender People Serve, Quinnipiac University National Poll Finds," August 3, 2017, https://poll.qu.edu/national/release-detail?ReleaseID=2477.

84. Quinnipiac University Poll, "U.S. Voters Trust Pelosi More than Trump."

85. White House, "Executive Order on Enabling All Qualified Americans to Serve Their Country in Uniform," January 25, 2021, https://www.whitehouse.gov/briefing-room/presidential-actions/2021/01/25/executive-order-on-enabling-all-qualified-americans-to-serve-their-country-in-uniform/.

86. White House, "Executive Order."

87. U.S. Department of Defense, "DOD Announces Policy Updates for Transgender Military Service," March 31, 2020, https://www.defense.gov/Newsroom/Releases/Release/Article/2557220/dod-announces-policy-updates-for-transgender-military-service/.

Bibliography

American Psychiatric Association. *Diagnostic and Statistical Manual of Mental Disorders* (DSM-5). Arlington VA: American Psychiatric Publishing, 2013.

Drew, Elizabeth. *On the Edge: The Clinton Presidency.* New York: Simon & Schuster, 1994.

Dunlap, Shannon, Ian W. Holloway, Chad E. Pickering, Michael Tzen, Jeremy T. Goldbach, and Carl Andrew Castro. "Support for Transgender Military Service from Active Duty United States Military Personnel." *Sexuality Research and Social Policy* 18 (2021): 137–43.

Elders, Joycelyn, Alan M. Steinman, George R. Browgn, Eli Coleman, and Thomas A. Kolditz. *Report of the Transgender Military Service Commission.* Santa Barbara CA: Palm Center, March 2014.

Gates, Gary J. *How Many People Are Lesbian, Gay, Bisexual, and Transgender?* Los Angeles: Williams Institute, University of California, Los Angeles, School of Law, April 2011.

Hembree, Wylie C., Peggy Cohen-Kettenis, Henriette A. Delemarre-van de Waal, Louis J. Gooren, Walter J. Meyer III, Norman P. Spack, Vin Tangpricha, and Victor M. Montori. "Endocrine Treatment of Transsexual Persons: An Endocrine Society Clinical Practice Guideline." *Journal of Clinical Endocrinology and Metabolism* 94, no. 9 (September 2009): 3132–54.

Menninger, William C. *Psychiatry in a Troubled World: Yesterday's War and Today's Challenge.* New York: Macmillan, 1948.

Moradi, Bonnie, and Laura Miller. "Attitudes of Iraq and Afghanistan War Veterans toward Gay and Lesbian Service Members." *Armed Forces and Society* 36, no. 3 (August 2009): 1–23.

RAND Corporation. *Sexual Orientation and U.S. Military Personnel Policy: An Update of RAND's 1993 Study.* Santa Monica CA: RAND, 2010.

Schaefer, Agnes Gereben, Radha Iyengar, Srikanth Kadiyala, Jennifer Kavanagh, Charles C. Engel, Kayla Williams, and Amii M. Kress. *Assessing the Implications of Allowing Transgender Personnel to Serve Openly.* Santa Monica CA: RAND, 2016.

Stephanopolous, George. *All Too Human.* Boston: Little, Brown, 1999.

U.S. Department of Defense. *Report of the Comprehensive Review of the Issues Associated with a Repeal of "Don't Ask, Don't Tell."* Washington DC: U.S. Department of Defense, November 30, 2010.

U.S. General Accounting Office. *Defense Force Management—DOD's Policy on Homosexuality.* GAO/NSIAD-92-98. Washington DC: General Accounting Office, June 12, 1992.

SEVEN

Formal Regulation, Cultural Enforcement

Managing Sexual Orientation and Gender Identity and Expression in the U.S. Military

JACQUELINE E. WHITT

In the United States, attitudes toward people whose sexual orientation, gender identity, or gender expression (SOGIE) is something other than straight, cisgender, and heterosexual have, until very recently, been negative—associated with perversion, deviance, mental illness, and criminality. Historically, those in the United States military who engaged in homosexual relationships or acts could face punishment, ostracism, or reprisal within or removal from the military. Not until 2011 could gay, lesbian, and bisexual people serve openly, and while many celebrate new norms and cultural acceptance, full integration is yet incomplete. For transgender people and those whose gender identity or expression does not fit neat binary norms, the situation has been, and remains, a problematic mix of formal regulation and informal control. Even so, gay, lesbian, bisexual, transgender, and queer (LGBTQ) people have always served in military organizations, and the occurrence of homosexual behaviors by military service members and in military contexts is unsurprising.

Sexual orientation and gender identity and expression have been explicitly managed through law, policy, and regulation, and changes in these policies and their enforcement reveal a complex relationship between the state, society, the military, and the bodies of individual military service members. But not all management has been formal. In the past, as well as today, norms, tradition, and culture within the military have all exerted tremendous pressure on military service members to conform to a relatively narrow set of expectations related to sexuality and gender. These expectations, deeply tied to binary gender norms about masculinity and femininity, have resulted in disparate enforcement and outcomes for men and women.

Given the relationship between the U.S. military and American society, four key factors have shaped the military's management of SOGIE. First, prevailing social, cultural, and political attitudes and expectations about SOGIE informed how the military approached these same topics. Second, the military is an arm of the state, so military policies and regulations related to SOGIE reflected the state's priorities and interests related to the same: the military was an institution through which a state's priorities were enacted. Third, military leaders argued that the military had institutional and organizational interests (to include good order and discipline, unit cohesion, readiness, and effectiveness) that compelled policy and regulation regarding SOGIE. Finally, there are the interests and actions of individual service members resisting or supporting the military's regulation of sexual orientation and gender identity.

Importantly, the military's regulation of sexual orientation and gender identity or expression was never absolute—there were always exceptions to how policies were enforced, and in many cases LGBTQ people thrived in military service, and their contributions were revered. Such exceptions to the dominant culture, law, and policy help underscore the complexity of managing sex and gender within a military context. The "management" of sexual orientation and identity in the military relied both on the regulation of "sex" and on mechanisms through which those regulations were bent, ignored, or reinterpreted in light of changing norms and arguments about military effectiveness. Military spaces also afforded LGBTQ people the ability to *manage* their own identities and experiences; they managed the institution as well.

The inclusion of people other than cisgender heterosexual men in the military prompted active management by military leaders and service members who wished to preserve the idea of the military as a heteronormative and masculine space. In the United States, such management only increased in importance in a gender-integrated military, which also coincided with the bureaucratization of the state, the professionalization of the military, and the development of a medical-scientific understanding of gender, sex, and sexuality. Military management of SOGIE is deeply tied to understandings of what it means to be a "man" or a "woman" in the military, and LGBTQ people have both challenged and altered what those ideas meant. Ultimately, many of the concerns about policies directed toward managing sexuality and gender identity and expression in the U.S. military point to fundamental and persistent unease with the role of *women* in the modern military, and the importance of maintaining binary definitions and roles that characterize the military (and combat, especially) as *masculine* space. Concerns, expressed through policy and reinforced through culture, have particularly centered around *effeminate* gay men, *butch* lesbians, and male to female transgender troops.

Laws, Policies, and Regulations: Managing Military SOGIE through Policy

That homosexuality and homosexual acts were, until recently, criminalized in both military and civilian contexts is essential to any discussion about the military's management of SOGIE.[1] Even without a formal ban on military service by LGBTQ people, military leaders could seek out, prosecute, and discharge people for expressing same-sex desires or for engaging in same-sex sexual behavior or other perceived sexual deviance. But how these policies were enacted and enforced reveals the difficulties military leaders had in managing questions related to SOGIE.

Before the late nineteenth century, the American military and its leaders lacked the mental construct of "sexuality" as a human characteristic (whether innate, environmental, or a result of choice). Thus, in this era, the management of SOGIE was predominantly about managing *behavior*. Sexual acts with a partner of the same sex were considered deviant, unnatural, and perverse, as were *all* nonprocreative sexual acts. But even then military leaders dealt with questions of (male) homosexual desire and behavior inconsistently. Two cases from the Revolutionary War era illustrate the tension between upholding moral and disciplinary codes and the concession that deviant behavior could be tolerated in circumstances where it was to the organization's benefit to do so. In some instances same-sex relationships were punished, as in the case of Lieutenant Frederick Gotthold Enslin, who was caught with a male private at Valley Forge in 1778, convicted of sodomy, and drummed out of the army.[2] In the case of Friedrich Wilhelm von Steuben, however, who aided General George Washington in drilling and professionalizing the Continental Army, suspicions about homosexual behavior and intimate same-sex relationships were politely ignored.[3]

In the first part of the twentieth century, the military's regulation of SOGIE was primarily related to regulating the sexual *behavior* of men in uniform. In the middle of the twentieth century, the shift to a formal ban on homosexuals meant moving from reactive management (i.e., policing *behavior*), to proactive management (i.e., policing *identity*) as the military determined that LGBTQ people were categorically unfit (morally and mentally) for military service.[4] Progressive-era activists and policymakers linked sexuality, morality, and physical health and sought to influence policy across a wide spectrum of American public life, including military service. Progressives worried that the military environment could be particularly corrupting, and they sought to control their bodies accordingly. In World War I, the War Department adopted policies advocated by a "social purity" movement not only to protect soldiers from the dangers of drinking and sex but also to shore up democratic values and institutions.[5]

Alongside this broader progressive movement, the U.S. military began formally to use law, policy, and regulation to actively manage men's sexual behaviors toward the end of World War I. The Articles of War first explicitly banned sodomy in 1916; the initial ban was related only to assault and was later expanded to include consensual sexual relations. The eventual inclusion of consensual same-sex relations in the regulation reflected an emerging belief that there were people for whom "deviant" sexual behaviors were not simply discrete acts, but were instead part of a broader sexual identity, and that those people were unlike those with "normal" sexual desires.[6]

In the wake of World War I, politicians and citizens worried, especially, that perverts and sexual deviants were weakening the moral and physical well-being of young men who enlisted in military service. The concern in port cities was especially high. In March 1919, in Newport, Rhode Island, the U.S. Navy undertook a covert operation, executed by volunteers or "decoys" who were to seduce or entice suspected service members into engaging in "acts of kissing, anal penetration, and/or receiving fellatio or hand masturbation," so the navy could rid the city of "cocksuckers and rectum receivers."[7] The operation resulted in more than twenty arrests, and ultimately both Secretary of the Navy Josephus Daniels and Under Secretary of the Navy Franklin D. Roosevelt received a congressional rebuke. The political concern, however, was with the investigation's methods, rather than its purpose.[8] Closely managing military bodies—to include the kind of sex they could engage in— was linked not only to protecting individuals' health and morality but also to protecting national security, as the purity of individual military bodies was taken to represent the purity of the national body politic.

As the initial estimates for personpower requirements for fighting World War II emerged, the military became more selective in screening men for service. At first the military services had that luxury. In October 1940 more than sixteen million men aged twenty-one to thirty-five registered for the draft. Psychiatrists, with newfound professional authority and trust, urged military leaders to exclude homosexuals from service. They also touted their ability to screen men for this particular characteristic and deemed them unfit for military service. These declarations required a host of policies, procedures, rules, and regulations for screening out and discharging homosexual men from military service.[9]

As always, though, theory deviated from reality. In practice personpower requirements in World War II were immense, and the systematic exclusion of any group presented problems. Gay men *did* enter the U.S. military during the war years—up to some 1.6 million (of about 16 million), if Alfred Kinsey's wartime surveys were accurate.[10] Gay and lesbian Americans who entered military service were, as Allan Berube argues, "in a double bind" and faced a significant dilemma as they "weighed the sacrifices and opportunities of military service against those of remaining civilians during a national emergency."[11]

By policy the military sought to exclude from military service those deemed "disruptive," and they used categories (often defined by psychiatrists) to characterize this unfitness for service. Psychiatrists categorized homosexuality, homosexual tendencies, cross-dressing, and other forms of sexual deviance alongside neurological, psychological, and other medical conditions, which warranted administrative separation or discharge from the U.S. military during the 1940s. Section VIII, "Inaptness or Undesirable Habits or Traits of Character," of Army Regulation 615-360 linked homosexuality and unfitness for military service in ways that influenced policies for decades. The November 26, 1942, revision included an instruction that "evidence of habits or traits of character [which included acting out behavioral disorders, alcoholism, and sexual perversions such as homosexuality] which serve to render his retention in the service undesirable" as sufficient reason for a (usually other than honorable) discharge.[12]

As homosexuality came to be understood as a category of identity, the military sought to manage and control it more strictly than when the prevailing belief was that homosexual acts were simply one type of deviant sexual behavior. Behaviors could be modified and categorized as separate from a holistic understanding of character and identity. But if homosexuality was a fundamental part of a person's identity, and homosexual acts were not incidental behaviors but an inextricable sign of someone's character and personhood, then there was no place for such people in the military. They were, by definition, disruptive to good order and discipline.

But these new regulations and psychiatric evaluations—even if they did not screen out homosexuals in practice (either because psychiatrists and officials did not want to do so, or because gay men and women understood they needed to hide their sexual preferences and activities from the screeners in order to gain entry into the military)—effectively introduced "to the military their idea that homosexuals were unfit to serve in the armed forces because they were mentally ill."[13] The connection between homosexuality and mental illness was the critical link in managing the military's treatment of lesbian, gay, and bisexual people between 1945 and 1993.

The twin postwar trends of state-building (i.e., the consolidation of power within the federal government over a host of issues previously thought to reside in the private sphere or with states) and the development of homosexuality as a category of identity best explain the formal ban on homosexuality in the U.S. military that held from 1949 to 1993.[14] The Department of Defense (DOD) adopted a clear policy statement, recommended by the DOD Personnel Policy Board: "Homosexual personnel, irrespective of sex, should not be permitted to serve in any branch of the Armed Forces in any capacity, and prompt separation of known homosexuals from the Armed Forces is mandatory."[15] The Uniform Code of Military Justice (which replaced the Articles of War) in 1951 criminalized sodomy in Article 125, now separated out and specified, rather than in a longer list of offenses: "Any person subject to this chapter who engages in unnatural carnal copulation with another person of the same or opposite sex or with an animal is guilty of sodomy." Service members who engaged in homosexual sex could also be prosecuted under Articles 133 and 134, which prohibited "conduct unbecoming an officer and gentleman" and offenses that undermine good order and discipline or that "bring discredit upon the armed forces" respectively.[16]

From 1947 to 1950, as the wartime army drew down, the rate of discharge for homosexuality was three times higher than it had been during the war. When the military needed fewer people to fill its ranks, it discharged members for infractions or deviations that could have, in wartime, been overlooked. This pattern repeated itself throughout the second half of the twentieth century. The rate remained relatively constant throughout the 1950s, except for a sharp decline in discharges in the navy during the Korean War.[17] Yet the execution of the policy to exclude homosexuals from military service required the judgment of many, especially recruiters, medical professionals, and commanders. These people in positions of authority applied discretion in individual cases, even as the institution doubled down on the rhetoric that defined homosexuality as (morally) incompatible with military service.

Between the 1950s and the 1990s, military policy remained consistent, but social and cultural values changed as LGBTQ people gained visibility and (slowly and unevenly) acceptance within American society. Homosexual men such as Tom Dooley were recognized for their honorable military service, even though he was forced out for his sexuality.[18] In 1973 the American Psychiatric Association removed "homosexuality" from its *Diagnostic and Statistical Manual* (DSM), which prompted significant sociocultural changes and represented evolving attitudes and beliefs among medical professionals.[19] In 1975 decorated Vietnam War veteran Leonard Matlovich was discharged from the air force for being gay; to stay in the service, he fought an extended legal battle, which was eventually settled in his favor, and was featured on the cover of *Time*.[20] The gay rights movement and the cultural zeitgeist of the 1970s seemed as if they might compel civilian leaders to push for a change in military policy. The military resisted mightily.

In 1981, in response to the challenge of the 1970s, the DOD pushed back. A revised DOD directive regarding enlisted administrative separations stated unequivocally, "Homosexuality is incompatible with military service." The presence of homosexuals (or people who engaged in homosexual behavior) "seriously impairs the accomplishment of the military mission." The directive laid out reasons designed to withstand a legal challenge: "The presence of such members adversely affects the ability of the armed forces to maintain discipline, good order, and morale; to foster mutual trust . . . ; to ensure the integrity of the system of rank and command; to facilitate assignment and worldwide deployment of service members who frequently must live and work in close conditions affording minimal privacy; to recruit and retain members of the armed forces; to maintain the public acceptability of military service; and to prevent breaches of security."[21] Over time the arguments against military service by gays, lesbians, and bisexuals moved from claiming that such individuals were psychologically and morally unfit to focusing on issues of good order and discipline, unit cohesion, readiness, and effectiveness.[22] These justifications clearly echoed the arguments made in earlier decades about racial integration in the military.[23]

From 1994 to 2011, the formal ban on homosexuals' military service remained, but the policy was enforced differently under the legislation popularly known as Don't Ask, Don't Tell (DADT).[24] During the 1992 presidential campaign, Democratic candidate Bill Clinton promised to end the military's ban on gay and lesbian service members. The outcry from senior military officials and other influential political groups, including conservative evangelical Christians, was swift and vocal. When Clinton took office, DADT emerged as an apparent compromise, one that almost everyone hated, and service members who were separated under the policy continue to seek legal redress, albeit unsuccessfully.

The implementation of the DADT policy varied widely and reveals the complexity of managing SOGIE in the U.S. military. Individual service members, commanders, colleagues, confidants, family members, and others all had to make potentially fraught decisions about whether or how to approach questions of sexual orientation, personal identity, ethics, medical care, and family life. In a military culture where the nuclear family was highly valued, and spouses provided untold amounts of unpaid labor and emotional support, asking soldiers to conceal their sexuality and their most intimate personal relationships had clear consequences for career advancement, mentoring, and mental health.[25]

Between 1994 and 2010, the Servicemembers Legal Defense Network estimates that more than 13,000 service members were discharged under DADT. From 1994 to 2001, the rates of discharge were steady, if slowly rising, to just over 1,200 in 2001; the number of DADT-related discharges decreased after 2001, when the U.S. military increased its operational tempo with routine deployments to Afghanistan and Iraq. In relative terms these numbers were miniscule—representing less than one-tenth of one percent of the active duty force (the percentage would be even smaller if guard and reserve components were included in the calculation).[26] Still, the effect was chilling.

Over time social attitudes continued to liberalize, and the U.S. wars related to the so-called global war on terror, especially in Iraq and Afghanistan, again thrust military effectiveness (rather than personal characteristics) in the rhetorical spotlight. Around the world many modernized militaries in developed, Western countries allowed for open service in the military by lesbian, gay, and bisexual (LGB) people. Case law regarding sexual orientation also began to shift in favor of LGB people and against institutions with policies of exclusion or discrimination. In October 2010 a federal judge, Virginia Phillips, ordered the military to suspend and discontinue investigations under DADT. This case and the appeals process emerged as Congress began to draft legislation to repeal the 1993 law. The repeal effort began with an amendment to the 2011 National Defense Authorization Act, but failed by filibuster in the Senate. Senators Joe Lieberman and Susan Collins then introduced the DADT Repeal Act of 2010, which was signed into law in December of that year, and would take effect on September 20, 2011.

The current narrative is that the change was politically contentious, but that, when it was time to execute the policy, the inclusion of openly LGBTQ military service members was a nonevent and caused few noticeable effects on readiness or cohesion (as was the conservative fear). It was a policy that ended not with a bang, but a whimper.[27] This story deserves to be complicated by a careful examination of the experiences of LGB service members since the end of DADT. LGBTQ service members have continued to face discrimination and ostracism and have struggled to access culturally competent healthcare, counseling services, and religious support.[28] In addition to conducting oral history interviews of LGBTQ veterans and service members, historians should also mine the archives and media records and remember their training to work in the silences.

For transgender and intersex people, the story has been more complex, and at the time of this essay's writing, their status within the military is still unresolved as legal, political, and regulatory battles continue. Fundamental questions about the eligibility of transgender people to serve in the U.S. military and what medical care they must be provided remain open, and the military continues to use a binary gender construct to shape many of its regulations. In the way that policies sometimes do, the military's regulation of SOGIE has in some ways come full circle, focusing now on behaviors rather than identity.

Culture, Narratives, and Norms: Informal Means of Managing SOGIE

When it comes to managing sexuality, sexual orientation, and gender identity, culture is just as (if not more) important as policy in shaping norms, expectations, and behaviors. Institutions can manage sex through informal mechanisms, peer pressure, and organizational culture just as surely as they can through policy. Cultural considerations can be more persistent and resistant to change and thus offer leaders and organizations ways to reinforce traditional notions of sexuality and gender identity even in the face of changing policies.

While the formal policies on homosexuality in the twentieth century primarily focused on regulating, controlling, and managing the sexual behaviors and orientation of gay men, as women entered military service in larger numbers these rules and regulations expanded to include women and, in many cases, affected them disproportionately. Lesbians were particularly vulnerable to discharge from the military in the second half of the twentieth century, and the investigations into their sexual orientation and behaviors were more complicated than those for men. Beginning in World War II, investigations into women's sexuality often revolved around their performance of gender—that is, women who were "mannish" or who associated with "mannish" women, or who were simply close to other women, might for no other reason be identified as having lesbian tendencies.[29] The disparate impact of the same law on gay versus lesbian service members highlights the fraught relationship between sexuality and gender identity and expression for military organizations.

These gendered differences in enforcement revealed the more difficult problem of defining femininity vis-à-vis military service in light of the overwhelming American concern about controlling women's sexuality and sexual behavior. Lesbian, bisexual, and straight women had to navigate a host of contradictory norms, expectations, and traditions related to their appearance, perceived sexual availability, and private sexual desires. Ultimately women were discharged under regulations forbidding homosexual behaviors, relationships, or tendencies at much higher rates than men— for most of the period covered by DADT, women accounted for about 30 percent of DADT-related discharges, while making up only about 15 percent of the military force.[30] Many women believed that military regulations and cultural expectations left them with three choices. Mickiela Montoya, who served in the army in the 2000s, put it this way: "There are only three things the guys let you be if you're a girl in the military—a bitch, a ho, or a dyke."[31] None of the available choices were particularly appealing.

One set of stories serves to define the military and war as masculine space, the province of (cisgender, heterosexual) men, where women are excluded outright or decidedly out of place. The idea that military training, service, and combat is masculine territory that transforms boys into men is a pervasive one. Military organizations and leaders reinforce this notion, as do military memoirs, military literature, and other cultural referents. During the Cold War, the U.S. Army used slogans including "Join the Army, Be a Man" and "The Army Will Make a Man Out of You."[32] Until 1976 one of the U.S. Marine Corps's official slogans was "We're Looking for a Few Good Men." By associating military service with mature masculinity, these official and unofficial messages signaled that the military is the domain of men.

But the gendered messages contained in recruiting materials and wartime posters or other advertising have never been simple—what, after all, did it mean to "be a man"? Katherine Jellison argues that World War II–era poster art "encouraging young men to serve in the military, war plant, or farm field presented hyper-masculinized images of the male body that were meant to represent not only the strength, power, and resolve of American men but of the American nation itself."[33] In wartime posters and other materials, notions of masculinity were deeply intertwined with notions about sexuality, but in queerer ways than might be traditionally imagined. Recruiting posters, for example, emphasized a variety of masculine ideals, mixing the martial masculine with the (homo)erotic: muscular shirtless men, lithe young men in tight uniforms, phallic weapons and ammunition, depictions of close same-sex relationships.[34]

During the recruiting crisis of the 1990s, when all of the services save the Marine Corps failed to meet their goals, observers wondered aloud whether the military, by integrating women and moving away from its core warfighting functions, "had undercut its warfighting ethos and abilities and become too soft to attract young men." Faltering recruiting—failing to attract America's young men to military service—was also linked to skepticism about American combat effectiveness. If the military was insufficiently masculine, could it fight and win the nation's wars? These concerns continued into the early 2000s, and prominent analysts, even those who supported women's service in the military, suggested that the military would be well served by promoting "military service as a rite of passage to manhood." Other more vocal opponents suggested that young men would "flock to an all-male military."[35]

Defining war, combat, and the military as masculine spaces also had significant implications for the way the military set expectations for and managed (especially male) sexuality. Masculinity and heterosexuality were linked to define proper and normative manhood. But the reality of military life was often less clear-cut, as men formed close relationships with each other in the barracks and in combat. Another set of tropes and narratives regarding homosocial and homosexual relationships between men created some ambiguity about acceptable behaviors in this masculine space.

Officially, homosexual relationships and sexual acts were forbidden, deemed to threaten combat readiness, to reduce social cohesion, or to feminize the force, thus rendering it ineffective. Historically, the line between homosocial bonds and homoerotic behavior was a thin one. In the Sacred Band of Thebes, a Greek formation in which 150 pairs of male lovers formed an elite military unit, homosexual love was thought to strengthen, not degrade, effectiveness. Within modern contexts some traditions enabled same-sex encounters or bending of gender norms by doing so within tightly constructed boundaries. For example, cross-dressing for entertainment (see one marine unit's spoof of Carly Rae Jepson's "Call Me Maybe" music video) and initiation ceremonies, such as the naval tradition of "Crossing the Line," offered opportunities for sanctioned gender-transgressive behavior.[36] Under DADT discharge could be avoided if an instance of homosexual conduct was determined to be a "departure from the member's usual and customary behavior."[37] This provision was known colloquially as the "queen-for-a-day" rule.

But alongside these narratives of homosocial brotherhood, homoerotic love, and homosexual behaviors exist overwhelming examples where military culture associates homosexuality and effeminacy with weakness and unmilitary character. The words "pussy," "dyke," "bitch," "girl," "fairy," and "faggot" are intended as insults and hurled at recruits, used to describe enemies, and littered throughout marching cadences and soldiers' vernacular.

Because historically girls and women have not participated as soldiers in war, disguising oneself as a woman is a common trope for *avoiding* military service. In the contemporary cultural canon, the question of cross-dressing as a way to avoid military service became a running gag and storyline in the long-running sitcom

M*A*S*H. From his initial appearance in the first season, Corporal Maxwell Klinger dresses in women's clothing in an attempt to secure a Section 8 discharge. But even in a show that routinely flouts military culture and signals mildly subversive messages, as Klinger takes on more responsibility, his maturation is reflected in the fact that he stops cross-dressing and angling for a Section 8 discharge, confirming both his masculinity and value to the unit.

This trope raises questions about how women choose to perform their gender and femininity in the context of their military service. When women serve as soldiers, sailors, airmen, and marines, what should they look like? How should uniforms be designed for women? To what extent would a "gender-neutral" uniform be possible or desirable? Should uniforms elide or accentuate difference? How should military women dress when they are off duty? How should they wear their hair? Should they wear makeup? Finding the right balance was (and is) difficult. In the 1940s the War Department's Bureau of Public Relations worked to reassure the public that women who joined the Women's Army Auxiliary Corps would be neither "Amazons rushing into battle" nor "butterflies fluttering free."[38] These issues persist today, with debates about uniforms, hairstyles, and physical fitness standards at the fore.[39] Race and ethnicity complicate these questions even further, especially with regard to grooming standards (i.e., policies about hair and hairstyles) and uniform fit. In the late 2010s, all of the services considered redesigning some or all pieces of women's uniforms, and these moves were hotly contested and fiercely debated.

Both popular culture and real-world examples demonstrate some of these tensions and highlight how we understand the performance of gender within the military. In film one might look to Lieutenant Jordan O'Neil in *GI Jane* (1997). O'Neil is selected as the first woman to attend an elite navy training course. The (female) senator behind the back-room deal selects O'Neil because she is the most traditionally feminine of the candidates. As O'Neil begins her training, her long hair and her curvy body are obstacles. But as she navigates the training, her physical transformation is marked. She shaves her head. Her muscles become pronounced. She stops having her period. She moves in with the men. And in the final training exercise, when she is being hazed by the movie's antagonist, she gains the unyielding support of her classmates as she screams, "Suck my dick." The transformation from feminine to masculine is crystal clear. But the transformation is costly. O'Neil is accused of being a lesbian because of her friendship with a female physician. Her husband distances himself from her success. The senator betrays her. O'Neil eventually succeeds, but it would be a stretch to call the film's ending a happy one.

In the real world, one might compare the "before and after" images of the first women to successfully complete Ranger School— Kristen Griest, Shaye Haver, and Lisa Jaster—that accompanied much of the media coverage of their accomplishments. In the "before" picture, Griest and Haver were usually shown as West Point cadets, dressed in the formal dress gray uniform and with long hair and conventionally feminine features. In the "after" picture, they sported shaved heads and were dressed in combat utilities, their bodies virtually indistinguishable from their male classmates. Jaster was older (a major) when she graduated, and her status as a mother was frequently highlighted. The physical transformation was important, as was the definition of these women as *women*.

If women's service, as women, has been suspect, stories of women disguising their gender to pass as men in order to serve are more celebrated, and they also reveal important ways in which both policy and culture serve to manage gender identity and expression. The ubiquity of stories of women dressing as men to serve in the military suggests this type of gender-bending expression is both more common and more culturally acceptable. Joan of Arc, Deborah Sampson, Cathy Williams (who enlisted in the U.S. Army as William Cathay) are hailed as military heroes and examples of women overcoming social and cultural expectations to serve in the military honorably and well.[40]

In all of these cases, cultural pressures, norms, and expectations reinforce the idea that gender expression is a central feature of military identity. The construction of military masculinity—and the selective adoption of traditionally feminine traits as a contrast to the dominant culture—is important not only for men. Aaron Belkin has persuasively argued in *Bring Me Men* that women can also access authority granted by the performance of military masculinity "on the basis of their relationship to the armed forces or to military ideas."[41] Claiming this authority has been particularly important for a number of women veterans who are seeking political office, often running against older white male incumbents with little or no record of military service.

In the age of social media, where virality is key to gaining name recognition and campaign donations, Mary Jennings "MJ" Hegar, Amy McGrath, and Kim Olson have produced viral campaign videos that emphasize their military and combat service and their identity as women. They show pictures of themselves in uniform and face the camera in bomber jackets; they talk about combat deployments and bombing the Taliban; they tell potential voters that they'll fight for them, just as they fought to open up opportunities for women in the military.[42]

For these women, however, the performance of military masculinity must be carefully balanced with the performance of traditional femininity. Hegar's video also shows her at home with her family, with a children's toy helicopter juxtaposed with the door of the helicopter she flew in combat. Olson notes that her call sign was "JETMOM," and the pictures that accompany her talk prominently show her family. McGrath speaks about her mother, a polio survivor who graduated from medical school, and about her children. Belkin reminds us that "women can exploit and embody masculinity, but . . . in the minds of most scholars and most Americans, the *ideal* of military masculinity has been predicated on a rejection of the unmasculine."[43] Women in the public eye can rarely, if ever, fully reject the unmasculine.

For men—regardless of their sexual orientation—military service has provided space and experiences that defined and cemented their masculine identity. There has not been a singular or monolithic military masculinity, but the idea that military service could make someone a man has been persistent and pervasive. For women who join the military, the coming-of-age narrative is more problematic. Army veteran and author Kayla Williams has poignantly said, "No woman joins the military to become a man," and she asserts that, as a result, women veterans who write about their military experiences do not always fit neatly within the canon.[44] There is no parallel construction about war, combat, or military service turning "girls" into women.

Rather than their gender identity and expression being normatively connected to their identity as a soldier, sailor, airman (and it is always air*man*), marine, or guardian, women's gender identity and expression could be seen in direct competition with their military identity. Recruiting materials and training materials emphasize that you could be a "soldier" and a "lady." Imagine the same thing being told to men: it's almost impossible because, culturally, "soldier" is coded as masculine.

Conclusion: Centering LGBTQ Voices

While the U.S. military and its leaders have sought to manage issues surrounding sexual orientation and gender identity and expression in order to maintain "good order and discipline" and to reinforce the idea of the military as a masculine space, we also know that LGBTQ individuals have served (and continue to serve) in the U.S. military, even in the face of laws, regulations, and cultures that have been specifically exclusionary. Thus, we must also ask how the experiences of LGBTQ people can inform our understanding of both policy and culture: How have LGBTQ people experienced the management of their sexuality or gender identity or expression? How have they resisted or acquiesced to such management? How has the open presence of LGBTQ service members changed military culture, especially when compared to past instances of explicit exclusion? The willingness of LGBTQ people to speak and write about their experiences in the military with scholars and policymakers, even when doing so could endanger their careers and even their personal safety, is a testament to the fact that management is not a one-way relationship, and their voices have created a rich archive for historians.[45]

When we center the voices of LGBTQ people, even the idea of military leaders "managing" sexual orientation and gender identity and expression is problematic. It highlights the fundamental tension between acknowledging that LGBTQ people have been and are serving in uniform, and the desire to control and subordinate military bodies, including how sex, sexuality, and gender are enacted by those bodies. While military leaders have sought to manage LGBTQ people within their ranks—balancing moralistic antigay arguments with a pragmatic need to use military manpower most efficiently—LGBTQ people also exercised agency. They joined for a variety of reasons, interpreted their military service differently, and created space for themselves in an often-hostile environment. LGBTQ people *managed* their military experiences and identities as well.

The study of LGBTQ and SOGIE history within the context of the U.S. military is inseparable from American political history and the history of the gay rights movement. Academics, policymakers, and activists continue to be involved in legal and policy battles about transgender military service. The debates are ongoing, and the highly politicized, historical questions about these topics coalesce at a history-policy-advocacy nexus. Organizations such as the Palm Center, the Modern Military Association of America (which merged with OutServe-SLDN), the National Center for Transgender Equality (NCTE), the Intersex Society of North America, the National LGBTQ Task Force, and the Council for Global Equality are involved in producing research, advising on matters of policy, and advocating for broader inclusion of LGBTQ individuals throughout society and public institutions, including the U.S. military. This history-policy-advocacy nexus is important because it informs current historical work as scholars cover the span of American military history to explore issues related to sexuality, sexual orientation, and gender identity and expression.

The attempt to manage homosexual behavior, sexual orientation, gender identity, and gender expression has been a constant feature of military organizations. In the United States, this management has been both formal and informal; it has involved both regulation and resistance; and it has changed over time as social values have changed. Importantly, the issues of sexual orientation and gender identity and expression have been intimately linked. It is impossible to understand the military's conception of and response to homosexuality without also delving into how the military (and its members) understand what it means to be a man or a woman.

The U.S. military's attempts to manage SOGIE demonstrate that military masculinities, to borrow Belkin's phrase, are fundamentally related to power, authority, and authenticity. The complex construction of military masculinities demands that military personnel take on both masculine and unmasculine roles.[46] Finally, we see policy and culture regarding the management of SOGIE within the military as tied to the maintenance of patriarchy—the power of men—despite a rhetorical commitment to diversity. One must think only so far as poorly designed and delivered Sexual Harassment/Assault Response and Prevention (SHARP) training or the centrality of sex and gender in scandals such as Tailhook or Marines United to understand that the U.S. military manages SOGIE through both official and unofficial means, often with conflicting aims and mixed results.

While people who are not cisgender straight men have been integrated into the contemporary American military, it does not follow that the *management* of SOGIE has disappeared. The management simply looks different; it selects different targets and sets new priorities. The ground is shifting, not stable, both in terms of policy and culture.

Notes

1. The landmark Supreme Court case *Lawrence v. Texas* (539 U.S. 558 [2003]) legalized consensual same-sex relationships nationwide in the United States and invalidated sodomy laws still on the books in thirteen states.

2. Frank, *Unfriendly Fire*, 1.

3. See Benemann, *Male-Male Intimacy in Early America*, 93–109; and Shilts, *Conduct Unbecoming*, 3.

4. For a scholarly examination of the historical construction of sex and gender as categories, see Laqueur, *Making Sex*; on the shift from policing behavior to policing identity, see Canaday, *Straight State*, 59.

5. Reilly, "Perilous Venture for Democracy"; see also Bristow, *Making Men Moral*.

6. Frank, *Unfriendly Fire*, 5.

7. Zane, "I Did It for the Uplift," 279.

8. Zane, "I Did It for the Uplift," 282.

9. Berube, *Coming Out under Fire*, 1–2, 12–21.

10. Berube, *Coming Out under Fire*, 3.

11. Berube, *Coming Out under Fire*, 4.

12. Bernucci, "Forensic Military Psychiatry," 487.

13. Berube, *Coming Out under Fire*, 33.

14. Canaday, *Straight State*, 3–4. On the Lavender Scare, which sought to rid the federal government of homosexual employees, see Johnson, *Lavender Scare*; and Shibusawa, "Lavender Scare and Empire."

15. U.S. Department of Defense policy quoted in Berube, *Coming Out under Fire*, 261.

16. Uniform Code of Military Justice, Stat. 109, 10 U.S.C. §§ 801–946 (May 1950). The prohibition against consensual sodomy was lifted with the National Defense Authorization Act of 2014, which was signed into law by President Barack Obama.

17. Berube, *Coming Out under Fire*, 262.

18. Shilts, *Conduct Unbecoming*, 25–26.

19. Drescher, "Out of DSM."

20. Estes, *Ask and Tell*, 185–87.

21. U.S. Department of Defense Directive 1332.14 (1981).

22. Herek, "Why Tell If You're Not Asked?" in Herek et al., *Out in Force*, 197–225; MacCoun, "Sexual Orientation and Military Cohesion," in Herek et al., *Out in Force*, 157–76; and Kier, "Homosexuals in the U.S. Military."

23. Bailey, "Introduction," in Bristol and Stur, *Integrating the U.S. Military*, 1–2; Whitt and Perazzo, "Military as Social Experiment," 9; Frank, *Conduct Unbecoming*, 26–27, 60–63.

24. Section 654 of Title 10 of the U.S. Code "Policy Concerning Homosexuality in the Armed Forces."

25. See first-person accounts collected in Seefried, *Our Time*.

26. Lehring, *Officially Gay*, 139–40; Bender, "Continued Discharges"; Burrelli, "Don't Ask, Don't Tell." It is unknown how many people may have left the military voluntarily during the years DADT was in place.

27. Charles McLean and Peter Singer suggested this would be the predominant narrative based on the experience of LGB integration in allied militaries. McLean and Singer, "Don't Make a Big Deal of Ending Don't Ask Don't Tell: Lessons from U.S. Military Allies on Allowing Homosexuals to Serve," Brookings Institute, May 27, 2010, https://www.brookings.edu/opinions/dont-make-a-big-deal-of-ending-dont-ask-dont-tell-lessons-from-u-s-military-allies-on-allowing-homosexuals-to-serve/. For other representative commentary from both sides of the political spectrum, see Jack Drescher, "Coming Out and Fitting In—The Post-'Don't Ask, Don't Tell' Era Begins," Fox News Opinion, September 20, 2011, https://www.foxnews.com/opinion/coming-out-and-fitting-in-the-post-dont-ask-dont-tell-era-begins; and Ian S. Thompson, "At DADT Repeal's One-Year Anniversary, Refusing to Turn Back the Clock," *Huffington Post*, September 19, 2012, https://www.huffpost.com/entry/at-dadt-repeals-one-year-anniversary-refusing-to-turn-back-the-clock_b_1894817.

28. Several studies contribute to a more complete understanding of the post-DADT military experience for LGBTQ service members. See, for example, Alford and Lee, "Toward Complete Inclusion"; Rich et al., "Don't Drop the Soap"; and Huffman and Schultz, *End of Don't Ask, Don't Tell*.

29. Wilson-Buford, *Policing Sex and Marriage*, 127; Canaday, *Straight State*, 177–213.

30. Under DADT, specifically, see Thom Shanker, "Don't Ask, Don't Tell Hits Women Much More," *New York Times*, June 23, 2008, https://www.nytimes.com/2008/06/23/washington/23pentagon.html; Gates, "Discharges"; on disparate impact before DADT, see Banner, "It's Not All Flowers and Daisies."

31. Montoya quoted in Benedict, *Lonely Soldier*, 167. See also Herbert, *Camouflage Isn't Only for Combat*; and Williams and Staub, *Love My Rifle More than You*.

32. Arkin and Dobrofsky, "Military Socialization and Masculinity," 155.

33. Jellison, "Get Your Farm in the Fight," 9.

34. Parkes, "'Men Working Together!'"

35. Brown, *Enlisting Masculinity*, 38–39.

36. On the participation in cultural memes such as this one, see Silvestri, "Mortars and Memes"; on Crossing the Line, see Hersh, "Crossing the Line."

37. Title 10 of the U.S. Code § 654(b) (1) (A).

38. Herbert, *Camouflage Isn't Only for Combat*, 3.

39. Enloe, "Constructing the American Woman Soldier"; Cohn, "How Can She Claim Equal Rights"; Burke, *Camp All-American*, 94–95.

40. Warner, *Joan of Arc*; Klass, *Soldier's Secret*; Tucker, *Cathy Williams*.

41. Belkin, *Bring Me Men*, 6.

42. Hegar, "Doors"; McGrath, "Told Me"; Olson, "Battles." Valerie Plame, a CIA operative whose identity was revealed in 2003, uses similar imagery and claims to martial masculinity in her campaign launch video, "Undercover."

43. Belkin, *Bring Me Men*, 6.

44. Bell, "Conversation with Kayla Williams," 75.

45. On experiences under DADT, see Estes, *Ask and Tell*. Allan Berube's *Coming Out under Fire* incorporates numerous stories from World War II–era service members. Randy Shilts interviewed more than one thousand people for his book *Conduct Unbecoming*. The Library of Congress's Veteran's History Project includes a collection of oral history interviews from LGBTQ veterans in "Speaking Out" and "Serving in Silence."

46. Belkin, *Bring Me Men*.

Bibliography

Alford, Brandon, and Shawna J. Lee. "Toward Complete Inclusion: Lesbian, Gay, Bisexual, and Transgender Military Service Members after Repeal of Don't Ask, Don't Tell." *Social Work* 61, no. 3 (2016): 257–65.

Arkin, William, and Lynne R. Dobrofsky. "Military Socialization and Masculinity." *Journal of Social Issues* 34, no. 1 (Winter 1978): 151–68.

Banner, Francine. "It's Not All Flowers and Daisies: Masculinity, Heteronormativity, and the Obscuring of Lesbian Identity in the Repeal of Don't Ask, Don't Tell." *Yale Journal of Law & Feminism* 24, no. 1 (2012): 61–117.

Belkin, Aaron. *Bring Me Men: Military Masculinity and the Benign Facade of American Empire, 1898–2001*. New York: Columbia University Press, 2012.

Bell, Jeri. "A Conversation with Kayla Williams." *O-Dark-Thirty* 3, no. 4 (Summer 2015): 75.

Benedict, Helen. *The Lonely Soldier: The Private War of Women*. Boston: Beacon, 2010.

Benemann, William. *Male-Male Intimacy in Early America: Beyond Romantic Friendships*. New York: Routledge, 2006.

Bernucci, Robert J. "Forensic Military Psychiatry." In *Neuropsychiatry in World War II: Zone of Interior*. Washington DC: Office of the Surgeon General, Department of the Army, 1966.

Berube, Allan. *Coming Out under Fire: The History of Gay Men and Women in World War II*. Chapel Hill: University of North Carolina Press, 1990.

Bristol, Douglas Walter, and Heather Marie Stur, eds. *Integrating the U.S. Military: Race, Gender, and Sexual Orientation since World War II*. Baltimore MD: Johns Hopkins University Press, 2017.

Bristow, Nancy K. *Making Men Moral: Social Engineering during the Great War*. New York: New York University Press, 1996.

Brown, Melissa T. *Enlisting Masculinity*. New York: Oxford University Press, 2012.

Burke, Carol. *Camp All-American, Hanoi Jane, and the High-and-Tight: Gender, Folklore, and Changing Military Culture*. Boston: Beacon, 2004.

Burrelli, David F. "'Don't Ask, Don't Tell': The Law and Military Policy on Same-Sex Behavior." Congressional Research Service, October 14, 2010.

Canaday, Margot. *The Straight State: Sexuality and Citizenship in Twentieth-Century America*. Princeton NJ: Princeton University Press, 2009.

Cohn, Carol. "'How Can She Claim Equal Rights When She Doesn't Have to Do as Many Push-Ups as I Do?': The Framing of Men's Opposition to Women's Equality in the Military." *Men and Masculinities* 3, no. 2 (2000): 131–51.

Drescher, Jack. "Out of DSM: Depathologizing Homosexuality." *Behavioral Sciences* 5, no. 4 (December 2015): 565–75.

Enloe, Cynthia H. "The Politics of Constructing the American Woman Soldier." In *Women Soldiers: Images and Realities*, 81–110. London: Palgrave Macmillan, 1994.

Estes, Steve. *Ask and Tell: Gay and Lesbian Veterans Speak Out*. Chapel Hill: University of North Carolina Press, 2007.

Frank, Nathaniel. *Unfriendly Fire: How the Gay Ban Undermines the Military and Weakens America*. New York: Thomas Dunne, 2009.

Gates, Gary. "Discharges under the Don't Ask/Don't Tell Policy: Women and Racial/Ethnic Minorities." Williams Institute, UCLA School of Law, September 2010.

Hegar, MJ. "Doors." YouTube, 3:28. June 20, 2018. https://www.youtube.com/watch?v=Zi6v4CYNSIQ.

Herbert, Melissa S. *Camouflage Isn't Only for Combat: Gender, Sexuality, and Women in the Military*. New York: New York University Press, 1998.

Herek, Gregory M., Jared B. Jobe, and Ralph M. Carney, eds. *Out in Force: Sexual Orientation and the Military*. Chicago: University of Chicago Press, 1996.

Hersh, Carie Little. "Crossing the Line: Sex, Power, Justice, and the U.S. Navy at the Equator." *Duke Journal of Gender, Law, and Policy* 9 (2002): 277–324.

Huffman, J. Ford, and Tammy Schultz, eds. *The End of Don't Ask, Don't Tell: The Impact in Studies and Personal Essays by Service Members and Veterans*. Quantico VA: Marine Corps University Press, 2012.

Jellison, Katherine. "Get Your Farm in the Fight: Farm Masculinity in World War II." Presidential address, June 8, 2017, printed in *Agricultural History* (2018): 5–20.

Johnson, David K. *The Lavender Scare: The Cold War Persecution of Gays and Lesbians in the Federal Government*. Chicago: University of Chicago Press, 2004.

Kier, Elizabeth. "Homosexuals in the U.S. Military: Open Integration and Combat Effectiveness." *International Security* 23, no. 2 (1998): 5–39.

Klass, Sheila Solomon. *Soldier's Secret: The Story of Deborah Sampson*. New York: Henry Holt, 2009.

Laqueur, Thomas. *Making Sex: Body and Gender from the Greeks to Freud*. Cambridge MA: Harvard University Press, 1990.

Lehring, Gary L. *Officially Gay: The Political Construction of Sexuality by the U.S. Military*. Philadelphia: Temple University Press, 2003.

McGrath, Amy. "Told Me." YouTube, 2:01. August 1, 2017. https://www.youtube.com/watch?v=CcjG2fK7kNk.

Olson, Kim. "Battles." YouTube, 3:12. June 18, 2018. https://www.youtube.com/watch?v=OLtxLWJgHZo.

Parkes, Chris. "'Men Working Together!': The Queer Masculinity of World War Two Propaganda." *Notches*, March 5, 2019. http://notchesblog.com/2019/03/05/men-working-together-the-queer-masculinity-of-world-war-two-propaganda.

Plame, Valerie. "Undercover." YouTube, 1:21. September 9, 2019. https://www.youtube.com/watch?v=ICW-dGD1M18.

Reilly, Kimberley A. "'A Perilous Venture for Democracy': Soldiers, Sexual Purity, and American Citizenship in the First World War." *Journal of the Gilded Age and Progressive Era* 13, no. 2 (April 2014): 223–55.

Rich, Craig, Julie Kalil Schutten, and Richard A. Rogers. "'Don't Drop the Soap': Organizing Sexualities in the Repeal of the U.S. Military's 'Don't Ask, Don't Tell' Policy." *Communication Monographs* 79, no. 3 (2012): 269–91.

Seefried, Josh. *Our Time: Breaking the Silence of "Don't Ask, Don't Tell."* New York: Penguin, 2011.

Shibusawa, Naoko. "The Lavender Scare and Empire: Rethinking Cold War Anti-Gay Politics." *Diplomatic History* 36 (2012): 723–52.

Shilts, Randy. *Conduct Unbecoming: Gays and Lesbians in the U.S. Military*. New York: Ballantine, 1994.

Silvestri, Lisa. "Mortars and Memes: Participating in Pop Culture from a War Zone." *Media, War & Conflict* 9, no. 1 (April 2016): 27–42.

Tucker, Philip Thomas. *Cathy Williams: From Slave to Female Buffalo Soldier*. Mechanicsburg PA: Stackpole, 2002.

Warner, Marina. *Joan of Arc: The Image of Female Heroism*. Berkeley: University of California Press, 1999.

Whitt, Jacqueline E., and Elizabeth Perazzo. "The Military as Social Experiment: Challenging a Trope." *Parameters* (Summer 2018): 5–12.

Williams, Kayla, and Michael Staub. *Love My Rifle More than You: Young and Female in the U.S. Army*. New York: W. W. Norton, 2006.

Wilson-Buford, Kellie. *Policing Sex and Marriage in the American Military: The Court-Martial and the Construction of Gender and Sexual Deviance, 1950–2000*. Lincoln: University of Nebraska Press, 2018.

Zane, Sherry. "I Did It for the Uplift of Humanity and the Navy: Same-Sex Acts and the Origins of the National Security State, 1919–1921." *New England Quarterly* 91, no. 2 (June 2018): 279–306.

PART 4

Sexual Assault and Prevention

EIGHT

Problematic Policies and Far-Reaching Consequences

Historicizing Sexual Violence in the U.S. Military

KELLIE WILSON-BUFORD

Policing sexual violence has been a central component of the efforts of the U.S. military to manage the sexualities of its service members—and its national and global reputation—since the Revolutionary War. Long before rape and sexual assault became a national and international policy issue in the wake of the 1991 U.S. Navy Tailhook scandal, military officials struggled to define "sexual violence" and implement policies to prevent it. Part of this struggle was rooted in the military's lack of jurisdiction over servicemen's perpetration of capital crimes into the twentieth century. But even in circumstances where commanders had jurisdiction, the scarcity of official service policies on sexual assault from the Revolutionary War to the Cold War suggests that military leaders did not view sexual violence as an institutional problem in need of sustained and systematic intervention. Consequently, policies implemented before congressional adoption of the Uniform Code of Military Justice (UCMJ) in 1950 were reactive and situational rather than preemptive and systematically implemented.

Although the UCMJ granted the military jurisdiction over sexual crimes and streamlined definitions of sexual assault across all service branches, varying interpretations of what constituted consent and procedural due process undermined efforts to punish sexual predators during the Cold War. So, too, did gendered assumptions and definitions that informed the creation of law and policy and normalized male sexual violence by placing the burden of proof on sexual assault victims. The military was not exceptional in this regard, as many of its sexual violence policies and procedures drew from and often mirrored those in U.S. civil law.

Despite a plethora of policy changes, congressional studies, and scholarship aimed at military sexual violence reform in the past three decades, the problem of managing American military sexual violence is more important now than it has ever been. Mapping the military's historic policies and practices related to sexual violence is critical for contextualizing current policy debates and offering effective solutions. Though the challenges researchers face, given the sensitive nature of the subject and the paucity of sources, are daunting, this work has far-reaching implications for improving social justice and the future of military efforts to manage sexual violence.

This essay is divided into three sections. The first section traces the U.S. military's efforts to manage sexual violence from the Revolutionary War through World War II to illustrate how the absence of official policies and competing jurisdictional issues left commanders to manage this problem on their own. The growth of the military during and after World War II and the subsequent rise in reported incidents of sexual violence prompted the creation of military rape and sodomy statutes in 1950, in Articles 120 and 125 of the UCMJ. The second section analyzes some of the gendered assumptions, definitions, and precedents in military case law during the Cold War that have undermined efforts to effectively enforce Article 120 since the UCMJ's adoption. The third section addresses potential challenges researchers of military sexual violence face and suggests sources and directions for future scholarship.[1]

Evolution of Military Policy and Management of Sexual Violence, 1776–1945

Tracing the history of the words "rape" and "sodomy" and military efforts to manage these crimes illustrates how policies on sexual violence were, from the military's inception, reactive and often formed in response to servicemen's perpetration of sexual crimes. How did the army manage sexual violence in its formative years? Officially, it did not. In fact, the word "rape" did not appear in the Articles of War, the military's code of conduct, until 1874. Carnal knowledge, or the rape of a minor, did not appear in the military criminal code until 1950, and nonconsensual sodomy made its first appearance in the twentieth century. From the original Articles of War in 1775 until 1863, military courts lacked jurisdiction over capital crimes, including rape, statutory rape, and murder. Instead commanders were required to turn over servicemen accused of capital offenses against civilians for prosecution and punishment in accordance with local civilian laws. The 1776 Articles of War did not specifically identify rape or sodomy as an offense, but alluded to rape among other capital offenses.[2]

Despite the requirement that commanders turn over capital offenses committed by servicemen to local civil courts, records from the Revolutionary War through the American Civil War illustrate that trials by court-martial for capital offenses occurred, though with what degree of frequency is uncertain.[3] Some commanders created their own policies to manage troops' sexual violence. In the absence of any official policy criminalizing rape, for example, General George Washington issued a special order on New Year's Day 1777 to his Continental Army forbidding the "plundering of any person" in order to distinguish "brave Americans" from infamous British or Hessian ravagers: "It is expected that humanity and tenderness to women and children will distinguish brave Americans, contending for liberty, from infamous mercenary ravagers, whether British or Hessians."[4] Washington enforced this policy, at least once, by sentencing to death Thomas Brown of the Seventh Pennsylvania Regiment after he was twice convicted of rape.[5] Likewise, General Winfield Scott issued his own orders to manage troops' violence against citizens in Mexico during the Mexican-American War. In his General Order 20, issued in February 1847, Scott forbade a long list of criminal acts including the rape and murder of Mexican civilians by U.S. troops. Men who committed these crimes were subject to military tribunals, the historical precedents of modern-day military commissions.[6]

The early navy was governed by a different set of policies than the army and suffered from "a confused and almost unworkable tangle of contradictory documents that were its rules and regulations."[7] Realizing that leaving naval captains without the authority to try men at courts-martial led to uncontrolled mayhem, Congress enacted the Articles for the Better Government of the Navy in 1800, which granted captains court-martial jurisdiction over servicemen who, "when on shore, plunder, abuse, or maltreat any inhabitant, or injure his property in any way."[8] Nonconsensual sexual crimes would likely have been included among the umbrella terms "plunder, abuse, or maltreat." The absence of sodomy from the navy criminal code was especially surprising given that this new code was modeled after the Royal Navy's Articles of War, which had condemned sodomy as a capital crime worthy of the death sentence since the 1660s.[9] Despite the absence of official policy criminalizing sodomy in the early navy, however, captains occasionally court-martialed sailors for this most "unnatural" and "detestable" crime, although it is unknown whether these instances were nonconsensual.[10] Similar to their army counterparts who created policies to address sexual violence as it occurred, some navy commanders attempted to regulate their men's sexual transgressions on a case by case basis, though "the absence of clear and well-ordered rules . . . meant that actual regulation at sea was the product of individual personalities and the caprice of commanders."[11]

The realities of the American Civil War prompted a change in the policy requiring commanders to turn over capital offense cases to civilian courts. According to Colonel William Winthrop, "The lack of functioning civilian courts and the prohibition against the use of courts-martial for civilian capital offenses meant that occupied territories did not have a forum to prosecute soldiers accused of rape and other civilian capital crimes."[12] Partly in response to Union soldiers' acts of sexual violence against southern women, Congress passed the National Forces Act in March 1863, giving commanders exclusive jurisdiction over soldiers accused of capital offenses in times of rebellion, insurrection, or war.[13] By the time this bill passed, "more than thirty Union soldiers had been court-martialed for varying crimes of sexual misconduct, twenty-four of whom were found guilty and two of whom were executed."[14] Nor did the army keep these prosecutions secret from the public. For instance, the army publicized the conviction of First Lieutenant George W. O'Malley of Company E, 115th Regiment Pennsylvania volunteers, for attempted rape and conduct unbecoming an officer and a gentleman. O'Malley was dishonorably dismissed, stripped of all pay and allowances, sentenced to hard labor for six years, and declared "forever incapable of holding any office of trust, honor or profit, under the United States."[15]

Periodicals of the times are scattered with descriptions of courts-martial for "conduct unbecoming" and behavior "prejudicial to good order and discipline," but the vague descriptions accompanying many of these charges leave us to wonder whether sexual misconduct was lumped under the umbrella term "conduct unbecoming." While the National Forces Act gave the military exclusive jurisdiction over capital offenses including arson, robbery, and murder, it neither mentioned nor defined rape or sodomy, nor did it grant commanders jurisdiction over capital crimes in times of peace.[16] If the Civil War army's court-martial system was, as historians E. Susan Barber and Charles F. Ritter argue, "not designed to deal with issues of sexual justice," the same is true of the army and navy's justice systems preceding the American Civil War.[17] This was partly the result of an absence of official policy acknowledging and defining rape, carnal knowledge, and sodomy, and partly because the existing Articles of War required commanders to turn troops accused of sexual crimes over to local civil jurisdictions.

The end of the Civil War ushered in an era of expanded command authority to manage sexual violence despite an absence of official policy defining rape. Not only did commanders sometimes continue to exercise prosecutorial authority over their own troops' sexual violence; some civilian leaders in the occupied South also authorized commanders to oversee the prosecution of rape and other crimes committed by civilians. In Florida, for example, Colonel John T. Sprague of the Seventh Infantry assumed jurisdiction over all "offences [*sic*] committed by the military forces" even though the war had ended. The acting general and provisional governor also authorized Sprague to oversee the prosecution of capital offenses including rape and murder committed by civilians in accordance with local laws. Assuring distressed civilians that "Colonel Sprague promises to give the hearty support of the military authorities to the civil law," civil authorities granted commanders peacetime jurisdiction over crimes of sexual violence committed by both troops and civilians.[18] But military policy was slow to catch up. Despite some commanders' efforts to manage troops' sexual violence in the absence of official policy from the Revolutionary War to the Reconstruction era, rape was not added to the Articles of War until 1874, and even then military jurisdiction only extended to capital crimes, including rape, in times of war, insurrection, or rebellion.[19]

Did the "Indian Wars" on the plains in the second half of the nineteenth century constitute a time of war, insurrection, or rebellion? One wonders if the sexual mutilation of Cheyenne women and children's bodies at the infamous Sand Creek Massacre in 1864 contributed to the eventual inclusion of rape in the Articles of War, though rape could hardly begin to describe the behavior of Colonel John M. Chivington's First and Third Colorado Cavalry Regiments. At a congressional investigation, men of the two regiments testified that the morning after the massacre, there was not a single dead body that had not been sexually mutilated. Corporal Amos C. Miksch testified to men "pull[ing] out the [dead] bodies of the squaws, pull[ing] them open in an indecent manner, and cut[ting] out the privates." Lieutenant James Connor also witnessed the bodies of women and children whose private parts had been cut out and exhibited on sticks, and he also "heard of numerous instances in which men had cut out the private parts of females and stretched them over the saddle-bows and wore them over their hats while riding in the ranks." Or perhaps rape was finally included in the 1874 Articles of War in part due to the "ghastly, unprintable disclosures" regarding "the stalking spectre of rape" that befell Nez Perce women at the hands of U.S. troops. Chief Joseph, leader of the Nez Perce, highlighted the savagery of General O. O. Howard's cavalry units when he asked, "Can the white soldiers tell me of one time when Indian women were taken prisoners and held three days and then released without being insulted?"[20]

Though the inclusion of rape (carnal knowledge and sodomy were still excluded) in the 1874 Articles of War marked a positive turning point in the military's acknowledgment that troops' sexual violence could no longer be ignored in official policy, the Articles of War did not define the crime, leaving commanders to interpret for themselves what constituted rape. In the absence of a definition, leaders typically borrowed the common law definition prevalent in most American jurisdictions at the time: "The unlawful carnal knowledge of a woman forcibly and against her will and consent."[21] This seems to have been Lieutenant Johnson's working definition of rape when he sent a cablegram to the *Atlanta Constitution* in 1898 publicizing atrocities committed by U.S. troops in Cuba. In what became known as the "Santiago Outrages," Lieutenant Johnson charged men of the Fifth Mississippi and Eighth Illinois Regiments with being "worse than the Spaniards . . . running wild, looting residences and stores and even going so far as to commit highway robbery, arson and rape." Foreshadowing a common practice of racialized scapegoating in the twentieth century military, some of the officers involved blamed "negro soldiers" who were recruited from the "slums of New Orleans" for the "insult[s] [to] defenseless women."[22] Though Colonel H. H. Sargent, commander of the Fifth Mississippi Regiment, assured the press that he would investigate and prosecute all soldiers involved in perpetrating these outrages, the extent to which he and other commanders in the Spanish Caribbean and the Philippines prosecuted rape crimes in the fledgling American empire needs more sustained scholarly attention.

The expansion of the U.S. military after the Spanish-American War highlighted the inadequacies of existing policies on sexual violence. For commanders overseeing occupations in Latin America and the Pacific between 1899 and America's entry into World War I, for example, the existing Articles of War did not authorize them to prosecute soldiers for sexual violence because this time frame did not technically constitute a time of war, insurrection, or rebellion. But some troops' abusive conduct toward civilians in the fledgling American empire began to undermine U.S. interests and plant seeds of anti-Americanism. In Latin America, for example, as historian Alan McPherson argues, "rape added an element of gendered terror" to U.S. Marine Corps occupations of Haiti, the Dominican Republic, and Nicaragua from 1912 to 1934, so much so that marines' "attitude of permissiveness, fed by the occupations' monopoly of force, bred widespread fear among occupied women" and generated hostile backlash from Dominican and Nicaraguan men. Rapes of Nicaraguan "margaritas" were apparently so common they "became a staple of the propaganda of Sandino and his defenders."[23] Rumors such as these, and the negative public response they received, likely played a role in Congress's decision in 1916 to expand the military's jurisdiction over troops' sexual crimes committed outside the territorial limits of the United States during peacetime.[24]

Surely this expanded jurisdiction would have been helpful for the commander of a marine private in Haiti who victimized fourteen-year-old Elanor Charles by catching her when she was walking with her mother, dragging her into the bushes, raping her, and inserting his penis into her mouth, or for the commander of a group of marines who demanded "obscene services from the women folks [in the Nicaraguan countryside] for which reason many of them ran away." Despite this evidence, McPherson notes that "Marine files on Nicaragua contain no evidence of rape," leading him to conclude that "rape appeared to be among the least punished offenses."[25] This seems to suggest that some commanders—in various occupations in Latin America at least—chose not to court-martial troops for crimes of sexual violence despite their expanded authority to do so.

Incidents like those experienced by Elanor Charles in Haiti likely prompted the inclusion of assault with intent to commit sodomy, which included oral and anal sex, in the 1916 Articles of War (consensual sodomy was added as a felony crime in 1920).[26] These additions and the surveillance apparatus they unleashed in the post–World War I era signaled a new phase in the military's management of both sexual violence and sexual perversion. As historian Margot Canaday illustrates, the criminalization of both nonconsensual and consensual sodomy "involved not merely a reactive but also a proactive and preemptive kind of policing" that necessitated the growth of "sophisticated screening and surveillance mechanisms."[27] But the Articles of War in 1916 and 1920 did not alter the substantive law on rape. Although the 1916 changes expanded the military's jurisdiction over all common law felonies in the United States during peacetime (including manslaughter, mayhem, robbery, larceny, and arson), rape and murder were still excluded, requiring commanders to turn over service members accused of these crimes to local jurisdictions for prosecution.[28]

Despite commanders' authority to prosecute rape and assault with intent to commit sodomy during World War I, very little is known about the scope of sexual violence committed abroad at the hands of U.S. servicemen. We know that the U.S. military had policies in place to manage prostitution and venereal disease, and that this policing was part of a larger effort to minimize incidents of rape that leaders assumed would inevitably occur if troops could not get their sexual needs met in brothels.[29] We also know that liaisons between U.S. troops and local women proliferated during and after the war.[30] But significant gaps remain in our understanding of the nature, scope, and outcomes of U.S. military sexual violence during and after World War I.

Scholarship on sexual violence during World War II is more abundant, revealing sexual exploitation and abuse by U.S. troops in both Allied and Axis nations. Robert J. Lilly's *Taken By Force*, for instance, analyzes military court records and estimates that over seventeen thousand rapes occurred in England, Germany, and France during World War II.[31] French L. MacLean's pathbreaking work, *The Fifth Field*, reveals that between December 1941 and April 1946 the U.S. Army charged 2,799 soldiers with rape or murder, 96 of whom received death sentences. Of these 96 the majority were African American soldiers.[32] Mary Louise Roberts's *What Soldiers Do* highlights the pervasiveness of sexual racism in France, revealing that commanders disproportionately targeted African American soldiers for rape in 1944.[33] Racism also played a role in Allied nations' failure to prosecute the Japanese military's systemic sexual abuse of Asian women, as Yuki Tanaka illustrates in *Japan's Comfort Women*.[34] This failure, Tanaka argues, was the result of Allied complicity in the sexual abuse and exploitation of Asian women. While studies such as these provide a useful starting point for mapping the scope of sexual violence during World War II, some scholars estimate that close to two million U.S. court-martial records from the war still remain unexamined, leaving many gaps in our understanding of the military's management of sexual violence during World War II.[35]

Management of Sexual Violence under the Uniform Code of Military Justice since 1950

Congressional adoption of the UCMJ in 1950 ushered in a new era in the military's efforts to manage sexual violence.[36] For the first time in U.S. history, military courts were granted jurisdiction over all crimes committed by service members in the army, navy, marines, air force, and coast guard, regardless of where the offenses occurred or whether the U.S. was in a time of war or peace. Prior to the creation of the UCMJ, the army, navy, and air force (established in 1947) operated under separate systems of military justice. Marines were caught in between, subject to army laws while on land and navy laws while at sea. The Elston Act of 1948 proposed to bring all branches under one military justice system in an effort to centralize the prosecution of criminal conduct and humanize what critics called an archaic justice system. Also known as the Military Selective Service Act, this act proposed to increase the size of the U.S. armed forces to accommodate the ever-growing demands of the U.S. containment policy during the Cold War.[37]

Expanding the military justice system across all branches and creating a military appellate court—the Court of Military Appeals—to manage troops' criminal conduct and ensure due process was central to this effort. The UCMJ streamlined service efforts to manage sexual violence by defining and criminalizing rape, statutory rape, and sodomy and establishing procedural safeguards for accused service members. Article 120, UCMJ combined the offenses of rape (Art. 120a) and carnal knowledge (Art. 120b) and defined rape as "the commission of an act of sexual intercourse with a female not his wife, by force and without her consent."[38] Article 125 prohibited both consensual and nonconsensual sodomy.[39] The courts also used the general articles, Articles 133 (conduct unbecoming an officer and a gentleman) and 134 (conduct prejudicial to good order and discipline), to enforce accepted notions of morality, decency, and deviance in the military community.[40] With over a century and a half of evidence pointing to inadequate sexual violence policies that ranged from nonexistent to vague to haphazardly implemented, the UCMJ granted military courts unprecedented authority to prosecute sexual violence—authority that was critical for managing sex (and the American military's reputation) in the postwar world as servicemen and their families expanded to the farthest reaches of the globe.

But gendered definitions of who constituted a legitimate rape victim undermined the effectiveness of the UCMJ's sanctions against sexual violence. The original Article 120, for example, echoed the common law definition of rape, which prohibited a male from

WILSON-BUFORD

engaging in "an act of sexual intercourse with a female not his wife, by force and without her consent."[41] By criminalizing rape against women only, the UCMJ left male victims without legal recourse for their sexual victimization until 1992 when Congress, in an effort to model revisions to civil rape laws, modified Article 120(a) to make the offense of rape gender neutral.[42] Even then male victims of sexual violence were deterred from reporting in the Don't Ask, Don't Tell era of 1994–2011, "when the suggestion that a service member was homosexual could lead to ostracism, punishment, and discharge."[43] Further, by defining rape as a crime that could only be committed by a man against "a woman not his wife," Article 120 denied the existence of and thus inadvertently condoned marital rape until Congress removed the spousal rape exemption from the UCMJ in 1992 in keeping with civil law.[44] Under the spousal exemption, husbands could not be charged for raping their wives based on the common law theory that sex was an implicit part of the marriage contract. Though the United States and the U.S. military were hardly unique in enforcing the spousal rape exemption until the last decade of the twentieth century, this practice undermined command efforts to manage sexual violence within military families by rendering service wives defenseless against their husbands' sexual predation.[45]

So, too, did military courts' endorsement of the spousal privilege, which often shielded child sex offenders from conviction. Originating in American common law where judges historically considered wives to be incompetent witnesses in cases involving their husbands, the spousal privilege protected husbands on trial from their wives' damning testimony when that testimony implicated husbands in criminal activity. Military courts during the Cold War often upheld the spousal privilege at the expense of child victims of sexual violence, as a "necessary [measure] to preserve . . . the relationship of husband and wife."[46] In the 1958 case of U.S. Army Sergeant Benn, for example, an appellate court overturned Benn's guilty conviction of attempted carnal knowledge and indecent sexual acts with a minor female because the admission of his wife's testimony at the original trial violated Benn's spousal privilege.[47] The same occurred in 1963 when the Court of Military Appeals (CMA), the military's version of the U.S. Supreme Court, let Sergeant Massey go free despite incontrovertible evidence that he raped his nine-year-old daughter multiple times. Ruling that Mrs. Massey's testimony was inadmissible because it violated Sergeant Massey's spousal privilege, the military high court, in attempting to protect the accused's rights to procedural due process, undermined the minor victim's chance for justice that Article 120(b) was intended to protect.[48] This insidious pattern—and the gendered assumptions that justified it—inadvertently shielded military child sex offenders from prosecution. In fact the sheer absence of official policy until 1950 prohibiting carnal knowledge suggests that the military justice system prior to 1950 was not equipped to manage sexual violence against children. In the absence of statutory rape provisions, prosecutors used the general articles, Articles 133 and 134, incorporating the carnal knowledge or statutory rape statute of the jurisdiction in which the offense occurred to court-martial military members who engaged in sexual intercourse with minors under the legal age of consent.[49]

Gendered precedents that blurred the boundaries of consent and placed the burden of proof on victims further undermined Article 120's effectiveness. Take the "mere non-consent" doctrine, for instance, which was established in the case of Marine Corps Private First Class Thomas L. Rogers, who raped a blind elderly Korean woman in 1951. The victim, who spoke very little English, testified that she "lost her senses" at the time of the alleged assault because Private Rogers kidnapped her, accidentally flipped the vehicle that he used to drive her to a deserted field, and then raped her. The victim claimed she was unable to resist because her arm was "uncoupled," and she could only shout "many times." Despite medical evidence showing contusions on the right side of her body, the defense attorney questioned the legitimacy of her story, arguing that if the victim had really lost her senses she would not have been able to "relate in detail the circumstances that occurred throughout the entire incident." Despite the court's acknowledgment that Rogers "had intercourse with her," and that he "willfully, maliciously and without justifiable cause . . . caught hold of and carr[ied] [the victim] away against her will and despite her protestations," the court ruled that the victim's "lack of consent was not sufficiently established to constitute the offense of rape."[50]

Ultimately, the court determined that the victim's testimony was not as credible as that of the accused.

Drawing on precedents in civil courts that placed the burden of proof on victims of sexual assault, the Naval Board of Review reasoned that the "mere non-consent of a female to intercourse . . . does not constitute the crime of rape."[51] The evidence of kidnapping, physical injury, and intercourse was not enough to convict Private Rogers of rape. Instead, because the victim's "mere vocal protestation and a pretense of resistance" were insufficient to show her lack of consent, Rogers escaped a rape conviction (which was punishable by death or life imprisonment) and was charged with a lesser offense of "abusing an inhabitant." Though his punishment was not explicated in the court transcript, this pattern of convicting a sexual predator with a lesser offense was common for sexual violence courts-martial in the second half of the twentieth century. But what would it have taken to convince the court that this nameless victim resisted to the extent of her ability given her old age, blindness, and physical injuries sustained from being kidnapped against her will? If the court, when contemplating the issue of consent, concluded that this elderly blind woman who spoke little English actually consented to intercourse with a complete stranger with whom she could barely communicate, much less see, what did this mean for other (more fortunate?) victims whose physical and linguistic capacities rendered them—in the courts' eyes—even more capable of resisting an assault? If "mere vocal protestation" did not constitute a lack of consent, what did? And at what point did a "pretense of resistance" cease to be a performance and become real?

The answers to these questions had disturbing implications for victims of military sexual violence. By ruling that verbal protestation in the form of screaming and shouting was a "mere pretense of resistance," the Rogers court effectively condoned the age-old adage "No means yes," making a mockery of victims' efforts to resist assault. The 1951 and 1969 versions of the *Manual for Courts-Martial* captured this gendered bias by advising legal officials that "it is true that rape is a most detestable crime . . . ; but it must be remembered that it is an accusation easy to be made, hard to be proved, but harder to be defended by the party accused, though innocent."[52] The assumption underlying this statement was that the accused, rather than the victim, was the person telling the truth. Though the military's practice of doubting the credibility of sexual violence victims was in keeping with most jurisdictions around the world in the second half of the twentieth century, in a legal environment where all-male courts were trained to question victims' credibility and assume that women were responsible for their own victimization, it is not surprising that crimes of military sexual violence proliferated despite Article 120's prohibition against rape and carnal knowledge.[53]

The military's legal definition of a "prostitute" further blurred the boundaries of consent and blamed victims for their sexual victimization. In the 1951 Barcomb case, the courts defined a prostitute as "a woman who indiscriminately offers her body for sexual intercourse for hire, but includes as well *a woman who submits to indiscriminate sexual intercourse which she invites or solicits by word or act or any device* [emphasis added]."[54] A prostitute, according to this definition, was any woman who "invited" or "solicited" sexual intercourse "by word or act or any device" irrespective of financial compensation. Virtually any woman, then, could have been a prostitute depending on how the courts interpreted a woman's actions or behaviors. The CMA overturned Barcomb's charge for pandering of a minor because the original review board's inclusion of the victim's deposition supposedly violated Barcomb's right to a fair trial. The "prostitute" in question was a minor female named Pansy Jones, whom the CMA deemed an incompetent witness at the original trial because she exhibited "extreme emotional instability."[55] By casting any woman or minor female as a prostitute whose words, acts, or any other devices represented her supposed submission to indiscriminate sex, women and girls bore the burden of having to prove beyond a reasonable doubt that their actions, whether intentionally or unintentionally, did not solicit the sexual advances of servicemen. Just as Article 120 made male victims of sexual assault a legal impossibility until 1992, so, too, did the courts' definition of a prostitute, which rendered men who submitted to "indiscriminate sexual intercourse" legal anomalies until 1969, when the CMA made the definition gender neutral.[56] Placing the burden of proof on sexual assault victims perpetuated a patriarchal legal system that deflected responsibility from male assailants whose sexual transgressions were, according to the prevailing logic, the natural consequences of women and girls' efforts to sexually entice servicemen.[57]

Procedural rules specific to rape cases exacerbated the challenges victims faced in trying to prove they were not responsible for their own sexual victimization. Similar to common law practice, in military courts nonconsensual sexual crimes were the only cases that required corroboration of victim testimony, yet very rarely did these crimes occur in the presence of witnesses (with the exception of gang rapes, which color the pages of military case law).[58] The impact of this rule on child victims was especially significant; military defense attorneys commonly attacked the credibility of child victims by claiming they misinterpreted or imagined their victimization. The fresh complaint rule complicated matters by associating the timing of a victim's complaint to their credibility.[59] In 1977 the CMA added more stipulations by ruling that the fresh complaint, in order to be admissible as evidence of a victim's credibility, had to be made while the victim was "in a state of shock, outrage, agony and resentment—the adrenergic circumstances which prompted the report."[60] This rule put victims' perceived credibility at the mercy of authorities whose subjective interpretations of what constituted shock, outrage, agony, and resentment varied. Perhaps most damning to victims' chances for sexual justice was the evidentiary rule that allowed a victim's sexual history to serve as evidence of their credibility.[61] The assumption that chastity equated to credibility was a powerful tool that men wielded to justify their own (and other men's) sexual predation. Given the courts' liberal definition of a prostitute, any woman's sexual history prior to marriage could be used as evidence that she solicited and consented to sexual assault or harassment. Though reform efforts in the 1980s began to challenge these problematic procedural rules, Article 120 remained significantly unchanged until the last decade of the twentieth century.[62]

Civil courts' historic deference to and non-interference with military decisions further undermined the effectiveness of the UCMJ's sanctions against sexual violence. The U.S. Supreme Court's 1950 Feres Doctrine, for example, which made it illegal for military service members or veterans to sue the military for injuries sustained during military service, has hindered military sexual violence victims' attempts to seek justice in civil courts.[63] In the 2011 case *Cioca et al. v. Rumsfeld et al.*, over a dozen military sexual trauma survivors sought monetary damages on the grounds that the Department of Defense deprived them of their constitutional rights to substantive and equal due process by contributing to a military culture of tolerance for sexual crimes. The district court dismissed the suit, arguing that sexual assault and harassment were occupational hazards of military service and, as a result, victims of military sexual violence could not sue the military for damages. The appellate court upheld the district court's ruling, shielding the military from external accountability for its pervasive culture of tolerance for sexual violence.[64] But the recent landmark Supreme Court ruling in *U.S. v. Briggs* (2020) has broken precedent with historic civil court rulings that have abstained from interfering in military decisions and operations. At issue was whether the Court of Appeals for the Armed Forces (CAAF) erred in imposing a five-year statute of limitations on rape cases occurring between 1986 and 2006—contrary to its own long-standing precedent. In a unanimous 8–0 decision, the Supreme Court overruled the CAAF's decision on the grounds that the plaintiffs' prosecutions for rape were timely under the UCMJ, paving the way for more victims of military sexual violence to seek justice in military courts. While it remains to be seen how military courts will interpret and enforce this ruling (e.g., will this ruling apply strictly to rape cases or will it also apply to sodomy, indecent assault, and sexual harassment?), *U.S. v. Briggs* signifies the U.S. Supreme Court's willingness to intervene in military judicial decisions to broaden protections for military sexual violence victims.[65]

Research Challenges and Future Directions

The history of military efforts to manage sexual violence—though tragic and unsettling—has much to teach us about the contemporary sexual assault crisis in the U.S. armed forces. This history is more important now than ever, as the American military empire encircles the globe and as U.S. troops are stationed at nearly one thousand locations worldwide.[66] As continued acts of sexual violence by U.S. service personnel victimize people and threaten U.S. global interests, scholars of military sexual violence have an even greater responsibility to investigate, collaborate, and speak up. But researching this subject is challenging, not least because of the politically charged nature of the topic and the paucity of available sources. Gleaning an accurate picture of the scope of sexual violence in any war, location, or time period is difficult because historical sources rarely reflect the actual number of sexual assaults that occurred. The stigma of rape and fear of retaliation for reporting undoubtedly led (and continue to lead) many victims to decline to report their victimization. Finding sources before 1950 is especially challenging given the absence of a centralized repository for courts-martial for all branches of the armed forces. Because the management of sexual violence fell outside the military's jurisdiction in some capacity before 1950, tracking this data will require tenacious digging into archives of individual command units and local jurisdictions all across the country and wherever U.S. troops were stationed overseas. Mining newspapers for reports of military sexual violence could provide a useful starting point for research into local jurisdictions.

For researchers focusing on the second half of the twentieth century, the annually published *Court-Martial Reports* are indispensable, though surprisingly overlooked by scholars outside of military legal journals. Records of the Office of the Judge Advocate General for each of the service branches need to be scoured, as do the various branches' policies on sexual violence. Researching the personnel files for troops who were convicted of rape or sodomy would be useful, but privacy protections that bar public access to military personnel files until sixty-two years after the service member separated from the armed forces pose accessibility issues. So, too, do restricted and classified government documents that require declassification and redaction in order to be used. Oral histories of both perpetrators and victims of military sexual violence could provide insights that other sources do not. For researchers of military sexual violence in the past three decades, congressional hearings and governmental task force reports are important sources, as are official DOD and Veterans Affairs (VA) policies and reports. But the majority of these sources have focused almost exclusively on intramilitary (or military on military) sexual assault. So have victim advocacy groups such as the Service Women's Action Network (SWAN), which advocates exclusively for female service members who have been sexually victimized. There are few, if any, organizations that advocate for the children, military spouses, and local civilians—both American and foreign—who have been victims of U.S. military sexual violence. While resources, organizations, and research studies focusing on intramilitary assault are critical for providing data that can help foster military accountability, this focus perpetuates both public and scholarly silence about the largely uncharted history of military sexual violence against civilians, family members, and children in the United States and around the world.

Notes

1. This essay is not intended to be a comprehensive analysis of the history of military sexual assault policy (this would require multiple volumes), but rather a starting point for future research. My use of the phrase "sexual violence" in this essay encompasses both rape and nonconsensual sodomy, but where appropriate I distinguish between the two crimes.

2. American Articles of War (1776), reprinted in Winthrop, *Military Law and Precedents*, 964.

3. Winthrop, *Military Law and Precedents*, 972.

4. Commager and Morris, *Spirit of 'Seventy-Six*, 525.

5. Fitzpatrick, *Writings of George Washington*, 244.

6. Bray, *Court-Martial*, 88–89.

7. Bray, *Court-Martial*, 42.

8. United States v. Solorio, 483 U.S. (1987), 444.

9. Burg, "Sodomy, Masturbation, and Courts-Martial," 53–54.

10. Burg, "Sodomy, Masturbation, and Courts-Martial," 54–55.

11. Bray, *Court-Martial*, 42.

12. Winthrop, *Military Law and Precedents*, 667.

13. 12 Stat. 736 (1863).

14. Barber and Ritter, "Dangerous Liaisons," 4.

15. "Record of Court-Martial Case since July, 1, 1863," *Army and Navy Official Gazette*, October 13, 1863, 231.

16. Winthrop, *Military Law and Precedents*, 671.

17. Barber and Ritter, "Dangerous Liaisons," 4.

18. "The Military Departments," *Army and Navy Journal*, December 30, 1865, 294.

19. 18 Stat. 228 (1874).

20. Brownmiller, *Against Our Will*, 151–53.

21. Winthrop, *Military Law and Precedents*, 677.

22. "The Santiago Outrages Call Forth Attention," *Atlanta Constitution*, August 21, 1898, 3.

23. McPherson, *Invaded*, 97–100.

24. 39 Stat. 664 (1916).

25. McPherson, *Invaded*, 97, 100.

26. 39 Stat. 619 (1916), Bul. No. 25, WD (1920).

27. Canaday, *Straight State*, 58–59.

28. 39 Stat. 619, 664 (1916).

29. For a review of the existing literature on the military's management of prostitution and venereal disease, see Knaff, "Homos, Whores, Rapists, and the Clap," 269–86.

30. For a review of U.S. troops sexual liaisons with local civilians, see Alvah, "U.S. Military Personnel and Families Abroad," 247–68.

31. Lilly, *Taken by Force*.

32. MacLean, *Fifth Field*.

33. Roberts, *What Soldiers Do*.

34. Tanaka, *Japan's Comfort Women*.

35. Bray, *Court-Martial*, 263.

36. 64 Stat. 108 (1950).

37. 62 Stat. 604 (1948).

38. 1951 *Manual for Courts-Martial*, Pt. XXVII, para. 199(a).

39. 1951 *Manual for Courts-Martial*, Pt. XXVII, para. 204.

40. Wilson-Buford, *Policing Sex and Marriage in the American Military*.

41. 1951 *Manual for Courts-Martial*, Pt. XXVII, par. 199(a).

42. National Defense Authorization Act for Fiscal Year 1993, Pub. L. No. 102-484, 106 Stat. 2315, 2506 (1992).

43. Hillman and Walsham, "Rape, Reform, and Reaction," 288.

44. National Defense Authorization Act for Fiscal Year 1993, Pub. L. No. 102-484, 106 Stat. 2315, 2506 (1992). By 1993 all fifty states criminalized marital rape.

45. The assumption that sex was implicit in the marriage contract can be traced to the writings of Sir Matthew Hale. Sir Hale's treatise, *The History of the Pleas of the Crown*, greatly influenced American rape laws and the rules governing the criminal prosecution of rape allegations in American jurisdictions, including the American military. See Hale, *Historia Placitorum Coronae*, 627, as cited in "Sex Crimes and the UCMJ," 39.

46. Wilson-Buford, *Policing Sex and Marriage*, 85, citing United States v. McDonald, 32 CMR 692 (NBR 1963).

47. Wilson-Buford, *Policing Sex and Marriage*, 89, citing United States v. Benn, 28 CMR 424 (ABR 1958).

48. Wilson-Buford, *Policing Sex and Marriage in the American Military*, 89–90, citing United States v. Massey, 34 CMR 930 (1963) and United States v. Massey, 35 CMR 255 (1965). See also United States v. Osborne, 31 MJ 842 (NMCMR 1990).

49. For useful context on how sex crimes against children were handled in specific civilian jurisdictions, see Robertson, *Crimes against Children*; and Smith, *Sex without Consent*.

50. United States v. Rogers, 1 CMR 459 (NBR 1951).

51. *Rogers*, 1 CMR 459.

52. 1951 *Manual for Courts-Martial*, Pt. XXVII, para. 199(a).

53. For a global analysis of the history of sexual violence, see Bourke, *Rape*. See Estrich, *Real Rape*, for a careful analysis of American civil courts' practice of doubting the credibility of rape victims.

54. United States v. Barcomb, 3 CMR 623 (AFBR 1951).

55. United States v. Barcomb, 3 CMR 149 (1951).

56. See Wilson-Buford's analysis of United States v. Adams, 40 CMR 22 (1969) in *Policing Sex and Marriage*, 191–92.

57. My definition of patriarchy mirrors Cynthia Enloe's usage of the term, which she defines as "the structural and ideological system that perpetuates the privileging of masculinity," in *Curious Feminist*, 4.

58. 1951 *Manual for Courts-Martial*, Pt. XXVII, para. 199(a). For careful analyses of the history of civilian rape laws more broadly and procedural rules that undermined victims' chances for justice in courts, see Estrich, *Real Rape*; Rowland, *Boundaries of Her Body*; Smith, *Sex without Consent*; and Freedman, *Redefining Rape*.

59. 1951 *Manual for Courts-Martial*, Pt. XXVII, para. 142(c).

60. United States v. Thompson, 3 MJ 168, 170 (1977).

61. 1951 *Manual for Courts-Martial*, Pt. XXVII, para 153(b).

62. For example, in 1980 President Carter signed Executive Order 12198, promulgating the Military Rules of Evidence (Mil. R. Ev.), which eliminated the corroboration requirement in sexual crimes, the fresh complaint rule, and included a rape shield provision that precluded evidence about a victim's sexual history. Cited in "Sex Crimes and the UCMJ," 26.

63. Feres v. United States, 340 U.S. 135 (1950).

64. Cioca v. Rumsfeld, 720 F.3d 505 (4th Cir. 2013).

65. United States v. Briggs, 592 U.S. ____ (2020). At the time this chapter went to press, this is the most recent citation for this case.

66. Vine, *Base Nation*. For general critiques of the U.S. military empire, see also Lutz, *Bases of Empire*; Gillem, *America Town*; and Johnson, *Blowback*.

Bibliography

Alvah, Donna. "U.S. Military Personnel and Families Abroad: Gender, Sexuality, Race, and Power in the U.S. Military's Relations with Foreign Nations and Local Inhabitants during Wartime." In *The Routledge History of Gender, War, and the U.S. Military*, edited by Kara Dixon Vuic, 247–68. New York: Routledge, 2018.

Barber, E. Susan, and Charles F. Ritter. "Dangerous Liaisons: Working Women and Sexual Justice in the American Civil War." *European Journal of American Studies* 10, no. 1 (2015): 1–15.

Bray, Chris. *Court-Martial: How Military Justice Has Shaped America from the Revolution to 9/11 and Beyond.* New York: W. W. Norton, 2016.

Brownmiller, Susan. *Against Our Will: Men, Women, and Rape.* New York: Faucett, 1975.

Bourke, Joanna. *Rape: Sex, Violence, History.* London: Virago, 2007.

Burg, B. R. "Sodomy, Masturbation, and Courts-Martial in the Antebellum American Navy." *Journal of the History of Sexuality* 23, no. 1 (January 2014): 53–78.

Canaday, Margot. *The Straight State: Sexuality and Citizenship in Twentieth-Century America.* Princeton NJ: Princeton University Press, 2009.

Commager, Henry Steele, and Richard B. Morris, eds. *The Spirit of 'Seventy-Six.* Indianapolis: Bobbs-Merrill, 1958.

Enloe, Cynthia. *The Curious Feminist: Searching for Women in a New Age of Empire.* Berkeley: University of California Press, 2004.

Estrich, Susan. *Real Rape.* Cambridge MA: Harvard University Press, 1987.

Fitzpatrick, John C., ed. *The Writings of George Washington from the Original Manuscript Sources, 1745–1799.* Vol. 19. Washington DC: U.S. Government Printing Office, 1937.

Freedman, Estelle. *Redefining Rape: Sexual Violence in the Era of Suffrage and Segregation.* Cambridge MA: Harvard University Press, 2013.

Gillem, Mark L. *America Town: Building the Outposts of Empire.* Minneapolis: University of Minnesota Press, 2007.

Hillman, Elizabeth L. "Front and Center: Sexual Violence in U.S. Military Law." *Politics and Society* 37, no. 1 (March 2009): 101–30.

Hillman Elizabeth L., and Kate Walsham. "Rape, Reform, and Reaction: Gender and Sexual Violence in the U.S. Military." In *The Routledge History of Gender, War, and the U.S. Military,* edited by Kara Dixon Vuic, 287–300. New York: Routledge, 2018.

Johnson, Chalmers. *Blowback: The Costs and Consequences of the American Empire.* New York: Holt, 2004.

Knaff, Donna B. "Homos, Whores, Rapists, and the Clap: American Military Sexuality since the Revolutionary War." In *The Routledge History of Gender, War, and the U.S. Military,* edited by Kara Dixon Vuic, 269–86. New York: Routledge, 2018.

Lilly, Robert J. *Taken by Force: Rape and American GIs in Europe during World War II.* New York: Palgrave Macmillan, 2007.

Lutz, Catherine, ed. *The Bases of Empire: The Global Struggle against U.S. Military Posts.* New York: New York University Press, 2009.

MacLean, French L. *The Fifth Field: The Story of the 96 American Soldiers Sentenced to Death and Executed in Europe and North Africa in World War II.* Atglen PA: Schiffer, 2013.

Manual for Courts-Martial, United States. Washington DC: U.S. Government Printing Office, 1951.

McPherson, Alan. *The Invaded: How Latin Americans and Their Allies Fought and Ended U.S. Occupations.* New York: Oxford University Press, 2014.

Roberts, Mary Louise. *What Soldiers Do: Sex and the American GI in World War II France*. Chicago: University of Chicago Press, 2013.

Robertson, Stephen. *Crimes against Children: Sexual Violence and Legal Culture in New York City, 1880–1960*. Chapel Hill: University of North Carolina Press, 2005.

"Sex Crimes and the UCMJ: A Report for the Joint Service Committee on Military Justice." 2005. http://www.dod.mil/dodgc/php/docs/subcommittee_reportMarkHarveyl-13-05.doc (in author's possession).

Smith, Merril D., ed. *Sex without Consent: Rape and Sexual Coercion in America*. New York: New York University Press, 2001.

Tanaka, Yuki. *Japan's Comfort Women: Sexual Slavery and Prostitution during World War II and the U.S. Occupation*. London: Routledge, 2002.

Vine, David. *Base Nation: How U.S. Military Bases Abroad Harm America and the World*. New York: Metropolitan, 2015.

Wilson-Buford, Kellie. *Policing Sex and Marriage in the American Military: The Court-Martial and the Construction of Gender and Sexual Deviance, 1950–2000*. Lincoln: University of Nebraska Press, 2018.

Winthrop, William. *Military Law and Precedents*. 2nd ed. Washington DC: Government Printing Office, 1920.

NINE

Managing Harassment and Assault in the Contemporary U.S. Military

AMANDA BOCZAR

One day each year, as part of a short-lived tradition, and a bold change to the normal sea of well-pressed gray classroom uniforms, cadets at the U.S. Military Academy at West Point attended their courses in blue jeans and a T-shirt reading "It's on Us." The shirts supported the national anti–sexual assault and sexual harassment campaign established by President Barak Obama and Vice President Joe Biden in 2014. Hosted on Denim Day, the event recognized a criminal case where the Italian Supreme Court ruled against a rape victim because of the tightness of her jeans.[1] Following a Pentagon report showing 48 percent of cadets had experienced unwanted sexual contact, a number far higher than the military's overall rates, West Point's current superintendent, Lieutenant General Darryl Williams, replaced the event in 2019 in favor a of full day of gender and racial diversity workshops.[2] Despite the shifting approaches, the academy continues to hope to open a dialogue among cadets who will almost certainly face issues of assault or harassment in their ranks after graduation. Annual training and efforts to implement discussions of rape into the curriculum have yet to spark drastic change. West Point, however, is not unique among military institutions attempting to normalize discussion of sexual assault in the services. Enlisted and officer ranks across branches all undergo regular prevention training, but statistics remain discouraging. In recent years assaults at every level have necessitated changes in policy.

Bluntly, the military has a sexual assault problem. Aggressive campaigns from the service academies to the Pentagon have failed to slow the number of reports, which showed a 38 percent increase between 2016 and 2018. Since the service-wide adoption of "zero tolerance" policies after the 1991 Tailhook scandal, initiating the contemporary era in military policy, the efforts have disappointed time and again.[3] Some officials, including the former superintendent of West Point Lieutenant General Robert L. Caslen Jr. have argued that the increase in reporting is a positive sign of change. In 2017 he testified in front of Congress that increased reports do not necessarily mean increased crimes, but an increased level of confidence in victims that their reports would be taken seriously. More victims are also willing to report openly without using restricted reporting methods that keep their identities hidden, but limit the ability to prosecute.[4] Caslen's point reflects the increase in the number of cases prosecuted via courts martial each year, but various studies, including the 2018 Department of Defense (DOD) report on sexual assault, estimate that anywhere between two-thirds to four-fifths of victims do not report such crimes.[5]

This chapter will discuss the evolution of the U.S. military's response to incidents of sexual assault and harassment within the services since World War II, with an emphasis on the dramatic increase in attention the topic received following the 1991 Tailhook scandal, in which the navy authorized a cover-up of the assaults of approximately ninety service members (eighty-three of whom were women) at an aviation conference. While assaults against female service members occur at statistically higher rates and are the focus of this chapter, assaults were—and still are— targeted against both women and men and can be perpetrated by either gender. Male victims historically report their crimes even less frequently than women, citing hazing, embarrassment, threats to their masculinity and chances for promotion, and—before the elimination of sodomy laws in 2003—the risk of being charged with a crime.[6]

The chapter begins with the influx of female service members during World War II, Korea, and the Vietnam War and examines the policy of gender segregation as a deterrent to assault. While the branches certainly never condoned rape, victims in this era often found that their commanding officers discouraged reporting or prosecution when an attack did take place. The military's 1978 gender integration led to an increase in attention on sexual encounters between service members but failed to decrease assaults. The lack of accountability is partly tied to the 1950 court precedent of *Feres v. United States*, which found that a member of the military could not hold the government liable or sue it for compensation for wrongdoing that occurred during their service.[7] The military has successfully included rape under this umbrella, keeping itself safe from cases brought by victims who place blame for their trauma on the training, retaliation for reporting, or overall lack of prosecution of offenders.

The chapter will then turn to the publicity received by the 1991 Tailhook scandal, and the steady increase in anti–sexual assault training all service branches implemented in its aftermath. While the DOD was managing the fallout of Tailhook, the government separately instituted Don't Ask, Don't Tell, a policy that allowed gay men and lesbians to serve so long as they did not disclose their sexual orientation, but mandated the discharge of those who revealed their homosexuality or who engaged in "homosexual activity." DADT was criticized for the closeting of service members and limiting their rights within the services. By not being allowed to openly serve, LGBTQ service members risked their careers if they attended events with partners, and their families were not be eligible for benefits. DADT also undermined the reporting of sexual assault, as LGBTQ service members who were victims of sexual assault feared their reports might lead to questions regarding their sexuality and to being forced out of the service.[8]

More recently, individuals have sought to hold the military or the U.S. government accountable for their inability to mitigate assault. The 2011 Supreme Court case *Cioca vs. Rumsfeld* challenged the *Feres v. United States* precedent, for example, by moving to sue the DOD for tolerating a culture that permitted assault. While the case failed, it received considerable publicity and kept pressure on the military services to keep working toward reducing the numbers of intraservice assaults. While outside the scope of this chapter, sexual assaults perpetrated by Americans against foreign nationals in and outside combat zones further compounded the pressure on the DOD to hold its own accountable through character-based training and more prosecutions, which, as seen in the West Point example, has yet to result in a significant reduction of crimes. Since World War II, and especially after the Tail-hook scandal, the military has consistently adapted to address sexual assault prevention, prosecution, and recovery to align with the evolution of the service branches and to respond to changing perceptions of acceptable behavior in American society. The process has been met with considerable skepticism about the effectiveness of programs from both inside and outside of the military, but efforts continue.

Sexual Harassment and Assault from World War II to the Vietnam War Era, 1943–77

The introduction of women into nonauxiliary positions in the armed forces in the 1940s, albeit in gender-segregated units, forged unprecedented pathways to new and exciting careers. The move also introduced women into male-dominated, strictly hierarchical organizations whose members held mixed opinions on the appropriate roles of women within them. Women enlisted across the services, including in the newly formed Women's Army Corps (WAC), seeking opportunities to serve their country in roles not previously available outside the nursing corps, the only corps that allowed military women to travel abroad regularly before 1943. Female service members experienced "episodic harassment" from their male counterparts during World War II, and military leaders worried about the potential of sexual assault and sometimes imposed policies intended to protect servicewomen from men in uniform.[9]

Part of the U.S. military's growth following World War II included the institution of the Uniform Code of Military Justice in 1951. President Truman approved the *Manual for Courts-Martial* via executive order, which included a provision against rape and carnal knowledge. The manual indicated "no limitation" to the possible punishments for rape.[10] The institute of the law into record, however, failed to change the culture within the services that allowed for assaults against its own members to go undocumented.

Female service members' accounts of rape during the Korean and Vietnam Wars indicate their lack of trust in the system, due in part to military leaders' failure to enforce regulations or pursue offenders. Many of the women who have shared their accounts in recent years felt they could not fairly seek prosecution at the time. Their accounts are often similar, of assaults perpetrated by assailants with more power or leverage, of fear of violence and repercussions if they resisted the attacks, of their isolation from potential witnesses, and of the feeling that they could not or were discouraged from filing official reports. Speaking about her experiences as a nurse during the Korean War era, for example, Maurine McFerrin DeLeo recounted how two pilots (therefore officers) drove her home from a party and took turns raping her. Because she had known of another servicewoman who was severely beaten for fighting back during a rape on a previous occasion, she did not physically resist to the fullest extent possible. When DeLeo reported the assault, her commanding officer agreed to "check into" the case and found the individuals, but they denied her story. If the men were disciplined, she never learned of it. She believed that nothing happened to the men.[11]

In the Vietnam War, a total of 7,500 to 11,000 women served in gender-segregated military units ranging from nursing to communications and logistics.[12] Historian Heather Stur shows that, in Vietnam, male U.S. soldiers viewed both American servicewomen and the local female population as potential sexual partners, but imagined Asian women as hypersexual and American women as girls next door who were, simultaneously, chaste and "objects of illicit male desire and sexual frustration, and, at an extreme, victims of violence."[13] From basic training onward, women found themselves in a military dominated by men, and with little change to the culture of harassment remembered by female World War II veterans. Reflecting on her arrival for clerical training after basic, First Sergeant Linda Earls stated, "Fort Knox, Kentucky was not a pleasant situation for women."[14] Earls recalled that any time the women left their barracks, male soldiers shouted at and harassed them. Similarly, Sergeant Linda McClenahan recalled that high fences and barbed wire surrounded her WAC detachment's female barracks in Vietnam. She estimated that 50,000 American men and only 125 American women were posted at Long Binh, the enormous army base near Saigon, prompting the army policy of segregating the male and female barracks so distinctly.[15]

McClenahan's experiences in Vietnam illustrate military failures to confront sexual assault. The sergeant, who worked in confidential communications, was gang-raped and robbed by a group of fellow soldiers, including one she knew. The incident shook her to the core of her deep religious values and her faith in army justice (although she did return to her religion and now serves as a Dominican nun). She immediately asked to speak to her captain, who offered her the opportunity to go to the hospital, which she refused out of embarrassment. McClenahan, however, faced resistance higher up in command and encountered hostile responses from male leadership. After being prescribed a sedative for her trauma, she had a negative encounter with a new chaplain to whom she had turned for support. One captain told her that the assailant claimed that McClenahan had organized the encounter and accepted payment for having sex with the men. Her entire chain of command discouraged her from pursuing the case, suggesting the risks of reporting the rape by asking her to consider "what do we women expect anyway, throwing ourselves into the middle of a man's war." A female captain expressed concern that going after the perpetrators would likely damage only McClenahan's career and not theirs, and she "reluctantly" advised McClenahan not to take further action.[16] McClenahan, like many other victims, agreed not to pursue charges. She had been a quickly promoted, highly specialized sergeant who worked with classified communications and code throughout her service, and she was forced to choose her career over prosecuting her assailants due to a fear of retribution. Such concerns persist into the twenty-first century.

The Vietnam War presented challenges for the U.S. military that went beyond internal sexual assaults, as service members' rapes of foreign victims garnered international attention and sparked widespread challenges of the military's handling of assault. Stories of violence against civilians appeared in newscasts, and activists shared detailed descriptions of rapes of women and girls. Daily army military police records indicate that significantly more assaults were reported to local MPs than were officially charged, as commanders failed to follow up on or to prosecute the cases.[17] Given how few cases the branches prosecuted, especially considering available evidence, they gained a reputation for tolerating assault.[18] Since Vietnam the global community has grown more critical of the military's misbehavior abroad and demanded changes to what they viewed as weak assault policies across the services.

From Gender Integration to Scandals, 1978–2004

Following the Vietnam War, the 1978 gender integration of the armed forces brought women into closer contact with their male counterparts.[19] The decision allowed women to transfer into units across the armed forces, with the exception of combat units, increasing their mobility and placing them within command structures dominated by men who may or may not have supported gender integration. When the first women granted admission to the service academies in 1976 graduated in 1980 and commissioned into an integrated armed forces, "male prejudice against women proved to be their biggest obstacle"—at least according to the Women in Military Service for America Memorial's history. That problem has continued throughout the postintegration era and placed female victims of assault and harassment into potentially difficult situations, with male members in their command structure dismissing their accounts.[20] A Pentagon survey from 1988 found that more than 90 percent of victims did not report the crimes to their chain of command out of fear they might be blamed instead.[21]

The 1991 Tailhook scandal was an important turning point in military handling of sexual assault, in part because it brought both harassment and assault to the attention of the mainstream media and Congress. The U.S. Navy scandal and cover-up occurred during the annual Las Vegas convention attended by hundreds of high-ranking naval officers and aviators, an event that had a reputation for raucous behavior. In 1991, after being assaulted by dozens of men in a hallway known as "the gauntlet," Lieutenant Paula Coughlin followed her chain of command to immediately report the "verbally, physically, and sexually abusive" behavior.[22] She reported the assault to her superior, Admiral Jack Snyder, the next morning and persisted in trying to get him to make a public response to the crimes for over five weeks. He ignored her claims in what one licensed social worker and researcher called a "classic power failure."[23]

The story became public and the military was forced to respond, but the thousands of interviews conducted by over 270 U.S. Navy and DOD agents only resulted in two named suspects.[24] This cover-up, acknowledged in part by Acting Secretary of the Navy H.

Lawrence Garrett III, led to an inspector general's investigation that named 117 officers for sexual misconduct; most, however, were "administratively punished; none were convicted."[25] The scandal triggered an erosion of confidence in the military's ability to police itself on issues of sexual harassment and assault, but Congress remained, and still remains, hesitant to strip that power from the services.

Following Tailhook and the follow-up barrage of congressional hearings and reports, the military publicly doubled down on the concept of a "zero tolerance" policy for assailants in sexual assault crimes.[26] Within the confines of military posts, however, crimes and their cover-ups persisted. In 1996 a story broke detailing the pattern of harassment and assaults that took place against female soldiers at the army's Aberdeen Proving Ground in Maryland. The contrast between Tailhook and Aberdeen is striking, as the army, aware of the fallout of the Tailhook scandal, immediately started working to get details on the events; the focus on zero tolerance after 1992 drove the military to make a show out of investigating and prosecuting at Aberdeen.[27] Responding to over fifty victim reports, the army tried twelve men, all African American, for their crimes at Aberdeen; nonetheless, only two received jail time. (The disproportionate convictions of Black soldiers for rape dates to World War II, raising questions about race inequality in military legal systems.)[28] At Aberdeen higher-ranking officers retired to avoid any formal charges.[29]

Historian Josh Cerretti argues that Aberdeen shows that, despite the increasing interest in sexual harassment and assault, the military enacted few meaningful policy changes and so participated in a "militarization of sexual violence."[30] His research contrasts the personal nature of the Aberdeen assaults with the "depersonalized mass sexual assaults" at Tailhook and suggests that the responses to such events are not simply stepping stones to more rights and additional protection policies.[31] Accusations of harassment, assault, inappropriate affairs between trainees and officers, and an overall hostile environment at Aberdeen received press attention for months. While not an immediate response to Aberdeen, the military did eventually approve a ban on fraternization between instructors and trainees in the ranks in 2016.[32]

Since 1976 the service academies have suffered from high rates of harassment and assault and struggled to implement effective sexual harassment and assault prevention measures. They report higher levels of both than the military at large. The persistence of sex crimes at the academies raises important questions about leadership and the formation of an elite officer corps that is already familiar with the crisis of sexual assault and with prevention efforts at the time of their commission. As of 2019 all four service academies had superintendents who graduated from their respective institutions after integration, which may change their approach to policies and investigations.

The military's inability to decrease the volume of crimes in institutions designed to mold leaders of character presents a striking contradiction to their missions. Anecdotally, most cadets at West Point during my two years as a postdoctoral fellow in their history department expressed concern and empathy when discussing rape in American history, but they also confessed to training burnout. The academic focus of the academies resulted in more frequent and theoretical discussions of assault scenarios than in the military as a whole, and cadets joked about their mandatory Sexual Harassment/Assault Response and Prevention (SHARP) training and whether they could even give their buddies a congratulatory tap on the shoulder without consent. But students also regularly discussed cases of assaults and rapes that involved cadets both on and off post, and the issue was never far from their minds.

One of the most notable examples of sexual harassment and assault at the service academies came out of the Air Force Academy in 2003. An anonymous email alleging that the academy had failed to act on reports of sexual assault triggered multiple internal and government investigations not only at the Air Force Academy but at the other service academies as well.[33] The report from the air force inspector general, however, found "no evidence of intentional mishandling or willful neglect on the part of any Academy official."[34] Because they must prove intention, such investigators face the difficult task of showing that decisions intentionally discourage prosecution, whether explicitly or implicitly. Scholars and journalists, however, have an opportunity to assess the military's decisions from outside its ranks, and their analyses of implicit dissuasion suggest ways that the armed forces might improve their command climate. The authors of the more than sixty-page 2004 *Denver Post* exposé "Betrayal in the Ranks" investigated events at the Air Force Academy as the third of three major instances of military violations against their members, starting with Tailhook and then Aberdeen, and the findings of this series should encourage examination of cases outside these big three.[35]

Developing an Accountability Culture, 2005–Present

Military attempts to deal with sexual harassment and assault generally focus on prevention, not on the causes of sexual assault. From a military standpoint, prevention is a critical step, because by preventing sexual assault the military can eliminate the extremely high financial, emotional, and political burdens and costs.[36] That approach, however, tends to be victim-focused. For decades the DOD has emphasized proactive vigilance from potential victims rather than attempting to profile and identify possible perpetrators. As such, prevention policies have largely failed to look at the root causes of sexual assault.

The military puts an emphasis on victims defending themselves, as well as taking on the burden to provide enough evidence to their chain of command that the case has reasonable cause to pursue. Leaders promote vigilance and advocate that service members travel in pairs "of the same sex for mutual assistance and support" in what the army calls its "battle buddy system" to "protect" them from "sexual assault/harassment, discrimination, and [reduce] the risk of suicide."[37] Recently, Fort Bragg in North Carolina has taken this system a step further through the use of gamification of assault training with a "SHARP escape room" where a battle buddy must answer assault training questions to free her or his partner, who in the scenario is an assault victim.[38] The gamification is no doubt an effort to fight off training burnout, but the effort to make serious training fun has currently unknown effectiveness, repercussions on the command climate, and mental health impacts for actual survivors.

Prevention measures and prosecution rules might dissuade some, but they have certainly not stopped attacks. At times prosecutions have made life more difficult for survivors of sexual assault; for example, military regulations encouraged prosecutors to obtain as many reports of the alleged event as possible, even if a victim reported anonymously. In closed settings like isolated posts or aircraft carriers, such policies sometimes led to repeated assaults and retaliation for reporting. In response the DOD introduced alternative reporting methods. Beginning in June 2005, the DOD instituted options for restricted reporting, which allows victims to inform the DOD and to receive medical and psychological care for their injuries "without triggering the official investigative process or notification to command."[39] While anonymous reporting limits the ability to prosecute, it improves the understanding of assault rates and provides an outlet to victims. Nonetheless, because they remain anonymous, they do not help to raise public consciousness of the problem of sexual assault in the military.

Other military policies that have no direct relationship to those on sexual assault also shape military responses. For example, the 2011 Supreme Court case brought by Kori Cioca and fifteen other veteran and active duty victims of physical and sexual assault against former secretaries of defense Donald Rumsfeld and Robert Gates included women who found themselves targets of investigations for adultery because their attackers were married at the time of their rapes.[40]

Policies against homosexuality in the United States and the armed forces have historically added an additional layer of complexity. Prior to the decriminalization of homosexuality, which remained illegal in some states until 2003 and partially illegal in the military until 2013, soldiers faced considerable personal and professional risk if accused of homosexual behavior, and under DADT (1994–2011), accusations of LGBTQ sexual orientations could lead to a discharge and the end of one's career.[41] Assailants used such restrictions, threatening to "reveal" that servicewomen were lesbians, as a tactic to force them into coercive sexual encounters.[42] In this way predators could use their victim's sexual orientation—or even her concern that such suspicions could sabotage her career—as a tool for harassment.

Assumptions that only women are victims of rape also have slowed appropriate responses. Men are also targeted by perpetrators, but report more diverse motivations for attacks against them than do women. The numbers of DOD men who reported assault move from a high of 1.8 percent in 2006 to a low of 0.6 percent in 2016, with what the DOD labeled as no change by 2018.[43] Women reported that men they knew typically acted alone in attacks against them. Male soldiers, however, reported that roughly half of attacks came at the hands of male perpetrators, 30 percent from women, and 13 percent of "offenders were a mix of men and women acting together."[44] While percentages remain far lower for assaults on men, the fact that men make up the great preponderance of military troops translates these rates into a striking number of total assaults—in the tens of thousands—each year. More research on the assaults of men will help to uncover a fairer representation of sex crimes across the four services.

Military admissions criteria may also play a role in continuing rates of sexual assault. According to the 2012 documentary *The Invisible War*, 15 percent of navy recruits had "attempted or committed rape before entering the military." This number is twice as high as the equivalent civilian population, supporting the idea that the military offers what psychologist and Brigadier General Loree Sutton has called "a target-rich environment for a predator."[45] The lack of attention to predator behavior or tendencies, along with the relatively low rates of prosecution, allowed perpetrators to target victims repeatedly. Scholars such as Nathaniel Franks have also linked the moral waivers increasingly offered during the U.S. wars in Iraq and Afghanistan, as the army and navy struggled to fill their ranks, to sexual assault; Franks discusses the case of army infantryman Private First Class Steven Green, who murdered family members of Abeer Qassim Hamza al-Janabi during her rape and murder in Iraq in 2006. Green had enlisted after leaving jail for his third misdemeanor and was discharged for a personality disorder only a month after the killings. Franks compares the "733 ex-convicts" who received morality waivers with the loss of 742 service members who were discharged as a result of DADT to suggest that gender and sexuality discrimination may have encouraged the services to offer more morality waivers and thus increase crimes within the armed forces.[46]

Military leadership also admits to a culture of "toxic masculinity" as part of their problem in enacting change.[47] Elisabeth Jean

Wood's description of the militarized masculinity approach to warfare as "based on sharp distinctions between genders: to become men, boys must become warriors. The result is that combatants represent domination of the enemy in highly gendered terms and use specifically sexual violence against enemy populations."[48] The link also applies to cases of assault within American forces, whereby soldiers found that they could use their positions of authority to control the minority female populations within their ranks. Gender integration of the armed forces placed women in closer contact than foreign women, making them easier targets for assault when deployed.[49]

To help fight the ever-expanding sexual harassment and assault problems, the federal government mandated that the military present statistics to Congress in regular intervals. An amendment to the Ike Skelton National Defense Authorization Act of 2011 required the DOD to compile and publish an "annual report regarding sexual assaults involving members of the Armed Forces and improvement to sexual assault prevention and response program."[50] The amendment came in the wake of criticism of the military and federal government for failing to protect service members. The Sexual Assault Prevention and Response (SAPR) program centers on reducing "the number of sexual assaults involving members of the Armed Forces, whether members are the victim, alleged assailant, or both," as well as improving "response of the Department of Defense, the military departments, and the Armed Forces to reports of sexual assaults involving members of the Armed Forces, whether members are the victim, alleged assailant, or both," as well as assaults involving their dependents.[51] Part of SAPR's program involves familiarizing service members with their rights and with the Uniform Code of Military Justice that defines military law and with the specific definitions outlined until Article 120.[52]

Also in 2011 the case of *Cioca v. Rumsfeld* drew public attention to the problem of sexual assault in the military, though the case failed as judges all the way to the Supreme Court relied on the precedent of *Feres*. Each of the sixteen plaintiffs described physical and mental distress from their attacks and argued that the "defendants' acts and omissions in their official capacities contributed to a military culture of tolerance for the sexual crimes perpetrated against them."[53] Cioca was discharged from the coast guard as a result of severe jaw injuries received when she was hit across the face during the assault by an individual who continued to serve despite her reports. Although it failed to overturn the 1950 case, the suit set off a series of new efforts within the armed forces and the government that defined contemporary military policy debates over harassment and assault.

Following the legal failure of *Cioca v. Rumsfeld* and the attention garnered by the documentary *The Invisible War*, lawmakers sought to build on data collection programs to mandate military change. Senator Kirsten Gillibrand (D-NY) introduced the Military Justice Improvement Act to the floor of the Senate in 2013.[54] If passed Gillibrand's bill would have granted "independent military prosecutors the authority to decide whether to convene courts-martial for sexual assault cases and other serious crimes punishable by confinement of more than one year," thus removing decisions about prosecution from the military chain of command.[55] At the same time, the DOD reworked its internal policies to increase transparency about its procedures and started to advertise its SAPR programs.[56] Members of Congress, including Gillibrand, hoped to build on these moves, as well as on the 2012 decision by Secretary of Defense Leon Panetta to remove authority from immediate supervisors to a higher point in the chain of command "at the level of brigade commander or Navy captain."[57]

Proposals opposing or amending Gillibrand's program, including a policy proposal from Senator Claire McCaskill (D-MO), stalled momentum for the legislation.[58] Many of McCaskill's suggestions, including a provision that stipulated that a civilian review should take place if a military prosecutor does not pursue a case, were adopted into the 2014 U.S. defense budget.[59] Years later the suggestion to remove various degrees of power for prosecution from the military resurfaced as the most contentious point of discussion over the division of power between the military and the federal government. At the time, however, neither plan succeeded, as McCaskill's plan passed the Senate but later stalled, and Gillibrand revised and resubmitted her program again in 2017.

Amid this lack of legislative advancement, the DOD reported a 38 percent increase in sexual assaults between 2016 and 2018.

The increase means assaults reached approximately 20,500 cases, something acting Secretary of Defense Patrick M. Shanahan called "unacceptable."[60] (As a minority of only 20 percent of military service members, women disproportionately made up 68 percent of assault victims.) Faced with an ineffective track record, leadership redefined the problem of sexual assault as primarily one of military readiness. In this context the DOD consistently runs statistics and introduces new prevention programs led by teams of primarily current or former service members, but have thus far refused to give up their control over prosecution. In addition to military resistance to civilian prosecutors, the Supreme Court repeatedly declines to hear cases to reverse *Feres v. United States*, which would allow service members to hold the military liable for wrongdoing.

While prosecution is still handled internally, the military is increasingly prosecuting those charged with committing sexual assault. Increased prosecution, however, has failed to discourage rape culture. The military found cause for disciplinary action in 65 percent of the cases that reached the prosecution stage in fiscal year 2018, but the DOD estimates that nearly 80 percent of victims never report their cases.[61] In addition, the military appeals court's decisions to overrule cases, including the 2017 conviction of a West Point cadet for rape, erode confidence in the military justice system and the value of reporting.[62]

In 2019, building on the 2005 program of restricted reporting, the DOD initiated the CATCH program to help "Catch a Serial Offender."[63] The program allows victims to file a restricted report that discloses evidence identifying the perpetrator, and if their information matches a previous submission, they are given the chance to convert their report to unrestricted. An unrestricted report results in the opening of a criminal investigation, but the victim can also decline and choose to end all contact or allow the CATCH staff to contact them for up to ten years with other matches. Since most assailants have more than one victim, DOD hopes CATCH will lead to a larger evidence pool against attackers to build more effective cases.[64] As a new program, its effectiveness and use of the data present two key areas for researchers to monitor regarding prosecution in the coming years.

Finally, going beyond prevention, prosecution, and increased awareness of the impact of gender and sexual orientation, some are beginning to examine the impacts of sexual assault–related physical trauma and emotional post-traumatic stress. The Veterans Administration and women's equality groups have worked together to establish clinics to address rapes, assaults, and attempted rapes, under the term "military sexual trauma."[65] The coinage of the term is significant, as it names the problem and so helps to allow creation of new pathways to treating physical and mental health issues stemming from sexual attacks. The impact of attacks on soldier psychology and the impacts of PTSD are only just becoming clear and will require considerably more research as scholars work to uncover the lasting impacts the unprecedented levels of assault will have on the military in the years to come. But greater awareness of long-term impact must focus on the troops. The coast guard medically discharged Kori Cioca two months before she qualified for veteran's benefits, and despite her need for jaw surgery resulting from her assault while serving, the Veterans Administration refused to cover the costs. Cioca's failed fight highlights some of the inherent flaws in military policy regarding post-traumatic health care benefits.[66]

Conclusion

In spring 2019 a new debate over military sexual harassment and assault broke out over the release of convicted service members. The legal struggles stem from a statute of limitations law that states cases from 1986 to 2006 must be brought within five years or the perpetrator can be freed, even if convicted. New legislation sponsored by congressman and former army staff sergeant Bryan Mast (R-FL) sought to provide a voice for the House's General Council on cases related to rape in the military and to eliminate a statute of limitation on sex-based crimes in the military.[67] In the summer of 2019, the Supreme Court again refused to hear a case that would overrule the *Feres* doctrine. That fall the secretary of defense was ordered to deliver a report to Congress on the number of individuals who brought accusations of sexual assault and were investigated or prosecuted themselves for a crime resulting from a subsequent investigation—in other words, a report on retribution taken against victims.[68]

In December 2020 the Supreme Court finally ruled on the statute of limitations issue in an 8–0 decision that determined the five-year limits did not apply to cases of rape in their hearing of the *United States v. Briggs*. U.S. Air Force Lieutenant Colonel Michael Briggs was originally tried in 2014 for the 2005 rape of a female sergeant. Briggs had confessed on a recorded call to his victim that he was sorry for raping her and was convicted. Due to the loophole regarding rapes before 2006 having a five-year statute of limitations, however, he won an appeal in military court along with other servicemen who had similar convictions, and he was released. The U.S. Air Force hailed the decision, praising how it "boosts Air Force efforts to combat sexual assault," by restoring the convictions of three servicemen and setting precedent for pursing conviction.[69] Whether any of these initiatives or legal victories for victims can reduce crimes, however, remains to be seen.

The sheer volume of tens of thousands of cases of sexual harassment and assault against American service members every year, not to mention the high rates of victims in conflicts around the world, has created a policy crisis within the military. Since 1951 UCMJ has officially prohibited rape and defined it as a crime with unlimited consequences. While enforcing that code has proven exceedingly difficult for the services, recent civilian interest has sparked renewed efforts in mitigating assaults. From 2013 to 2016 alone, legislators presented thirty-six bills, including budgeting documents, that address the issue of military sexual assault.[70] Most of these efforts stalled or were referred up to other committees without being voted on. The DOD continues to create task forces to investigate policies and prosecution records, and efforts to prevent sexual assault and harassment evolve daily.[71] Still, policy changes for sexual assault have come slowly for the military, and those that have passed have yet to produce a meaningful shift in soldier behavior.

Notes

1. West Point Parents, April 11, 2017, https://www.facebook.com/WestPointParents/posts/denim-day-at-west-point-the-us-military-academy-cadets-staff-and-faculty-are-wea/10155343137470572/.

2. "West Point Sets Aside Day to Confront Sexual Harassment," *Army Times*, February 26, 2019, https://www.armytimes.com/news/your-army/2019/02/26/west-point-sets-aside-day-to-confront-sexual-harassment/.

3. Michael Winerip, "Revisiting the Military's Tailhook Scandal," *New York Times*, May 13, 2013, https://www.nytimes.com/2013/05/13/booming/revisiting-the -militarys-tailhook-scandal-video.html.

4. *Overview of the Annual Report on Sexual Harassment and Violence at the Military Service Academies*, statement of Lieutenant General Robert L. Caslen Jr., superintendent, U.S. Military Academy, 115th Cong., 1st sess., May 2, 2017, https://www .govinfo.gov/content/pkg/CHRG-115hhrg25834/html/CHRG-115hhrg25834.htm.

5. Kirby, *Invisible War*; "DOD Annual Report on Sexual Assault in the Military, FY 18," accessed September 17, 2021, https://www.sapr.mil/sites/default/files/DoD _Annual_Report_on_Sexual_Assault_in_the_Military.pdf.

6. Nelson, *For Love of Country*, 42–43, 67; Dave Philipps, "Six Men Tell Their Stories of Sexual Assault in the Military," *New York Times*, August 10, 2019, https:// www.nytimes.com/interactive/2019/09/10/us/men-military-sexual-assault.html; C. Todd Lopez, "Male Hazing Most Common Type of Sexual Assault, Expert Reveals," *Army Times*, April 15, 2016, https://www.army.mil/article/166188/male_hazing_most _common_type_of_sexual_assault_expert_reveals.

7. "Feres Doctrine," Legal Information Institute, Cornell Law School, accessed July 19, 2021, https://www.law.cornell.edu/wex/feres_doctrine; Kevin M. Lewis, "The Feres Doctrine: Congress, the Courts, and Military Servicemember Lawsuits against the United States," Congressional Research Service, June 5, 2019, https://fas .org/sgp/crs/misc/LSB10305.pdf; Daniel v. United States, 587 U.S., 1 (2019).

8. Nathaniel Franks, *Unfriendly Fire*.

9. Melissa Ziobro, "'Skirted Soldiers': The Women's Army Corps and Gender Integration of the U.S. Army during World War II," National Museum of the U.S. Army, June 21, 2016, https://armyhistory.org/skirted-soldiers-the-womens-army -corps-and-gender-integration-of-the-u-s-army-during-world-war-ii/.

10. *Legal and Legislative Basis, Manual for Courts-Martial United States*, 1951, VI, 199, https://www.loc.gov/rr/frd/Military_Law/pdf/CM-1951.pdf.

11. Estes, *Ask and Tell*, 49–50.

12. Stur, *Beyond Combat*, 7.

13. Stur, *Beyond Combat*, 68–69.

14. First Sergeant Linda Earls, interview by Lieutenant Colonel David Siry, West Point Center for Oral History, August 26, 2016.

15. Sergeant Linda McClenahan, interview by Lieutenant Colonel David Siry, West Point Center for Oral History, April 27, 2018.

16. McClenahan, interview.

17. USARV/1st Infantry Division, Provost Marshal—Military Police Desk Blotters, 01/13/1967–02/17/1970, Boxes 4–8, NARA.

18. Brownmiller, *Against Our Will*, 98–99; Turse, *Kill Anything That Moves*, 166–67, 242.

19. Bellafaire, "The Women's Army Corps."

20. Women in Military Service for America Memorial, "Women Entering the Military Academies," Women's Memorial, accessed July 19, 2021, https://www .womensmemorial.org/history/detail/?s=women-enter-the-military-academies.

21. Herdy and Moffeit, "Betrayal in the Ranks," 34.

22. Nelson, *For Love of Country*, 57.

23. Nelson, *For Love of Country*, 58.

24. Quoted in Nelson, *For Love of Country*, 58.

25. Herdy and Moffeit, "Betrayal in the Ranks," 34.

26. Nelson, *For Love of Country*, 54–56.

27. O'Neill, "Sex Scandals in the Gender-Integrated Military," 68.

28. Kaplan, *Interpreter*, 7.

29. Philip Shenon, "Commander at Aberdeen to Retire over Affair," *New York Times*, June 3, 1997, https://www.nytimes.com/1997/06/03/us/commander-at-aberdeen-to-retire-over-an-affair.html.

30. Cerretti, "Rape as a Weapon of War(riors)," 804.

31. Cerretti, "Rape as a Weapon of War(riors)," 803.

32. 10 U.S.C. 893a: Art. 93a., "Prohibited Activities with Military Recruit or Trainee by Person in Position of Special Trust," accessed July 19, 2021, https://uscode.house.gov/view.xhtml?req=granuleid:USC-prelim-title10-section893a&num=0&edition=prelim.

33. Air Force Inspector General, Report to SECAF, "Summary Report Concerning the Handling of Sexual Assault Cases at the United States Air Force Academy," September 14, 2004, 1, https://web.archive.org/web/20090513235422/http://www.af.mil/shared/media/document/AFD-060726-033.pdf.

34. Air Force Inspector General, "Summary Report," 17.

35. Herdy and Moffeit, "Betrayal in the Ranks," 5.

36. Nelson, *For Love of Country*, 189–213.

37. Memorandum from Lieutenant Colonel Cedric G. Lee for CDR/1SG—HQ/A, B, C, "Policy Letter 7—Battle Buddy System," U.S. Department of the Army, June 19, 2018, https://sill-www.army.mil/30ada/2-6/docs/Policy%20letter%206-%20Battle%20Buddy%20System.pdf.

38. Meghann Myers, "Fort Bragg Created a Sexual Assault 'Escape Room' but It's Not What it Sounds Like," *Army Times*, April 9, 2019, https://www.armytimes.com/news/your-army/2019/04/09/fort-bragg-created-a-sexual-assault-escape-room-but-its-not-what-it-sounds-like/.

39. U.S. Department of Defense Sexual Assault Prevention and Response, "DOD Annual Report on Sexual Assault in the Military, FY 18," accessed July 19, 2021, 4, https://www.sapr.mil/sites/default/files/DoD_Annual_Report_on_Sexual_Assault_in_the_Military.pdf; U.S. Department of Defense Sexual Assault Prevention and Response, "Restricted Reporting," accessed July 19, 2021, https://www.sapr.mil/restricted-reporting; U.S. Department of Defense, "Sexual Assault Prevention and Response (SAPR) Program Procedures," May 24, 2017, https://www.esd.whs.mil/Portals/54/Documents/DD/issuances/dodi/649502p.pdf.

40. Kirby, *Invisible War*.

41. National Defense Authorization Act for Fiscal Year 2014, HR 3304, 113th Cong., 2013–14; 10 U.S.C. 925: Art. 125, Kidnapping, January 1, 2019, https://uscode.house.gov/view.xhtml?req=(title:10%20section:925%20edition:prelim).

42. Nathaniel Franks, *Unfriendly Fire*, 181–82.

43. The 2018 level for DOD men was 0.7 percent, but the report labels this 0.1 percent change as a no change in their summary; "DOD Annual Report on Sexual Assault in the Military, FY 18," accessed July 19, 2021, https://www.sapr.mil /sites/default/files/DoD_Annual_Report_on_Sexual_Assault_in_the_Military.pdf.

44. "DOD Annual Report on Sexual Assault in the Military, FY 18."

45. Kirby, *Invisible War*.

46. Franks, *Unfriendly Fire*, 244; for a detailed assessment on morality waivers, see Banner, "Immoral Waiver."

47. Lucas Daprile, "USC Presidential Finalist Says Comments on Sexual Assault Were Taken Out of Context," *The State*, April 29, 2019, https://www.thestate.com /news/local/education/article229799329.html; Kirby, *The Invisible War*.

48. Wood, "Rape during War," 402.

49. Monahan and Neidel-Greenlee, *Few Good Women*, 405–6.

50. Public Law 111-383, Stat. 4137, 2011, https://www.govinfo.gov/content/pkg /PLAW-111publ383/html/PLAW-111publ383.htm.

51. Section 1601, Public Law 111-383, Stat. 4137, 2011, https://www.govinfo.gov /content/pkg/PLAW-111publ383/html/PLAW-111publ383.htm.

52. U.S. Department of Defense, "SAPR and the Uniform Code of Military Justice," accessed July 19, 2021, https://www.sapr.mil/sapr-and-ucmj.

53. *Cioca v. Rumsfeld*, U.S. Fourth Circuit Court of Appeals, No. 12-1065, July 23, 2013, http://www.ca4.uscourts.gov/opinions/Published/121065.p.pdf.

54. Military Justice Improvement Act of 2013, S.1752, 113th Cong., 2013–14.

55. Military Justice Improvement Act of 2017, S.2141,115th Cong., 2017–18.

56. U.S. Department of Defense, "DOD Sexual Assault Prevention and Response Initiatives," 2013, https://archive.defense.gov/news/DodsexualAssault PreventionandResponseInitiatives.pdf; U.S. Department of Defense, "Sexual Assault Prevention and Response (SAPR) Program Procedures," May 24, 2017, https://www .esd.whs.mil/Portals/54/Documents/DD/issuances/dodi/649502p.pdf.

57. Nancy Montgomery, "Policy Change Strips Unit Commanders of Deciding how to Handle Reported Rapes," *Stars and Stripes*, June 3, 2012, https://www .stripes.com/news/europe/germany/policy-change-strips-unit-commanders-of -deciding-how-to-handle-reported-rapes-1.179463.

58. Nora Caplan-Bricker, "Claire McCaskill Defends her Controversial Stance on Military Sexual Assault," *New Republic*, March 6, 2014, https://newrepublic .com/article/116899/military-sexual-assault-vote-senator-claire-mccaskill-her-bill.

59. Spencer Ackerman, "Senate Approves U.S. Defence Budget Plan with Sexual Assault Reforms," *Guardian*, December 20, 2013, https://www.theguardian.com /world/2013/dec/20/congress-passes-ndaa-defense-budget-sexual-assault-reform.

60. Dave Philipps, "'This Is Unacceptable': Military Reports a Surge of Sexual Assaults in the Ranks," *New York Times*, May 2, 2019, https://www.nytimes.com /2019/05/02/us/military-sexual-assault.html.

61. U.S. Department of Defense Sexual Assault Prevention and Response, "DOD Annual Report on Sexual Assault in the Military, FY 18," accessed July 19, 2021, https://www.sapr.mil/sites/default/files/DoD_Annual_Report_on_Sexual_Assault_in_the_Military.pdf.

62. Meghann Myers, "Overturned West Point Rape Case Sends 'Hugely Negative Message,' Former Air Force Prosecutor Says," *Army Times*, June 5, 2019, https://www.armytimes.com/news/your-army/2019/06/05/overturned-west-point-rape-case-sends-hugely-negative-message-former-air-force-prosecutor-says/.

63. C. Todd Lopez, "New DOD Program Leaves Predators Nowhere to Hide," U.S. Department of Defense, August 5, 2019, https://www.defense.gov/explore/story/Article/1926005/new-dod-program-leaves-sexual-predators-nowhere-to-hide/.

64. Lopez, "New DOD Program Leaves Predators Nowhere to Hide."

65. Enloe, *Banana, Beaches, and Bases*, 159.

66. Kirby, *Invisible War*.

67. Yaremi Farinas, "New Legislation Aimed at Protecting Survivors of Military Rape," CBS News, April 26, 2019, https://cbs12.com/news/local/new-legislation-aimed-at-protecting-survivors-of-military-rape.

68. 10 U.S.C. 1561, "Complaints of Sexual Harassment: Investigation by Commanding Officers," 2019, https://uscode.house.gov/view.xhtml?req=(title:10%20section:1561%20edition:prelim).

69. Charles Pope, "Unanimous Supreme Court Ruling Boosts Air Force's Effort to Combat Sexual Assault," U.S. Air Force, December 16, 2020, https://www.af.mil/News/Article-Display/Article/2448527/unanimous-supreme-court-ruling-boosts-air-forces-effort-to-combat-sexual-assault/.

70. "Military Sexual Assault: Chronology of Activity in the 113th–114th Congresses and Related Resources," Congressional Research Service, May 16, 2019, https://fas.org/sgp/crs/natsec/r43168.pdf, 19–21.

71. U.S. Department of Defense, "Sexual Assault Accountability and Investigation Task Force," April 30, 2019, https://media.defense.gov/2019/May/02/2002127159/-1/-1/1/SAAITF_REPORT.PDF.

Bibliography

Archives and Manuscript Materials

NARA. RG 472, Records of U.S. Forces in Southeast Asia, 1950–75. National Archives and Records Administration, College Park MD.

Published Works

Bailey, Beth, and David Farber. *The First Strange Place: The Alchemy of Race and Sex in World War II Hawaii*. Baltimore MD: Johns Hopkins University Press, 1992.

Banner, Francine. "Immoral Waiver: Judicial Review of Intra-Military Sexual Assault Claims." *Lewis & Clark Law Review* 17, no. 3 (2013): 723–87.

Bellafaire, Judith A. "The Women's Army Corps: A Commemoration of World War II Service." CMH Publication 72-15. U.S. Army Center of Military History. Accessed July 19, 2021. https://history.army.mil/brochures/WAC/WAC.HTM.

Brownmiller, Susan. *Against Our Will: Men, Women, and Rape*. New York: Fawcett, [1975] 1993.

Cerretti, Josh. *Abuses of the Erotic: Militarizing Sexuality in the Post–Cold War United States*. Lincoln: University of Nebraska Press, 2019.

——— . "Rape as a Weapon of War(riors): The Militarization of Sexual Violence in the United States, 1990–2000." *Gender & History* 28, no. 3 (2016): 794–812.

Clark, Janine Natalya. "Making Sense of Wartime Rape: A Multi-Causal and Multi-Level Analysis." *Enthnopolitics* 13, no. 5 (2014): 461–82.

Enloe, Cynthia. *Bananas, Beaches, and Bases: Making Feminist Sense of International Politics*. 2nd ed. Berkeley: University of California Press, [1989] 2014.

——— . *Maneuvers: The International Politics of Militarizing Women's Lives*. Berkeley: University of California Press, 2000.

Estes, Steve. *Ask and Tell: Gay and Lesbian Veterans Speak Out*. Chapel Hill: University of North Carolina Press, 2007.

Feimster, Crystal N. "'How Are the Daughters of Eve Punished?' Rape during the Civil War." In *Writing Women's History: A Tribute to Anne Firor Scott*, edited by Elizabeth Anne Payne, 64–78. Jackson: University Press of Mississippi, 2011.

Franks, Nathaniel. *Unfriendly Fire: How the Gay Ban Undermines the Military and Weakens America*. New York: St. Martin's, 2009.

Frederick, Jim. *Black Hearts: One Platoon's Descent into Madness in Iraq's Triangle of Darkness*. New York: Broadway, 2010.

Henry, Nicola. *War and Rape: Law, Memory, and Justice*. New York: Routledge, 2011.

Herdy, Amy, and Miles Moffeit. "Betrayal in the Ranks." *Denver Post*, extra digital newsbook. 2004. https://extras.denverpost.com/justice/tdp_betrayal.pdf.

Kaplan, Alice. *The Interpreter*. Chicago: University of Chicago Press, 2005.

Kirby, Dick, dir. *The Invisible War*. Los Angeles: Cinedigm, 2012.

Monahan, Evelyn M., and Rosemary Neidel-Greenlee. *A Few Good Women: America's Military Women from World War I to the Wars in Iraq and Afghanistan*. New York: Anchor, 2011.

Moore, Eileen C. "To Combat Sexual Assault in the Military, Womanpower Is Essential." GP *Solo* 35, no. 1 (January–February 2018): 38–41.

Nelson, T. S. *For Love of Country: Confronting Rape and Sexual Harassment in the U.S. Military*. New York: Hayworth, 2002.

O'Neill, William L. "Sex Scandals in the Gender-Integrated Military." *Gender Issues* 16, nos. 1–2 (Winter–Spring 1998): 64–85.

Pryor, John B. "Sexual Harassment in the United States Military: The Development of the DOD Survey." Report #DEOMI-88-6. Defense Equal Opportunity Management Institute, Patrick Air Force Base FL. September 30, 1988. https://apps.dtic.mil/dtic/tr/fulltext/u2/a207047.pdf.

Roberts, Mary Louise. *What Soldiers Do: Sex and the American GI in World War II France*. Chicago: University of Chicago Press, 2013.

Stur, Heather. *Beyond Combat: Women and Gender in the Vietnam War Era.* New York: Cambridge University Press, 2011.

Sturdevant, Saundra Pollock, and Brenda Stoltzfus. *Let the Good Times Roll: Prostitution and the U.S. Military in Asia.* New York: Norton, 1993.

Thoman, Jay, and Erika Andresen. "The Military's Campaign against Sexual Assault." GP *Solo* 35, no. 3 (May 2018): 40–44.

U.S. Congress, House of Representatives, Subcommittee on Military Personnel of the Committee on Armed Services. *Overview of the Annual Report on Sexual Harassment and Violence at the Military Service Academies.* 115th Cong., 1st sess., May 2, 2017. https://www.govinfo.gov/content/pkg/CHRG-115hhrg25834 /html/CHRG-115hhrg25834.htm.

Vuic, Kara Dixon. *Officer, Nurse, Woman: The Army Nurse Corps in the Vietnam War.* Baltimore MD: Johns Hopkins University Press, 2010.

Weaver, Gina Marie. *Ideologies of Forgetting: Rape in the Vietnam War.* Albany: State University of New York Press, 2010.

Wood, Elisabeth Jean. "Conflict-Related Sexual Violence and the Policy Implications of Recent Research." *International Review of the Red Cross* 96, no. 894 (2014): 457–78.

———. "Rape during War Is Not Inevitable: Variation in Wartime Sexual Violence." In *Understanding and Proving International Sex Crimes,* edited by Morten Bergsmo, Alf Butenschon Skre, and Elisabeth J. Wood, 389–419. Beijing: Torkel Opsahl, 2012.

———. "Variation in Sexual Violence During War." *Politics and Society* 34, no. 3 (2006).

Wood, Elisabeth Jean, and Nathaniel Toppelberg. "The Persistence of Sexual Assault within the U.S. Military." *Journal of Peace Research* 54, no. 5 (2017): 620–33.

Zimmerman, Jean. *Tailspin: Women and War in the Wake of Tailhook.* New York: Doubleday, 1995.

PART 5

Gender, Sexuality, and Combat

Combat Exclusion Policies and the Management of Gender Difference in the U.S. Military

ELIZABETH MESOK

On January 11, 2005, President George W. Bush assured the American public that there were "no women in combat."[1] The declaration came in the midst of the early years of the U.S.-led occupation of Iraq, where American military women were regularly participating in direct ground combat in violation of official Pentagon policy. During the wars in Iraq and Afghanistan, the policies barring women from ground combat were nearly impossible to enforce, given both the irregular nature of counterinsurgency warfare and military commanders' belief that having female soldiers and marines present on combat missions to interact with civilians would contribute to mission effectiveness. Yet Bush's unequivocal denial of women's involvement in combat—despite all evidence to the contrary—speaks to the United States' complicated history of needing women's military labor while insisting on their exclusion from combat, an exclusion that was often rhetorical and not always reflected in the reality of women's experiences at war.

This chapter explicates the historical origins of this paradox, beginning with the debates over expanding women's military roles in the early 1970s, when the transition to the All-Volunteer Force (AVF) and the anticipated ratification of the Equal Rights Amendment (ERA) prompted a reimagining of women's military labor. There were few debates over women and combat prior to the 1970s, as military women were predominantly conceptualized as supplemental and needed to "free" men to fight or prevent men from being drafted. For instance, the Women's Armed Services Integration Act, which established permanent roles for women in the military in 1948, was based on the need to harness the nation's "womanpower" in order to make men available for the "rougher and more actives duties" of combat.[2] Along with limiting women's overall presence in the armed forces to 2 percent, the Integration Act also contained provisions prohibiting the assignment of navy women to ships other than hospital and transport ships, and navy and air force women to combat aircraft, suggesting that women, of course, were never imagined as "equal" military subjects to be fully integrated alongside men.[3] Indeed, the Integration Act was passed just two months prior to Executive Order 9981, which ended racial segregation and promised "equality of treatment and opportunity for all persons in the armed services without regard to race, color, religion or national origin"—with no mention of sex or gender.[4] While the Integration Act created permanent roles for women in the military, it also codified women as a fundamentally different category of military subject and marked gender difference, unlike racial or religious difference, as something to be regulated and maintained rather than assimilated. The management of women's presumably innate gender difference occurred in large part through combat exclusion policies, which attempted to mark combat labor as definitively the work of men.

Given the constitutional mandate of a civilian-controlled military, decisions regarding the utilization of women in the military are overwhelmingly made by Congress and influenced by political will, albeit with the input of military leadership and considerations of military necessity. Historically, both military and civilian advocates of expanding women's military roles have focused on the role of armed service in securing women's full citizenship and equality; on the largely arbitrary definition of "combat" and the fact that despite assignment restrictions women were often still exposed to combat; and on the need for women's military labor. Arguments against women's participation in combat were, broadly speaking, rooted in the belief that women are inherently different than men. Some claimed that women's lack of physical strength and emotional durability would erode unit cohesion and negatively impact military readiness. Others argued that women symbolize motherhood and the creation of life, and therefore men will naturally be inclined to protect them at the expense of mission objectives and their own safety, or that allowing women to act "like men" will lead to the degradation of traditional social mores and family values. Arguments opposing women in combat conflate the concepts of gender and sex; gender identity is understood as emanating from the biological differences between men and women and thus is ahistorical and immutable.

Congressional debates over women's access to combat roles grappled with two, often competing, interests: the need to meet the labor needs of the military, which significantly increased following the end of the draft in 1973, and the need to maintain social constructions of gender. Women, here, were considered to be in need of men's protection, and excluding women from combat served to protect both women's material bodies while in the theater of war and women's feminine virtue as well as the gendered social order. Importantly, the construction of femininity imagined to be in need of protection is an inherently racialized construction rarely extended to Black women and women of color. Despite the preoccupation with racial difference that shaped debates regarding the integration of Black soldiers in the immediate postwar era, later debates over women's military roles among congressional and military leadership were largely silent on the issue of women's racial difference and implicitly shaped by a construction of femininity that imagined "women" to be white.

Combat exclusion policies that focused on protecting women and their allegedly inherent femininity also, by extension, worked to protect the masculine coherence of the military institution. As Susan Jeffords writes in her study of masculinity and the Vietnam War, "War *is* the spectacle of the masculine bond. It is the optimal display of masculine collectivity in America, since battle, as defined by American culture, is an exclusively male activity."[5] Throughout the late twentieth century, women's gradual entrance into spaces that were once all-male threatened the presumably natural relationship between men, masculinity, and warfare. Until its repeal in 2013, the combat exclusion policy worked to stabilize this relationship by symbolically and materially excluding women's feminine difference from the defining activity of both the military and masculinity: direct ground combat warfare. If, as Jeffords argues, war is "the most efficient structural space for the figuration of gender difference," combat exclusion policies can be read as symbolically reaffirming that differentiation even as it was materially disrupted. However, even as restrictions barring women from combat roles were officially rescinded in 2013, presumptions of difference remain. Policies excluding women from combat were not lifted because Congress and military leadership recognized that women were necessarily equal to men, but rather because gender difference was identified as a tool for fighting nontraditional warfare.

The definition of "combat" is central to the debates over women's exclusion, and yet there is no singular, stable definition of the term any more than there is a singular, stable definition of "women." Is combat defined by a spatial location on the battlefield, by the act of engaging an enemy, or by a job title? Further, how has the evolution of U.S. warfare transformed an understanding of what constitutes combat and combatants? Within U.S. counterinsurgency campaigns—both before and after the emergence of the global war on terror—differentiating between combat and noncombat positions and between combatants and noncombatants is difficult if not impossible.[6] As retired U.S. Air Force colonel Lory Fenner notes, "Our doctrine and tactics, as well as our strategy, recognize that in modern warfare there is little distinction between combatants and noncombatants; all are at risk."[7] This chapter analyzes how the combat exclusion policy worked historically, as feminist historian Linda Kerber observes, as a "social marker rather than a substantive boundary" and a means by which to affirm the difference between men and women—until that very difference was named as a key asset to waging population-centric counterinsurgency warfare.[8]

Arguments against Women's Entrance to the Military Service Academies in the Early 1970s

In the early 1970s, the transition to the AVF and the burgeoning women's movement catalyzed sweeping changes for women in the U.S. armed forces. In 1972, largely owing to concerted feminist advocacy against legally codified gender inequalities, Congress passed the ERA, an amendment that had been consistently defeated since its initial introduction in 1921. The congressional passage of the ERA sparked debates over women's role in the armed forces, in particular whether the amendment's ratification would require women to register for the draft or allow them to serve in combat. Women's equal rights activists, including the National Organization for Women (NOW), advocated for the elimination of sex-based restrictions in employment and the expansion of military roles for women, asserting that equality for women in the military was a necessary precondition for women obtaining full citizenship. Conservative forces opposed to the women's liberation movement and intent on preventing the ERA's ratification, however, argued that legislating gender equality would have devastating social effects. Anti-ERA forces seized upon the issue of women in the military to highlight the destruction such an amendment would bring, particularly given that the amendment did not include specific language exempting women from the draft.[9] The 1970s were thus marked by debates over women's military service, debates that served as a conduit for deeper political arguments against women's equality and for the maintenance of traditional gendered social and economic arrangements.

The congressional passage of the ERA and the ensuing debates over women's role in the military occurred, however, simultaneously with the transition to the AVF and an increased need for women's military service. The Department of Defense (DOD) and military leadership, anticipating both the labor shortage that would accompany the end of the draft and the ratification of the ERA, began to explore options on how best to utilize women in the services. In 1972 the Central All-Volunteer Task Force provided a plan for meeting All-Volunteer Force objectives by "increasing use of women to offset any shortage of men."[10] Aware of the pending ERA, the report reflects the DOD's intention to "make Military and Civilian service in the Department of Defense a model of equal opportunity for all regardless of race, sex, creed, or national origin"—a shift from the postwar language of Executive Order 9981, which made no reference to sex or gender.[11] However, based on the restrictions codified in the Integration Act, women were prohibited from serving aboard combat aircraft and naval vessels and the task force acknowledged that they, in line with the services, were making recommendations for the utilization of women based on the assumption that "military women will not participate as active members of combatant units."[12] Asserting that women's military labor would be used to support rather than directly enact combat warfare was crucial given the expectation that the ratification of the ERA would challenge combat exclusion policies as unconstitutional.

In August 1972 an ad hoc committee known as the ERA Committee was established by the army chief of staff to study how the amendment's anticipated ratification would affect the army. The committee made a number of recommendations, including that, regardless of whether the ERA was ratified, the army should continue to employ women only in noncombat roles but should also allow for the enrollment of women in the U.S. Military Academy, the army's service academy in West Point, New York. However, military leadership overwhelmingly balked at the idea of admitting women to the service academies and insisted that, since the academies were intended to train men for combat leadership roles, women should not be permitted to attend. In 1972 and 1973 congressional proposals to admit women to the military academies were opposed by the DOD, the services, and the chairman of the House Armed Services Committee. In September 1973 two congressmen filed suit against the Air Force Academy and the Naval Academy, alleging that their refusal to consider women for admittance was unconstitutional.[13] In June 1974 the court found in favor of the defendants, stating that "the admissions policy of the Navy and Air Force Academies is reasonably related to furthering a legitimate governmental interest— the preparation of young men to assume leadership roles in combat where necessary to the defense of the nation."[14] As long as women remained barred from combat roles, the court reasoned, there was no reason to admit them to military service academies.

Congress, however, was persistent, and in the spring and summer of 1974, hearings were held on the proposition that women should be allowed admittance to the academies. The proposal was met with great resistance from military leadership, who testified as to why women should not be allowed to serve in combat and therefore should be denied entrance to the service academies. The opposing arguments, laden with essentialist and patronizing rhetoric, overwhelmingly focused on maintaining women's exclusion from combat and repeatedly emphasized the importance of respecting the allegedly innate difference between men and women. For instance, Lieutenant General Albert P. Clark, superintendent of the

U.S. Air Force Academy, argued that to ignore "the physiological and biological difference between the sexes and the resulting evolutionary differences in their roles in society" would be a grave mistake: "For this nation to open combat roles to our women, short of a dire emergency, in my view, offends the dignity of womanhood and ignores the harsh realities of war."[15] For Clark the difference between the sexes and the question of whether women were capable of withstanding and competing in combat was far less important than the need to protect the "dignity of womanhood" and, by extension, the gendered social order.

Women also constructed arguments based on an assumption of women's innate difference and thus unsuitability for combat roles. For instance, Jacqueline Cochran, the former head of the Women Airforce Service Pilots (WASPS), argued that women had "no business" being in the academies or in combat, since "a woman's primary function in life is to get married, maintain a home and raise a family."[16] Despite the fact that Cochran herself stood as evidence that women *could* serve in combat—she testified to flying bombers and taking enemy fire during World War II—she was adamant that women should remain excluded from combat warfare based on the fact that women were, quite simply, different from men. During her testimony, when asked to elaborate as to why combat should be the exclusive responsibility of men, Cochran replied, "Because they are men and we don't have to do it because we are women."[17] This tautological argument—that men should serve in combat because they are men and women should not serve in combat because they are women—characterizes much of the opposition to women in combat in the late twentieth century. Indeed, Cochran's testimony suggests that the combat exclusion policies worked to symbolically differentiate men and women more than they reflected women's actual abilities. In other words, excluding women from combat maintained that men and women were innately different. To allow women in combat would disrupt essentialized notions of women's biological difference as predictive of her physical, intellectual, and emotional capacities, destabilize the gender binary of masculine and feminine, and threaten the symbolic order of both society and the military.

Importantly, the 1974 congressional hearings on women's admittance to the service academies reveal the interdependence of the definition of "combat" and the definition of "women." For instance, when asked whether the definition of combat was fixed or whether it needed to be revisited, Clark was emphatic: "I don't think combat is going to change. It hasn't changed for thousands of years . . . and I don't think we should inject our women into that role if we don't have to."[18] This statement, which ignores the monumental changes to combat warfare wrought by the invention of air power and other technological advances, represents a desire for combat to remain fixed and known in order for there to be clear boundaries that would demarcate where "our women" do not belong. Similarly, when asked to define combat, General Fred Weyand, army vice chief of staff, began by referencing the specific branches of the army—the arms of infantry, air defense, artillery, and armor—as well as "those elements that are expected to look at the enemy face-to-face" and engage in "close physical contact with the enemy forces."[19] However, in the next breath, Weyand emphasized, "This whole business of what is a combat role, of course, is very pertinent to the issues that you are considering, because we repeat over and over again that we do not believe that our daughters, or our women, should engage in combat."[20] Regardless of the technical definition of combat, it is something that "our women" and "our daughters" should not do. Indeed, women's exclusion from combat was often the only stable characteristic of combat; combat is fluid, it changes historically and in response to new technology, it differs between the services, but at the very least, it is defined as an activity exclusively performed by men. In the end Congress argued that women's exclusion from combat was not relevant to the decision as to whether or not admit women to the service academies, signaling a commitment to advancing women's military equality. On October 7, 1975, to the shock and dismay of most military leadership, Public Law 94-196 was signed into law, requiring the service academies to admit women.

Combat Aircraft and Ships and the Arbitrariness of Women's Combat Exclusion: Debates in the Late 1970s

While the 1975 decision to admit women to the service academies certainly expanded women's military opportunities, the combat exclusion policies continued to constrain their career advancement, particularly in the navy and the air force. Specifically, Section 6015 of U.S. Code Title 10 prohibited assignment of women in the navy and Marine Corps to ships or aircraft engaged in combat missions, and Section 8549 prohibited assignment of women in the U.S. Air Force to aircraft engaged in combat missions. There was, however, no formal restriction on the assignment of women in the army, with Section 3012 granting the secretary of the army the authority to determine how women should be assigned.

The reason for the army's discretion in the assignment of women can be traced back to the congressional hearings on the Integration Act, where army leadership presented convincing arguments that future wars would make differentiating combat from noncombat zones impossible and inefficient. As Colonel Mary Hallaren, the director of the Women's Army Corps testified, "Modern warfare makes us vulnerable in our own backyard," and "when the house is on fire, we don't talk about a woman's place in the home. And we don't send her a gilt-edged invitation to help put the fire out."[21] The army recognized, even then, that the future of warfare would require flexibility in determining how best to utilize women, regardless of combat and noncombat designations, and that there would be no time to be constrained by the trappings of gender conventions. As Major General Jeanne Holm of the U.S. Air Force writes, "Because the Army was unable to come up with an adequate, acceptable definition of combat, Congress elected to leave this matter to be sorted out by the Secretary of the Army so long as clearly understood the intent of Congress, which was *no combat for women*."[22]

For years the Defense Advisory Committee on Women in the Services (DACOWITS) and the DOD had recommended granting the secretaries of the navy and the air force the same flexibility in assigning women. Following the 1975 decision to admit women to the service academies, the DOD continued to press for increased flexibility in women's assignments, given the anticipated graduation of the first classes of women in 1980. In late 1977 Deputy Secretary of Defense Charles Duncan urged Congress to repeal the laws and to authorize the secretary of defense to decide where and how military women should be utilized. The House rejected Duncan's proposals and instead passed a bill to modify Section 6015, which allowed women to serve on permanent duty on hospital and transport ships, while maintaining women's exclusion from combat ships and aircraft.[23] This legislation followed the *Owens v. Brown* class-action sex discrimination lawsuit against the navy, which found that Section 6015 denied navy women their constitutional right to equal protection. In the ruling against the navy, Judge John J. Sirica argued that Section 6015 "tends to suggest a statutory purpose more related to the traditional ways of thinking of women than to the demands of military preparedness."[24] The decision to allow women to serve on some ships, but not all, reveals the largely arbitrary nature of women's exclusion from combat but also offered a glimmer of hope that the "traditional way of thinking of women" had perhaps begun to shift.

A year later the DOD, recognizing that the combat exclusion policies limited the ability of the AVF to meet its labor needs, provided Congress the first official definition of combat in the history of the U.S. military: "The term 'combat' refers to 'engaging an enemy or being engaged by an enemy in armed conflict.' Under current practices, a person is considered to be 'in combat' when he or she is in a geographic area designated as a combat/hostile fire zone. . . . These definitions apply to men and women of all the services."[25] With an eye toward easing restrictions on the utilization of women, the DOD recognized that, despite being classified as noncombatants, "women have served in combat in many skills during World War II, Korea, and Vietnam. Army nurses have served in combat for over a hundred years."[26] Importantly, the DOD recognized the ambiguity of the term "combat" and the arbitrariness of using such a shifting designation as a basis for women's assignment: "Since the word 'combat' has historically been used to include such a broad range of activities, the Department of Defense does not believe that the term provides a useful basis for expanding the opportunities for women in the services."[27] Because of the barriers they posed to increasing the use of women in the navy and air force, the DOD recommended the repeal of Sections 6015 and 8549.

In November 1979 and February 1980, the House Armed Services Subcommittee on Military Personnel held hearings on DOD-sponsored bills to rescind Sections 6015 and 8549 and permit women on combat ships and aircraft. The bills were debated in a social and political climate marked by the defeat of the ERA and a growing conservative backlash against the women's movement, both of which decreased congressional willingness to legislate women's equality. While women in combat had always been a controversial and divisive issue, advocates of women's military equality were "blindsided" by the deeply conservative and oppositional testimony offered at the hearings, from both the military and civil organizations.[28] In a significant shift from mandating the services academies to admit women just four years prior, Congress now gave conservative voices center stage to wage arguments against expanding women's military roles based on the need to uphold traditional "family values" and gender arrangements.

During the hearings supporters of expanding women's roles offered reasoned arguments rooted in legal analysis and social science data, insisting that combat restrictions were based not on logic but on paternalistic notions of women's supposedly inherent need for protection, a protection that could no longer be guaranteed within modern theaters of war. Indeed, keeping women off combat ships and aircraft worked only to deny women's equality, they argued, for nothing could definitively guarantee a service member's safety while at war. Drawing on similar logic used by the army in 1948 Integration Act hearings, Antonia Handler Chayes, under secretary of the air force, argued, "In any future war, I have no doubt women will face more severe risks of injury, just as U.S. civilians will. What we achieve by barring women from combat roles is an obstacle to career advancement, and little enhancement of protection."[29] Further, advocates linked women's military service to citizenship rites. As Diana Steele, a lawyer with the American Civil Liberties Union (ACLU), argued, "Until both the responsibilities and the rights of citizenship are shared on a gender-neutral basis, women will continue to be considered less than full-fledged citizens."[30]

On the opposing side, conservative political and religious organizations as well as military leadership—despite the fact that the bills were supported by the DOD—offered testimony against allowing women to serve on combat ships and aircraft. Steeped in Christian morality and calls to preserve traditional American values, in which women are imagined as innately and exceptionally feminine, opposing testimony called for women's protection and thus women's exclusion from all combat roles. As historian Beth Bailey notes, many opponents of expanding women's military roles argued that "Americans should hold to the timeless truths, to the divine wisdom, to the traditional values that defined the differences between men and women."[31] For instance, General William Westmoreland, former chief of staff of the army, testified against women in combat based on the supposedly natural roles that men and women have always played: "Traditionally in our society the warrior has been the man. It has been the man who society has called on, called upon to destroy, and the woman has been called upon to create."[32] Representative Larry McDonald (D-GA), who opposed the bills and denounced "leftist support for the feminization of the Armed Forces," answered pointedly when asked why women should not be allowed in combat: "Because in our society, we have women as sweethearts, as wives, as mothers, and as daughters," and as long as we exist in "a civilization that gives a special homage to women," the American public will not accept women in combat.[33]

For these opponents allowing women to serve aboard combat aircraft and ships would threaten the "special homage" afforded to women, the honor and meaning of being a woman. Speaking to the allegedly eternal character of womanhood, Charles Cade, the operations director of Moral Majority, a conservative political organization founded by Baptist minister Jerry Falwell, testified that allowing women in combat would be a "violation of God's creation," as their "sensibilities will be offended in the rough environment of simulated combat. They will become defeminized, denatured; in truth, less than they were created to be."[34] Here, the constructedness of femininity is exposed: women are presumed to be naturally, innately feminine, but femininity must be cultivated, performed, and, above all, protected. Allowing women to engage in combat roles would, according to such testimony, potentially disrupt women's ability to fulfill their feminine destiny and thus threaten the civilizational order of society.

Other opponents of women serving in combat argued that for a woman to desire such an occupation was not just unnatural and ungodly, but pathological. Psychiatrist Harold M. Voth testified that women who want to serve in combat have "profound psychologic difficulties which may cause them to veer away from the most classic feminine identity."[35] In line with the ideology of feminine domesticity, Voth believed women should be naturally fulfilled by the pleasures of the home, motherhood, and marriage. Desiring to be "like men," as Voth argued, could be characterized as an "antifemininity or masculinity complex" that causes women to "want what the male has rather than strive for more recognition and greater reward for *what women are* and contribute best to society." For Voth, as for many opponents of women in combat, gender identity emanates from biological difference and, therefore, is fixed; quite simply, he argued, "a woman cannot become a man any more than a man can become a woman."[36] The very fact that individuals such as Voth—who also believed that the feminist movement was contributing to the degradation of family life, and that women would prefer to remain in the home if it were not for economic pressures—were given visibility during these hearings suggests that the depth of resistance to women in combat was about much more than concerns over military readiness or national security. Testimony such as Voth's bespeaks a hostility not just to women's equality but to what such equality might result in: exposing the fictiveness of the gender binary and fundamental shifts to gendered social and economic arrangements.

Indeed, opposing testimony overwhelmingly focused on the imperative of protecting women's femininity. Paradoxically, concerns about protecting femininity implicitly recognized gender as malleable and fluid, even as the femininity to be protected was understood as natural and immutable. Opponents, here, were equally concerned about maintaining a clear gender binary. The protection of men's masculinity was central. If women's exposure to combat risked defeminizing or denaturing women, as Voth argued, allowing women in combat would also risk men's emasculation—it would threaten to strip them of the very thing that definitively made them men. Former marine infantry commander James Webb made a related argument in an article published in the *Washingtonian* in 1979 and included in the hearings. In particular Webb argued that men in the service academies are "stronger and more aggressive" than their civilian counterparts: "They play hard. They drink hard. They are physical, often comically abusive among each other. They are not trying to prove their manhood; they are celebrating their masculinity."[37] Indeed, the service academies had long existed as institutions devoted to crafting men into warriors; the recent decision to allow women to infiltrate previously male-only space provoked resentment and even violence against women. Jeff McFadden, a 1979 Naval Academy graduate, is quoted in Webb's article as saying, "Males in the society feel stripped, symbolically and actually. I wonder if that doesn't tie into the increase in rapes over the past decade. Rape is a crime of revenge, not passion. In any event, the real question isn't the women. The real question is this: Where in this country can someone go to find out if he is a man? And where can someone who knows he is a man go to celebrate his masculinity?"[38] Allowing women to perform the same tasks as men destabilizes the gender binary and undermines "masculinity." It also exposes the fictiveness of the supposedly natural relationship between men, masculinity, and combat warfare. As women advance through the ranks of the military, as they demonstrate their physiological and intellectual capacity, men risk losing exclusive access to cultivating the behavior and obtaining the character traits that definitively make them men.

Further, as referenced here by McFadden, the topic of sexual violence is present throughout most opponents' testimony. Despite the insistence that in American society women are "sweethearts" to be respected and protected, most who opposed allowing women in combat recognized that women were also at risk of violence at the hands of American men. McFadden's pondering that men's threatened masculinity was related to the rise in rape was mirrored in Webb's prediction that sexual violence will increase as clearly defined gender roles are degraded: "Introducing women into combat units would greatly confuse an already confusing environment, and would lessen the aggressive tendencies of the units, as many aggressions would be directed inward, toward sex, rather than outward, toward violence."[39]

Tottie Ellis, the national vice president of the conservative women's group Eagle Forum, called out the hypocrisy of feminists who "go on and on about battered wives" and simultaneously call for women to be placed in combat, which "would open the gates to rape from the enemy as well as from our own men."[40] Phyllis Schlafly, the president of the anti–women's rights group STOP ERA, noted that the "rape rate" in the services was twice as high as in civilian life. She then asked, "How could anyone be surprised?"[41] Ellis and Schlafly's insistence that sexual violence would be an inevitable, if regrettable, outcome of integrating women further into combat roles countered the idea that men are, by definition, supposed to protect women. Webb also saw rape as the consequence of combat integration. He argued that the aggression required of men at war would be "directed inward, toward sex," suggesting that men's frustration with the breakdown of clearly defined gender roles would result in sexual violence as a means to insist on sexual differentiation and to reimpose such gender boundaries between masculine and feminine.[42]

Overall, opposing testimony hardly even addressed the issue at hand—whether to permit women to serve on combat aircraft and ships. Instead, opponents seized an opportunity to issue dire warnings about military women's threat to the social order, with some individuals calling for the removal of women from uniform altogether. The arguments presented by opponents made it clear that they were less interested in protecting women from physical harm and more interested in protecting the social construct of womanhood. In the end the hearings concluded without a decision on whether to repeal the combat exclusion policies barring women from combat aircraft and ships.

New Roles and New Rules for Women in Combat in the 1980s and 1990s

Despite the resistance to expanding women's roles, the number of women in the military continued to grow, particularly with the end of conscription in 1973. From the time the 2 percent ceiling was lifted in 1967 until 1980, the number of women in the forces had tripled.[43] In response to the growing presence of women in the force, the military continued to create new rules to mitigate women's exposure to combat, rules that U.S. military interventions of the 1980s and 1990s proved ineffective. In 1983, for example, the army instituted the Direct Combat Probability Coding (DCPC), which barred women soldiers not just from combat roles, but also from being "collocated" with—or assigned in close proximal relation to—direct combat units, a distinction confusing for army leaders to implement in practice. For instance, during the U.S invasion of Grenada that same year, four U.S military policewomen were deployed only to be sent back to Fort Bragg by a commander who was concerned about women's exposure to danger.[44]

In 1988, following an assessment of the existing policies as ambiguous and contradictory, the DOD adopted the "Risk Rule," a single standard against which all services were to evaluate the assignment of women. This new policy mandated that women be excluded from combat and noncombat positions on "grounds of risk of exposure to direct combat, hostile fire, or capture, provided that the type, degree, and duration of risk is equal to or greater than that experienced by associate combat units (of similar land, sea, or air type) in the same theaters of operation."[45] The Risk Rule exposed the arbitrariness of using combat and noncombat designations as a basis for women's assignment in its recognition that some jobs classified as "noncombat" might actually place women in greater danger than jobs designated as "combat."[46] Ultimately, the Risk Rule's reliance on spatial location to accurately predict the likelihood of combat exposure proved untenable. In the 1989 invasion of Panama, more than 150 deployed women soldiers were reported to have been in close proximity to combat, with accounts of women even leading units in combat.[47]

While the policies of the 1980s demonstrated the difficulty of clearly excluding women from harm when deployed to theaters of war, the Persian Gulf War brought the issue of women and combat to the attention of the American public, generating what feminist theorist Ilene Rose Feinman calls "a concern at times approaching national obsession."[48] Women comprised more than 12 percent of the armed forces deployed to the Persian Gulf, and their participation in and exposure to combat was, for the first time in U.S. military history, widely visible to the American public. The media, dubbing the war a "mom's war," ran stories on mothers leaving behind their children, aligning "women" with heterosexuality and motherhood.[49] However, at the same time that the media was associating military women with the creation of life, the public was faced with the reality of women at war, a reality that included the capture and imprisonment of two women and the death of twelve others.[50] As feminist international relations scholar Cynthia Enloe observed at the time, "The always artificial categories of 'combat,' 'near combat,' and 'non-combat' may indeed be crumbling in the desert."[51]

Congress reflected their awareness of the arbitrariness of such barriers when they passed the 1992/93 Defense Authorization Bill in the spring of 1991, which repealed the restrictions on women flying combat aircraft. However, Public Law 102-190, the legislation that formally rescinded the limitations on assignment of women to combat aircraft, also established the Presidential Commission on the Assignment of Women in the Armed Forces to assess the laws and policies governing the assignment of women in the military. The commission, which Feinman calls "a compromise and a stall on the enforcement of Public Law 102-190," was formed in response to conservative resistance toward women's growing presence in the armed forces following the Gulf War.[52] Of the fifteen commissioners appointed by the Bush administration, six were women, more than half were military leadership, and the majority held predetermined opinions *against* women in combat.[53] Insisting that the question was less about whether women can fly combat aircraft and more about whether they should, the commission's final report revealed the deep resistance to expanding roles for women in the military, as they recommended against the enforcement of Public Law 102-190 and the assignment of women to combat-mission aircraft. The commission also recommended that women should be overwhelmingly banned from combat assignments, including direct ground combat units, amphibious craft and submarines, combat-mission aircraft, and Special Forces. They did, however, acknowledge that "there are circumstances under which women *might* be assigned to combat positions."[54] Even this extremely cautious recommendation was too extreme for five of the commissioners, who detailed their objections in a separate section of the report titled "Alternative Views."

The deeply conservative objections offered in the alternative section of the report reflect the opposition against expanding women's military roles seen in the 1979 hearings. The opposing commissioners argued that, unequivocally, there are no circumstances in which women should ever be allowed in combat. In opposition to some witnesses' claims that allowing women in combat would actually enhance military effectiveness, or that allowing women in combat was the right of women as citizens, these opponents focused on the "deep-seated cultural and family values millions of American hold and are still teaching their children."[55] Echoing the ominous warnings heard in the 1979 hearings, these commissioners warned that allowing women to serve in combat would cause "monumental and irreversible" damage to American culture and society.[56] Indeed, the commissioners write, "the successful integration of women into combat units could occur only if we as a society undergo a cultural change discouraging men from protecting women. . . . Good men respect and defend women. Women should not be required, as the price for equality, to sacrifice this fundamental principle that governs a civilized order."[57] According to this logic, allowing women to serve in combat roles is only possible if gender norms that identify "women" as passive and in need of protection, and "men" as active defenders, are dismantled. The "fundamental principle" of gender differentiation, which is challenged by women's mere presence in a once all-male institution, is reaffirmed through the distinction of "combat" and "noncombat." Indeed, as an army veteran stated in his testimony before the commission, "The distinction between combat and noncombat is purely descriptive and never definitive. The only reason it is made at all is to say where women may serve or where they may not serve. The line between the two is always drawn arbitrarily."[58] Here the differentiation of men and women is constituted along the lines of combat and noncombat—or, in other words, the insistence on the differentiation of combat and noncombat is needed to ensure the differentiation between men and women.[59]

The commission's final report was sent to President Bush on November 15, 1992, following his loss of the presidential election to Bill Clinton. Given this political shift, along with broad public support of women following their performance in the Gulf War, the commission's recommendation against the enforcement of Public Law 102-190 was disregarded. By April 1993 Secretary of Defense Les Aspin had called for the opening of as many combat roles as possible under the law. By the end of 1993, Congress had also repealed the naval combat ship exclusions.[60] In addition, Secretary Aspin established an Implementation Committee to review the Risk Rule, which found that, based on the experiences in Operation Desert Storm, the rule was no longer relevant, as there were no assignments within a theater of war that could be definitively without the risk of combat. In response, Aspin issued the Direct Ground Combat Definition and Assignment Rule in January 1994, which allowed women to serve in combat support groups close to, but not on, the front lines, while maintaining their exclusion from serving in infantry, armory, Special Forces, and field artillery positions. Women could not be assigned to units "below the brigade level whose primary mission is to engage in direct combat on the ground," or "where units and positions are doctrinally required to physically collocate and remain with direct ground combat units that are closed to women."[61] While the 1988 Risk Rule opened an approximately 30,000 positions, its repeal opened an additional 32,700 U.S. Army positions and 48,000 Marine Corps positions to women.[62]

Until 2013 military commanders used the Pentagon's 1994 combat exclusion policy along with a 1992 army regulation to determine women's assignments.[63] However, both policies contained language that was difficult to interpret as well as to implement, as the two directives offered conflicting definitions and guidance in a number of key areas. For instance, a study of the two policies found that "neither the Army nor the DOD assignment policies for military women are clearly understandable. . . . There is no shared interpretation of the meanings of many of the words used in the policy, including *enemy, forward* or *well forward,* and *collocation.*"[64] Furthermore, as military legal scholar Jeffrey S. Dietz points out, while both the 1992 DOD policy and the army regulation comprise an exclusion policy that "attempts to both exclude women from exposure to the enemy and to exclude women from roles where their mission is to locate and engage the enemy," these policies were elaborated following the Gulf War and with the expectation that the military would continue to engage in conventional armed conflicts.[65] The counterinsurgency warfare of Iraq and Afghanistan was nonlinear and irregular—in short, it was unpredictable and omnipresent. The experience of American women in Iraq and Afghanistan would render the 1994 combat exclusion policy, which referred to a spatially discernible battlefield with distinct rear and forward areas and clearly identifiable enemy combatants, obsolete.

Iraq and Afghanistan and Reevaluation of Gender Difference for Twenty-First-Century Military Strategy

In late 1998, at the request of the Senate Committee on Armed Services, the Government Accountability Office (GAO) reviewed the 1994 ground combat exclusion policy and found that the definition of direct ground combat did not "reflect the less predictable nature of emerging post–Cold War military operations that may not have a well-defined forward area on the battlefield."[66] While there was a clear recognition that the nature of military operations would inevitably change, the DOD had no plans to reconsider the exclusion policy "because, in its view, there is no military need for women in ground combat positions because an adequate number of men are available."[67] What military leaders and policymakers did not foresee, however, was the specifically gendered need for women that would emerge in Iraq and Afghanistan.

Indeed, in the early stages of the Iraq occupation, the U.S. Army established a program that attached teams of women soldiers to marine combat units in order to have U.S. military women interact with Iraqi women civilians during home raids and at checkpoints. Known as "Lioness teams," these ad hoc units were created to address Islamic restrictions on the mixing of men and women, or what military commanders called "unforeseen cultural circumstances" that reportedly made it difficult for American men to search Iraqi women.[68] In Afghanistan in 2009, the U.S. Marine Corps developed Female Engagement Teams (FETS) to enable access to Afghan women, a strategy military commanders believed necessary to win a population-centric counterinsurgency.[69] One year later the Army Special Operations Command created Cultural Support Teams, which sent all-women teams out on special operations missions. All three iterations of these all-women counterinsurgency teams assumed the stability of women's gender difference and the presumably universal signification of the feminine gender as less threatening and thus more approachable. In other words, military commanders assumed that a gendered identification—a shared sisterhood—would emerge between Afghan and

Iraqi women and American women, transcending other power differentials present in a military occupation. According to this logic, Iraqi and Afghan women would recognize American military women as more benevolent and empathetic than their male counterparts, and therefore the all-women counterinsurgency teams would be more successful in engaging civilian populations. At the same time, these teams also relied on gender's fluidity, as women counterinsurgents were routinely exposed to combat and had to strategically tack back and forth between different roles coded as both masculine and feminine, often within the same mission.[70]

These teams, along with the unpredictable nature of counterinsurgency warfare more broadly, raised concerns about the relevance of the combat exclusion policy.[71] Indeed, the media focused on the fact that, in contradiction to official policy, American military women were routinely exposed to and engaging in direct ground combat. A 2005 editorial in the *New York Times* argued that "the daily car bombings, suicide atrocities, and insurgent raids show that no area of Iraq, from Humvee patrols to chow halls, is a safe haven for the occupation troops, male or female."[72] The media emphasized how the Pentagon policy was "being tested" in Iraq, "where the lack of a defined front line and insurgent guerilla tactics expose female troops to deadly situations."[73] Further, while the policies banning women from combat had long been justified as necessary to protect women from death or capture, as well as the American public from the horror of daughters or mothers returning home from war in body bags, the anticipated public outcry never came. In 2006, following the death of West Point graduate Lieutenant Emily Perez, the sixty-fourth woman to be killed in Iraq or Afghanistan, the *New York Times* noted the silence: "Despite longstanding predictions that America would shudder to see its women coming home in coffins, Lieutenant Perez's death, and those of the other women, the majority of whom died from hostile fire . . . have stirred no less—and no more—reaction at home than the 2,900 male dead."[74]

With military labor already strained, commanders struggled to adhere to the combat exclusion policies that often prevented assigning women where they were needed. In 2004, as part of its reorganization to meet the demands of nontraditional warfare, the army created new mixed-sex forward support companies that would be located with combat battalions in order to provide immediate support. However, congressional Republicans balked at the idea, arguing that it would violate the 1994 exclusion policy that prohibits collocation with direct ground combat units.[75] In May 2005 House Armed Services Committee chairman Duncan Hunter and Military Personnel Subcommittee chairman John McHugh introduced an amendment to the 2006 National Defense Authorization Bill that would explicitly ban women in the army from being assigned to forward support companies. In a press release, Hunter stated, "Rocket-propelled grenades, machine gun fire and all the other deadly aspects of war *will make no distinction between men and women* on the front lines. The nation should not put women into the front lines of combat."[76] Duncan's statement, once again steeped in protectionist rhetoric, expresses concern for the danger that women will face if assigned to forward support companies. However, his statement can also be read as indicting the lack of "distinction between men and women" or the absence of gender differentiation, as itself a harm that must be prevented.

After the amendment passed along party lines on May 11, 2005, Democratic members of the House Armed Services Committee expressed their strong opposition in a letter written to Chairman Hunter. The committee members argued that they, along with army leadership, believed the amendment would dangerously impede the ability of military commanders to make decisions in the best interest of their objectives, undermine unit morale and cohesiveness, and weaken the overall force of the armed services.[77] Indeed, U.S. Army Lieutenant General James L. Campbell, director of army staff, sent a letter to Congress stating his opposition to the amendment, which, if passed, would close 21,295 positions that were currently open to women.[78] In response Representative McHugh offered an alternative amendment that would legally codify the 1994 Pentagon exclusion policy, as well as require congressional approval for the opening of any new positions to women. This version of the amendment also passed along a party-lines vote. However, in the House Armed Services Committee report on the bill, twenty-four Democratic members and one Republican member submitted additional views once again expressing their disappointment with the amendment. These committee members argued that codifying the 1994 Pentagon exclusion policy without further study was ill advised, particularly while in the midst of a war which rendered such an exclusion policy obsolete: "The modern battlefield has changed so that there is no longer a clear distinction between the front lines and what has traditionally been regarded as relatively secure rear areas."[79] In addition, the committee members argued that this amendment would send the message that women's service in Iraq and Afghanistan was not valued and "may well drive qualified women out of the service and away from already struggling recruiters. . . . The message the bill's language sends can only compound the nation's already difficult challenge to fill the ranks."[80] Given the reservations of both congressional members and military leadership, the provision codifying the 1994 Pentagon policy was struck from the final legislation passed by Congress.[81]

While Congress recognized that codifying the combat exclusion policy would jeopardize the military's objectives in Iraq and Afghanistan, they were also not yet willing to rescind the policy. For nearly a decade, a policy inconsistent with irregular warfare and therefore "not actionable" continued to govern the assignment of military women in theater in Iraq and Afghanistan.[82] However, concerted activism by military women's rights advocacy groups and a shifting understanding of what difference and diversity meant for military effectiveness continued to push the conversation forward. For instance, in April 2011, the Military Leadership Diversity Commission (MLDC), established by Congress to evaluate diversity among military leaders, released the final report of the first commission to study equal rights and opportunities in the military since 1962.[83] In their recommendations the commission argued that the lack of gender, racial, and ethnic diversity in military leadership was a serious impediment to the military's effectiveness and efficiency, and that any barriers to the advancement of racial and ethnic minorities and women should be identified and eliminated. Their recommendations included repealing the combat exclusion policy: "An important step in this direction is that DOD and the Services eliminate combat exclusion policies for women, including removing barriers and inconsistencies, to create a level playing field for all servicemembers who meet the qualifications."[84] Reports by DACOWITS in 2010, 2011, and 2012 all included the recommendation to eliminate gender-based restrictions on military assignments. In February 2012 the DOD announced that it would make changes to the 1994 combat exclusion policy that would result in opening more than fourteen thousand new positions to women.[85]

At the same time that Congress was being pressured to formally acknowledge the reality of women serving in combat, the constitutionality of the 1994 combat exclusion policy was being challenged in federal courts. In November 2012 four military women, along with the military women's rights organization Service Women's Action Network, filed suit against the DOD, alleging that women are "categorically" excluded from more than 238,000 positions in the armed forces *solely because they are women*."[86] Further, the complaint alleged that not only is the combat exclusion policy obsolete given that "the battlefields in Iraq and Afghanistan lack any clear boundaries or front lines" but that "the unique circumstances and demands of fighting in Iraq and Afghanistan have led to a greater need for women on the ground."[87] Although not explicitly defined, these "unique circumstances" likely refer to the need to have women available to engage with civilians in order to wage successful population-centric counterinsurgency. Indeed, two of the plaintiffs were assigned to FETs where they served alongside male infantry marines and "wore the same body armor as the infantrymen, carried the same weapons as the infantrymen, and, along with infantrymen, regularly encountered ground combat."[88] Women were tapped to serve on FETs because they were women— and yet it was within this space that they proved they were capable to participate in combat, like men. Within months the 1994 combat exclusion policy was repealed. Announced by memorandum on January 24, 2013, Secretary Panetta and Chairman of the Joint Chiefs of Staff Martin Dempsey directed all services to open any positions and units previously closed to women.[89]

In Iraq and Afghanistan, with military operations occurring in civilian spaces, the U.S. military recognized the importance of eliminating all barriers to women's participation in warfighting. As the MLDC argued, the elimination of the combat exclusion policy was necessary because modern military operations "are executed in complex, uncertain, and rapidly changing environments. Men and women representative of the U.S. population and with different skills, experiences, and backgrounds are needed to respond to new and emerging threats."[90] To meet these threats, the MLDC called for the military to "harness these differences in ways that increase operational effectiveness."[91] Gender difference, which had for the majority of U.S. military history been identified as an impediment to military cohesion and effectiveness, was identified as a tool to be harnessed and leveraged for the future of nontraditional warfare. The repeal of the combat exclusion policy in 2013 did not render gender difference irrelevant. Rather, such a decision suggests that the emergence of population-centric counterinsurgency warfare has identified gender difference as more relevant than ever.

Notes

1. Rowan Scarborough and Joseph Curl, "Despite Pressure, Bush Vows 'No Women in Combat,'" *Washington Times*, January 12, 2005, https://www.washingtontimes.com/news/2005/jan/11/20050111-101005-5277r/.

2. Senate Committee on Armed Services, Women's Armed Services Integration Act of 1947, 23.

3. Women's Armed Services Integration Act, Public Law 80-625, June 12, 1948.

4. President's Committee on Equality of Treatment and Opportunity in the Armed Services, *Freedom to Serve*, xi.

5. Jeffords, *Remasculinization of America*, 73.

6. See O'Connell, "Combatants and the Combat Zone."

7. Fenner and DeYoung, *Women in Combat*, 61.

8. Kerber, *No Constitutional Right*, 267.

9. For a historical overview of the debates over the ERA, the draft, and women in combat, see Feinman, *Citizenship Rites*, 111–30. For an analysis of the draft and gender-based discrimination, see Decew, *Combat Exclusion*.

10. U.S. Department of Defense, *Utilization of Military Women*, 1.

11. U.S. Department of Defense, *Utilization of Military Women*, 1.

12. U.S. Department of Defense, *Utilization of Military Women*, 5.

13. Edwards v. Schlesinger, 377 F. Supp. 1091 (DDC 1974).

14. House Committee on Armed Services, *Admission of Women*, 190.

15. House Committee on Armed Services, *Admission of Women*, 135.

16. House Committee on Armed Services, *Admission of Women*, 255.

17. House Committee on Armed Services, *Admission of Women*, 260.

18. House Committee on Armed Services, *Admission of Women*, 147.

19. House Committee on Armed Services, *Admission of Women*, 176.

20. House Committee on Armed Services, *Admission of Women*, 176.

21. Senate Committee on Armed Services, *Women's Armed Services Integration Act of 1947*, 43.

22. Holm, *Women in the Military*, 118–19. Emphasis in original.

23. The bill, HR 7431, was later signed into law as Public Law 95-485.

24. Quoted in Holm, *Women in the Military*, 337.

25. Senate Committee on Appropriations, *Appropriations for Fiscal Year 1979*, 32. Section 303, Public Law 95-79 requested the secretary of defense to provide the definition to Congress.

26. Senate Committee on Appropriations, *Appropriations for Fiscal Year 1979*, 33.

27. Senate Committee on Appropriations, *Appropriations for Fiscal Year 1979*, 33.

28. For an excellent discussion of the hearings, see Bailey, *America's Army*, 166–71.

29. House Committee, *Women in the Military*, 56.

30. House Committee, *Women in the Military*, 256.

31. Bailey, *America's Army*, 167.

32. House Committee, *Women in the Military*, 81.

33. House Committee, *Women in the Military*, 50.

34. House Committee, *Women in the Military*, 291.

35. House Committee, *Women in the Military*, 228.

36. House Committee, *Women in the Military*, 225.

37. House Committee, *Women in the Military*, 364.

38. House Committee, *Women in the Military*, 367.

39. House Committee, *Women in the Military*, 363.

40. House Committee, *Women in the Military*, 251.

41. House Committee, *Women in the Military*, 236.

42. For analysis of sexual violence and the construction of gender in the U.S. military, see Mesok, "Men, Masculinity, and Sexual Violence."

43. Defense Advisory Committee on Women in the Services, "Changing Roles of Women in the Armed Forces," 1983, C-5, Littauer Library, Harvard University.

44. Kamarck, *Women in Combat*, 3–4.

45. U.S. Department of Defense, *Task Force on Women in the Military*, v.

46. Feinman, *Citizenship Rites*, 146–48.

47. Feinman, *Citizenship Rites*, 155–56.

48. Feinman, *Citizenship Rites*, 160.

49. Feinman, *Citizenship Rites*, 161.

50. Enloe, "Gendered Gulf," 225.

51. Enloe, "Gendered Gulf," 218.

52. Feinman, *Citizenship Rites*, 174.

53. See Feinman, *Citizenship Rites*, 174–97.

54. Presidential Commission, *Women in Combat*, 22. Emphasis added.

55. Presidential Commission, *Women in Combat*, 46.

56. Presidential Commission, *Women in Combat*, 59.

57. Presidential Commission, *Women in Combat*, 60–61.

58. Quoted in Dietz, "Breaking the Ground Barrier," 86.

59. Combat designations are also needed to ensure combat pay, determined by risk. See Gould and Horowitz, *History of Combat Pay*.

60. U.S. General Accounting Office, *Gender Issues*, 2.

61. Les Aspin, secretary of defense, "Direct Ground Combat Definition and Assignment Rule," memorandum, January 13, 1994, https://www.govexec.com/pdfs /031910d1.pdf.

62. Dietz, "Breaking the Ground Barrier," 98.

63. AR 600-13.

64. RAND, *Assessing the Assignment Policy*, xiv. Emphasis in original. See also Dietz, "Breaking the Ground Barrier," 98–102.

65. Dietz, "Breaking the Ground Barrier," 101.

66. U.S. General Accounting Office, *Gender Issues*, 4.

67. U.S. General Accounting Office, *Gender Issues*, 7.

68. Commander Richard Carby as quoted in *Lioness*, dir. Meg McLagan and Daria Sommers (New York: Room 11 Productions, 2008), DVD.

69. See Pottinger et al., "Half-Hearted."

70. For a thorough discussion of the racialized and gendered elements of female counterinsurgency teams, see Mesok, "Affective Technologies of War."

71. For an analysis of the ground combat exclusion policy within the wars in Iraq and Afghanistan, see McSally, *Women in Combat*.

72. "Chauvinism at the Battlefront," *New York Times*, May 20, 2005, A20.

73. "Female Troops in Iraq Exposed to Combat," CNN International, June 28, 2005, www.cnn.com/2005/WORLD/meast/06/25/women.combat.

74. Lizette Alvarez, "Jane, We Hardly Knew Ye Died," *New York Times*, September 24, 2006, https://www.nytimes.com/2006/09/24/weekinreview/24alvarez.html.

75. Ann Scott Tyson, "Panel Votes to Ban Women from Combat," *Washington Post*, May 12, 2005, https://www.washingtonpost.com/archive/politics/2005/05/12 /panel-votes-to-ban-women-from-combat/616f06c5-9645-4c9f-bec5-7b3bccd57186/.

76. Press release, House Armed Services Committee chairman Duncan Hunter, May 11, 2005, quoted in "Restrictions on Assignments of Military Women: A Brief History," National Women's Law Center, Washington DC, 2015.

77. Letter from twenty-seven members of Congress to Duncan Hunter, U.S. House of Representatives, May 17, 2005, quoted in "Restrictions on Assignments of Military Women."

78. Ann Scott Tyson, "More Objections to Women in Combat Ban," *Washington Post*, May 18, 2005, https://www.washingtonpost.com/wp-dyn/content/article /2005/05/17/AR2005051701356.html.

79. House Committee on Armed Services, Authorization Act for Fiscal Year 2006, 509.

80. House Committee on Armed Services, Authorization Act for Fiscal Year 2006, 510.

81. National Defense Authorization Act for Fiscal Year 2006, Public Law No. 109-163.

82. RAND, *Assignment Policy for Army Women*, 68.

83. National Defense Authorization Act for Fiscal Year 2009, Public Law No. 110-417.

84. Military Leadership Diversity Commission, *From Representation to Inclusion*, xvii.

85. U.S. Department of Defense, *Report to Congress*.

86. Hegar v. Panetta, 12 CV 6005 (ND Cal. 2012) at 1. Emphasis in original.

87. Hegar v. Panetta, 12 CV 6005 (ND Cal. 2012) at 1.

88. Hegar v. Panetta, 12 CV 6005 (ND Cal. 2012) at 7.

89. Memorandum on Elimination of the 1994 Direct Ground Combat Definition and Assignment Rule from the Secretary of Defense and Chairman of the Joint Chiefs of Staff for the Secretaries of the Military Departments, Acting Under Secretary of Defense for Personnel and Readiness, and Chiefs of the Military Services, January 24, 2013, https://dod.defense.gov/Portals/1/Documents/WISRJointMemo.pdf.

90. Military Leadership Diversity Commission, *From Representation to Inclusion*, xviii.

91. Military Leadership Diversity Commission, *From Representation to Inclusion*, xviii.

Bibliography

Bailey, Beth. *America's Army: The Making of the All-Volunteer Force.* Cambridge MA: Harvard University Press, 2009.

Decew, Judith Wagner. "The Combat Exclusion and the Role of Women in the Military." *Hypatia* 10, no. 1 (Winter 1995): 56–73.

Dietz, Jeffrey S. "Breaking the Ground Barrier: Equal Protection Analysis of the U.S. Military's Direct Ground Combat Exclusion of Women." *Military Law Review* 207 (2011): 86–154.

Elshtain, Jean Bethke. *Women and War.* Chicago: University of Chicago Press, 1987.

Enloe, Cynthia. "The Gendered Gulf." In *Seeing Through the Media: The Persian Gulf War,* edited by Susan Jeffords and Lauren Rabinovitz, 211–28. New Brunswick NJ: Rutgers University Press, 1994.

Fenner, Lorry M., and Marie E. de Young. *Women in Combat: Civic Duty or Military Liability?* Washington DC: Georgetown University Press, 2001.

Gould, Brandon R., and Stanley A. Horowitz. "History of Combat Pay." *Eleventh Quadrennial Review of Military Compensation* (2011): 207–66.

House Committee on Armed Services. *National Defense Authorization Act for Fiscal Year 2006.* 109th Cong., 1st sess., May 20, 2005.

House Committee on Armed Services, Subcommittee No. 2. *Admission of Women to the United States Military Academy.* 93rd Cong., 2nd sess., May 29; June 4, 5, 12, 18, 19; July 16, 19; and August 8, 1974.

House Committee on Armed Services Military Personnel Subcommittee. *Women in the Military.* 96th Cong., 1st and 2nd sess., November 13–16, 1979, and February 11, 1980.

Jeffords, Susan. *The Remasculinization of America: Gender and the Vietnam War.* Bloomington: Indiana University Press, 1989.

Kamarck, Kristy N. *Women in Combat: Issues for Congress.* Washington DC: Congressional Research Service, 2016.

Kerber, Linda K. *No Constitutional Right to be Ladies: Women and the Obligations of Citizenship.* New York: Hill & Wang, 1998.

McSally, Martha. "Women in Combat: Is the Current Policy Obsolete?" *Duke Journal of Gender Law and Policy* 14 (2007): 1011–59.

Mesok, Elizabeth. "Affective Technologies of War: U.S. Female Counterinsurgents and the Performance of Gendered Labor." *Radical History Review* 123 (October 2015): 60–86.

———. "Men, Masculinity, and Sexual Violence in the U.S. Military." In *Sexual Violence against Men in Global Politics,* edited by Marysia Zalewski, Paula Drumond, Elisabeth Prügl, and Maria Stern, 57–70. New York: Routledge, 2018.

Military Leadership Diversity Commission. *From Representation to Inclusion: Diversity Leadership for the 21st-Century Military.* Arlington VA: Military Leadership Diversity Commission, 2011.

O'Connell, Mary Ellen. "Combatants and the Combat Zone." *University of Richmond Law Review* 43, no. 3 (March 2009): 845–64.

Pottinger, Matt, Hali Jilani, and Claire Russo. "Half-Hearted: Trying to Win Afghanistan without Afghan Women." *Small Wars Journal* 18 (2010).

Presidential Commission on the Assignment of Women to the Armed Forces. *Report to the President.* Washington DC: U.S. Government Printing Office, November 15, 1992.

President's Committee on Equality of Treatment and Opportunity in the Armed Services. *Freedom to Serve: Equality of Treatment and Opportunity in the Armed Services.* Washington DC: Government Printing Office, 1950.

RAND National Defense Research Institute. *Assessing the Assignment Policy for Army Women.* Arlington VA: RAND, 2007.

Senate Committee on Appropriations. *Department of Defense Appropriations for Fiscal Year 1979, Part 3—Operation and Maintenance.* 95th Cong., 2nd sess., March 16, 1978.

Senate Committee on Armed Services. *Women's Armed Services Integration Act of 1947.* 80th Cong., 1st sess., July 2, 9, 15, 1947.

U.S. Department of Defense. *Report: Task Force on Women in the Military.* Washington DC: U.S. Department of Defense, January 1988.

———. *Report to Congress on the Review of Laws, Policies and Regulations Restricting the Service of Female Members in the U.S. Armed Forces.* Washington DC: U.S. Department of Defense, 2012.

———. *Utilization of Military Women.* Washington DC: U.S. Department of Defense, December 1972.

U.S. General Accounting Office. *Gender Issues: Information on DOD's Assignment Policy and Direct Ground Combat Definition.* Washington DC: General Accounting Office, October 1998.

ELEVEN

Brothers in Arms?

Combat, Masculinity, and Change in the Twenty-First-Century American Military

CHRISTOPHER HAMNER

On December 3, 2015, Secretary of Defense Ash Carter stepped to the podium in the Pentagon briefing room to deliver a major statement regarding American military policy. Standing before a blue background bearing the Pentagon seal, the nation's top Department of Defense official announced plans to open all combat assignments to women. "I'm directing all the military services to proceed to open all military occupational specialties to women 30 days from today," Carter told the assembled reporters. Services would furnish his office with their plans to integrate women into those positions the following month. The decision, Carter said, was the result of his careful review of studies from the U.S. Army, Navy, Air Force, Marine Corps, and Special Operations Command exploring whether any remaining combat positions warranted continued exclusion on the basis of sex.[1]

The *New York Times* described the announcement as "groundbreaking" and "historic," and in many ways it was.[2] At the time nearly 10 percent of military positions, all in the combat arms, remained closed to women. The new policy would open some 220,000 slots to female service members. "There will be no exceptions," Carter informed the press. Under the new regulations, women would be allowed "to drive tanks, fire mortars and lead infantry soldiers into combat." Women would finally be eligible for a broad swath of elite branches; as Carter noted, "They'll be able to serve as Army Rangers and Green Berets, Navy SEALs, Marine Corps infantry, Air Force parajumpers and everything else that was previously open only to men."[3]

Carter was guided in his decision, he said, by a pair of interconnected principles. First, "mission effectiveness is most important." Second, the implementation would be based on "rigorous analysis of factual data." Pronouncing the plan "evidence-based, and iterative," the secretary of defense argued that the new policy would not compromise the ability of the military to fight. Indeed, Carter maintained that a military that no longer excluded women from combat roles would not just be more fair but more effective in combat, since it would emerge "better able to harness the skills and perspectives that talented women have to offer."[4]

The image of women in the infantry, exchanging fire with enemy soldiers and sustaining losses in close ground combat, challenged some powerful and long-standing assumptions about warfare, soldiering, and gender. Many of those assumptions have deep if frequently unexamined roots. At the center is the powerful understanding of the battlefield as a profoundly masculine space: combat is the activity that both tests manhood and proves manhood. In many ways it represents not just a uniquely male endeavor but *the* archetypal male endeavor. That idea permeates much of the writing on warfare, from the social sciences, literature, and history to recruiting posters. It represents a potent and persuasive part of the way that many Americans, particularly the lay public, reflexively imagine battle. The notion of women facing the test of combat—and potentially passing it—threatened some deep-seated beliefs about the nature of masculinity and male identity, particularly male sexual identity.

The idea of combat as naturally male is ubiquitous. In a 2000 article in the *Journal of Strategic Studies*, the prominent military historian Martin van Creveld issued a sweeping assertion that "from the beginning of history, war has been an almost exclusively male affair and those who took part in it were often extolled as the most manliest of men."[5] Van Creveld's assertion echoed decades of observations and theorizing about the profoundly gendered nature of battle. Samuel Stouffer's groundbreaking 1949 study of World War II GIs, *The American Soldier*, offered a strikingly terse summary of the expectation against which combat soldiers judged and policed the behavior of their comrades: "Be a man." Acknowledging that ideas about masculinity varied among different American groups, Stouffer's researchers nonetheless identified a "core" set of masculine values that applied in the military: "Courage, endurance and toughness, lack of squeamishness when confronted with shocking or distasteful stimuli, avoidance of display of weakness in general, reticence about emotional or idealistic matters, and sexual competency."[6] Stouffer's team of social scientists viewed the notion of combat as a test of manhood as one of the critical things that kept GIs functioning amid the punishing and terrifying environment of the battlefield. "The man who lived up to the code of the combat soldier had proved his manhood," they concluded, and a soldier who passed this test "could take pride in being a combat man and draw support in his role from this pride."[7]

The American Soldier formally codified an observation that generations of soldiers had already made: that battle was at once a demonstration of manhood and a test of it. Musing on the factors that kept the soldiers in his regiment fighting on the battlefields of the Civil War, college-professor-turned-soldier Joshua Lawrence Chamberlain listed factors from pride to discipline to the bond of comradeship—but the first and overarching theme was "simple manhood."[8] Nor are these ideas confined to American soldiers and scholars. Shakespeare's 1599 history *Henry V* finds the young Prince Hal rallying his outnumbered troops as a "band of brothers" on the eve of the Battle of Agincourt. In the famous St. Crispin's day speech, the future king urges the soldiers to steel their resolve for combat with a paean to their masculine honor. Those slumbering comfortably at home during the feast day, their captain assures them, will wish they had fought instead; those safe at home would later "hold their manhoods cheap" when presented with veterans of the battle.[9]

Shakespeare's language, in turn, inspired the title of Stephen Ambrose's bestselling hagiography of World War II's 101st Airborne Division, *Band of Brothers*, itself the source of a ten-episode miniseries with the same title. *Band of Brothers* is typical of American war movies, a genre overflowing with images of traditional masculinity: grim, stoic men laboring in miserable circumstances to overcome some threat or complete some mission, over taglines like "Leave no man behind," "The mission is a man," and "When the order came to retreat, one man stayed."[10] Seminal works on the psychology of combat in the 1940s and 1950s, like S. L. A. Marshall's *Men against Fire* and Roy Grinker and John Spiegel's *Men under Stress*, carry in their very titles the controlling assumption that combat is fundamentally and essentially a male activity.

A bedrock idea runs through these depictions of ground combat: that the battlefield is inextricably male, a place where men work furiously with their male comrades to kill other men. In one sense, then, Carter's 2015 announcement signaled an important, tectonic shift in American military personnel policy. Ground combat, long framed as male by its very nature, would finally be open to women.

In another sense, however, Carter's announcement represented another evolutionary step in an ongoing, generational discussion about the place of women in the military and in combat. That debate—sometimes dryly scientific, sometimes highly emotionally charged—unfolded in the years since the close of World War II. It gained momentum with the 1973 introduction of the all-volunteer force, and again with Secretary of Defense Les Aspin's 1993 decision to allow women to fly combat aircraft and to serve aboard combat ships. In the broader sweep of evolving U.S. military personnel policy, then, Carter's 2015 announcement was hardly unanticipated. Just two years earlier, Secretary of Defense Leon Panetta had withdrawn the rule preventing women from serving in combat units and instructed the U.S. military to review its standards and policies for implementation no later than the beginning of 2016.[11]

The 2015 announcement that combat would officially be open to women met with a variety of responses. Some hailed it as a milestone in gender equality. The *New York Times* quoted Katelyn van Dam, an attack helicopter pilot in the Marine Corps who deployed to Afghanistan: "I'm overjoyed," she said. "Now if there is some little girl who wants to be a tanker, no one can tell her she can't."[12]

Others welcomed the new policy but viewed it as a belated official recognition of what had already been true on the ground for nearly a decade and a half. As Carter himself noted in his remarks, the new policy was announced "even though women have often found themselves in combat in Iraq and Afghanistan over the past 14 years."[13] Through the lens of those two conflicts, the secretary's formal statement was less a groundbreaking new policy than an overdue acknowledgment of the reality of American warfighting in the twenty-first century. Those formless, asymmetric wars had no easily defined battle front, and no safe area to the rear. Everyone who deployed to a combat theater shared some of the risk. Women went into dangerous areas; women carried weapons; women died from hostile action. Existing combat restrictions had allowed women to serve under fire in combat but prevented them from doing so officially. In that sense the 2015 announcement simply forced official policy to catch up with reality.

Response to Carter's announcement in official quarters proved noticeably less enthusiastic. In the halls of Congress, the reception was conspicuously lukewarm. Representative Mac Thornberry and Senator John McCain, chairs of the Armed Services Committees in the House and Senate, issued a joint statement noting that "Secretary Carter's decision to open combat positions to women will have a consequential impact on our service members and our military's warfighting capabilities" without offering even a word of support for the new proposal.[14]

The response from some uniformed senior leaders was similarly unenthusiastic. General Joseph E. Dunford Jr., a former Marine Corps commandant who was in December 2015 serving as the chairman of the Joint Chiefs of Staff, did not attend Carter's press conference. The Marine Corps, alone among the military branches, had requested exceptions for certain combat positions based on their own year-long internal study, which suggested that integrating women would hurt the fighting ability of those units. Carter's 2015 statement denied the marines' request on the basis that the U.S. military is "a joint force," and that the most sensible decision would be one that applied "to the entire force." Dunford released a statement later that day offering decidedly tepid support for the new policy, the bare minimum his office required. "I have had the opportunity to provide my advice on the issue of full integration of women into the armed forces," Dunford's message read. "In the wake of the secretary's decision, my responsibility is to ensure his decision is properly implemented."[15]

Outside the government the community of soldiers, veterans, national security intellectuals, and political pundits who comment on military policy were quick to respond. Many of the most negative responses to the new policy were not so measured in their tone as the official statements from within the government. To a vocal segment, Carter's announcement appeared as a dire threat to the distinctly male "warrior culture" of the combat arms. Opponents cast the inclusion of women in ground combat units as a dangerous social experiment with two potentially disastrous consequences. First, it would degrade the ability of the armed forces to fight and win the nation's wars. Second, women's participation in combat would needlessly imperil the lives of America's fighting men, who would no longer be able to depend on the physical strength, endurance, and bravery of their fellow soldiers. Such sentiments had simmered for decades in debates over personnel policy, common threads in an ongoing discourse.

Some of those objections came from scholars. For example, the historian van Creveld had long lamented the "feminization of the armed forces of many developed countries," which, he argued, was "part symptom, part cause, of the decline of those forces." The larger the proportion of women in the military, van Creveld held, "the less likely it is to undertake serious wars."[16]

Other opposition to women in combat units came from within the ranks of active-duty soldiers and marines. These too pre-dated Carter's 2015 announcement. "It's the worst decision that the military could make," a marine who had deployed to Afghanistan and Iraq told a *New York Times* columnist in 2013. That sergeant suggested that the negative response to the idea of women in combat was the rule rather than the exception in his service: "I haven't met an infantry Marine, from senior leadership to lower levels, that has been in agreement with the change." The new policy, he held, would cause "major problems" when implemented. "Even females I talk to think it's a crazy idea—completely off the wall."[17]

Online, resistance to the new policy was even more full throated. Skeptics were quick to cast the announcement as another victory for a vaguely defined sense of "political correctness," and the debate over personnel policy became another front in the ongoing culture wars. Over the preceding ten years, a significant part of the national conversation migrated off the op-ed pages of traditional print newspapers and the pages of academic and professional journals to newer platforms: blogs like the national security–focused *War on the Rocks*; sites like the popular military satire *DuffelBlog*;

and the comments sections of the *New York Times*, the *Wall Street Journal*, the *National Review*, and virtually every traditional publication that hosts an online edition.

Those new platforms, in turn, opened the conversation to individuals and groups who previously lacked a convenient means to enter the national discourse. One effect has been to amplify some of the uglier parts of the debate. The internet maxim "Never read the comments" is especially useful advice in this arena; even on fairly staid sites like the *New York Times*' online edition, the level of vitriol can quickly skyrocket when the subject turns to women in combat. More conservative analogs often became loud echo chambers populated by commenters who viewed the possibility of women in the combat arms as an existential threat to military culture if not the military itself.

Amid the clamor of voices eager to weigh in the idea of women in ground combat, there emerged no apparent consensus over the effect or desirability of allowing women to serve in the combat arms. Indeed, there was little agreement even as to who ought to be given a voice in the debate itself. Opponents of gender integration frequently brandished their military service or combat experience as a trump card that should by definition override the input of civilians, be they politicians or scholars. Responding to a *New York Times* story on Carter's announcement, a reader who took the name "RetiredArmy" criticized the "dictatorial tone" of "this non-elected bureaucrat" who was "ignoring the input of senior leaders who actually know best." That reader cast the new policy as "traitorous," a "purposeful endangerment to combat readiness designed to weaken the fighting capability of American forces."[18] Another commenter expressed deep concern at the idea of civilians—worse, civilian *politicians*—interfering in the central policy decisions of the military with an ominous-sounding prediction: "We shall see the wisdom of not only a person making the decision with no military experience, backed by a political machine that has few, if any military experience [*sic*], when the rubber meets the pavement. A long sustained ground war."[19]

Online forums allow commenters to claim whatever military experience they assert, and the purported credibility that goes with it, without fear of fact-checking. Many of those who responded to articles published online chose monikers with conspicuous military overtones: writing in to the *New York Times*, the emphatically named "Force6Delta" argued that "academic decisions have NO place in the reality of, and during, combat," because civilians had no understanding of combat and no concern for the ramifications of their policy directives. "The stench of elections, careerism and promotion," he noted sourly, "permeates every decision and action being made. . . . Those who make life and death decisions that will cause veterans to go into REAL, prolonged, daily, savage, vicious and violent combat should be required to participate in, and see, hear, and smell, the results of the killing and being killed their decisions will cause to happen." To that commenter the decision to open the combat arms to women flew in the face of "decades of harsh EXPERIENCE," a "disgusting" and "tragic" decision whose supporters were "naive, politically correct, and despicable."[20]

Nor were these dire warnings about allowing civilians to participate in the decision-making process confined to pseudonymous online commenters. "The disagreement over this issue isn't so much a divide between Republicans and Democrats," argued the *Weekly Standard* the day after Carter's 2015 announcement. Nor was it even a simple disagreement between men and women. Rather, the disagreement reflected an even starker divide, "between the men and women who have actually served in the Marine Corps and civilians who think they know better."[21] Or, as a columnist for the *Washington Free Beacon*, a conservative news site, wrote acidly, "Who cares what the Marines think about winning in combat when questions of social progress are on the table?"[22]

Debate over military personnel policy—who should be allowed to serve, and under what conditions—stretches back centuries. In various incarnations it has focused on the service of African Americans; African American service in the combat arms; racial segregation within the service branches; and homosexuals (and later, during the Don't Ask, Don't Tell era, openly serving homosexuals) in uniform. Indeed, many of the arguments made regarding the implication of gender-integrated ground combat units, both in support and against, repeated versions of arguments that had been presented in earlier iterations of this national debate. (The

2015 *New York Times* article noted this last feature, describing Carter's announcement as "the latest in a long march of inclusive steps by the military, including racial integration in 1948 and the lifting of the ban on gay men and lesbians serving openly in the military in 2011.")[23] Participants in the debate, particularly those opposed to women in combat, did not always acknowledge the history of those interconnected debates and arguments, perhaps because the dire predictions about collapsing military discipline, performance, and effectiveness made in those earlier cases did not materialize when those groups joined the ranks.

The image of female soldiers in American infantry armies collided with an enduring if implicit national conception of ground combat as an exclusively masculine domain. And yet American women have fought in battle since the War of Independence. Deborah Sampson famously disguised herself as a man and enlisted in a Massachusetts regiment as "Robert Shurtleff." Binding her breasts allowed her to pass as a smooth-faced scout for a year and a half, suffering multiple wounds while serving in Manhattan and at the siege of Yorktown. (At one point Sampson dug a musket ball out of her own thigh in order to prevent a doctor from discovering her secret.) Only after she took sick in the summer of 1783 and fell unconscious did a physician's examination reveal that "Robert Shurtleff" was in fact a woman. Sampson's service in combat was not a wholly unique example: the record suggests that more than 240 women disguised themselves in order to enlist in the Union and Confederate armies during the American Civil War.[24]

But those women were exceptional cases, and none fought openly as women. In the first half of the twentieth century, American combat soldiers were exclusively men. Congress formally codified the policy with the 1948 Women's Armed Services Integration Act, which allowed for women to serve as regular members of the armed forces during peacetime even as it simultaneously excluded them from service in combat. Those provisions remained in force until 1993, when women became eligible to serve in combat aviation positions. A 1994 policy, the Direct Ground Combat Definition and Assignment Rule, restricted women from joining any unit below the brigade level "whose primary mission is to engage in direct combat on the ground."[25]

Yet even when they were issued, those updated policies did not necessarily reflect the reality on the ground. A 1991 editorial in the feminist journal *off our backs* pointed out that five women had been killed in the Gulf War by hostile action, with another two taken prisoner. That evidence already suggested to some that statutes restricting women's participation in combat were "an anachronism."[26] By the time Carter gave his press conference in 2015, the U.S. military had already been engaged in Afghanistan and Iraq for more than a dozen years. While women serving in those theaters had not formally been part of the combat arms, the formless nature of the counterinsurgency efforts meant that the line between "combatant" roles and combat support was murky and ill-defined. A 2012 editorial in the *New York Times* noted that, as of the first decade of those wars, more than 130 American women had died fighting in Iraq and Afghanistan, and another 800 had been wounded.[27]

The twenty-first-century steps toward opening ground combat to women, and particularly the responses those policy changes generated, opened a fascinating window into broader American ideas about military service, combat, and gender. The discourse throws into sharp relief some explicit and some implicit assumptions about battle and what it represents in the contemporary American imagination.

Proponents of officially opening ground combat to women generally made two broad kinds of arguments. The first and most entrenched argument spoke to basic fairness: closing off those positions to female service members denied them important opportunities for advancement within the military. A second revolved around combat efficacy: incorporating women into the combat arms could increase the effectiveness of those units by drawing on the largest possible pool of talent. The two positions were not mutually exclusive, and supporters of opening the combat arms to women had plenty of empirical examples from the historical record to draw upon in making their case.

The argument about fairness was hardly a new one. The first Gulf War in the 1990s saw many women serving with distinction under fire. That accumulated real-world evidence led to a wave of articles and essays noting that continued discrimination against women in combat lacked a strong basis in fact. A 1992 *New York*

Times editorial noted that it was difficult to maintain the idea that "courage" was exclusively or even primarily a male trait in the face of so many concrete counterexamples. "Female astronauts, fire-fighters, police—and the 35,000 women who served in the Persian Gulf war—have taught America a valuable lesson," it argued. "Courage and competence have no gender."[28] A quarter century later the *Times* returned to that earlier observation, highlighting the basic injustice. "Women have long chafed under the combat restrictions," it noted, "which allowed them to serve in combat zones, often under fire, but prevented them from officially hold-ing combat positions, including in the infantry, which remain crucial to career advancement." By refusing to recognize the real-ity of their service, "the military has unfairly held them back."[29] Indeed, the idea that prohibiting women from serving in the com-bat arms, and thus barring them from the professional opportu-nities, promotions, salary, and pensions those positions afforded, had already been the subject of 1992 lawsuit brought by two army reservists arguing that the military's discrimination, based solely on their gender, had restricted their opportunities and violated the equal protection clause.[30]

Supporters of opening the combat arms to women acknowl-edged that framing the policy in terms of fairness could lead to some second-order concerns about equal treatment. Would women be required to register for the Selective Service like their male counterparts? Would women in the military be assigned to the combat arms, regardless of preference, as men are? Reporters at Carter's 2015 press conference questioned the secretary directly about whether the new policy would reopen the debate about women and the Selective Service. Noting that the issue was cur-rently a matter of litigation, Carter admitted, "I don't know how that will turn out."[31]

Basic fairness provided one argument in favor of opening the remaining military jobs to female service members. It highlighted an important American ideal and referenced previous, successful arguments in favor of opening parts of the military to groups previ-ously excluded. But opening the combat arms to women, supporters held, had an important concrete benefit as well: equal opportu-nity would actually make the military *more* effective in combat.

That reasoning unfolded along two lines. First was the idea that, by drawing on a larger pool of talent, the military could fill important roles with the most highly qualified personnel. Second was the idea that warfare in the twenty-first century called for a much broader set of skills and capabilities than simple brute strength. In particular, the kind of asymmetric counterinsurgency warfare that dominated much of the first two decades of the twenty-first century benefited from the presence of women in combat units. Where the logic surrounding basic fairness existed in part in the abstract, these two arguments about improved combat performance took on a decidedly pragmatic tone.

Carter referenced the first directly at his 2015 press conference. "When I became secretary of defense, I made a commitment to building America's force of the future," he told reporters. "In the 21st century that requires drawing strength from the broadest possible pool of talent. This includes women."[32] His statement echoed hundreds of similar observations: no modern organization could reasonably argue that it was uniformly filling *all* its positions with the most highly qualified individuals while simultaneously excluding half of the adult population from consideration. Carly Lohrentz, the first female F-14 fighter pilot in the U.S. Navy, offered that argument in a 2013 editorial in the pages of *Time* magazine: "Lifting this ban is about increasing military effectiveness. If we want the most effective fighting force, we need to recruit and assign the most qualified individuals for the job."[33]

A second argument regarding the increased efficacy of gender-integrated combat units focused on the particular kinds of military action that dominated American warfighting in the first two decades of the twenty-first century. Kyleanne Hunter, a marine combat helicopter pilot and political scientist, made precisely that argument in a September 2015 article from *War on the Rocks*, a popular website devoted to national security issues. In "We Need What Women Bring to the Fight," Hunter urged a broader understanding of "combat effectiveness," one that recognized that military action was not simply a matter of putting fire on targets but the "ability to shape the international arena to favor our larger strategic aims." Evolving challenges in battle required a change in approach: "New threats require new tactics."[34] The nature of the fighting that absorbed the majority of America's military efforts following the 2002 and 2003 invasions of Afghanistan and Iraq suggested that presence of women actually made the units *more* combat-effective. Counterinsurgency in particular requires movement within a population and direct engagement with all its members, not just military-aged men. All-male American units operating in areas with cultural or religious prohibitions against certain kinds of interactions between men and women found themselves at a material operational disadvantage.

American men who had served in combat zones with Female Engagement Teams, or FETs (a program that attaches female soldiers to male units to facilitate interactions with the local population), attested to the importance of that support, particularly in regions in which religious customs prevent women from speaking or being alone with men. "Having them in squads may help because they will constantly be learning about women that men can't speak to," one marine observed. "The women the FETs would speak to may have insight on IED's or enemy locations or other information that may be helpful that the male population is afraid to bring to our attention."[35] And the indisputable evidence from the long wars in Iraq and Afghanistan had begun to change some minds about whether female soldiers could function under fire. "I honestly didn't think about women in combat much until Iraq," an army officer told a reporter. There he witnessed women in military police units under heavy fire. "I encountered female soldiers that were in the same firefights as us, facing the same horrible stuff, even if they weren't technically in combat units." His experience taught a simple lesson: "They could fight just as well as I could, and some of those women were tremendous leaders. It gave me such respect."[36]

Those who supported opening ground combat to women deployed both kinds of arguments to make their case and substantiated the logic with empirical examples. Opponents found those arguments unconvincing, to say the least. A 2019 opinion piece in the *Wall Street Journal* described Carter's 2015 announcement as "a misguided social experiment that threatens military readiness and wastes resources in the service of a political agenda."[37] Some opponents took issue with the idea of "fairness" itself, reframing the concept in terms of the male soldiers who, they argued, would be unjustly disadvantaged in battle by the presence of women in their units. "Putting women into close combat roles isn't fair to the men who will be relying on them," claimed one *National Review* writer. It was not fair, either, to the women themselves, "who will find themselves continuously at a deadly disadvantage."[38] Viewed in that light, a retired Marine Corps general claimed, "'fairness' is an obscenity. Fairness is about individuals." The very notion, he argued, ran counter to fundamental military values: "It's selfish. And selfishness can kill."[39]

But most opponents of the move to fully integrate women into combat units largely conceded the abstract point regarding fairness. Opening all parts of the military to women would indeed make the institution as a whole more equal and more equitable. But opponents differed greatly on the importance and desirability of equitability as a meaningful goal when it came to ground combat. They frequently cast the very idea of fairness as ill informed or misguided. A vaguely defined reproach of "political correctness" accompanied many of these dissents. Critics castigated what they viewed as the prioritization of abstract notions like justice over harsh reality. An online comment from a 2015 *New York Times* story described Carter's announcement as a "big win for liberal political correctness." Misplaced notions of fairness, that commenter argued, would run a predictable course when the "first woman SEAL who causes a fellow SEALS death because she could not keep up in the physical exertion department will cause the family of the dead to file a lawsuit for allowing women in the SEALs in the first place." That commenter warned knowingly of a policy "which will truly damage the military. . . . Only then," he concluded confidently, "will liberals have claimed their final victory."[40]

But even some of the most ardent opponents of gender integration acknowledged the logic of the claim regarding fairness even as they found ways to minimize its importance. It was the second claim—the idea that female soldiers could actually improve overall combat effectiveness rather than undermine it—with which opponents took sharpest issue. They argued, often fiercely, that the incorporation of women into combat units would degrade combat performance, perhaps catastrophically. Opponents often couched their arguments in heightened emotional terms, setting abstract ideas of fairness against the image of dead soldiers in body bags and flag-draped coffins. Male soldiers, they held, would die unnecessarily because their unit's effectiveness had been needlessly and fatally compromised by the presence of female soldiers who were, quite simply, not up to the task of fighting. Such rhetoric amplified the stakes of debate as an existential threat to male warriors if not national security itself. Those arguments emphasized the risks involved in overturning established norms. "Maybe women can join the infantry and succeed, but many of us are not sure," wrote a marine combat veteran. "There's more at stake here than equal opportunity and political correctness."[41] A retired marine general posed a stark choice in his criticism of the idea of female combat soldiers: "If I'm wrong, the cost may be denied opportunity to strong and impressive young women. If *you're* wrong, our national security is shaken and there is a butcher's bill to pay. . . . Make your choice," he implored readers. "The line forms on the left."[42]

Opponents of officially opening ground combat roles to women lodged four broad objections. Three related to the presumed deleterious consequences that the inclusion of female soldiers would have on combat performance. The fourth revolved around what might be termed America's "social values": the effects that seeing women in the combat arms, or seeing mangled female bodies on a battlefield, might have on the nation's self-perception and ideals.

Two of the first three objections dealt with the ability of individual women to meet the demands of ground combat. Here opponents stressed biological differences that they believed rendered women less suitable for battle. First was the argument that women were physically weaker and thus incapable of the exertions ground combat requires. (That argument often accompanied a parallel objection that mandating women's inclusion in combat units would result in lower physical standards across the board, watering down the performance of *all* soldiers, male and female, as the military struggled to get women qualified for combat units.) A second, overlapping argument held that women were by nature less able to handle the psychological strains of battle: the fear, the misery, the discomfort, the shock of seeing friends' bodies disfigured by enemy fire, the necessity of killing.

The third objection lodged against including women in combat units was the broadest, most amorphous, and in many ways the most contentious and the most revealing. That line of argument held that the presence of women, even those judged to be personally capable of bearing up to the physical and psychological strains of command, would disrupt group dynamics within combat units, to disastrous effect. Gender-integrated combat units would forfeit the bonds of trust and mutual interdependence that enabled soldiers to function in the unforgiving environment of battle. Those social relationships—the "cohesion" of military units—has played a long and controversial history in soldiers' and scholars' understanding of combat performance and behavior. The idea that integrating women into combat units would damage or destroy the invisible social glue that held those units together was both the most profound and the most abstract objection to gender desegregation in the combat arms. It also recalled previous debates over military personnel policy from the late 1940s to the twenty-first century: opponents of racial integration, of homosexual service generally, and of openly serving homosexuals had deployed the same warnings about the erosion of unit cohesion in previous iterations of the larger ongoing debate surrounding military personnel policy.

A final objection to the inclusion of women in combat units had little to do with combat effectiveness or victory on the battlefield and everything to do with American sensibilities. It was largely an aesthetic objection: not that women would compromise combat performance, but that dead and wounded female soldiers would violate Americans' sense of decorum—in short, that Americans should not have to see their daughters coming home in body bags.

Each of these objections built upon ideas and assumptions that proponents tended to portray as self-evident truths. Combat is an intensely physically demanding activity, and the average woman does not have the size and physical strength of the average man. "Humping a hundred pounds, man, that ain't easy, and it remains the defining physical requirement of the infantry," said one exercise scientist who conducted a multiyear study of the marines. It was a matter of "practical reality," he judged, that "the preponderance of women will not be able to do the job."[43] A marine staff sergeant agreed. "The physical aspect is obvious," he said. While a handful might be able to meet the strength requirements, "the majority of women cannot carry 125 pounds of gear for five to ten kilometers and then aid a wounded Marine while under fire."[44]

Some early experiments with female marines in training exercises provided anecdotal support for the idea that military training inflicted special punishment on female skeletal structure and musculature. A young marine NCO who spent months in training camps in North Carolina and California witnessed this phenomenon up close, as the other women in her cohort steadily succumbed to a series of injuries. "I was stressing out because all my girlfriends started getting hurt," she told a reporter. "They're all getting this common injury from hips. I was waiting to feel something in my hips and I never did." She was one of only two women in two platoons to complete the nine-month experiments.[45] Another female marine rolled the same ankle repeatedly on daily training hikes. Six days before her platoon completed its round of assessments, she withdrew after concluding that the infantry was not a good fit. "It sucked; it really sucked," she said. "I wouldn't do this experiment again."[46]

The observation that female physiology differs from men's struck few on either side of the debate as controversial. A 1992 editorial in the *New York Times* recognized the reality: "To put a woman in a role that demands muscles she doesn't have is a disservice to everyone."[47] Supporters of integrating the combat arms did not hide from the fact that women's bodies differed from men's. Carter acknowledged the demonstrated reality in his 2015 press conference: "Studies say there are physical differences," he noted.[48] Some women would be able to meet those standards; many men already could not.

Whether the material significance of those physical differences could be accommodated through rigorous standards and testing, or whether they represented a disqualifying obstacle on their own, proved much more controversial. Some differences between the average male body and the average female body were fairly obvious; how to accommodate those differences, or whether they could be accommodated at all, was not. Supporters of gender integration argued that physical standards, administered rigorously and fairly, could address the differences. Opponents argued that opening the combat arms to women would necessarily result in an across-the-board lowering of standards to ensure that some women qualified for the prized slots. Carter acknowledged the possibility of that appearance and moved to preempt it in his remarks: "There must be no quotas or perception thereof."[49] Opponents agreed with the statements in principle: integration could only work, read a 2013 *New York Times* editorial by a former marine staff sergeant who served in Iraq and Afghanistan, given "a minimum strength qualification that is the same for both sexes" even though members of both sexes would not qualify. That rigorous standard was necessary, he argued, because "weak infantry Marines will get people killed." But the writer rejected the assurances from civilians that standards would be fairly administered and rigorously maintained, guaranteeing readers they could "bet your future earnings that the current effort to integrate the infantry will not cease with a few extraordinary females, but will eventually accommodate a social engineering goal by changing standards."[50]

Opponents of women in the combat arms leveled a second, parallel concern about women's innate ability to withstand combat separate from the differences in raw physical strength. That objection argued that even those women able to face the physical stresses of battle would be unable to bear the psychological strains. Being a combat soldier "isn't just about uncomfortable living situations" and physical exertion, a combat veteran wrote in his *New York Times* editorial. Combat meant "kill or be killed, blood, entrails and fear"—demands, the writer suggested, that drew upon qualities women simply could not muster.[51]

The notion that combat places unique emotional burdens on its participants—burdens that not everyone could bear—was not a new one. The colossal psychological stresses attached to facing enemy fire had been used in the first years of the Civil War to argue against using African American soldiers in battle. Few northerners in 1861 doubted the physical strength and stamina of African American bodies, but only white men, the argument held, possessed the will, discipline, character, and courage to maintain their composure amid a hail of bullets to withstand the test of combat. Others would simply come undone in the chaos.

References to the immense psychological demands of ground combat resurfaced in subsequent iterations of the debate over soldiering. In 1993 testimony before the House Committee on Armed Services, an army colonel emphasized the psychological strains of battle over the physical ones. Combat fitness, he argued, came down to a simple, urgent question: "Down there we need to know: Will he fight?" The list of burdens a combat soldier had to overcome was more psychological than physical: "Will he be there when the going gets tough? Is he willing to take a hill in the pouring rain, walk in among the enemy dead, see their bloated bodies . . . the trash, the filth, the piles of excrement . . . the stench of that mixed with that horrible sweetish smell of rotting flesh? Is he willing to push a dead soldier out of a fox hole so he can get into it? Is this guy willingly [*sic*] to aim his weapon right at somebody and kill them?" How would powerful emotional bonds affect performance? "Can he take it if his best friend, the guy he went through basic training with and shared a hole with for the past 3 months, gets shot through the middle of the forehead and he has to sit there with the body all night?" Interestingly, that 1993 statement was offered as part of an earlier debate over personnel, one exploring the possibility of lifting the ban on homosexuals in the military. The language underlines how deeply entwined ideas about masculinity and combat service have been for decades. And in a prescient phrase, the colonel added that "if the answer to all of these questions is yes, then we don't care if he is white or black or brown or red or yellow. . . . We don't give a damn if he is gay. We wouldn't even care if he were a she."[52]

Plenty of opponents rejected the notion that women could bear the psychological burdens of ground combat. Some scrambled to marshal empirical data to demonstrate women's innate unsuitability for battle, as did one *National Review* editorial that referenced a BBC News story about a Hungarian study showing that women were less likely to take action when confronted with images of danger, offered as evidence that women's impediments in combat were biologically hard-wired.[53]

Both of the first two objections revolved around individual women's fitness for battle. Both allowed for the possibility that at least some number of exceptional women might be able to face the physical and psychological demands of combat, no matter how small that pool of outliers was likely to be. Even some of the most vocal opponents of gender integration in the combat arms acknowledged that truth. "There unquestionably are women who can pass any physical challenge the military may require," argued Newbold, the retired marine general.[54] "We should celebrate those who succeed and encourage others. They are worthy role models, and certainly not just to women." A commenter to the *New York Times* article even suggested that women might have some psychological advantages over men: "If you want endurance female physiology beats [male] hands down everytime." For "ferocious protection of family," look to women for "ruthless[ness.]"[55]

But even many opponents who allowed that a small group of exceptionally talented women might meet the individual standards still saw potential catastrophe in adding female soldiers to male combat units. They were quick to emphasize that physical attributes were not the sole, or even most important, factor in battle. Newbold asserted that in combat "we expect the collective entity to persevere because it has a greater will and fighting spirit, and not because it is bigger, faster, or more agile. The championship team in virtually any professional sport may only coincidentally be the most physically talented, but it most assuredly will be the most cohesive." He offered a simple suggestion: "Why not appreciate the same ingredients in infantry units?"[56]

More than any other part of the debate, the argument over women's presumed effect on group dynamics in combat units laid bare some of the deepest and often unspoken assumptions about the gendered nature of the battlefield and what fighting demanded of combatants. It opens an especially contentious debate in that it revolves not around what women in combat *do* but what they *represent*. Viewed against the backdrop of cohesion, the threat women pose to combat effectiveness comes not from a particular action that a female soldier might take or fail to take under fire but from the way her simple presence might affect the way male soldiers think and behave.

That idea has appeared repeatedly throughout the debates over integrating women into ground combat units. A Marine Corps veteran writing in the *New York Times* characterized it as a "common concern voiced by male Marines" who wondered whether they themselves "might react differently to seeing female infantrymen in danger, wounded or even killed." That possibility was damaging no matter how effective female marines' own performance under fire was if their simple presence meant that men might "respond in ways that could endanger a mission if they tried to protect a female colleague." The author held that the impulse was so deeply-ingrained by masculine culture that it was all but reflexive: "My dad taught me, as I'm sure other men were taught, to protect women when they are in harm's way. Combat is harm's way. Will men involuntarily look out for the woman to their left more than the man to their right?"[57] Another marine, who followed the corps's experiment integrating women in training exercises (and who began the experiment in favor of incorporating women into those units) later wrote an essay explaining why his observations had changed his mind. It was not the fitness of the women themselves, but the way that "the female variable in this social experiment has wrought a fundamental change in the way male [non-commissioned officers] think, act and lead," he wrote.[58]

A final concern about the negative effects women in ground combat units would have on group cohesion revolved around the possibility of sexual temptation and fraternization that their presence would raise in previously all-male environments. Female service members were among the first to note that sexual dynamics were an unavoidable part of being in the minority in the overwhelmingly male environment of the military. Early in her memoir of her experience as a woman in the army, *Love My Rifle More than You*, Kayla Williams introduced that idea starkly: "Right into it: Sex is key to any woman soldier's experiences in the American military." (Williams also described the tortured dynamics of heterosexual attraction in the military—particularly on the men's side—by defining the casual put-down lobbed at women by male service members, "Queen for a Year": "A female soldier who becomes stuck-up during her deployment due to an exponential increase in male attention." Williams notes wryly that the term is "used disparagingly.")[59] Male service members reported similar dynamics; in the marines' gender-integration experiments, a male lance corporal described how relationships between men and women in the platoon could turn romantic, "a change that is sadly for the worse, not the better."[60]

Arguments about the purported deleterious or dangerous effects on unit cohesion have a long history in debates over American personnel policy. Opponents of racial desegregation in the army used them to argue that African American and white GIs could not develop the requisite trust necessary to fight alongside one another in integrated units. Opponents of homosexuals in the military (and, later, openly serving homosexuals) deployed similar arguments to argue that heterosexual soldiers simply could not trust comrades that they worried harbored a secret sexual attraction to them.

Among those who study combat performance, "cohesion" as a blanket explanation for combat motivation and combat effectiveness has a checkered history. Supporters, frequently practitioners or military veterans, take its power as self-evident if fundamentally inscrutable to those who have not fought themselves; for most veterans the idea that soldiers fight primarily because of the bonds of trust, affection, and mutual interdependence remains the widely accepted orthodox explanation to explain a variety of behaviors in combat.[61] Skeptics, frequently within the academy, have pointed out a variety of problems with using the idea of these social bonds to explain performance in battle.[62]

One problem stems from the simple difficulty of describing precisely the nature of the bonds that form among members of a combat unit. Veterans themselves frequently suggest that only those who have been under fire can understand the way the experience transforms the members of a combat unit. Newbold, the retired marine general, described the process as a kind of "alchemy" and noted that it was difficult for practitioners to explain to civilians "much as it is difficult for those of faith to explain their conviction to an atheist."[63] That reasoning does not strike many civilian scholars as particularly persuasive.

A second problem with using cohesion as a broad explanation for combat motivation and combat performance is the lack of strong empirical evidence or data to connect the strength of social bonds among members of a unit with their collective performance in combat. Numerous studies from history, political science, and sociology have suggested that while the strong bonds of affection among the members of small combat units are very real, they are neither necessary nor sufficient by themselves for units to fight effectively.[64]

Finally, those who argue that group cohesion is a critical part of combat function are sometimes at a loss to explain its precise mechanics, why the presence of women would affect it, and why their effect would be negative. Aside from the potential for sexual fraternization among members of a combat unit, the conclusion that female soldiers will erode cohesion in combat units is often presented as self-evident. "This selflessness is derived from bonding, and bonding from shared events and the unquestioning subordination of self for the good of the team," Newbold offered in his essay. "But what destroys this alchemy—and, therefore, combat effectiveness—are pettiness, rumor-mongering, suspicion, and jealousy. And when fighting spirit is lessoned, death is the outcome."[65] The author did not explain why the presence of female soldiers would necessarily increase pettiness, rumor-mongering, suspicion, and jealousy. Nor do most veterans who tout the importance of cohesive bonds to effective combat performance grapple with the studies that describe the negative effects of those bonds—sexual bullying, indiscipline, insubordination—that sometimes appear even in all-male groups with strong social cohesion.[66]

And while suggestions that women would disrupt the cohesion of combat units remains a majority position, it is hardly universal. One marine corpsman pointed out that "men and women will both bleed red on the battlefield." He did not think that gender would affect the way he thought about his comrades ("If you lose a woman on the battlefield I don't think it would bother me mentally more than losing a man") and suggested that "you would have developed that same bond with them as you did with the other men. It will be no different."[67]

The myriad empirical problems with using social cohesion to explain combat performance have led many scholars to replace it with a parallel phenomenon: "task cohesion." Rather than the bonds of affection and familial emotion that characterize social cohesion, task cohesion revolves around the commitment of members of a group to a specific mission, regardless of their personal feelings for one another. Unlike social cohesion task cohesion has demonstrated and measurable effects on battlefield performance.

Julia Bringloe, an army medic who worked as part of helicopter medical evacuation team and who received the Distinguished Flying Cross with Valor for her service, described her experience in combat zones in terms that strongly resemble task cohesion. "As the only female in my platoon, when I first got there . . . you know, the first month was rough, without a doubt," she recalled. Male soldiers "weren't sure if I was going to be able to handle myself when I came in contact." But their apprehension eventually gave way when she "finally did my first mission and got shot at and got my patient on board and did my job and dropped my patient off." Those actions altered the dynamic of the team noticeably: "And then all of a sudden everybody talked to me." Nor did she necessarily see the phenomenon as primarily the product of gender dynamics. "We sort of treat everyone like that until you get your first mission in," she observed, concluding that, "now, those people I work with are my brothers."[68] Those observations echoed a 2014 statement from army general and chairman of the Joint Chiefs of Staff Martin Dempsey: "Trust transcends gender."[69]

Running throughout all of the objections—about women's physical and psychological fitness as well as their purported effect on cohesion within groups—is a persistent, unshakeable belief that ground combat is by its very nature a male activity. Ground combat is not just enduring unpleasant living conditions, wrote a former combat marine. "It's kill or be killed, blood, entrails and fear. We are a brotherhood; a collection of ragtag men who hunt and kill the enemy and travel to undesirable places to do even more undesirable things."[70] Newbold asserted that male biology was an essential part of close combat: men in their teens and twenties, he suggested, "are overloaded with testosterone, supremely confident about their invincibility, and prone to illogical antics." While those characteristics sometimes created trouble in civilian life, "the same traits are, by the way, nearly ideal for direct ground combat."[71]

Those ideas hearken back to some of the earliest scholarly work on combat performance. Samuel Stouffer's team argued in 1949 that the "code of masculinity," and men's desire to live up to it, was instrumental in overcoming the powerful instincts for self-preservation long enough to perform in combat. Those who failed to measure up risked losing their "social manhood." (Stouffer included typical jibes with unsubtle gendered accusations: "Whatsa matter, bud—got lace on your drawers?" and "Christ, he's acting like an old maid.") Losing that social manhood carried with it "a strong likelihood of being branded a 'woman,'" which Stouffer described as "a dangerous threat to the contemporary male personality."[72] A great deal rests on that understanding of the battlefield as unalterably masculine. If battle is the ultimate test of manhood, what would it mean if women were present? What would the test mean if some women passed it as well? How critical are the "brothers" to the "band of brothers" phenomenon?

A final objection to the widespread employment of women in combat revolved around not combat performance but the policing of traditional gender boundaries. It reflected a fairly widespread set of beliefs about acceptable roles broken down by gender. Heather Wilson, a retired U.S. Air Force officer and Rhodes scholar, addressed the question of women in combat in two parts—"Can They?" and "Should They?"—in a 1993 article in the *National Interest*. She argued that evidence and historical experience had made it "increasingly difficult to sustain" arguments that women could not perform combat jobs (in combat aircraft and aboard naval vessels, in this case). Setting aside performance, the idea of women in combat had reopened a debate about what Wilson termed "social values"—that is, "what we are as a nation and what we should be." A "traditionalist" view held that women "should be protected, not the protectors"; traditionalists viewed women as "the givers of life" and argued that "combat is or ought to be against a woman's nature." Though Wilson placed herself firmly in the camp in favor of allowing women to fly combat missions and serve on warships, she acknowledged "a genuine fear among those who hold these views of the social consequences if we were to allow the primary nurturers in our society to be combatants."[73]

Similar ideas about what the broader American public would tolerate in battle reappeared in the twenty-first-century iteration of the debate. One online commenter to the *New York Times* urged readers to "imagine a war, and in combat, a number of American service women are captured. Now imagine what happens next. War is ugly business." That writer was open to some kinds of gender equality within the armed forces; women should be allowed some roles. "But putting them in harms way is NOT the same as putting a man in harms way."[74] "It's a fear of the unknown," said one marine. "I've never seen a woman get killed or wounded. In my mind they may resemble my wife and I don't know how I would react." Gender was simply irrevocably tied to warfare: "It's one thing to see a man injured or killed but a woman, now that's a different story."[75]

None of the arguments against gender integration in the combat arms derailed the process, and the military branches moved forward with their plans to open their ranks to qualified women. Even before Carter's December 2015 announcement, those changes were visible. Two women had graduated from U.S. Army Ranger School—one of the most demanding programs in the army—the previous August, with another to follow that October. Not six months after Carter's announcement, Captain Kristen Griest, one of the first two women to complete Ranger School, became the first female army infantry officer.

But neither did these and other early successes end the debate over the wisdom of allowing women to serve in the combat arms. A particular feature of the current iteration of the debate over military personnel policy is its seeming intractability. Writing for *War on the Rocks* just after the first two women completed Ranger School, two political scientists (one a retired army general) suggested that the sight of two women "clearly overcoming the arduous physical demands long touted as barriers to women serving in ground combat roles will effectively end the debate as to whether women are up to the physical and mental demands that duty in infantry, armor, or special operations requires." The two had established their physical and mental toughness far beyond any reasonable expectation; as the authors pointed out, most men in the combat arms were not graduates, and only two-fifths of the men who began the course completed it.[76]

But the objections to women in combat were never solely or even mainly about individual women's physical and mental toughness. Opening the combat arms to women brought together a bundle of broad and long-simmering concerns about men, women, traditional gender roles, and the powerful if inexpressible maleness of the battlefield. With the lines so starkly drawn—recall Newbold's "Line forms to the left" warning—there seems little in the way of new data or evidence to persuade the most determined on either side.

Part of that is the difficulty of identifying agreed-upon metrics. There is no way to measure qualities like "psychological resilience" and "unit cohesion" that can satisfy both sides. The historical record proves equally frustrating. Proponents can point to other nations' successful experiments with women in combat; opponents can counter that those countries and their militaries differ from the United States in important ways. The weight afforded personal impressions, "common sense," and anecdote further complicates the discourse, especially when so much of that evidence is steeped in deeply held assumptions about the gendered nature of the battlefield. Absent any way to persuade the most fervent believers on either side, the process creeps on.

Notes

1. Ash Carter, "Department of Defense Press Briefing by Secretary Carter in the Pentagon Briefing Room," U.S. Department of Defense, December 3, 2015, https://www.defense.gov/Newsroom/Transcripts/Transcript/Article/632578/department-of-defense-press-briefing-by-secretary-carter-in-the-pentagon-briefi.

2. Matthew Rosenberg and Dave Philipps, "All Combat Roles Now Open to Women, Defense Secretary Says," *New York Times*, December 3, 2015, https://www.nytimes.com/2015/12/04/us/politics/combat-military-women-ash-carter.html.

3. Carter, December 2015 briefing.

4. Carter, December 2015 briefing.

5. Van Creveld, "Less than We Can Be," 1.

6. Stouffer et al., *American Soldier*, 131.

7. Stouffer et al., *American Soldier*, 134.

8. Chamberlain *Passing of the Armies*, 20.

9. William Shakespeare, *Henry V*, 4.3.18–67.

10. In addition to "The mission is a man," Steven Spielberg's 1998 *Saving Private Ryan* also carried the taglines "The greatest challenge for eight men . . . was saving one" and "There was only one man left in the family, and the mission was to save him." A viewer must sort through a warehouse of titles to find a tiny handful of popular films that do not reflect and reinforce the idea of battle as a specifically and exclusively male world. Ridley Scott's 1997 GI *Jane*, which depicts the trials of a woman attempting to become the first to complete the navy's rigorous SEAL training, and the 1997 film adaptation of *Starship Troopers* (which includes a gender-integrated twenty-third-century "mobile infantry" unit fighting an insectoid alien menace) are rare exceptions.

11. Kamarck, *Women in Combat*, 1.

12. Rosenburg and Philipps, "All Combat Roles Now Open."

13. Carter, December 2015 briefing.

14. Rosenburg and Philipps, "All Combat Roles Now Open."

15. Rosenburg and Philipps, "All Combat Roles Now Open."

16. Van Creveld, "Less than We Can Be," 1–20.

17. Thomas James Brennan, "Women in Combat? Some Marines React," *New York Times*, January 29, 2013, https://atwar.blogs.nytimes.com/2013/01/29/women -in-combat-some-marines-react/.

18. Online comment from "RetiredArmy" on Rosenburg and Philipps, "All Combat Roles Now Open." The article received 407 comments before the *Times* closed the discussion. https://www.nytimes.com/2015/12/04/us/politics/combat -military-women-ash-carter.html, accessed October 14, 2019.

19. Online comment from "Roy" on Rosenburg and Philipps, "All Combat Roles Now Open."

20. Online comment from "Force6Delta" on Rosenburg and Philipps, "All Combat Roles Now Open."

21. John McCormack, "Obama Admin's Ruling on Women in Combat Will Endanger Marines," *Weekly Standard*, December 4, 2015, https://www.washingtonexaminer .com/weekly-standard/a-draft-for-women.

22. Aaron MacLean, "Progress Comes to the Military," *Washington Free Beacon*, December 4, 2015, https://freebeacon.com/national-security/progress-comes -to-the-military/.

23. Rosenburg and Philipps, "All Combat Roles Now Open."

24. Blanton and Cook, *They Fought Like Demons*.

25. "Women's Armed Services Integration Act of 1948," Public Law 625, 62 Stat. 356, June 12, 1948; U.S. Department of Defense, Direct Ground Combat Definition and Assignment Rule, January 13, 1994.

26. "Women in Combat . . . ," 8.

27. "Women in Combat," *New York Times*, June 3, 2012, https://www.nytimes .com/2012/06/04/opinion/women-in-combat.html.

28. "Women in Combat: Maybe? Yes?" *New York Times*, November 28, 1992, https://www.nytimes.com/1992/11/28/opinion/women-in-combat-maybe-yes.html.

29. Rosenburg and Philipps, "All Combat Roles Now Open."

30. "Women in Combat: Maybe? Yes?"

31. Carter, December 2015 briefing.

32. Carter, December 2015 briefing.

33. Carey Lohrenz, "Time for Some Fearless Leadership," *Time*, January 30, 2013, https://nation.time.com/2013/01/30/time-for-some-fearless-leadership/.

34. Kyleanne Hunter, "We Need What Women Bring to the Fight," *War on the Rocks*, September 21, 2015, https://warontherocks.com/2015/09/we-need-what -women-bring-to-the-fight/.

35. Brennan, "Women in Combat?"

36. Rosenburg and Philipps, "All Combat Roles Now Open."

37. Heather MacDonald, "Women Don't Belong in Combat Units," *Wall Street Journal*, January 16, 2019, https://www.wsj.com/articles/women-dont-belong-in -combat-units-11547411638.

38. Mike Fredenburg, "Putting Women in Combat Is an Even Worse Idea than You'd Think," *National Review*, July 15, 2015, https://www.nationalreview.com/2015 /07/women-in-combat-military-effectiveness-deadly-pentagon/.

39. Gregory Newbold, "What Tempers the Steel of an Infantry Unit," *War on the Rocks*, September 9, 2015, https://warontherocks.com/2015/09/what-tempers -the-steel-of-an-infantry-unit/.

40. Online comment on Rosenburg and Philipps, "All Combat Roles Now Open."

41. Brennan, "Women in Combat?"

42. Newbold, "What Tempers the Steel."

43. Rosenburg and Philipps, "All Combat Roles Now Open."

44. Brennan, "Women in Combat?"

45. Hope Hodge Seck, "Grunt Life: Marines Dish on the Corps' Women in Combat Experiment," *Marine Corps Times*, September 7, 2015, https://www .marinecorpstimes.com/news/your-marine-corps/2015/09/07/grunt-life-marines -dish-on-the-corps-women-in-combat-experiment/.

46. Seck, "Grunt Life."

47. "Women in Combat: Maybe? Yes?"

48. Carter, December 2015 briefing.

49. Carter, December 2015 briefing.

50. Brennan, "Women in Combat?"

51. Brennan, "Women in Combat?"

52. Lucian Truscott, testimony before the House Committee on Armed Services, in *Policy Implications of Lifting the Ban on Homosexuals in the Military*, 103rd Cong., 1st sess., May 4–5, 1993, 1–2, 4–6.

53. Fredenburg, "Even Worse Idea."

54. Newbold, "What Tempers the Steel."

55. Online comment on Rosenburg and Philipps, "All Combat Roles Now Open."

56. Newbold, "What Tempers the Steel."

57. Brennan, "Women in Combat?"

58. Seck, "Grunt Life."

59. Williams, *Love My Rifle*, 18.

60. Thomas Gibbons-Neff, "Marine Corps' Women-in-Combat Experiment Gets Mixed Results," *Washington Post*, September 8, 2015, https://www.washingtonpost .com/news/checkpoint/wp/2015/09/08/marines-women-in-combat-experiment -gets-mixed-results/.

61. Wong et al., *Why They Fight*.

62. MacCoun, "What Is Known"; MacCoun et al., "Social Cohesion."

63. Newbold, "What Tempers the Steel."

64. MacCoun et al., "Social Cohesion," 646–54.

65. Newbold, "What Tempers the Steel."

66. Anthony King, "Here's Why Women in Combat Will Work," *War on the Rocks*, December 1, 2014, https://warontherocks.com/2014/12/heres-why-women-in-combat-will-work/.

67. Brennan, "Women in Combat?"

68. Katey van Dam, "Women in Combat Arms: Just Good Business," *War on the Rocks*, February 25, 2015, https://warontherocks.com/2015/02/women-in-combat-arms-just-good-business/.

69. Martin Dempsey, "Dempsey's Message on Women in Combat," *Defense One*, January 28, 2014, https://defenseone.com/ideas/2014/01/dempseys-message-women-combat-trust-transcends-gender/77690/.

70. Brennan, "Women in Combat?"

71. Newbold, "What Tempers the Steel."

72. Stouffer et al., *American Soldier*, 131.

73. Wilson, "Women in Combat," 76.

74. Online comment from "John" on "Women in Combat Jobs," *New York Times*, December 5, 2015, https://www.nytimes.com/2015/12/06/opinion/sunday/women-in-combat-jobs.html.

75. Brennan, "Women in Combat."

76. David Barno and Nora Bensahel, "35 Years, Two Rangers, and the End of the Brass Ceiling," *War on the Rocks*, September 8, 2015, https://warontherocks.com/2015/09/35-years-two-rangers-and-the-end-of-the-brass-ceiling/.

Bibliography

Blanton, DeAnne, and Lauren Cook. *They Fought Like Demons: Women Soldiers in the American Civil War*. Baton Rouge: Louisiana University Press, 2002.

Chamberlain, Joshua Lawrence. *The Passing of the Armies: An Account of the Final Campaign of the Army of the Potomac Based Upon Personal Reminiscences of the Fifth Army Corps*. New York: G. P. Putnam's Sons, 1915.

House Committee on Armed Services. *Policy Implications of Lifting the Ban on Homosexuals in the Military*. 103rd Cong., 1st sess., May 4–5, 1993.

Kamarck, Kristy. *Women in Combat: Issues for Congress*. Washington DC: Congressional Research Service, 2015.

MacCoun, Robert. "What Is Known About Unit Cohesion and Military Performance." In *Sexual Orientation and U.S. Military Personnel Policy: Options and Assessments*, 283–331. Washington DC: RAND National Defense Research Institute.

MacCoun, Robert, Elizabeth Kier, and Aaron Belkin. "Does Social Cohesion Determine Motivation in Combat? An Old Question with an Old Answer." *Armed Forces and Society* 32, no. 4 (2006): 646–54.

Stouffer, Samuel A., Arthur A. Lumsdaine, Marion Harper Lumsdaine, Robin M. Williams Jr., M. Brewster Smith, Irving L. Janis, Shirley A. Star, and Leonard S. Cottrell Jr. *The American Soldier: Combat and its Aftermath*. Vol. 2. Princeton NJ: Princeton University Press, 1949.

Van Creveld, Martin. "Less than We Can Be: Men, Women, and the Modern Military." *Journal of Strategic Studies* 23, no. 4 (2000): 1.

Williams, Kayla. *Love My Rifle More than You: Young and Female in the U.S. Army.* New York: W. W. Norton, 2005.

Wilson, Heather. "Women in Combat." *National Interest* 32 (Summer 1993): 75–77.

"Women in Combat . . ." *off our backs* 21, no. 7 (July 1991): 8.

Wong, Leonard, Thomas Kolditz, Raymond Millen, and Terrence Potter. *Why They Fight: Combat Motivation in the Iraq War.* Carlisle Barracks PA: Strategic Studies Institute, U.S. Army War College, 2003.

TWELVE

"The Juice Ain't Worth the Squeeze"

Resisting Gender Integration in Special Forces

ALESHA E. DOAN AND SHANNON PORTILLO

The juice isn't worth the squeeze. I don't see possibly how the
combat effectiveness could be raised to the point where it would
offset the troubles it'll cause. It isn't going to be value-added.
We're not going to gain enough to make it worth it.

—BRIAN, Special Forces operator, 2014

On January 24, 2013, Secretary of Defense Leon Panetta and Chairman of the Joint Chiefs of Staff General Martin Dempsey announced that the Department of Defense (DOD) had repealed the 1994 Direct Ground Combat and Assignment Rule (DGCAR), which restricted women from serving in combat positions. This policy change applied to all military branches, but it had the most significant impact on the army because the percentage of positions closed to women was much greater compared to the air force and the navy, where most positions were already open to women, or to the marines, where the number of women serving was relatively minimal.[1] By time DGCAR was rescinded, more than 280,000 women had been deployed as support personnel for ground combat units operating in Iraq and Afghanistan; more than 800 women were wounded, and over 130 died.[2] Touting the contributions women have made to the military, Secretary Panetta stated in the announcement that "women have shown great courage and sacrifice on and off the battlefield, contributed in unprecedented ways to the military's mission and proven their ability to serve in an expanding number of roles."[3]

In their joint memorandum, Secretary Panetta and General Dempsey required military departments to provide detailed plans for implementing the new policy change by May 15, 2013, and established a deadline of January 1, 2016, for "expeditiously" integrating women into previously unavailable positions. In addition, the memorandum left the armed forces with an option to request an exception to the policy change by that date, stating, "Any recommendation to keep an occupational specialty or unit closed to women must be personally approved first by the Chairman of the Joint Chiefs of Staff, and then by the Secretary of Defense." It goes on to clarify that "exceptions must be narrowly tailored and based on a rigorous analysis of factual data regarding the knowledge, skills and abilities needed for the position."

This dramatic shift in policy recognized what many military leaders, politicians, and civilian advocates for gender equality had long asserted: the combat exclusion policy was at odds with the de facto reality that women were already engaged in direct combat.[4] While many heralded the change, the prospect of integrating women into all units, including those within Army Special Operations Forces (SOF), faced resistance from the cloistered all-male units, many of whom were hoping SOF units would be exempted from the policy. Even though a considerable amount of research had been conducted to guide the army's implementation strategy for gender integration following Secretary Panetta and General Dempsey's announcement, specifically the two-year Gender Integration Study commissioned by Headquarters, Department of the Army, the focus was on the conventional army rather than Special Forces (SF). As leaders grappled with deciding whether to request an exception for SOF, they sought out research "based on a rigorous analysis of factual data" to help inform the decision.

Our research, done with the cooperation of U.S. Special Operations Command, was designed to identify and examine the potential barriers and benefits of integrating women into the SF 18-series military occupational specialty. It was conducted in 2013–14, after DGCAR was rescinded but when Special Operations (SO) was still considering requesting an exemption to the policy change. Our goal was to provide information to army leaders to help inform their decision. Toward that end we conducted twenty-seven focus groups, with a nonrandom sample of 198 participants during multiday site visits across five military bases. Twenty-three focus groups con-

DOAN AND PORTILLO

sisted of active duty male SF operators serving as enlisted soldiers, warrant officers, and commissioned officers and four focus groups with women serving as enlisted soldiers and commissioned officers working in units housed in army SO.[5] We used the data to develop two surveys that were administered to all male SF operators and all female operators assigned to Special Operations Command.[6]

Based on our findings, we concluded that the largest barrier to integrating women into SF is cultural opposition to integration, rather than material or physical barriers. Men were overwhelmingly negatively predisposed to integration in SF, and their concerns were largely premised on gender tropes: narratives based on prevalent stereotypes of women and men. Participants largely defined gender along binaries heavily steeped in patriarchal and heteronormative assumptions that structured their behavior toward female colleagues and shaped the day-to-day cultural norms of SF. Brian's adage that "the juice isn't worth the squeeze" captures the sentiment of many male soldiers who have concluded that women's value to combat missions is questionable and would create untold "troubles" ultimately undermining of the masculine culture and thus the "functioning" of the military. Couching disapproval of gender integration in terms of the mission of the military—"combat effectiveness"—masks the systemic impact of the ways in which gender tropes reinforce military norms and behavior. Although women were much more supportive of gender integration, they also subscribed to these pervasive tropes. Male and female soldiers occasionally challenged them, but given the dominant culture of the organization, their voices were typically dismissed by their peers.

As we argue in this chapter, most SF soldiers drew on traditional gender stereotypes and tropes to resist integration. Men, along with a surprisingly significant percentage of women, founded their opinions about integration on gender stereotypes and anecdotal experiences rather than empirical facts. After providing a brief history on the DGCAR and some background on SF, we examine how male and female soldiers' reliance on gender tropes structures their behavior, which reinforces existing gender hierarchies. Soldiers conceptualized masculinity in opposition to femininity, and male soldiers frequently used their female colleagues as foils to illustrate what masculinity is not in SF. Gendered stereotypes function as informal behavioral management tools that continue to define and manage sex, reinforcing the construction of SF as a masculinized space where women are othered and constructed as outsiders.

Women and Combat

Formal roles for women in the military are still relatively recent; however, women's involvement with the military is long-standing and pre-dates the official founding of the nation, dating back to the 1775 Revolutionary War.[7] In more modern history, nearly 33,000 women served in the military during World War I. By World War II, this number increased dramatically to approximately 350,000, as female service members helped assuage the military's manpower shortage by filling administrative and nursing positions. In efforts aimed at attracting women for service, the Women's Army Auxiliary Corps's original recruitment campaign included a plea to women to join the corps and "release a man for combat." Despite women's contributions to the war effort—including working in intelligence, supply, medicine, and communications, among other positions—their formal participation in the U.S. military began after World War II, with the explicit refusal that women would participate in combat.[8]

From its inception the management of sex, gender, and sexuality has been a central feature of the military, shaped by a labyrinth of combat and leadership exclusion policies, stemming from the 1948 Women's Armed Services Integration Act.[9] This act permitted women to have a permanent status in the U.S. Army, Navy, Air Force, and Marine Corps, but restrictions were placed on their participation. The number of women allowed in the army was restricted to 2 percent of enlisted soldiers, with female officers capped at 10 percent. Their ranks were restricted, and they were barred from combat aircrafts and ships.[10]

By 1967 the military removed the cap on women's participation and loosened ranking restrictions. These policy changes, however, did little to increase the number of women serving in the armed forces until the military shifted to an all-volunteer force and once again began targeting recruitment efforts at women. As women's roles in the military expanded during the ensuing years, many women achieved "firsts," including the first female major general, first female chaplain, and first female to complete navy flight school in 1973. Three years later the U.S. Air Force Academy, Naval Academy, and Military Academy started admitting women, and in 1978 Congress amended the 1948 Women's Armed Services Integration Act, opening the door for women to work on noncombat ships.[11]

As women gained a stronger foothold in the military, Congress sought clarification on their role in combat, convening a DOD Task Force on Women in the Military in 1988, which resulted in the creation and adoption of the Risk Rule. Under the Risk Rule, the military was permitted to close assignments to women that carried "risks of exposure to direct combat, hostile fire, or capture."[12] The Risk Rule, however, did not stand the test of time, and in 1994 Secretary of State Leslie Aspin rescinded it following Operation Desert Storm, where soldiers' on-the-ground experiences illuminated the challenges of delineating between assignments that were "at risk" compared to those that were not.[13]

During Operation Desert Storm, more women served in the military than any previous war in the United States, and 29 percent served in nontraditional positions. Over the course of deployment, male and female service members experienced similar levels of exposure to environmental hazards. Even more troubling for the implementation of the Risk Rule, 71 percent of women and 70 percent of men experienced at least one exposure to combat-related hazards in events such as a scud missile, artillery, rockets, or mortars explosion; engagement in small arms fire; or seeing dead or seriously injured people.[14] These realities reflected the changing nature of modern warfare, where "everyone in theater was at risk, and thus a risk-based policy was no longer appropriate."[15] Realizing the futility of the Risk Rule in the contemporary theater of war, the air force, navy, and marines repealed the ban on assigning women to combat aircrafts through the National Defense Authorization Act for Fiscal Years 1992 and 1993, but they continued to exclude women from assignments to "units below the brigade level whose primary mission is direct ground combat."[16]

Although the Risk Rule was rescinded in 1994, the Direct Ground Combat and Assignment Rule—largely modeled after the army's ground combat exclusion policy—stayed firmly in place for nearly a decade. In practice women were not allowed to work in infantry, artillery, or armor, as combat engineers, or in so units of battalion size or smaller.[17] The implementation of DGCAR closed approximately 15 percent of all positions across the armed forces to women, translating to about 142,000 (29 percent) positions in the army; 43,400 (25 percent) positions in the Marine Corps; 33,300 (9 percent) in the navy; and 2,300 (1 percent) in the air force.[18] The DOD's justification for the DGCAR was predicated on leaders' beliefs that public support for integration was tepid, that integration would create privacy issues for service members, and that women lacked the physical strength and stamina for combat. Consequently, leaders insisted that women "would not contribute to the readiness and effectiveness of those units."[19]

More than a decade later, following the U.S. military's protracted participation in conflicts in Iraq and Afghanistan, politicians, civilians, and some military leaders once again joined a growing chorus of opposition to DGCAR. Operation Iraqi Freedom began on March 20, 2003, and the conflict quickly illuminated the changing parameters of warfare because "enemy techniques blur the line between combat and noncombat situations on the ground."[20] Relying on established definitions of a linear battlefield—where a distinction was made between forward and rear operating areas—became more tenuous in the "nonlinear battlefields" of Iraq and Afghanistan.[21] Further complicating compliance with DGCAR, women frequently engaged in direct combat when they were deployed in a support unit for a combat unit, effectively rendering the definition of the "direct ground combat" contained in the policy as irrelevant to the reality of the contemporary battlefield.

With these realities on the horizon, the Duncan Hunter National Defense Authorization Act for Fiscal Year 2009 authorized the creation of the Military Leadership Diversity Commission (MLDC). The MLDC was created as a nonpartisan body to be populated with military and civilian leaders. Among its charges the commission was tasked with conducting "a comprehensive evaluation and assessment of policies that provide opportunities for the promotion and advancement of minority members of the Armed Forces,"

DOAN AND PORTILLO

which, among its other duties, included "the establishment and maintenance of fair promotion and command opportunities for ethnic- and gender-specific members of the Armed Forces at the 0-5 grade level and above."[22] Taking note of the historical absence of women in three- and four-star positions, advocates for gender equity pointed to the policies that excluded women from combat as one of the main culprits.

In 2011 the MLDC released a report, "From Representation to Inclusion: Diversity Leadership and the 21st-Century Military," that contained twenty recommendations designed to "develop future military leaders who represent the face of America."[23] Several of the recommendations were targeted at diversifying the pool of candidates considered for high-ranking leadership positions, conducting annual "barrier analyses" of policies and practices that derail ethnic, racial and gender minorities' career pathways, and establishing accountability metrics for measuring progress. But the most radical change—recommendation 9—urged officials to "eliminate the 'combat exclusion policies' for women, including the removal of barriers and inconsistencies, to create a level playing field for all qualified servicemembers."[24]

In February 2012, against this backdrop, U.S. Army Secretary John McHugh loosened one component of DGCAR—the collocation restriction—which was unique to the army's assignment policy and more restrictive than the DOD's version of the DGCAR. The restriction prohibited assigning women to units that "collocate routinely with units assigned a direct combat mission."[25] Although this policy modification opened over fourteen thousand additional positions to women, it only created more confusion and did little to clarify DGCAR.

Less than a year later, the DOD rescinded DGCAR, vowing to "successfully integrate women into the remaining restricted occupational fields within our military" and using gender-neutral "occupational performance standards."[26] The armed forces were given a three-year timeline for implementing integration by January 1, 2016. However, the services were permitted to request an exception to the policy change. SF was contemplating requesting an exception and began seeking out research.

Special Forces

Although using small-unit, unconventional warfare tactics stems back to the Revolutionary War, the first official SF unit was established in 1952 following the military's success of using specialized small-unit teams in World War II.[27] In 1954 SF adopted the green beret as part of their uniform to demarcate themselves from the conventional army. Today SF are an elite component of SO; less than 10 percent of the men who apply end up making it through screening and assessment. At the time of our study, there were no women in SF.

SF operators are trained to perform highly skilled missions around six key areas: counterinsurgency, unconventional warfare, direct action, foreign internal defense, special reconnaissance, and security force assistance.[28] Most of these areas involve preventing or disrupting terrorist activities, training other nations' military forces or insurgency movements, improving the defense capabilities of allied military forces, and gathering intelligence.[29] SF teams are regularly deployed in small-person units called Operational Detachment Alpha (ODA). When deployed SF operators often rely closely on each other, with no forward operating base or support teams. Even when they are training and stateside, most ODAS spend significant on-duty and off-duty time together.

Throughout the remainder of our chapter, we draw on data from focus groups and surveys to present the overarching gender narratives that emerged from participants in our study. Our data illustrate how male and female soldiers' behavior is often animated by underlying gender tropes, which are used to manage and reinforce a gendered hierarchy in SF despite the army's implementation of official policies that are intended to be gender-neutral.

Alpha Male

SF is a space defined by the homosocial nature of a male-only workforce, where exclusivity is part of the masculine identity. Male participants therefore perceived gender integration as antithetical to the espoused values of SF, even though women have been successfully integrated into other aspects of the military. Only 16 percent of male survey respondents strongly or somewhat agreed that "females should have the opportunity to serve in SF," compared to 70 percent of female survey respondents. Yet while most female respondents wanted women to have the opportunity to compete as individuals who may qualify to participate in SF, they nonetheless supported the normalized masculine identity of SF. Most survey participants reported that SF should remain masculine in nature if integrated. Roughly half of the women agreed or strongly agreed (56 percent) that SF should remain largely masculine, while most of the men (86 percent) agreed or strongly agreed with the same statement.

Although most men and women supported keeping SF a masculine space, men proudly embodied this identity. Using shorthand they often described themselves as quintessential "alpha males," a term that they used interchangeably with "hypermasculine," to encapsulate how they differed from men serving in the "conventional army" and women. In characterizing the alpha male, men described themselves as guys who liked to use vulgar language in the team room, were overly sexual, and embraced violence.

Compared to female soldiers, men consistently subscribed to and expressed a higher frequency of stereotyping, foregrounded in the larger context of the military's male identity. Succinctly capturing the group's sentiment, Mike stated, "We're all 18-series, type-A personalities. We can work around anything. But is [integration] something that we want to have to work around?" For many male soldiers, integration was described as an obstacle to be managed by circumventing or excluding women rather than working inclusively with them. Mike references 18-series, the military occupational specialty that demarcates SF, in essence conflating the MOS and maleness with his comment. Men would "work around" integration, rather than seeing it as a part of the work they do.

Their narratives presented a hypermasculine workplace culture grossly at odds with men's stereotypical description of women and femininity, which they used to underscore their opposition to integration. Referencing the hard-hitting, aggressive sports ethos of professional football, multiple SF members analogized the "testosterone-fueled" culture of SF to the National Football League (NFL), with no room or need for women. After making this comparison, Joel posed several questions to the focus group:

"Here's a question. They are so hell bent on doing this, on integrating women into every facet in the military, why don't they integrate women in the NFL? I mean it's the same concept." In a different focus group, Carter asked similar questions: "What's the difference between the professional organization like SF versus the NFL? Do they have the opportunity as a female to go play football in the NFL? So why should SF?" Both Joel and Carter articulate a common perception among male focus group participants: that the integration of women into SF was an unnecessary decision to symbolically "make women be seen as equals." Their comparison between SF and the NFL was used to underscore the absurdity of having women in these "alpha male" spaces, where women's physicality is comical next to men's. Pointing to these two distinct spaces, Joel and Carter managed expectations about gender—specifically, normalizing their belief that women do not belong everywhere. Like most other focus group participants, Joel and Carter concluded that if SF is forced to integrate, male members would have to make special concessions to compensate for women's physical limitations. Ironically, while men in our focus groups regularly touted SF as an elite space that uniquely uses intelligence, independent thinking, problem-solving, teamwork ability, and leadership skills as metrics of success, they often advocated for excluding women based solely on physical arguments.

Drawing more distinctions between alpha males and stereotypical females, men pointed out aspects of SF culture they believed would be off-putting to women. They buttressed their alpha male identity with their masculine identity outside of work, which they assumed was a universal identity for all Green Berets. Men frequently claimed that shared interests in extracurricular activities, such as hunting, drinking, shooting, and listening to rock and roll, strengthened and solidified male bonding among coworkers and fit the culture of SF. In describing their commonalities, Sam explained that team members shared "interest in the same things pretty much. We all like guns, we all like lifting weights, we all like women, we all like just being aggressive monsters on the battlefield. That's what we do." Sam referenced his heterosexuality and tied it to interest in guns and physicality to describe his version of the of alpha male that belongs in SF. He assumed that masculinity required men to "like" the same activities, and that women do not participate in these activities, despite the reality that female soldiers operate guns, lift weights, and perform on the battlefield. By integrating these activities into his definition of heterosexual masculinity, Sam articulated an environment where women could not be included. In his portrayal of masculinity, uniformity was expected, and this picture was shared by most men in the focus groups.

The alpha male narrative draws on soldiers' deep-seated beliefs that gender differences are biologically rooted, which they confirmed with their experiential knowledge drawn from interactions with female romantic partners and family members. During the focus groups, male participants deployed these anecdotes to illustrate the incompatibility between gender integration and the mission of SF. These men often claimed that their "natural instinct" to protect women would be problematic on integrated teams. As Paul argued, "Gender creates all kinds of expectations and gender norms and roles that we have deeply ingrained in us. Call it instinctual—wanting to protect the opposite sex. These things are good things normally in our society because they enable us to protect our loved ones, our sisters, our mothers. But in this situation, where warfighting is our primary mission, that disrupts our job. It doesn't enable us to do the job correctly because it creates a liability." Seconding Paul's perspective, Arnold pointed to men's "natural instinct to protect a lady" as a limitation to having women on a SF team. He went on to explain that a man's "protective mentality" would fire up around women—that regardless of whether he "spends a week with her, [or] spends ten weeks with her, [they're] going to develop that" protective shield around female colleagues.

Intertwining biological and socially constructed gendered expectations, men frequently made contradictory claims, simultaneously asserting that their treatment and understanding of women's fragility stemmed from their genetic makeup and upbringing. This was particularly heightened when men constructed their desire to protect women as part of their biological hardwiring to "protect" those who are weaker. Threading several of these stereotypes together, Stanley commented that "as a man I have a protective instinct over anything smaller, a child and a woman. I'm married, I have a wife. I look at her different. That's nature. I can't change it."

Stanley sees himself, and his role in SF, in terms he understands as completely "natural," based on gender roles framed by physical size and traditional nuclear family expectations. However, Stanley is oblivious to the fact that equating all women to children infantilizes women, which spills over to his perception of, and interactions with, female colleagues. Stanley's understanding of women as a group that needs to be protected stunted his ability to view female colleagues as equals who may potentially qualify and succeed in SF.

While Stanley pointed to his wife as a touchstone to illustrate men's protective instinct, Randall, after noting that he "[didn't] mean to sound caveman or chauvinistic," took a step further and stereotyped all men as protective and all women as seeking male protection: "There's an evolutionary digression when you get into a situation where females almost look for protection from a man. You can't train that. That's genetic." Randall went on to connect men's protective instinct with traditional nuclear family roles, which he also believed has a genetic base. "The basic instinct is that men and women get married, [have] kids, and all that stuff," he stated. "You can't get away from that. It's genetics." The potential presence of a woman on an SF team posed a disruption to Randall's heteronormative narrative, where "genetics" dictate gender roles and life events including marriage and children. Randall was adamant that having women on a team would distract men from the objectives of their mission because of men's protective instinct.

Approaching gender from a different angle that highlights physical attributes, Michael interjected a racial analogy into the conversation to further emphasize the biological differences between men and women: "So, a Black man and a white man. Still men. There's nothing genetically different other than the pigment of your skin. There's genetic differences between men and women, bottom line. I was never raised to look down on, or look up to, a Black man or protect a Black man, as where I was a woman. So, when genetically the same as me, we can move past race issues and be one in the same. We can't when you're not the same." Michael saw his desire to protect women as unmovable because it is rooted in biology. However, by muddling physiological differences with cultural expectations, Michael believed that interacting with women differently was not only justified but beyond his control.

DOAN AND PORTILLO

While women much less frequently offered such explanations, eight women made similar biologically grounded claims, characterizing men as "naturally protective." For women like Becca, being treated "as more of a little sister" by her male colleagues had its downside, even getting "in the way" at work. At times men's protective instinct created tension for Becca that hampered her ability to perform her job, but she had learned to accept that tension because, she said, it is ingrained in men's "human nature." Jennifer likewise described herself as a capable person, but she also understood that sometimes she must "swallow my pride a little bit [because] men in our culture and our society are protective of a woman," which she attributed to the "nature" of men.

Neither Becca nor Jennifer saw male protection as "a bad thing as long as it doesn't get in the way of the mission." Their perspectives were exceptional among the women, but not inconsequential. Both women were willing to acquiesce to men's protective instinct if it did not "interfere" with their ability to perform their job, even though they both acknowledged that, at times, it did. They are what feminist sociologists Anastasia Prokos and Irene Padavic refer to as the "foil" for the organization—meaning that Becca and Jennifer embraced and propped up a traditional gender trope where men are understood as natural protectors and women as the weaker sex in need of protection. Positioning themselves and other women as a group that should accept and accommodate men's "protective nature" functions as a "foil" that thwarts gender equity in the organization by reinforcing and maintaining the gendered hierarchy in the military. By accepting these exaggerated differences between men and women, Becca and Jennifer lend credibility to the underlying, yet prevailing, belief that women do not truly belong in the armed forces.

In male focus groups, discussions of protectionism also quickly dovetailed into discussions centered around spousal jealously, which men were concerned would escalate if they worked on an integrated team. Taylor discussed the stress that he would encounter if women were deployed with him: "Just another thing like on the home front here that [will] have an impact with women being with an ODA. The wives would be thinking, okay, this captain is—she's new and my husband's over there for nine months with this chick, and I don't know who she is. And it's just the way the women think. But to put one or two women in there that are in shape and fairly good-looking or whatever, it's going to cause a lot of issues with the wives back home." Taylor referenced jealousy and heterosexual relationship arrangements stateside that would, in his mind, naturally create stress for the men working in SF. The way Taylor and many of his colleagues discussed the inclusion of women into SF emphasized their potential role as romantic or sexual partners, which they constructed as an inevitable—and natural— consequence of having a mixed gender team. Kevin emphasized this point, saying, "And I think that biological factor is often just brushed to the side and we pretend that because it's 2013 we can all ignore it, but ultimately that's not the case."

Once again men in our study couched their concerns in the "natural" or heteronormative understandings of a family unit. Rather than viewing female colleagues as potential "brothers in arms," SF members constructed female colleagues as sexual temptresses who would exacerbate tensions on the home front. Kirk tried to emphasize the significance of his concerns by saying women, including his girlfriend, are focused on jealousy: "I would be more worried about the wives being jealous. If I was married, I wouldn't necessarily worry about sexual harassment but the wives. Even the girlfriends. We still all hang out, like, all the time. And so I know my girlfriend would be pissed if I was hanging out with [female colleagues]." Generalizing from experiences with his girlfriend, Kirk stereotyped all wives as being consumed by jealousy when their husbands spend time with women outside of their home. Kirk's girlfriend already struggled with the time he spent away from home on deployments and socializing with his male friends at home. Kirk believed that having women on an ODA would simply add an additional layer of discord to SF members' personal relationships.

Hygiene and Emotions

The men in our study commonly drew on unfounded assumptions about the functioning of women's bodies. Drawing on stereotypes, men discussed how women's menstruation, reproduction, and hygiene needs would compromise the mission-oriented nature of SF deployments and prevent women from successfully operating on an SF team.

In the male focus groups, participants pathologized women's embodied experience of menstruation and potential reproduction to frame their opposition to integration, claiming that women's biology would present limitations "down range." SF members repeatedly referenced menstruation to illustrate that women's bodies starkly contrast with the functioning of the bodies of men, which, by implication, do not need such attention and are therefore superior in the field. Menstruation was discussed as an unwanted medical "risk factor" that would require men to carry additional medical supplies. Pulling these themes together, Robert explained why women's bodies mark them as unfit for serving in the field: "I mean [the] potential for yeast infections and everything without being clean. A woman has a menstrual cycle and all that. These are all things that could definitely be complicated in a situation where you are just pretty filthy and you're living in a dirty environment and you have no way to take care of yourself." Although Robert did not articulate any misgivings about men's hygiene, his preoccupation with women's cleanliness revealed his larger unease with the prospect of having women on a SF team. Careful not to couch their opposition in terms of their own discomfort, men situated it in medical discourse that focused on the "risks" menstruation and irregular access to hygiene uniquely pose to women.

Men also pinned women's mood fluctuations to their menstrual cycle. Patrick explained to the group that all women, regardless of their professional role or rank, are to be avoided while they menstruate: "It's like a roller coaster with women. One week can be really good and then, all of a sudden, it's that time of the month and you can't even be around them." Chris also drew on his personal experience to highlight the emotional chaos menstruating women inject in a group. "I'm not being a jerk," he said. "I mean, hell, I've got five sisters, and I've got a wife. I know there's a period during the month that you're just, 'What the hell happened to you and who are you?'" Mirroring many men in the focus groups, Chris saw his knowledge of women—based on his personal relationships—as a source of expertise that he extrapolated to stereotype all menstruating women as overly sensitive and emotional.

Menstruation was held up by men as a tangible factor that demonstrated the unfitness of women to serve in SF, and to it they linked stereotypes about women's behavior. In doing so men were managing women's fitness for SF based on physiology while simultaneously propagating stereotypes about women's emotional instability.

While men portrayed menstruation as a liability, most women described it as a regular part of their lives. Summing up the impact of menstruation on her ability to work, Susan stated, "I can handle myself. I've done this since I was sixteen. This is part of my normal life." In contrast to their male colleagues, women did not view menstruation as a hygiene risk that would create additional health problems, compromise their emotional health, or affect their ability to perform in the field. Rather than seeing menstruation as central to their performance at work or identity, women described it as a normal part of their everyday lives.

Men often closely linked menstruation and hygiene to more complex stereotypes about women's weaker emotional endurance to voice their trepidation about integration. Summing up women's limitations, Eldon candidly admits, "I just don't think psychologically, emotionally, and physically that they are made to endure that hardship." Even men like Alex, who recognized that some women can handle the physicality of the job, women's potential to succeed on a SF team was discounted when he defaulted to gender tropes regarding women's supposedly weaker emotional constitution. He commented: "What makes a SF operator different than the rest of the army is not our weapons, not even our mission, but it's the guy that's selected because of his mental, physical, and emotional capability. Can some females who have the fitness and the mental fortitude to go out there and pass selection at the standard that's out there, can they do it? I believe there are females that can. I've seen them. Are there things that can be overcome that they can still do hygiene in a certain way that doesn't change the standard? Yes. It can be done. My concern is the emotional aspect."

Martin similarly recognized that some women "can make it through SF training," but like Alex, he expressed the belief that women simply don't have the same mental fortitude as men. "One of my concerns is that in these split-second scenarios where you have to make a decision, you have to make it quick, and you have to act on it. [Women] are indecisive and they're trying to process multiple things, connecting to it emotionally, and then freezing. This is just talking strictly about how men and women think and process information." Although Martin hasn't witnessed firsthand a woman "freezing" or being "indecisive" in the field, he nonetheless registered this concern. He also presented his speculations as a narrow and neutral read on women that was limited to their ability to "think and process information." Such assessments were not unique; many SF soldiers in our study described women's alleged emotionality and decisional incompetence, thereby marking women as a liability in the field. And the consequences for women extended beyond SF: men's widespread belief that emotion, rather than reason, drove women's decisions trailed women throughout the organization.

Perhaps surprisingly, women also offered negative gender stereotypes about women, but they drew on a different trope. After carefully noting how they, individually, were "different" or "atypical," nearly one-third of female focus group participants proceeded to stereotype other women, often describing them as the archetypical "mean girl," who was characterized as competitive, unsupportive, and eager to create drama. Women were far more likely to embrace this stereotype than their male colleagues. In sum women offered negative stereotypes of women on 167 occasions, or 28.6 percent of the time, whereas, among men, these numbers were 197, and 16.1 percent, respectively.

According to some of the female participants, women's unbridled competitive nature surfaced in multiple arenas, including physical fitness tests, career advancement, and male attention. Maddie bristled at physically competitive women, telling the group, "I'm so sick of the females that you get that come in immediately—'I did ninety-nine pushups. How much did you do?'" Shifting gears, Amaya claimed that women are excessively competitive when it comes to career advancement and seeking out male attention. After implicating all women, Amaya summed it up by saying, "I think honestly in the military women are really competitive toward each other, especially since there's such a small population."

Many female participants linked stereotypes that portrayed

women as unsupportive of each other to their claims about women's competitive nature. Participants also asserted that women behaved poorly when interacting with other women, but when these same women interacted with men, they were pleasant. Comfortably casting all women in this mold, Natalie said, "Any time I interact with any other female it's kind of like a little standoffish, more so than when they interact with other guys." Adding validity to Natalie's account of female colleagues, Bella made a point of letting the group know she has always gravitated toward "guys" because, unlike women, men "aren't bitchy" and "don't judge." She confessed to the group that she, too, prefers working with men, and that working with women was a "culture shock" that "just completely threw [her] off guard" because she "wasn't used to working with other females." Even though Bella had extremely limited experience working with other women, she perpetuated a gender trope that portrayed all women as undercutting of each other for their own career advancement. In this trope cattiness was the preferred method women used to "tear [each other] down" and generate harmful rumors about other women. Attempting to counter this trope, 23.6 percent of female participants pushed back, noting that men were just as guilty of indulging the rumor mill. A smaller percentage of male participants (14.3 percent) acknowledged that men also started rumors and enjoyed the "entertainment" value they provided.

But a key difference existed between the men and women in terms of how the rumor mill was described and used. Women saw rumors as a means for women to undercut or be catty to one another, to promote oneself over other women, and to stifle competition. In stark contrast, the men used rumors as a tool to help manage women. They described rumors as a way to isolate women during deployment, to illustrate the incompatibility between gender integration and cohesion, and, most of all, to highlight the "drama" women bring to the organization. Claiming to have "zero tolerance" for drama, Patrick succinctly summed up the issue as: "Women bring drama to the table. Women equals [sic] drama." Drama, in these discussions, often referred to a rift that developed between two men on a team. Alluding to the fracturing of cohesion, Joshua explained the problem of gender integration: "It's the cattiness; it's the clique forming on a team when you have a dude and chick. It's the sexuality of it. It makes a very unpleasant work environment."

Sexual Tension

As Joshua's comment suggests, men's belief that women bring drama was often closely related to their perception that the presence of women created sexual tension, which represented another of their key arguments against gender integration. Many soldiers described a "natural" sexual tension between men and women. Like many of his colleagues, R.J. had worked with female soldiers and was complimentary of their performance, but he believed gender integration "came at a price." That price was sexual tension and disharmony among the team, which R.J. viewed as a "natural phenomenon" that he attributed to the "attraction factor between a man and a woman, which creates an awkward environment" regardless of "how professional we want to be." An overwhelming majority of men—and, to a lesser degree, women—echoed his sentiments, viewing heterosexual indiscretions as "unavoidable," "a matter of time," and a sordid element of human nature.

Women's sexuality, according to most men, posed an inexorable distraction to teams. Assuming that men have a biological imperative to pursue women, Nick makes a heteronormative case for gender exclusion: "It's human nature. Men are attracted to women. We all can agree on that." Nick concluded that sexual tension is "human nature" and thus inevitable; therefore, "safeguards" cannot be "written into policy" to prevent it. Jimmy, based on his experiential knowledge, likewise framed sexual tension as impossible to avoid and harmful to the work environment: "You get the opposite sex in close quarters and a stressful environment a long way from home and things are going to happen. Guys who were focused on their mission completely lost their minds when the attractive females showed up" in support units. Jimmy's comments underscore men's perceptions of the disruptive influence "the attraction factor" could have on eroding professionalism on a team, which is particularly heightened if the women are deemed "attractive."

Men often attributed what they understood as their inability to control themselves around women to their alpha male personalities, which they saw both as biologically fixed and as necessary to succeed in sf. Ethan was irritated with what he perceived as conflicting professional expectations: to exhibit aggressive traits and simultaneously maintain sexual self-control: "The men you want for combat, the most driven, are also the most sexually driven men. And when you arouse one on purpose, it promotes the other as well." According to Ethan, sexual aggression goes hand in hand with being "driven," which is incompatible with having women on sf teams.

In these focus group exchanges, men did not blame women for sexual actions or intentions, but instead portrayed women's sexuality as a passive force. Noah reflected on his work experience with a woman, grousing that "the female that came to us was a distraction and there was, for a lack of better term, sexual frustration." Noah's comments made it clear that he didn't see the woman or her behavior per se as the problem; instead, it was the uncomfortable "sexual frustration" men experienced. However, Noah's stereotyping of men unintentionally places blame on the "female" who was a "distraction" simply by virtue of her presence, not by her actions. Jacob speculated that even more dire consequences would occur, adding that sexual tension, harassment, and even assault is "going to increase" if women are put in an environment where they are "secluded with alpha males." Even as he described the potential for male sexual violence against women, Jacob seemed unaware that his comments endorsed myths about sexual violence (e.g., victim-blaming) by positioning gender integration as the culprit rather than the behavior of a perpetrator. While few challenged portrayals of male sexuality as biologically fixed and uncontrollable, some men did push back. Isaac rejected the idea that the potential for sexual tension warrants preventing women from entering sf. He argued that, while some men may have a hard time containing themselves, not all men suffer from an absence of self-control: "I hate to point my finger at other sf guys, but it really falls on our shoulders that it's our fault, and I hate to say it, but why is it a big deal? Why can't you handle it, dude? The mentality around it just doesn't make sense to me."

Likewise, in a different focus group, after listening to his colleagues ruminate about women's sexuality as an on-site liability, Paul countered their stories with his own extensive experience working with women. "My experience was actually quite different than what's been voiced so far," he said. "They were absolutely an asset. I ran over 100 missions with them, over 250 with the team, and never once was I driven into their bed from sexual tension or something like that. It was just a professional relationship. We have grown men and introduce females to the equation and, all of a sudden, we become animals?" Taking an unpopular stand, Paul and Isaac suggested that their colleagues' claims were absurd and that they served primarily as "excuses" to oppose integration.

Female focus groups discussed sexuality in dramatically different terms than most of their male colleagues. Seeing sexual tension and aggression as neither biologically fixed nor inevitable, their conversations primarily centered on how their gender marked them as "different" or singled them out for unwanted attention, isolation, or harassment. Angela felt ill equipped to deal with the "dynamic" created by her presence, even though she consciously downplayed her sexuality. Likewise, Jennifer and Ellen did not "invite" male attention, but despite their own professionalism, they were subjected to unwelcome and unprofessional sexual attention during deployments. Jennifer elaborated, "I worked with the medics in the clinic. And one of the other men on the team needed that attention from his friends and he perceived that I was getting that attention. And we started noticing things would change. There were certain rules where we couldn't go certain places anymore on the base. And it got to the point where there was animosity in the air. And you could feel that it was towards us, for just being females and just trying to do our job." As Jennifer noted, although she was doing nothing more than her job, some of her male colleagues struggled with her presence on the base, effectively altering the dynamic for everyone. Nonetheless, male colleagues saw women as culpable for the "animosity in the air." Attempting to mitigate the tension, the commanding officer implemented rules and restrictions that limited women's mobility on the base "for just being females."

Echoing the dire need for cultural reform, Charlie confided to the focus group that her male colleagues used harassment as a management tool to segregate her on base. At Charlie's site her arrival threw her male colleagues off guard because they were expecting a man to arrive: "They thought I was a dude because of my name." Her isolation, and the harassment directed toward her, quickly escalated. "I guess you could say I've never experienced sexism until I got to Afghanistan," she said, "and I've never been so lonely in my life. They treated me horrible. I'm talking like a lesser human being. Like I'm sitting here eating and [they] knocked my dinner out from me, telling me, 'Clean that shit up, bitch.' That's how I was spoken to. [It was] just appalling."

As a petite, attractive woman of color, Charlie had been subjected to inappropriate innuendos and suggestive, racialized euphemisms in the past. However, this assignment transcended those experiences and entered a new terrain of harassment, which was ignored by her superiors. Even though Charlie's stateside superior was concerned and gave her permission to return early, she declined. Fearing that she would not receive "good" assignments in the future, and that she would acquire a reputation as being too soft or too girly, Charlie suffered in silence during this deployment.

Conclusion

Throughout this chapter we have examined how gender tropes shape soldiers' attitudes, which will likely structure women's experiences as they integrate into SF. The overt, brazen harassment targeted at Charlie is easily identifiable, but also exceptional. More common are the less visible obstacles to women's success that persist in the day-to-day work environment. One of our most persistent findings, across focus groups, was that participants normalized gender stereotypes, particularly when they opposed gender integration. Bringing awareness to the invisibility of stereotypes, and the way they shape the experiences of women and men in SF, is a first step to ensure that they are not reinforced in the culture of the organization.

As we have seen, both men and women relied on deeply embedded stereotypes about gender, and regardless of the specific stereotype employed, participants constructed gender in binary terms. While men belonged to the organization, women were outsiders. Thus, stereotypes supported a "gendered organizational logic"

DOAN AND PORTILLO

that structured the institution.[30] Although most participants were oblivious to their invocation of stereotypes, most of their opinions pertaining to integration and, as importantly, their daily behavior and interactions with colleagues were grounded in them. The few times individuals challenged gender tropes, their voices were quickly silenced by other focus group participants who confirmed the stereotypes for each other. Functioning as the "invisible hand" of management practices, stereotyping continues to reinforce and normalize gender hierarchies in the military and poses the largest obstacle for integrating women into all units in the armed forces.[31] Providing visibility to the gendered logic of the organization that is apparent in the norms, and actively pushing back on it, is a step in shifting to a more equitable culture.

After DGCAR was rescinded, the armed services conducted more than thirty primary studies, including our research, that were used by leaders to both inform their decision about requesting an exception to the policy change and their implementation of it.[32] On September 30, 2015, the secretaries of the Military Departments submitted their final recommendations to the secretary of defense. The commandant of the Marine Corps was the only one who requested an exception to the policy change, which would have kept 48,779 positions in the active and reserve components in the marines and the navy closed to women. The secretary of the navy rejected the request and then sent it to the secretary of defense. After review and consultation with the chairman of the Joint Chiefs of Staff, the secretary of defense opened all remaining occupations and positions to women, allowing for no exceptions.[33] Women can now formally apply to any military occupational specialty, including SO branches. Since the ban on women in combat was lifted, over a dozen women have earned their Army Ranger tab, and three women joined the marines infantry in January 2017. As of November 2018, the first woman successfully completed SF Assessment and Selection, and more women are expected to follow in the coming years.[34] However, rescinding the policy that denies women access to opportunities is not enough; the military must consider how it promotes integration by bringing awareness of gender tropes, understanding how they are used within the organization, and actively addressing them within the broader military culture.

Note on Methods

In 2013 and 2014 we explored the potential integration of women into SF with a project that relied on data collected from men in SF and women in SO.[35] Female participants in our study came from Civilian Affairs (CA), Military Information Support Operations (MISO), and Cultural Support Teams (CST)—all units within army SO. Each of these units serves as support for SF when they are deployed. CA and MISO are long-standing units that are gender integrated. CST is a newer unit, developed in response to current military conflicts. CSTs are exclusively female and recruited specifically to interact with women and children in Iraq and Afghanistan.

Our data were collected in 2013–14 after the DGCAR was rescinded, but when SO was still considering requesting an exception to the policy change. We used a sequential, mixed-methods design comprised of focus groups that were in turn used to design two surveys eliciting soldiers' opinions regarding the potential barriers and benefits of integrating women into SF.[36] Given the lack of data available on the topic, we were interested in developing a theory from soldiers' lived experiences and exploring how these experiences have shaped their beliefs about gender integration using grounded theory.[37] This methodology provided us with the flexibility to pursue unanticipated topics that surfaced during the focus groups and include them in subsequent groups, and ultimately our survey design.[38]

We conducted twenty-seven focus groups, using a semistructured script, with a nonrandom sample of 198 participants, during multiday site visits at five military bases. Twenty-three focus groups consisted of men, and four focus groups consisted of women; all focus groups lasted approximately two hours. The SF community is small, generally older, and less racially diverse compared to the broader army. Consequently, we were sensitive about collecting information from participants that could easily identify them. Pseudonyms are used for all participants, and we obtained human subjects' approval for this research. In designing the focus groups, we were sensitive to workplace hierarchy and tried to create groups that would foster uncensored opinions. To reduce potential power dynamics, in twenty-one of the focus groups we divided participants by rank with enlisted soldiers, warrant officers, and commissioned officers in separate groups. We also conducted three focus groups with full ODAs, which gave us an opportunity to observe how participants articulated, discussed, and at times revised their opinions among trusted members of their small group.

The four female focus groups were conducted after the male focus groups concluded, which was a function of logistics rather than design. These groups were configured differently due to the limited numbers of women serving in SO; they contained a mix of enlisted soldiers and commissioned officers. All of the focus groups were recorded, transcribed, and analyzed. The results of the analysis were then used to develop two surveys, which were used as an additional source of data that provided a more systematic perspective of soldiers' opinions about the barriers and benefits of gender integration, complementing the nonrandom sample of the focus groups.

The first survey was designed for all SF men; the population of U.S. SF men is 6,109. The second survey was designed for female CA, MISO, and CST enablers currently assigned to U.S. Army SO Command (n = 779). The surveys were administered online in 2014. In total the surveys yielded a sample size of 1,613 active-duty men and 88 National Guard men (27.8 percent response rate) as well as 214 active-duty women (27.6 percent response rate). The mean age of female survey respondents was 32 (ages ranged from 20 to 50 with a median of 31) and 37 for men (ages ranged from 24 to 55 with a median of 35). Most male respondents identified as white (n = 1,116, 80 percent), 7 percent (n = 99) identified as Black, 3 percent (n = 46) identified as Asian American, 3 percent (n = 46) identified as "other," and 6 percent (n = 93) responded they "don't know." Two-thirds of female respondents (n = 131, 64 percent) identified as white, 15 percent (n = 31) identified as Black, 11 percent (n = 22) identified as Asian American, 5 percent (n = 10) identified as "other," and 6 percent (n = 12) responded "don't know." Marriage and parenthood rates varied considerably across men and women; 78 percent (n = 1,083) of men were married, and 75 percent (n = 1,049) had children. For women 45 percent (n = 88) were married, and 44 percent (n = 86) had children.

In terms of work experience, the survey population had longer work experience compared to the general enlisted army population. Almost half (47 percent, n = 98) of female survey respondents had served in the military nine or more years (range = 0–25+); for male respondents this number was 78 percent (n = 1,287 with a range of 0–25+). In addition, most survey respondents had served in a combat zone (95 percent of men, n = 1,569 and 94 percent of women, n = 166). The survey respondents were also highly educated; 26 percent of women (n = 50) were college graduates, and an additional 33 percent (n = 64) had some postgraduate education. Among the men 29 percent (n = 404) were college graduates, and another 12 percent (n = 168) had postgraduate education.

Notes

Pseudonyms are used for all interviewees in this chapter.

1. Burrelli, "Women in Combat."

2. Burrelli, "Women in Combat."

3. U.S. Department of Defense news release no. 037-13, January 24, 2013, https://archive.defense.gov/Releases/Release.aspx?ReleaseID=15784.

4. Jimmie Keenan, "The DOD Combat Exclusion Policy," January 2008, https://www.globalsecurity.org/military/library/report/2008/ssi_putko-johnson.pdf; "Iraq Lacks Women Trained in Security," *Washington Times*, July 11, 2005, https://www.washingtontimes.com/news/2005/jul/11/20050711-122346-9856r/.

5. See "Note on Methods" in this chapter.

6. See "Note on Methods" in this chapter.

7. Skaine, *Women at War.*

8. U.S. Department of Defense, "Women in Defense of Our Nation."

9. Morden, *Women's Army Corps.*

10. Burelli, "Women in Combat."

11. U.S. General Accounting Office, "Gender Issues."

12. U.S. General Accounting Office, "Gender Issues."

13. Burelli, "Women in Combat."

14. Carney et al., "Women in the Gulf War."

15. Burelli, "Women in Combat."

16. U.S. General Accounting Office, "Gender Issues."

17. Burrelli, "Women in Combat."

18. U.S. General Accounting Office, "Gender Issues."

19. U.S. General Accounting Office, "Gender Issues."

20. Military Diversity Leadership Commission, "From Representation to Inclusion."

21. Military Diversity Leadership Commission, "From Representation to Inclusion."

22. Duncan Hunter National Defense Authorization Act for Fiscal Year 2009, Public Law 110-417, October 15, 2008.

23. Military Diversity Leadership Commission, "From Representation to Inclusion," viii.

24. Military Diversity Leadership Commission, "From Representation to Inclusion," 127.

25. U.S. Department of the Army, "Army Policy for the Assignment of Female Soldiers," 5.

26. Burelli, "Women in Combat."

27. U.S. Department of the Army, "Special Forces."

28. U.S. Department of the Army, "Special Forces."

29. U.S. Department of the Army, "Special Forces."

30. Acker, "Inequality Regimes."

31. Ridgeway, *Framed by Gender.*

32. U.S. Department of Defense, "Fact Sheet."

33. U.S. Department of Defense, "Fact Sheet."

34. Vanessa Romo, "Woman Qualifies for Special Forces Training, Could Be the First Female Green Beret," NPR, November 18, 2018, https://www.npr.org/2018/11/16/668771232/woman-qualifies-for-special-forces-training-could-be-the-first-female-green-beret.

35. For more on this work, see Doan and Portillo, *Organizational Obliviousness.*

36. Hess-Biber and Johnson, *Oxford Handbook.*

37. Charmaz, *Constructing Grounded Theory.*

38. Charmaz, *Constructing Grounded Theory.*

Bibliography

Acker, Joan. "Inequality Regimes: Gender, Class, and Race in Organizations." *Gender and Society* 4 (2006): 441–64.

Britton, Dana M. *At Work in the Iron Cage: The Prison as Gendered Organization.* New York: New York University Press, 2003.

Burrelli, David F. "Women in Combat: Issues for Congress." Congressional Research Service Paper no. 7-5700, 2013.

Carney, Caroline P., Tomoko R Sampson, Margaret Voelker, Robert Woolson, Peter Thorne, and Bradley N. Doebbeling. "Women in the Gulf War: Combat Experience, Exposures, and Subsequent Health Care Use." *Military Medicine* 168, no. 8 (2003): 654–61.

Charmaz, Kathy. *Constructing Grounded Theory: A Practical Guide through Qualitative Analysis.* Thousand Oaks CA: SAGE, 2006.

Doan, Alesha, and Shannon Portillo. *Organizational Obliviousness: Entrenched Resistance to Gender Integration in the Military.* London: Cambridge University Press, 2019.

Hesse-Biber, Sharlene, and Burke Johnson. *The Oxford Handbook of Multimethod and Mixed Methods Research Inquiry.* London: Oxford University Press, 2016.

Keenan, Jimmie O. "The DOD Combat Exclusion Policy: Time for a Change?" In *Women in Combat Compendium*, edited by M. M. Putko and D. V. Johnson, 21–25. Washington DC: Strategic Studies Institute, 2008.

Military Leadership Diversity Commission. "From Representation to Inclusion: Diversity Leadership for the 21st-Century Military: Final Report." March 15, 2011. https://diversity.defense.gov/Portals/51/Documents/Special%20Feature/MLDC_Final_Report.pdf.

———. "Women in Combat: Legislation and Policy, Perceptions, and the Current Operational Environment." Issue Paper #56, Office for Diversity, Equity, and Inclusion, U.S. Department of Defense. Accessed December 10, 2019. https://diversity.defense.gov/Portals/51/Documents/Special%20Feature/MLDC_Final_Report.pdf.

Morden, Bettie J. *The Women's Army Corps, 1945–1978.* Washington DC: Center of Military History, 1990.

Prokos, Anastasia, and Irene Padavic. "'There Oughtta Be a Law against Bitches': Masculinity in Police Academy Training." *Gender, Work, and Organization* 9, no. 4 (2002): 439–59.

Ridgeway, Cecilia L. *Framed by Gender: How Gender Inequality Persists in the Modern World.* London: Oxford University Press, 2011.

Skaine, Rosemarie. *Women at War: Gender Issues of Americans in Combat.* Jefferson NC: McFarland, 1999.

U.S. Department of Defense. "Fact Sheet: Women in Service Review (WISR) Implementation." Accessed July 27, 2021. https://DOD.defense.gov/Portals/1/Documents/pubs/Fact_Sheet_WISR_FINAL.pdf.

———. "Women in Defense of Our Nation." Accessed July 27, 2021. https://diversity.defense.gov/Portals/51/Documents/Resources/Docs/Factsheets/Women%20in%20Defense%20of%20our%20Nation.pdf.

U.S. Department of the Army. "Army Policy for the Assignment of Female Soldiers [Army Regulation 600-13]." Washington DC: U.S. Department of the Army, 1992.

———. "Special Forces." 2019. https://www.goarmy.com/special-forces/primary-missions.html.

U.S. General Accounting Office. "Gender Issues: Information on DOD's Assignment Policy and Direct Ground Combat Definition." 1998. https://www.gao.gov/assets/230/226446.pdf.

Afterword

BETH BAILEY, ALESHA E. DOAN, SHANNON PORTILLO,
AND KARA DIXON VUIC

Two decades into the twenty-first century, "managing sex" remains a fundamental military concern, even as today's force differs dramatically from that of the early twentieth century. No longer comprised mostly of young single men, the military of today is a diverse collection of Americans: single service members without children are joined by families, both "traditional" and nontraditional; the ranks include young parents and pregnant women, dual-uniform couples, gay men and women, teenagers and grandparents. These service members enjoy a much broader range of options than their predecessors. Women's roles have expanded in ways few female pioneers in military service could have imagined. The Uniform Code of Military Justice no longer labels sodomy a crime. Service members are now able to have families, to combine parenthood and career, to have sex with or to marry the partner of their choice (albeit subject to Uniform Code of Military Justice regulations barring "fraternization" and adultery). And yet few in the military would argue that the problems of sex have been resolved.

Women continue to confront specific hurdles related to sex and gender. Despite the removal of combat restrictions on women, they continue to wear body armor that, because it was designed for men and does not properly fit women's frames, often causes injury instead of preventing it. Sexual assault remains an intractable problem, affecting both women and men. Sex work continues to play a critical role in base economies around the globe, tying people and communities in nations such as South Korea to an American military presence. And trans people have found themselves in uncharted territory, as changing and often contradictory executive orders shifted not only the conditions but the possibility of their service.

As this collection suggests, none of these contemporary issues are completely new. Each has historical precedents and most claim a long and often complex history in which policy makers and individuals have worked together—or sometimes at odds—to confront them. The preceding chapters illustrate the evolution of military policies about sex: about the ways that military officials have sought to regulate sexual behaviors, along with matters of reproduction and family life, of biology and identity, as well as to manage or prohibit sexual violence and regulate the intersections among sex, gender, and combat.

Individually and collectively, these chapters show that changes in sexual policies were sometimes progressive, but not always. They reveal that change frequently came in intermittent fashion; that change was rarely linear, that it was often inconsistent, even contradictory. They make clear that the specific histories and institutional needs of the individual military branches shaped military policies. They demonstrate that broader forces of social change in civilian society played a critical, if sometimes unacknowledged, role in prompting and shaping change, highlighting the fact that, despite its legally "exceptional" status, the U.S. military never stood fully apart from the civilian society it defends. And in the end these chapters suggest that military policies and practices governing sex (in its various definitions) have played significant roles within and beyond the U.S. military.

Military attempts to manage sex affect the millions who serve in ways that range from the intimate to the professional. For that reason alone, our historical explorations have value. But because military service holds symbolic weight in American society, and because military debates over how to manage sex are frequently public in nature, military policies and practices indirectly affect the hundreds of millions of Americans who have not, and will never, serve in the nation's armed forces. Thus, the editors and authors of this work hope that our histories will inform the continuing struggles over sex as the U.S. military confronts both long-standing issues and new ones emerging in an ever-evolving sociopolitical landscape.

CONTRIBUTORS

Beth Bailey is Foundation Distinguished Professor at the University of Kansas, where she directs the Center for Military, War, and Society Studies. Her military history publications include *America's Army: Making the All-Volunteer Force* (2009) and the coedited volumes *Beyond Pearl Harbor: A Pacific History* (2019) and *Understanding the U.S. Wars in Iraq and Afghanistan* (2015). She is currently writing about how the U.S. Army, as an institution, tried to manage what army leaders often called the "problem of race" during the Vietnam War era.

Amanda Boczar is a digital teaching fellow at the University of South Florida, where she researches and develops innovative digital pedagogy for the college classroom. Dr. Boczar's research examines the intersections of warfare and sexuality in the twentieth century, with specific research interests in prostitution and sexual violence. Her first book, *Foreign Affairs: American Policy and the Making of Love and War in Vietnam*, is under contract with Cornell University Press. She was previously a postdoctoral fellow at the U.S. Military Academy West Point, where she served as the editor of the digital, interactive source readers *The West Point Guide to Gender and Warfare*, vols. 1–3.

Kellie Wilson-Buford is an assistant professor of history and director of the Secondary Social Studies Education program at Arkansas State University. Her book, *Policing Sex and Marriage in the American Military: The Court-Martial and the Construction of Gender and Sexual Deviance, 1950–2000*, was published by the University of Nebraska Press in 2018 as part of the Studies in War, Society, and the Military series. Her current book project, tentatively titled "Shattering the Silence: Sexual Violence and American Military Justice from the Korean War to the Present," traces military courts' efforts to manage service members' crimes of sexual violence since 1950.

Andrew Byers earned his PhD in history from Duke University, where he also served as a visiting assistant professor of history. He is the author of *The Sexual Economy of War: Discipline and Desire in the U.S. Army* (Cornell University Press, 2019). He researches the history of the regulation of the human body and the intersection of science, sexuality, and law in civilian and military contexts.

Susan L. Carruthers is professor of American studies in the Department of History at the University of Warwick; she previously taught for fifteen years at Rutgers University–Newark. Carruthers's work deals broadly with questions of how individuals, societies, and states have made sense of war and its aftermath in the twentieth and twenty-first centuries. She is the author of several books, including *Cold War Captives: Imprisonment, Escape, Brainwashing* (University of California Press, 2009), *The Media at War* (Palgrave Macmillan, 2011), and, most recently, *The Good Occupation: American Soldiers and the Hazards of Peace* (Harvard University Press, 2016), which was shortlisted for the 2017 PEN Hessell-Tiltman Prize. Her new book project uses the "Dear John" letter to explore how U.S. military and popular culture has attempted to script wartime romance and negotiate its rupture.

Alesha E. Doan is an associate professor at the University of Kansas and holds a joint appointment in the School of Public Affairs and Administration and the Women, Gender, and Sexuality Studies Department. Professor Doan's interdisciplinary research is guided by her broader interests in public policy, organizations, and gender and social equity, with a more specialized focus on reproductive policies. Her publications include articles in a variety of journals as well as three books: *Opposition and Intimidation: The Abortion Wars and Strategies of Political Harassment* (University of Michigan Press, 2007), *The Politics of Virginity: Abstinence in Sex Edu-*

cation (coauthored, Praeger, 2008), and *Abortion Regret: The New Attack on Reproductive Freedom* (coauthored, Praeger, 2019).

Christopher Hamner is an associate professor of history at George Mason University, specializing in the social history of American soldiers. His 2011 book, *Enduring Battle: American Soldiers in Three Wars, 1776–1945*, examines the experiences of American infantry soldiers under fire in the War of Independence, the Civil War, and World War II, analyzing the ways that individuals and small groups were motivated to face the terror and chaos of battle as technologies changed the experience of fighting on the ground. He has been a fellow at the Center for Military History and at Harvard University's John M. Olin Institute for Strategic Studies. From 2014 to 2016 he was a visiting professor at the U.S. Army War College, teaching courses on military strategy, planning, and operations.

Elizabeth Mesok is a researcher and consultant in the field of gender, peace, and security. Currently a senior researcher at swisspeace, a practice-oriented peace research institute in Bern, Switzerland, Mesok completed her PhD in American studies at New York University in 2013. As a postdoctoral fellow at Harvard University's Charles Warren Center for American History from 2013 to 2015, Mesok's work focused on sexual violence against women in the U.S. military and the instrumentalization of U.S. military women's affective labor for counterinsurgency in Iraq and Afghanistan. She is currently working on a research project about the recent emergence of gendered security strategies used to prevent violent extremism in military and development agencies in the Horn of Africa. In Switzerland she teaches courses on gender, war, and peacebuilding at the Graduate Institute of International and Development Studies in Geneva and the University of Basel. Her most recent publication on male-male sexual violence in the U.S. military can be found in the edited volume *Sexual Violence against Men in Global Politics*.

Shannon Portillo, PhD, is assistant vice chancellor of undergraduate programs at the KU Edwards Campus and an associate professor in the School of Public Affairs and Administration at the University of Kansas. Dr. Portillo takes an interdisciplinary approach to her work, drawing on organizational theories rooted in public administration and law and society to explore how rules and policies are carried out within public organizations. To date she has done work in a broad array of organizations, including the military, problem-solving courts, probation, restorative justice programs, administrative hearings, policing, higher education, and city management. Teaching and research interests include social equity, social justice, organizational theory, and law and public management. Her work has appeared in *Law & Policy*, *Administration & Society*, *Law & Social Inquiry*, *Journal of Public Administration Research & Theory*, and *Public Administration Review*.

Agnes Gereben Schaefer is associate director of the International Security and Defense Policy Center and a senior political scientist at the RAND Corporation. Her research specializations include issues related to U.S. military personnel policy, national security strategy, and emerging threats. Since joining RAND in 2005, Dr. Schaefer has conducted more than fifty studies for senior civilian and military leaders, including studies for the secretary of defense that assessed the implications of allowing transgender military personnel to serve openly, allowing gays and lesbians to serve openly in the U.S. military, and integrating women into the USMC infantry and Special Operations Forces. She has published articles in a range of journals and has been interviewed by many media outlets including the Associated Press, BBC, CBS News, CNN, the *Economist*, Fox News, NBC, PBS *News Hour*, *Time*, the *Wall Street Journal*, the *Washington Post*, and *USA Today*. Dr. Schaefer received her PhD from Syracuse University's Maxwell School of Citizenship and Public Affairs. Before joining RAND she was a postdoctoral research associate and lecturer at Princeton University's Woodrow Wilson School of Public and International Affairs.

Kara Dixon Vuic is the LCpl. Benjamin W. Schmidt Professor of War, Conflict, and Society in Twentieth-Century America at Texas Christian University. She is the author of *The Girls Next Door: Bringing the Home Front to the Front Lines* (Harvard University Press, 2019) and *Officer, Nurse, Woman: The Army Nurse Corps in the Vietnam War* (Johns Hopkins University Press, 2010). She also edited *The Routledge Handbook on Gender, War, and the U.S. Mil-*

itary (2017) and is coeditor (with Richard Fogarty) of the University of Nebraska Press's book series Studies in War, Society, and the Military. Her new book project examines historical debates about drafting women for the U.S. military.

Dr. Jacqueline E. Whitt joined the U.S. Army War College faculty in 2016. She teaches courses on the "Theory of War and Strategy" and "National Security Policy and Strategy," as well as electives on "War and Social Change" and "Great Books and Literature for Strategists." Her first book, *Bringing God to Men: American Military Chaplains, Religion, and the Vietnam War*, was published by the University of North Carolina Press in 2014 and in 2016 won the Richard W. Leopold Prize from the Organization for American Historians. Her current work examines how narrative has shaped American grand strategy since 1945. She also writes about and lectures on understanding the integration of women, LGBTQ people, and religious minorities in the contemporary American military.

John Worsencroft is an assistant professor of history and a research fellow at Louisiana Tech University. He earned his PhD in U.S. history from Temple University, and as a scholar he researches and writes about twentieth-century America through the interlocking themes of policy, gender, war, the military, and society. His book project, "A Family Affair: Military Service in America," is a history of family policies in the army and Marine Corps, exploring how military institutions and policies shape rights, obligations, and the meaning of citizenship in the United States. Before pursuing graduate studies, he was a U.S. Marine and fought in Iraq in 2003.

INDEX

abortion, 11, 88, 129–33; rates of, 131–32

abstinence, sexual, 1–2, 35, 37, 60, 78, 85

adultery, 43–44, 63–64; and rape cases, 64–65, 229

African Americans, 3, 29, 49, 51, 58–59, 81, 99, 226, 247, 292, 296; hypersexualization of, 25, 59; and racial integration, 158, 178, 246, 282–83, 290, 296; and WAC, 76, 81–82, 85

all-volunteer force (AVF), 5, 7, 9, 11, 71, 86, 100, 132, 154, 245, 248–49, 254, 278, 310; effect of, on family policy, 107, 121; effect of, on marriage policy, 63, 96–99, 113

American Civil Liberties Union (ACLU), 87, 104, 255

American Expeditionary Force, 24–25

The American Soldier (Stouffer), 276–77

The Army Family (Wickham), 95, 107–8

Army Nurse Corps, 2, 127–28

Army Officers' Wives Club, 104–5

Articles of War, 20, 28; and rape, 30–31, 198–205; and sodomy, 20, 174, 198–200, 202, 204

Aspin, Les, 111, 146–47, 261–62, 278, 311

Becraft, Carolyn, 104, 108

Biden, Joseph, 144, 160–62, 219

birth control, 7, 11, 80, 83–84, 88, 129–30; condoms as, 6, 23, 78, 84; the pill as, 7–8, 88

breastfeeding, 119–20, 134

brothels, 1, 46, 50, 52–55, 59; racial segregation of, 51

Bush, George H. W., 261

Bush, George W., 50, 149, 245

carnal knowledge, 198, 201–2, 206, 208, 222. *See also* rape

Carter, Ashton, 153–54, 162, 275–76, 278–83, 285–88, 291–92, 300

children, 3, 26, 102, 122; and childcare, 105, 109; illegitimate, 58–59, 60–61, 75, 86–87, 128

Cioca, Kori, 229, 234

Cioca et al. v. Rumsfeld et al., 212, 221, 229, 231–32

Civil Rights Act (1964), 128, 159

Civil War, U.S., 200–202, 277, 283, 292

Clark, Albert P., 250–52

Clinton, Bill, 146–48, 162, 178, 262

Collins, Susan, 95, 179

combat, 9–10; definitions of, 246, 248, 252–54, 260, 262–63, 267, 312; and masculinity, 13, 246, 257–58, 276–78, 283, 293, 298

combat exclusion, 13, 163; and efficacy, 284–89, 309; end of, 275–76, 278–79, 300, 307–8, 313; and fairness, 284–85, 287–88; and gender stereotypes, 309–10, 316–19, 323–29; opposition to repeal of, 279–82, 287–92; and physiology, 289–90, 320–22; and psychology, 292–94, 322; and unit cohesion, 294–98, 301

consent, sexual, 30–32, 197, 206; boundaries of, 208–11

contraceptives. *See* birth control

counterinsurgency, 245, 248, 263; women's role in, 264–65, 268–69, 286–87

cross-dressing, 174, 183–85, 183

343

policy (*cont.*)

sexual trauma, military, 234
sexual violence. *See* carnal knowledge; rape; sexual assault; sodomy
sodomy, 3, 8, 20, 31, 43, 145, 173–74, 212; and Articles of War, 198–202, 204; definition of, 32, 177, 206; and Uniform Code of Military Justice, 145, 177, 198, 206, 335
Special Forces (SF), 14, 308–9, 314; and alpha males, 315–17, 326; and gender exclusion, 261, 263; and masculinity, 309–10, 314–20
Stouffer, Samuel, 276, 298–99
Supreme Headquarters Allied Expeditionary Force (SHAEF), 47–49

Tailhook scandal, 189, 197, 220–22, 225–26
transgender personnel, 5, 335–36; ban of, 12, 143–44, 151–61; and health care, 143, 153–56, 158–59, 161, 163, 180; public opinion of, 144, 156, 160, 162–63; and readiness and unit cohesion, 143–44, 153–57, 161, 164, 172; recruitment and retention of, 143, 154, 157, 163. *See also* gender identity
transgender rights movement, 153
Truman, Harry, 124, 127, 222
Trump, Donald, 144, 155–60, 162

Uniform Code of Military Justice (UCMJ), 3, 197, 205–6, 222; and prostitution, 49–50, 56; and rape, 198, 205–12, 235; and sodomy, 145, 177, 198, 206, 335
United States v. Barcomb, 210
United States v. Briggs, 212, 235
United States v. Rogers, 208–9

van Creveld, Martin, 276, 280
venereal disease, 1, 3, 7, 10, 19, 26, 28, 37, 82, 130; association of, with prostitution, 20–21, 24–25, 34–35, 51–52; medical inspection for, 22–25, 28, 34–35, 51–52; and prophylaxis, 7, 24, 59, 78–79, 130; and race, 23–25, 59; rates of, among soldiers, 22; and readiness, 10, 22, 34; and WAC, 78–80, 86
Vietnam War, 4, 11, 71, 126–27; and birth control, 130–31; and marriage, 62; and masculinity, 247; and prostitution, 2, 53–57; and rape, 52, 55–57, 220, 223–24; and

recruitment, 95–99; and servicewomen, 254; and venereal disease, 59

War in Afghanistan, 71, 267–68, 278, 284, 287, 307, 312, 328; and abortion, 133; and Don't Ask, Don't Tell, 149–50, 179; and prostitution, 49; and recruitment and retention, 71, 230. *See also* counterinsurgency; Female Engagement Teams (FETS)
Wickham, John A., Jr., 95, 107–9, 112
wives, 28–29, 88, 101, 123; activism of, 97–98, 103–9; and birth control, 130–32; and labor, 99–101, 105; as moral influence, 63; and sexual assault, 207, 214
Women's Armed Services Integration Act, 125–26, 245–46, 249, 253, 255, 283, 310–11
Women's Army Auxiliary Corps (WAAC). *See* Women's Army Corps (WAC)
Women's Army Corps (WAC), 10, 126–27, 222–23, 253, 310; and Black women, 76, 81–82, 85; end of, 88–89; founding of, 73–76; and homosexuality, 72–73, 84, 88, 123; and public perception, 75–76, 78–84, 89, 130, 184; and recruitment, 76, 81, 85–86; regulations of, 77–80, 87; relation of, to U.S. Army, 76–79; reputation of, 71–73, 75–76, 78–80, 83–86, 88–89, 123; and scandal campaign, 72–73, 82–84, 86; and sexual hygiene program, 78–79
Women's Equity Action League (WEAL), 104, 108
women's movement, 11, 74, 86–89, 97–98, 103–4, 107–8, 121, 248, 255. *See also* feminism
World War I, 1, 4, 21, 31, 33–35, 37, 47, 95, 122, 174, 310; and homosexuality, 31–34, 174–75; and prostitution, 23–24; and sexual assault, 204–5, 226; and venereal disease, 23–25, 78; and women, 310
World War II, 2–3, 10–11, 13, 45–46, 85, 89, 95–96, 310; and family policy, 61–62, 122, 124; and homosexuality, 8, 145, 175, 181–82; and sexual assault, 205; and sexual behavior of soldiers, 10, 46–50; and sexual harassment, 222; and venereal disease, 20, 59, 78; and women, 254, 278, 310

Studies in War, Society, and the Military

Military Migration and State Formation: The British Military Community in Seventeenth-Century Sweden
Mary Elizabeth Ailes

Managing Sex in the U.S. Military: Gender, Identity, and Behavior
Edited by Beth Bailey, Alesha E. Doan, Shannon Portillo, and Kara Dixon Vuic

The State at War in South Asia
Pradeep P. Barua

Marianne Is Watching: Intelligence, Counterintelligence, and the Origins of the French Surveillance State
Deborah Bauer

Death at the Edges of Empire: Fallen Soldiers, Cultural Memory, and the Making of an American Nation, 1863–1921
Shannon Bontrager

An American Soldier in World War I
George Browne
Edited by David L. Snead

Beneficial Bombing: The Progressive Foundations of American Air Power, 1917–1945
Mark Clodfelter

Fu-go: The Curious History of Japan's Balloon Bomb Attack on America
Ross Coen

Imagining the Unimaginable: World War, Modern Art, and the Politics of Public Culture in Russia, 1914–1917
Aaron J. Cohen

The Rise of the National Guard: The Evolution of the American Militia, 1865–1920
Jerry Cooper

The Thirty Years' War and German Memory in the Nineteenth Century
Kevin Cramer

Political Indoctrination in the U.S. Army from World War II to the Vietnam War
Christopher S. DeRosa

In the Service of the Emperor: Essays on the Imperial Japanese Army
Edward J. Drea

American Journalists in the Great War: Rewriting the Rules of Reporting
Chris Dubbs

America's U-Boats: Terror Trophies of World War I
Chris Dubbs

The Age of the Ship of the Line: The British and French Navies, 1650–1815
Jonathan R. Dull

Of Duty Well and Faithfully Done: A History of the Regular Army in the Civil War
Clayton R. Newell and Charles R. Shrader
With a foreword by Edward M. Coffman

The Militarization of Culture in the Dominican Republic, from the Captains General to General Trujillo
Valentina Peguero

A Religious History of the American GI in World War II
G. Kurt Piehler

Arabs at War: Military Effectiveness, 1948–1991
Kenneth M. Pollack

The Politics of Air Power: From Confrontation to Cooperation in Army Aviation Civil-Military Relations
Rondall R. Rice

Andean Tragedy: Fighting the War of the Pacific, 1879–1884
William F. Sater

The Grand Illusion: The Prussianization of the Chilean Army
William F. Sater and Holger H. Herwig

Sex Crimes under the Wehrmacht
David Raub Snyder

In the School of War
Roger J. Spiller
Foreword by John W. Shy

On the Trail of the Yellow Tiger: War, Trauma, and Social Dislocation in Southwest China during the Ming-Qing Transition
Kenneth M. Swope

Friendly Enemies: Soldier Fraternization throughout the American Civil War
Lauren K. Thompson

The Paraguayan War, Volume 1: Causes and Early Conduct
Thomas L. Whigham

Policing Sex and Marriage in the American Military: The Court-Martial and the Construction of Gender and Sexual Deviance, 1950–2000
Kellie Wilson-Buford

The Challenge of Change: Military Institutions and New Realities, 1918–1941
Edited by Harold R. Winton and David R. Mets

To order or obtain more information on these or other University of Nebraska Press titles, visit nebraskapress.unl.edu.

CPSIA information can be obtained
at www.ICGtesting.com
Printed in the USA
LVHW110759140422
716120LV00006B/856